Houghton Mifflin Harcourt

Texas GO Math!

Volume 2

Texas GoMath!

Printed in the U.S.A.

ISBN 978-0-544-08675-3
12 13 14 15 16 0607 24 23 22 21
4500821533 C D E F G

Cover Image Credits: (building) ©MWaits/Shutterstock; (landscape) ©Radius Images/Corbis; (pier) ©Matthew Wakem/Getty Images; (Ibis) ©Joel Sartore/Getty Images.

Dear Students and Families,

Welcome to **Texas Go Math!**, Grade 5! In this exciting mathematics program, there are hands-on activities to do and real-world problems to solve. Best of all, you will write your ideas and answers right in your book. In **Texas Go Math!**, writing and drawing on the pages helps you think deeply about what you are learning, and you will really understand math!

By the way, all of the pages in your **Texas Go Math!** book are made using recycled paper. We wanted you to know that you can Go Green with **Texas Go Math!**

Sincerely,

The Authors

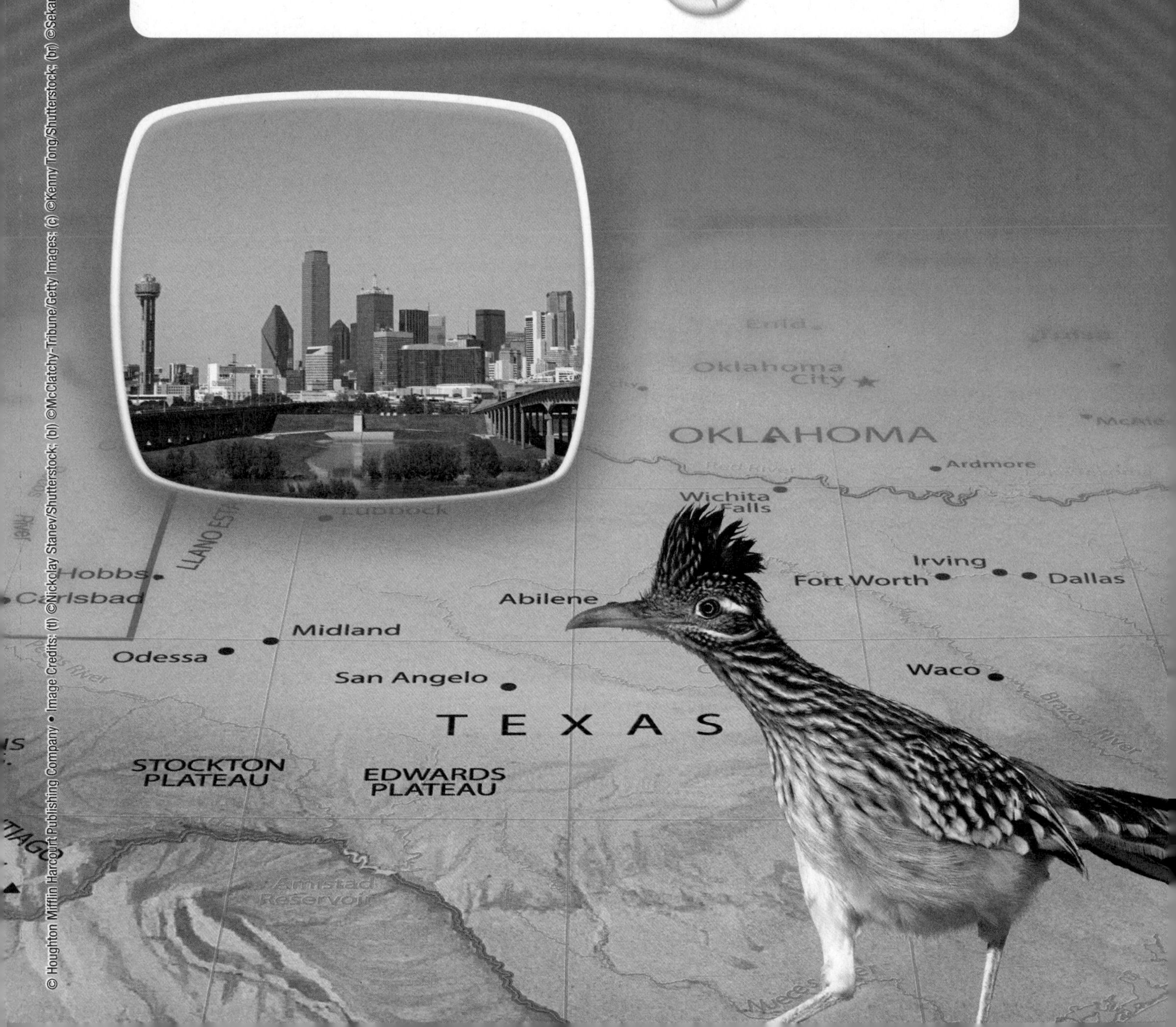

Texas GO Math!

Authors

Juli K. Dixon, Ph.D.
Professor, Mathematics Education
University of Central Florida
Orlando, Florida

Edward B. Burger, Ph.D.
President
Southwestern University
Georgetown, Texas

Matthew R. Larson, Ph.D.
K-12 Curriculum Specialist for Mathematics
Lincoln Public Schools
Lincoln, Nebraska

Martha E. Sandoval-Martinez
Math Instructor
El Camino College
Torrance, California

Consultant

Valerie Johse
Math Consultant
Texas Council for Economic Education
Houston, Texas

Volume 1

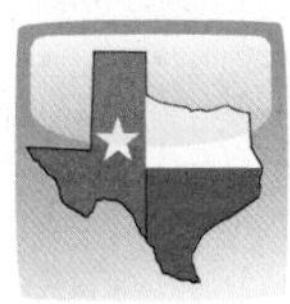

Unit 1 • Number and Operations: Place Value and Operations

Module 1 Place Value and Decimals

Module 2 Multiply and Divide Whole Numbers

Look for these:

H.O.T. Problems
Higher Order Thinking
Multi-Step Problems

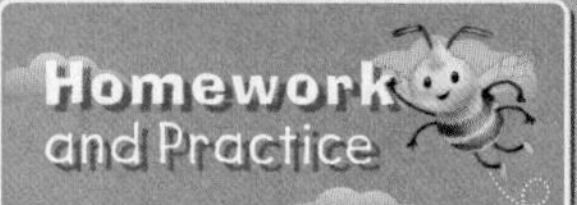

Homework and TEKS Practice in every lesson.

GO DIGITAL Resources

DIGITAL RESOURCES
Go online for the Interactive Student Edition with Math on the Spot Videos. Use *i*Tools, the Multimedia *e*Glossary, and more.

Module 3 Multiply Decimals

Module 4 Divide Decimals

Look for these:

H.O.T. Problems
Higher Order Thinking
Multi-Step Problems

GO DIGITAL Resources

DIGITAL RESOURCES
Go online for the Interactive Student Edition with Math on the Spot Videos. Use *i*Tools, the Multimedia *e*Glossary, and more.

Volume 1

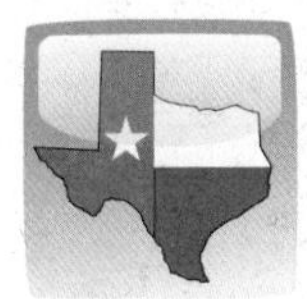

Unit 2 • Number and Operations: Fractions

Module 5 Add and Subtract Fractions

Module 6 Multiply and Divide Unit Fractions and Whole Numbers

Look for these:

H.O.T. Problems
Higher Order Thinking
Multi-Step Problems

Homework and TEKS Practice in every lesson.

Look for these:

H.O.T. Problems
Higher Order Thinking
Multi-Step Problems

Volume 1

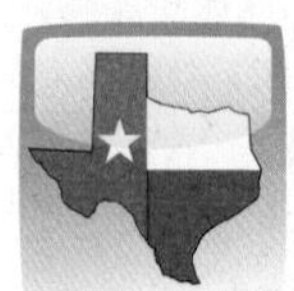

Unit 3 • Algebraic Reasoning

Module 7 Algebra • Expressions

Module 8 Algebra • Equations

GO DIGITAL Resources

DIGITAL RESOURCES
Go online for the Interactive Student Edition with Math on the Spot Videos. Use *i*Tools, the Multimedia *e*Glossary, and more.

Module 9 Algebra • Formulas

Module 10 Algebra • Patterns

Look for these:

H.O.T. Problems
Higher Order Thinking
Multi-Step Problems

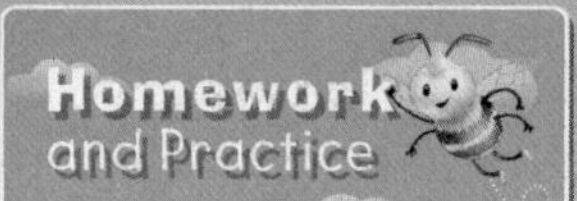

Homework and TEKS Practice in every lesson.

Volume 2

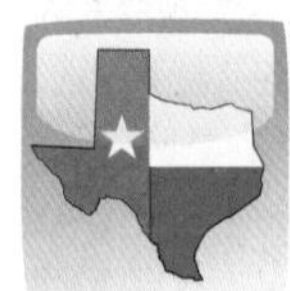

Unit 4 • Geometry and Measurement

Module 11 Two-Dimensional Figures

Module 12 Volume

Module 13 Convert Units of Measure

Look for these:

H.O.T. Problems
Higher Order Thinking
Multi-Step Problems

GO DIGITAL Resources

DIGITAL RESOURCES
Go online for the Interactive Student Edition with Math on the Spot Videos. Use *i*Tools, the Multimedia *e*Glossary, and more.

Module 14 Graphing

Look for these:

H.O.T. Problems
Higher Order Thinking
Multi-Step Problems

Volume 2

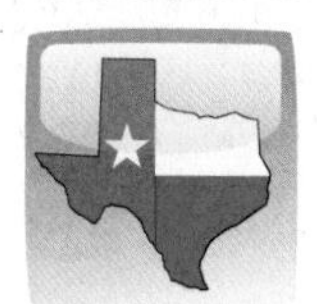

Unit 5 • Data Analysis

Homework and TEKS Practice in every lesson.

Module 15 Categorical Data

Module 16 Numerical Data

Volume 2

Unit 6 • Personal Financial Literacy

Module 17 Personal Financial Literacy

Look for these:

H.O.T. Problems
Higher Order Thinking
Multi-Step Problems

GO DIGITAL Resources

DIGITAL RESOURCES
Go online for the Interactive Student Edition with Math on the Spot Videos. Use *i*Tools, the Multimedia *e*Glossary, and more.

Unit 4

Geometry and Measurement

Show What You Know

Check your understanding of important skills.

Name ________________________

Measure Length to the Nearest Inch

Use an inch ruler. Measure the length to the nearest inch.

1. 

about _____ inches

2. 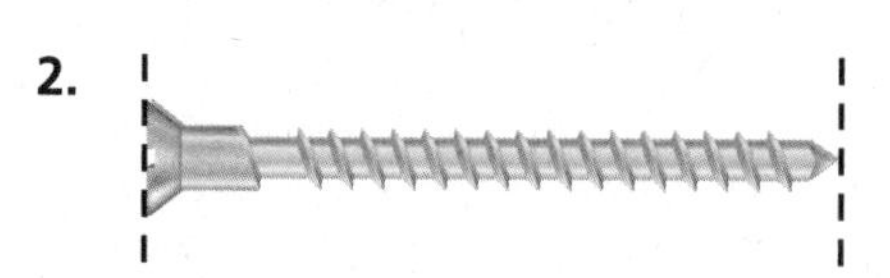

about _____ inches

Classify and Measure Angles

Classify the angle. Write *acute, right,* or *obtuse.*

3. 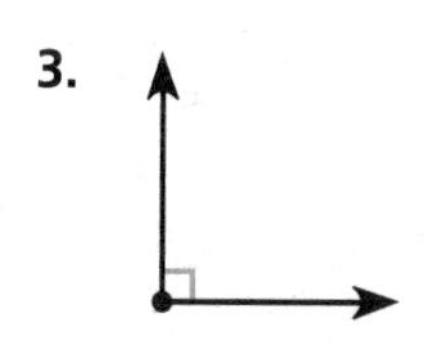

____

4. 

____

5. _______________

6. 

____

Describe Sides of Polygons

Write *intersecting, parallel,* or *perpendicular* to describe the numbered sides.

7. 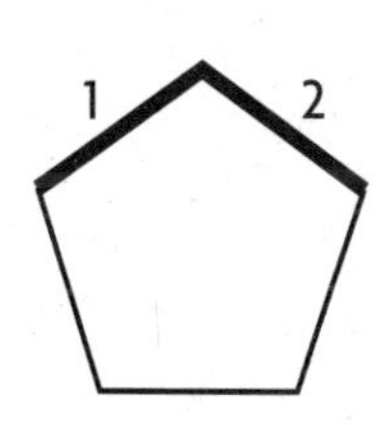

____

8. 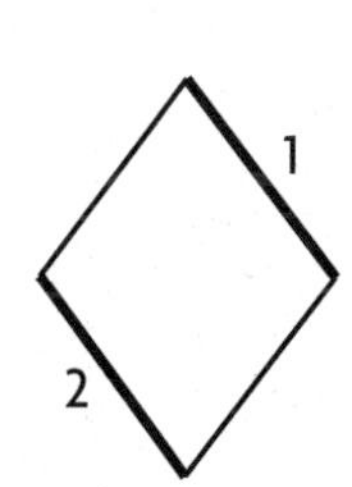

____

9. 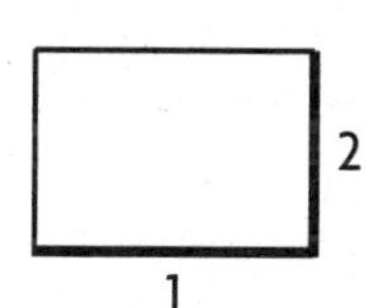

____

GO DIGITAL Assessment Options: Soar to Success Math

Vocabulary Builder

▶ Visualize It

Sort the checked words into the circle map.

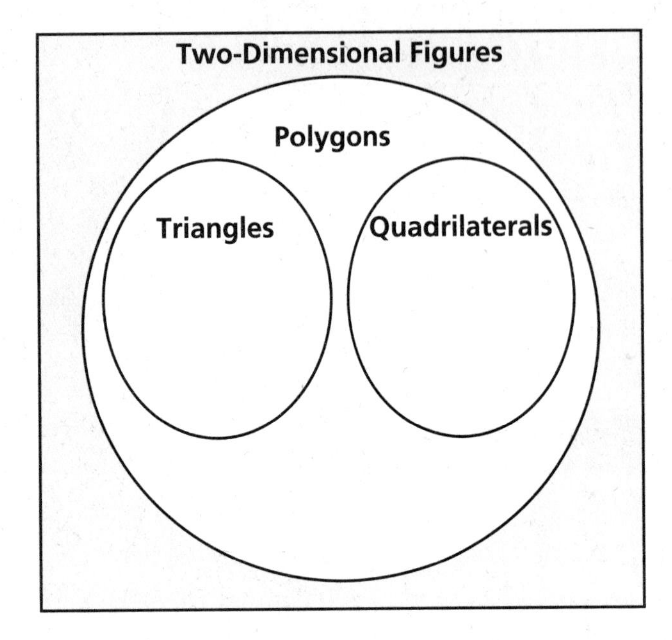

Review Words

✓ acute triangle
capacity
cubic units
✓ decagon
✓ hexagon
✓ obtuse triangle
✓ octagon
✓ parallelogram
quadrilateral
✓ rectangle
✓ rhombus
✓ right triangle
✓ trapezoid
volume

▶ Understand Vocabulary

Complete the sentences using the preview words.

1. The pair of numbers used to locate points on a grid is an

 ________________.

2. All sides and all angles are ________________ in a regular polygon.

3. The first number in an ordered pair is the ________________ and

 the second number in an ordered pair is the ________________.

4. A cube with length, width, and height of 1 unit is a

 ________________.

5. All three sides are the same length in a(n) ________________.

6. The point, (0, 0), also called the ________________, is where the *x*-axis and the *y*-axis intersect.

Preview Words

congruent
equilateral triangle
heptagon
isosceles triangle
nonagon
ordered pair
origin
polygon
regular polygon
scalene triangle
unit cube
x-axis
x-coordinate
y-axis
y-coordinate

• Interactive Student Edition
• Multimedia eGlossary

Name ______________________

Reading In reading, thinking about what you already know helps you to understand a new topic. You already know a lot about geometry. You can use what you know to move ahead.

Topic: Angles and lines

What do I already know?

1. Angles are measured in degrees.
2. An acute angle has a measure less than 90°.
3. Perpendicular lines intersect to form right angles.

Think
I remember classifying triangles by the measure of their angles.

Before beginning a module on geometry, Lauren lists three things she already knows.

Writing Think about all the words in your math vocabulary that relate to angles and lines, for example, *right angle*, *parallel lines*, and *obtuse angle*. Work with a partner to write five more things you know about the topic.

____

____

____

____

____

Get Ready Game

Three-in-a-Row

Object of the Game Identify and draw geometric figures.

Materials

- Counters
- 3-by-3 Grid
- Geometry Cards

Set Up

Give each player a 3-by-3 grid. Players shuffle the Geometry Cards and place them face down in a stack.

Number of Players 2–3

How to Play

1. Each player sketches the following geometric figures in any space on their grid:
   - acute angle
   - right angle
   - obtuse angle
   - acute triangle
   - right triangle
   - obtuse triangle

2. Students take turns turning over the top card from the stack.

3. Students place a counter over the drawing on their grid that matches the Geometry Card.

4. The first player to get three in a row horizontally, vertically, or diagonally is the winner.

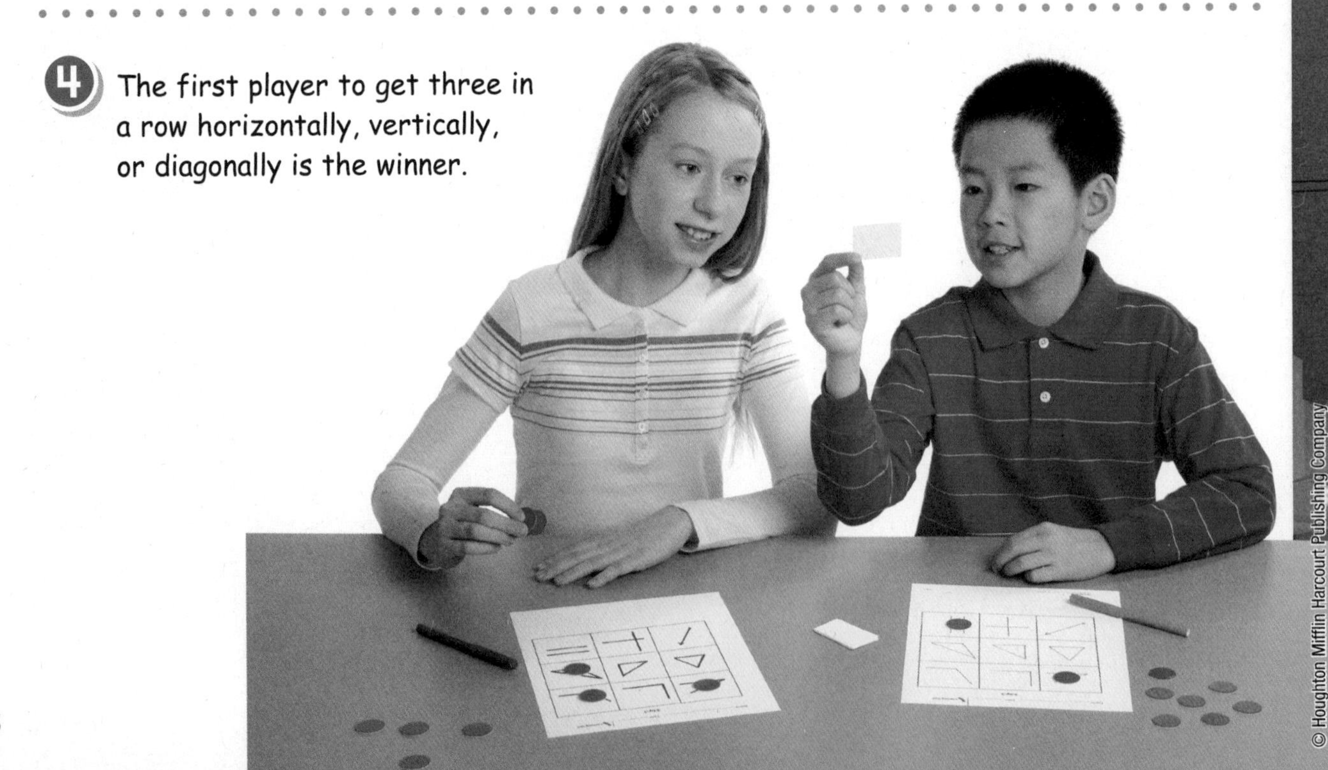

Name ____________________

11.1 Polygons

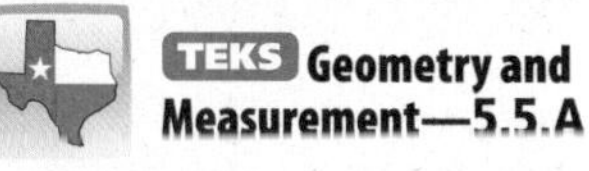

MATHEMATICAL PROCESSES 5.1.D, 5.1.E

Essential Question How can you identify and classify polygons?

Unlock the Problem (Real World)

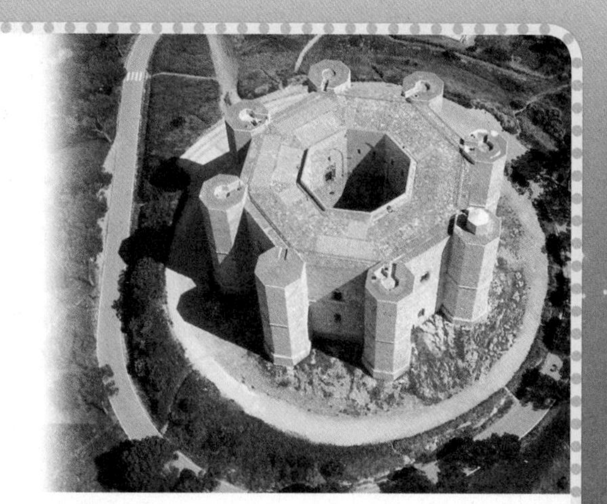

The Castel del Monte in Apulia, Italy, was built more than 750 years ago. The fortress has one central building with eight surrounding towers. Which polygon do you see repeated in the structure? How many sides, angles, and vertices does this polygon have?

A **polygon** is a closed plane figure formed by three or more line segments that meet at points called vertices. It is named by the number of sides and angles it has. To identify the repeated polygon in the fortress, complete the tables below.

Polygon	Triangle	Quadrilateral	Pentagon	Hexagon
Sides	3	4	5	
Angles				
Vertices				

Polygon	Heptagon	Octagon	Nonagon	Decagon
Sides	7	8		
Angles				
Vertices				

So, the ____________ is the repeated polygon in the Castel del Monte because it has ______ sides, ______ angles, and ______ vertices.

Math Idea

Sometimes the angles inside a polygon are greater than 180°.

Math Talk Mathematical Processes

What pattern do you see among the number of sides, angles, and vertices a polygon has?

Regular Polygons When line segments have the same length or when angles have the same measure, they are **congruent**. In a **regular polygon**, all sides are congruent and all angles are congruent.

regular polygon

All sides are congruent.

All angles are congruent.

4 cm 4 cm 4 cm 4 cm 4 cm
108° 108° 108° 108° 108°

You can write measurements to show congruent sides and angles.

not a regular polygon

Not all sides are congruent.

Not all angles are congruent.

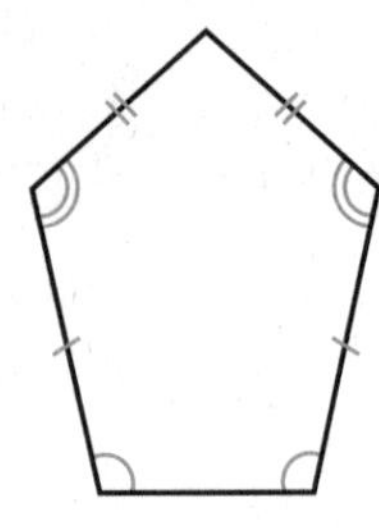

You can use the same markings to show the congruent sides and angles.

Try This! **Label the Venn diagram to classify the polygons in each group. Then draw a polygon that belongs only to each group.**

Congruent ______________ Congruent ______________

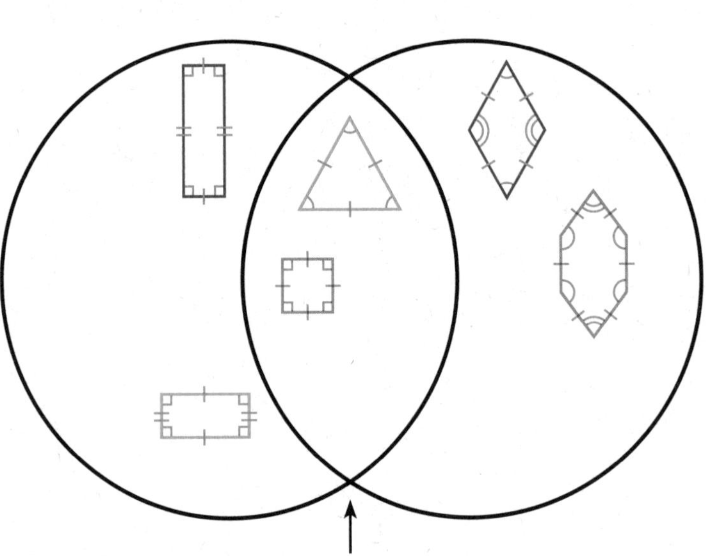

Regular ______________

Share and Show

Name each polygon. Then tell whether it is a *regular polygon* or *not a regular polygon*.

1.

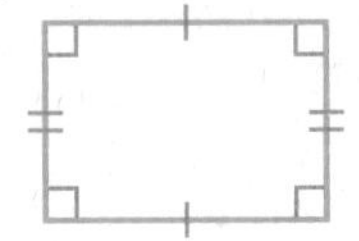

____

2.

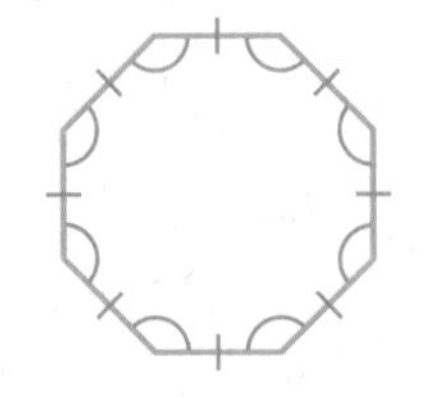

____

Name ______________________

3. 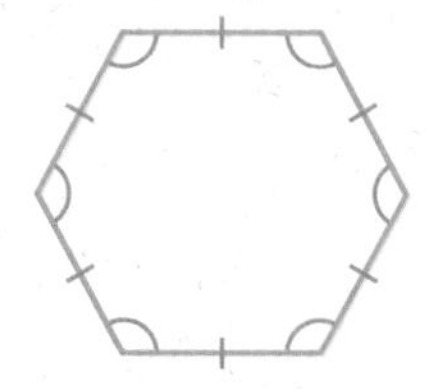

4. 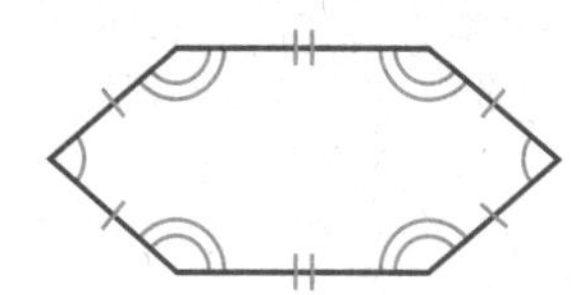

Problem Solving

5. H.O.T. Compare the polygons shown in Exercises 3 and 4. **Use Math Language** to describe how they are alike and how they are different.

6. Why do all regular pentagons have the same shape? **Explain.**

Problem Solving Real World

For 7–8, use the Castel del Monte floor plan at the right.

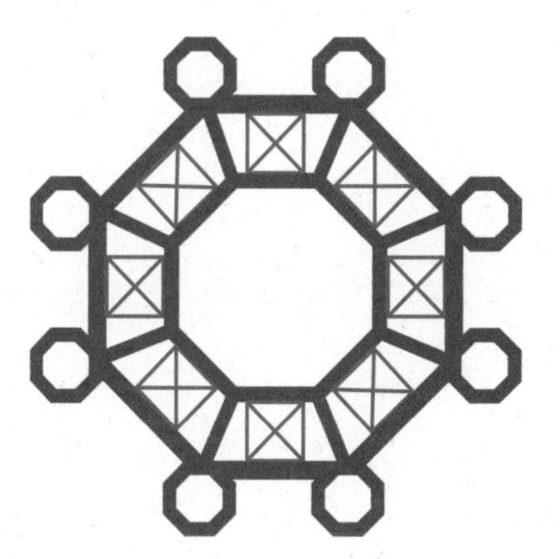

7. **Multi-Step** Which polygons in the floor plan have four equal sides and four congruent angles? How many of these polygons are there?

8. **Multi-Step** Is there a quadrilateral in the floor plan that is not a regular polygon? Name the quadrilateral and tell how many of the quadrilaterals are in the floor plan.

9. H.O.T. Look at the angles for all regular polygons. As the number of sides increases, do the measures of the angles increase or decrease? What pattern do you see?

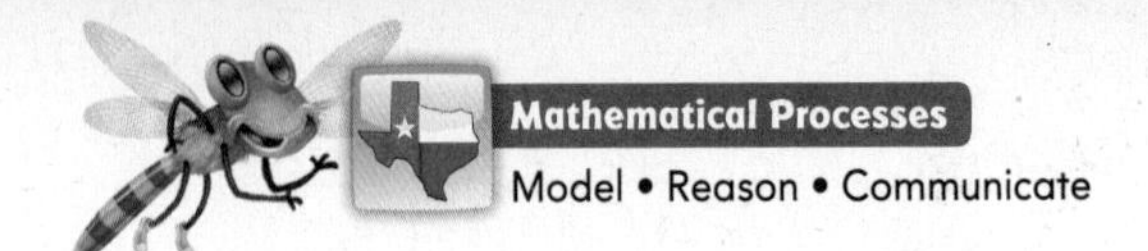

Daily Assessment Task

Fill in the bubble completely to show your answer.

10. Marianna would like to create a mosaic using pieces that have only four angles. Which shapes could Marianna use?

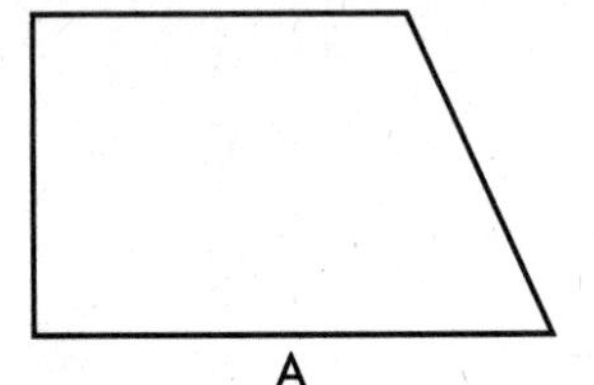

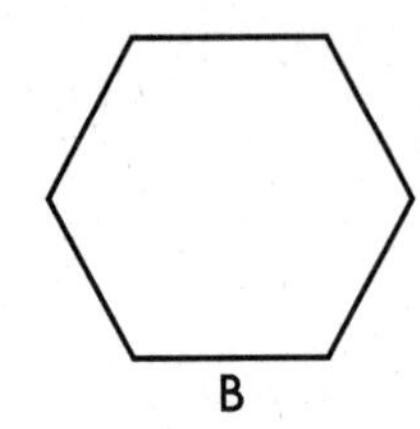

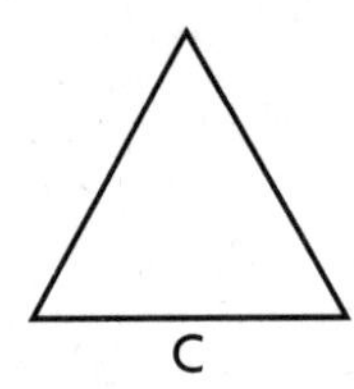

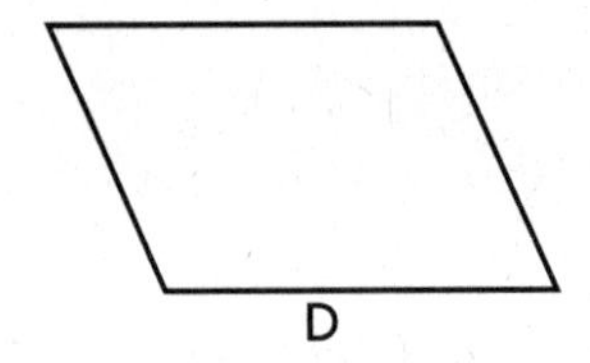

Ⓐ A and B   Ⓒ A and D

Ⓑ B and C   Ⓓ B and D

11. Lino found a small green piece of glass with this shape. What is the name of the shape? Is it regular?

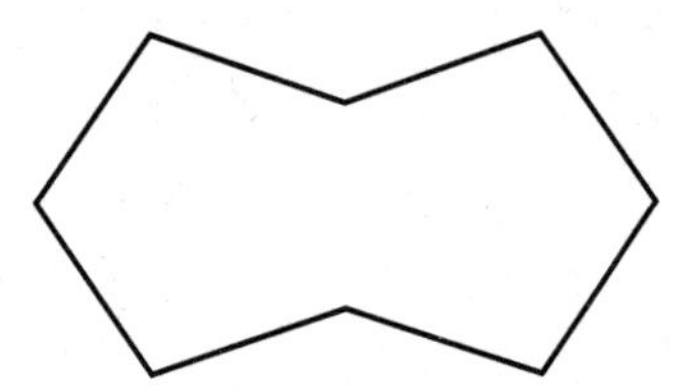

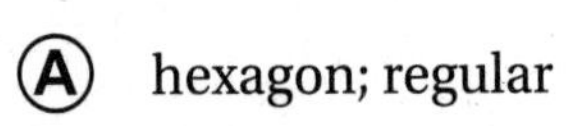
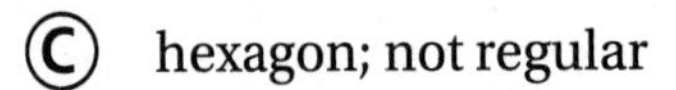

Ⓐ hexagon; regular   Ⓒ hexagon; not regular

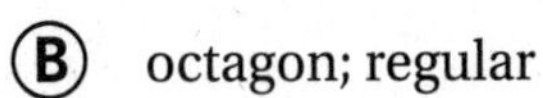

Ⓑ octagon; regular   Ⓓ octagon; not regular

12. **Multi-Step** Lois began a mosaic using congruent regular triangles. She first placed a triangle as a center piece. She then placed three triangles so that one side of each triangle lined up with one side of the original triangle. What shape was formed by the first four pieces?

Ⓐ regular hexagon   Ⓒ regular triangle

Ⓑ quadrilateral   Ⓓ nonagon

TEXAS Test Prep

13. Which of the following is a regular hexagon?

Ⓐ 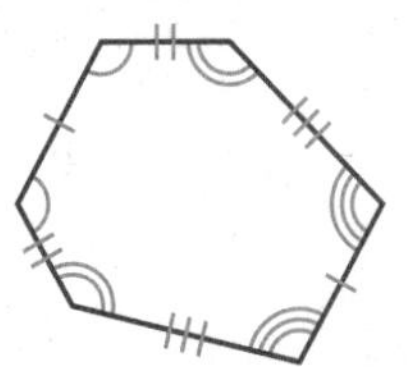

Ⓒ 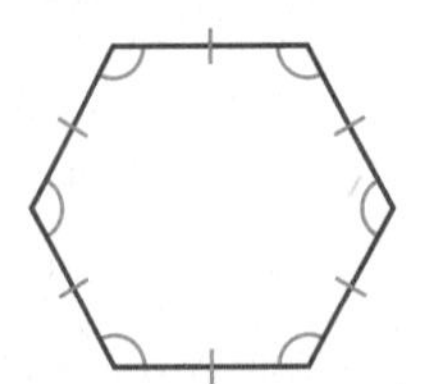

Ⓑ 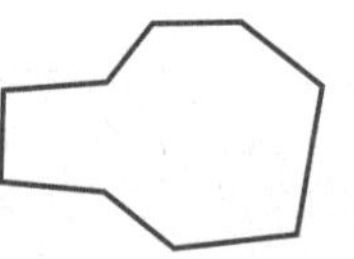

Ⓓ 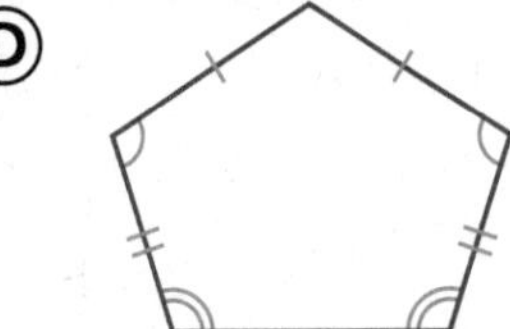

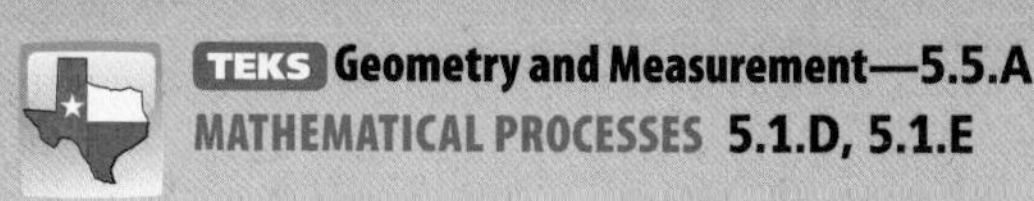

Name ___________________________

11.1 Polygons

Name each polygon. Then tell whether it is a *regular polygon* or *not a regular polygon*.

1. 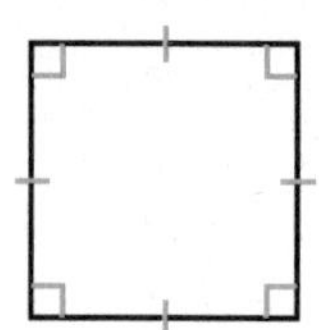

2. 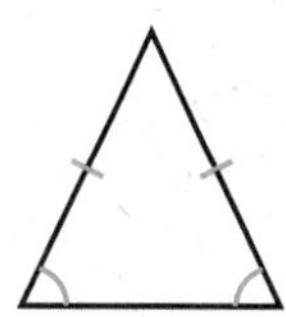

3. 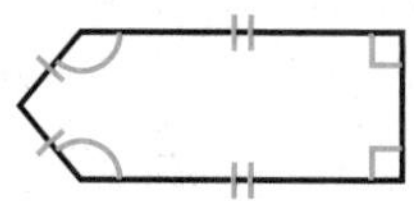

4. 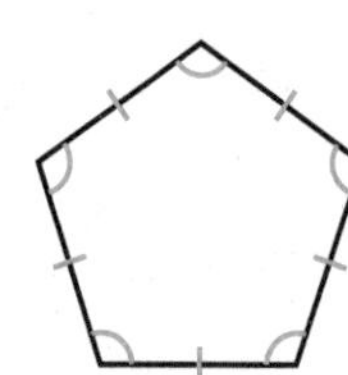

Problem Solving Real World

5. Chantal draws a polygon with seven congruent sides and angles. Name Chantal's shape. Is the shape a regular polygon? **Explain.**

6. Name the shapes that make up the Texas state flag. Are any of the shapes regular polygons? **Explain.**

Lesson Check

Fill in the bubble completely to show your answer.

7. Which of the following is a regular octagon?

Ⓐ 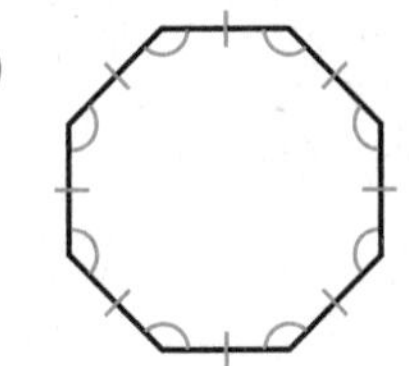

Ⓑ 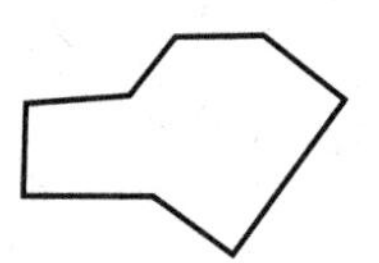

Ⓒ 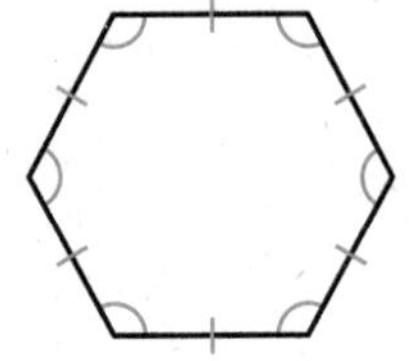

Ⓓ 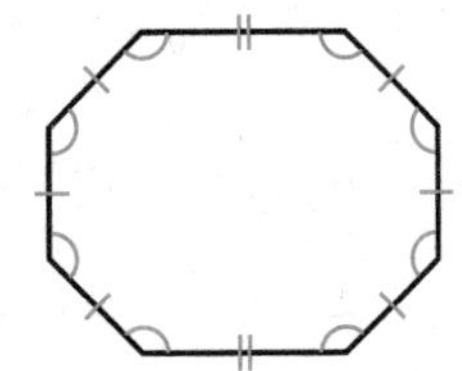

8. Bradley uses only regular polygons in his shape mobile. Which polygon could NOT be in Bradley's mobile?

Ⓐ 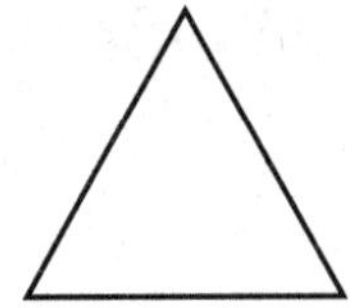

Ⓑ 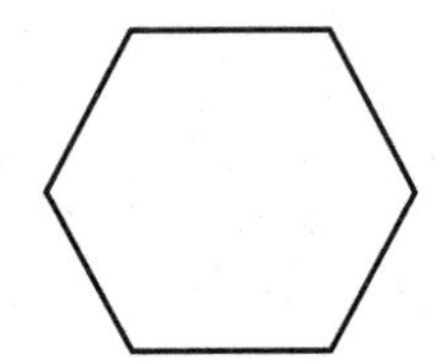

Ⓒ 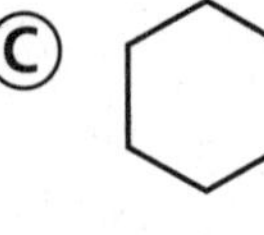

Ⓓ 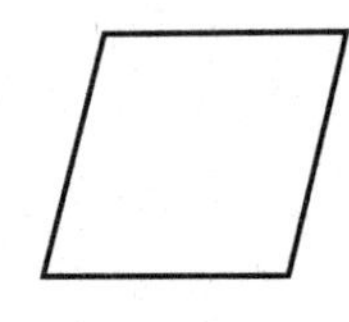

9. How many regular triangles are in this figure?

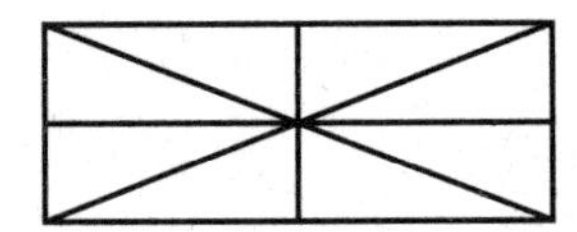

Ⓐ 0

Ⓑ 8

Ⓒ 4

Ⓓ 6

10. An artist made a pendant with the shape shown below. What is the name of the shape? Is it regular?

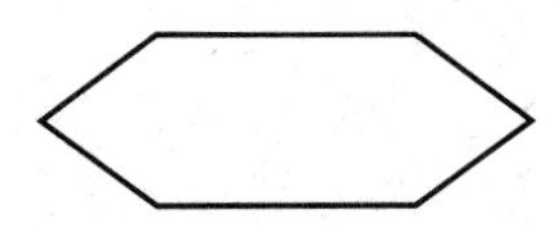

Ⓐ hexagon; regular

Ⓑ hexagon; not regular

Ⓒ octagon; regular

Ⓓ octagon; not regular

11. **Multi-Step** Which are the next two polygons in the pattern?

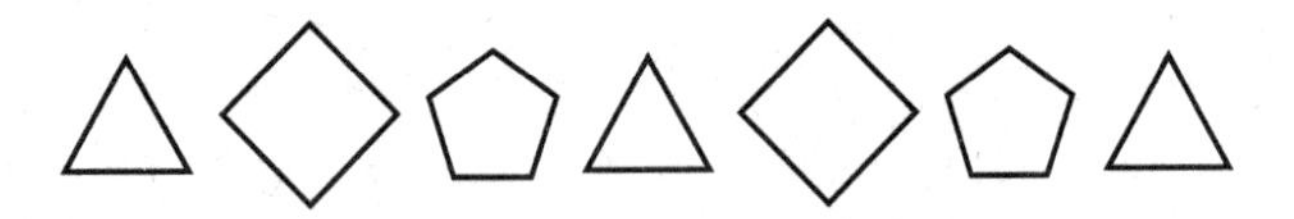

Ⓐ triangle; square

Ⓑ quadrilateral; triangle

Ⓒ quadrilateral; pentagon

Ⓓ pentagon; triangle

12. **Multi-Step** How can you classify the sides and angles of a square?

Ⓐ 2 pairs of congruent sides; 2 pairs of congruent angles

Ⓑ 4 congruent angles; 4 congruent sides

Ⓒ 0 congruent angles; 4 congruent sides

Ⓓ 2 pairs of congruent sides; 1 pair of congruent angles

Name ______________________

MATHEMATICAL PROCESSES 5.1.F, 5.1.G

11.2 Triangles

Essential Question How can you classify triangles?

Unlock the Problem

If you look closely at Epcot Center's Spaceship Earth building in Orlando, Florida, you may see a pattern of triangles. The triangle outlined in the pattern at the right has 3 congruent sides and 3 acute angles. What type of triangle is outlined?

Complete the sentence that describes each type of triangle.

Classify triangles by the lengths of their sides.

An **equilateral triangle** has ______ congruent sides.

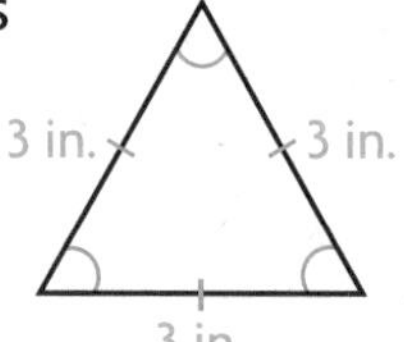

An **isosceles triangle** has ______ congruent sides.

3 in. 2 in. 3 in.

A **scalene triangle** has ______ congruent sides.

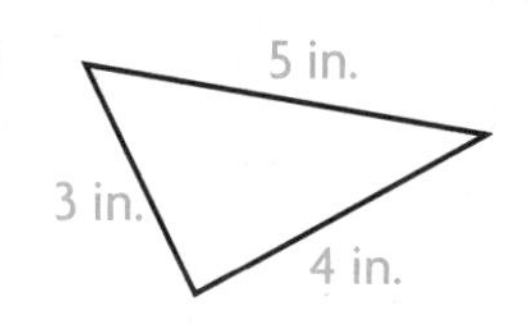

Classify triangles by the measures of their angles.

A **right triangle** has one 90°, or ____________ angle.

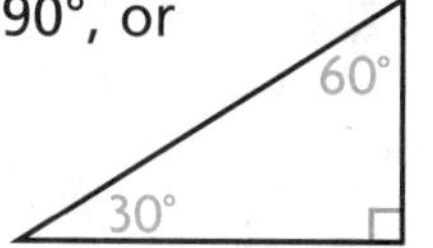

An **acute triangle** has 3 ____________ angles.

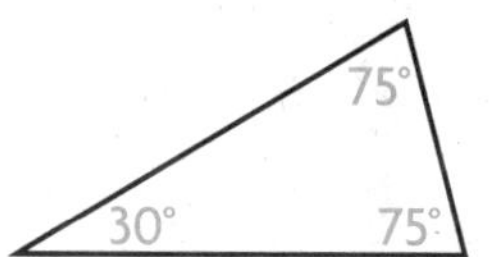

An **obtuse triangle** has 1 ____________ angle.

32° 18° 130°

The type of triangle outlined in the pattern can be classified by the length of its sides as an ____________ triangle.

The triangle can also be classified by the measures of its angles as an ____________ triangle.

Math Talk Mathematical Processes

Is an equilateral triangle also a regular polygon? Explain.

Classify triangle ABC by the lengths of its sides and by the measures of its angles.

Materials ■ centimeter ruler ■ protractor

STEP 1 Measure the sides of the triangle using a centimeter ruler. Label each side with its length. Classify the triangle by the lengths of its sides.

STEP 2 Measure the angles of the triangle using a protractor. Label each angle with its measure. Classify the triangle by the measures of its angles.

- What type of triangle has 3 sides of different lengths?

____

- What is an angle called that is greater than 90° and less than 180°?

____

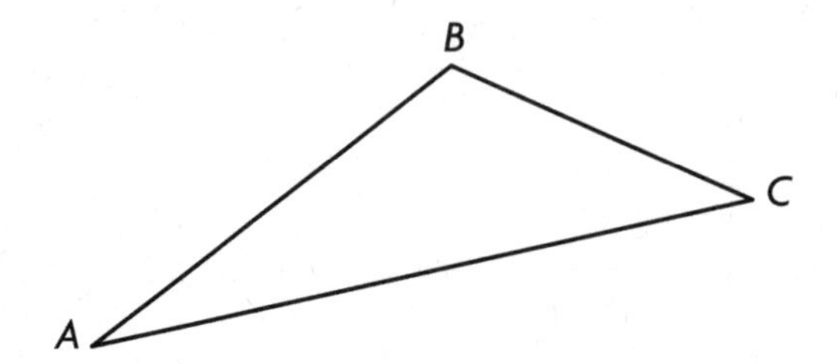

Triangle *ABC* is a _______ _______ triangle.

Try This! **Draw the type of triangle described by the lengths of its sides and by the measures of its angles.**

Triangle by Length of Sides			
		Scalene	**Isosceles**
Triangle by Angle Measure	**Acute**	Think: I need to draw a triangle that is acute and scalene.	
	Obtuse		

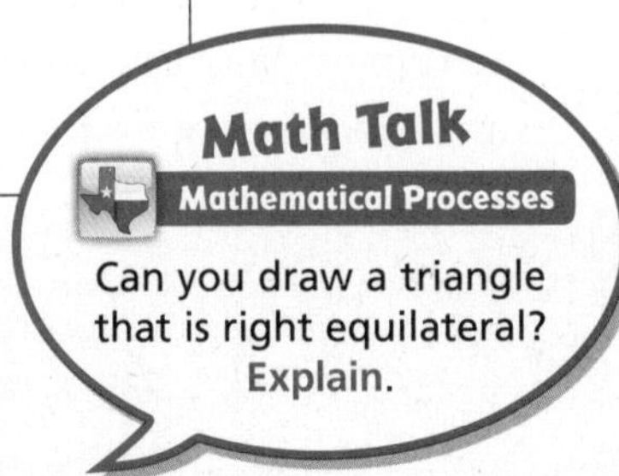

Name ___

Share and Show

Classify each triangle. Write *isosceles, scalene,* or *equilateral.* Then write *acute, obtuse,* or *right.*

1. 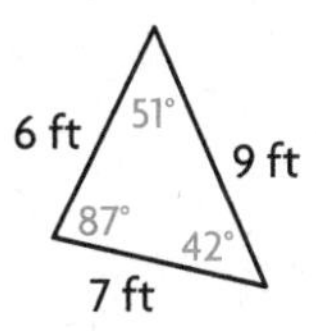

___ ___

2. 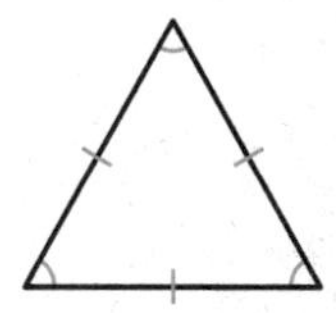

___ ___

3. 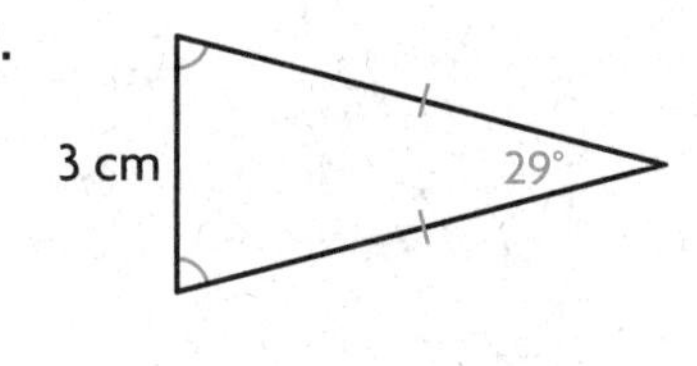

___ ___

Problem Solving

4. H.O.T. Can you tell that a triangle is obtuse, right, or acute without measuring the angles? Explain.

___

___

___

5. Multi-Step Draw 2 equilateral triangles that are congruent and share a side. What polygon is formed? Is it a regular polygon?

___

___

___

Problem Solving Real World

6. H.O.T. Analyze Shannon said that a triangle with exactly 2 congruent sides and an obtuse angle is an equilateral obtuse triangle. Describe her error.

___

___

Classify the triangles in the structures below. Write *isosceles, scalene,* or *equilateral.* Then write *acute, obtuse,* or *right.*

7. 

___ ___

8. 

___ ___

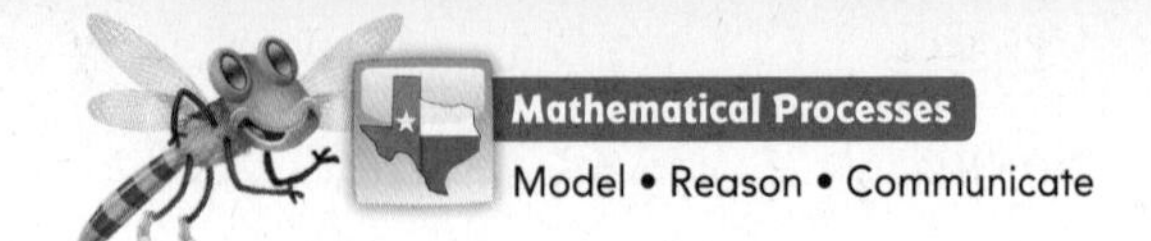

Daily Assessment Task

Fill in the bubble completely to show your answer.

9. Ricky drew a triangle with angles measuring 90°, 30°, and 60°, and no congruent sides. Which of these describes the triangle?

Ⓐ isosceles right

Ⓑ equilateral obtuse

Ⓒ scalene acute

Ⓓ scalene right

10. Which of these triangles is isosceles and obtuse?

Ⓐ 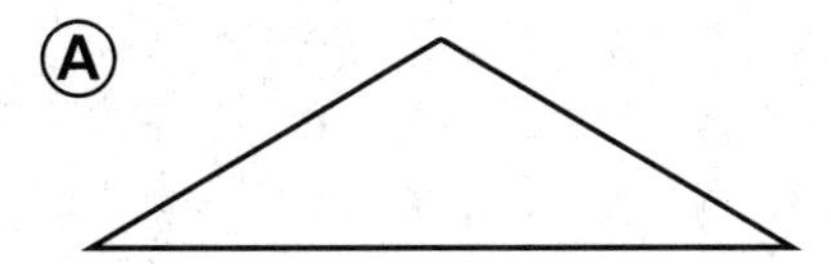

 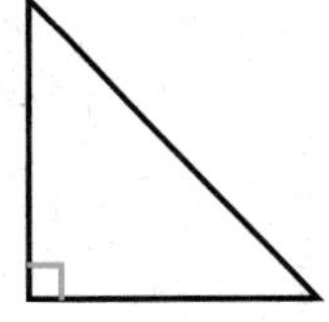

Ⓑ 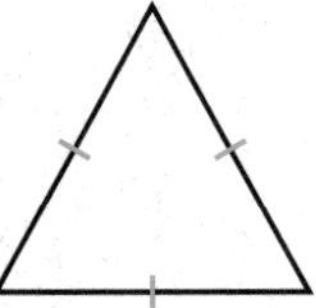

Ⓓ 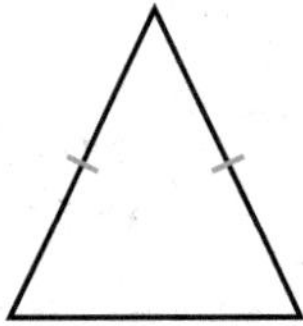

11. **Multi-Step** Jenna drew this triangle, and then drew the dotted line down the center. What type of triangle did she draw first? What triangles resulted from the dotted line?

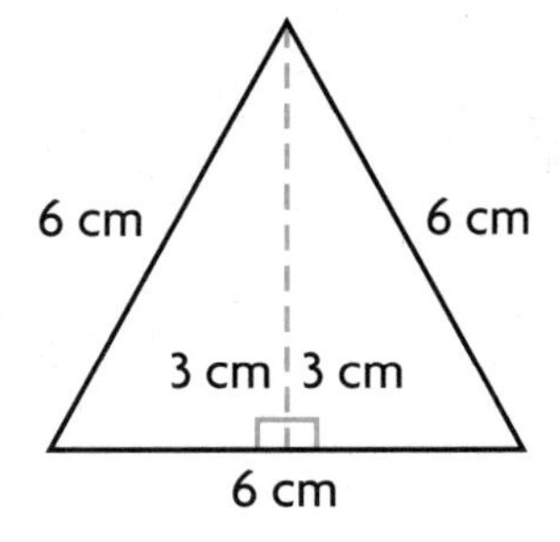

Ⓐ right; two scalene obtuse triangles

Ⓑ equilateral; two right triangles

Ⓒ scalene right; two right triangles

Ⓓ isosceles acute; two equilateral triangles

TEXAS Test Prep

12. Which kind of triangle has exactly 2 congruent sides?

Ⓐ isosceles

Ⓑ equilateral

Ⓒ scalene

Ⓓ right

Name ______________________

11.2 Triangles

Classify each triangle. Write *isosceles, scalene,* or *equilateral.* Then write *acute, obtuse,* or *right.*

1. 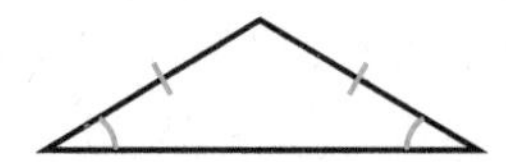

____

____

2. 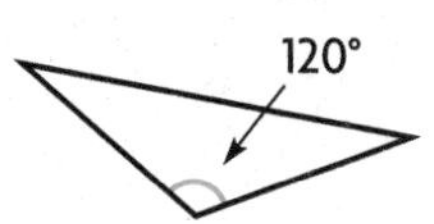

____

____

3. 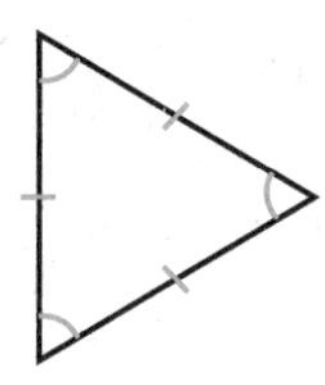

____

____

4. 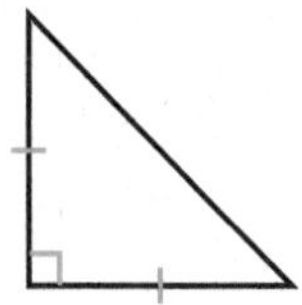

____

____

5. 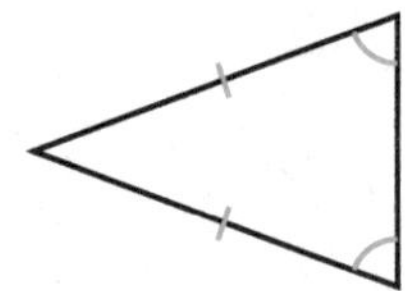

____

____

6. 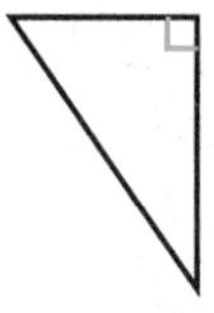

____

____

Circle the figure that does not belong. Explain.

7. 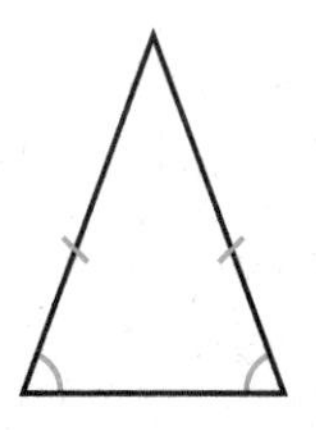  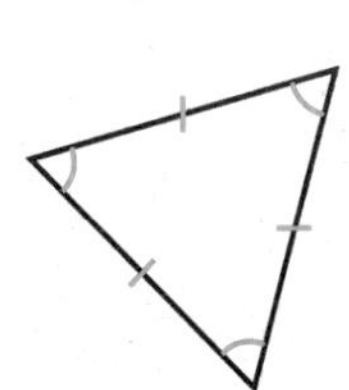

____

Problem Solving

8. Parker drew a triangle with no congruent sides and a 95° angle. Classify the triangle by the lengths of its sides and measures of its angles. Explain.

____

____

Lesson Check

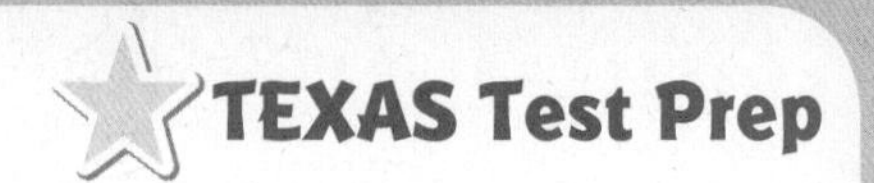

Fill in the bubble completely to show your answer.

9. Lindsay draws a right triangle and adds the measures of the right angle and one acute angle. Which is a possible sum of the two angles?

(A) 180°

(B) 45°

(C) 90°

(D) 120°

10. Which of these triangles is isosceles and acute?

(A) 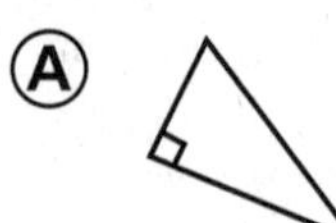

(B)  

(C) 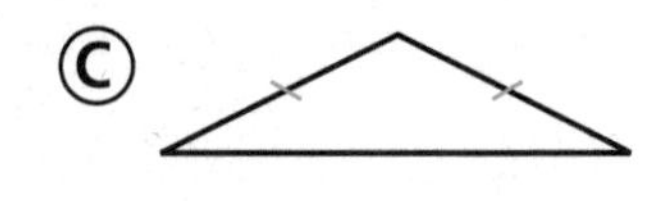

(D) 

11. Which kind of triangle has 3 congruent sides?

(A) right

(B) isosceles

(C) equilateral

(D) scalene

12. Which of the following is another way to classify a scalene triangle with one angle greater than 90°?

(A) acute

(B) obtuse

(C) right

(D) equilateral

13. **Multi-Step** Mrs. Bennett has a rug that is an equilateral triangle with a perimeter of 12 feet. Which could be the lengths of the sides of the rug?

(A) 4 ft, 4 ft, 4 ft

(B) 5 ft, 5 ft, 2 ft

(C) 3 ft, 3 ft, 3 ft

(D) 3 ft, 4 ft, 5 ft

14. **Multi-Step** Nathan cut a square tile in half for his kitchen floor design. He made one cut along a diagonal from one vertex to another vertex. Which triangles resulted from the cut?

(A) two scalene right triangles

(B) two isosceles obtuse triangles

(C) two isosceles right triangles

(D) two equilateral right triangles

Name ______________________________

11.3 Quadrilaterals

TEKS Geometry and Measurement—5.5.A

MATHEMATICAL PROCESSES
5.1.E, 5.1.G

Essential Question

How can you classify and compare quadrilaterals?

Unlock the Problem

A seating chart for a baseball field has many four-sided figures, or **quadrilaterals**. What types of quadrilaterals can you find in the seating chart?

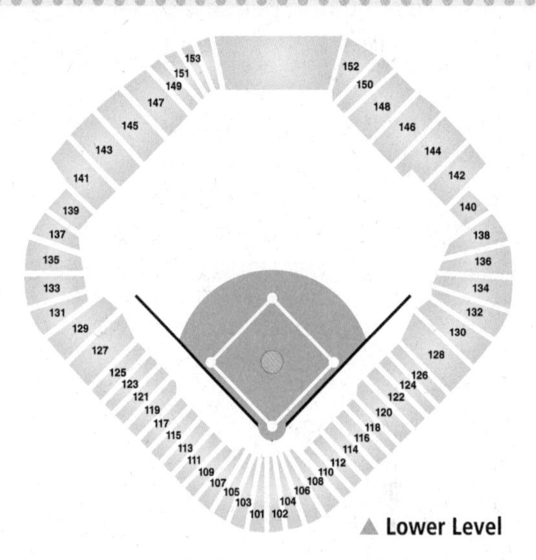

There are five special types of quadrilaterals. You can classify quadrilaterals by their properties, such as parallel sides and perpendicular sides. Parallel lines are lines that are always the same distance apart. Perpendicular lines are lines that intersect to form four right angles.

Complete the sentence that describes each type of quadrilateral.

A general quadrilateral has 4 sides and 4 angles.

A **parallelogram** has opposite ____________ that are ____________ and parallel.

A **rectangle** is a special parallelogram with ______ right angles and 4 pairs of ________________ sides.

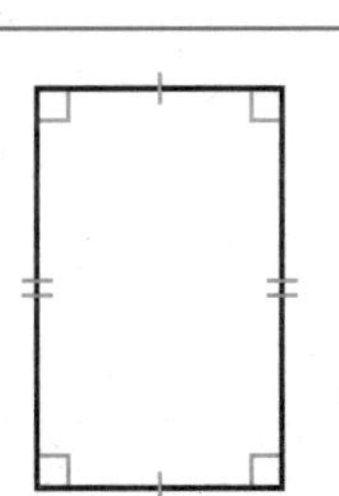

A **rhombus** is a special parallelogram with ______ congruent sides.

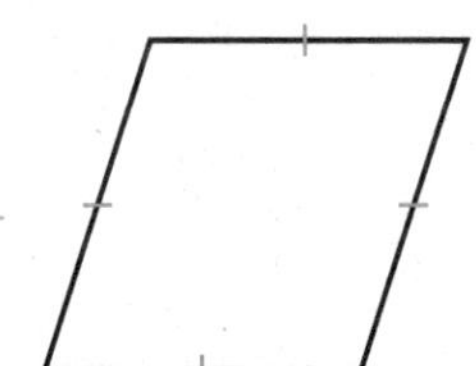

A **square** is a special parallelogram with ______ congruent sides and ______ right angles.

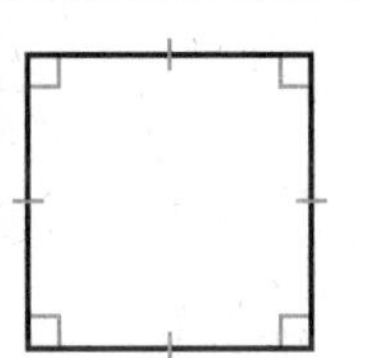

A **trapezoid** is a quadrilateral with exactly 1 pair of ____________ sides.

So, the types of quadrilaterals you can find in the seating chart of the field are ____

____.

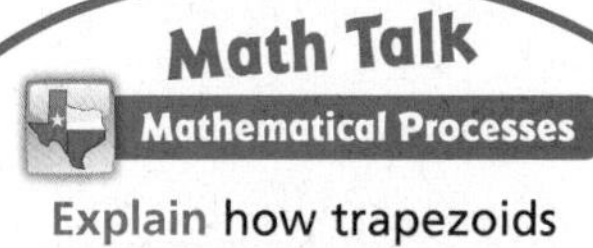

Explain how trapezoids and parallelograms are different.

Materials ■ quadrilaterals ■ scissors

You can use a Venn diagram to sort quadrilaterals and find out how they are related.

- Draw the diagram below on your MathBoard.
- Cut out the quadrilaterals and sort them into the Venn diagram.
- Record your work by drawing each figure you have placed in the Venn diagram below.

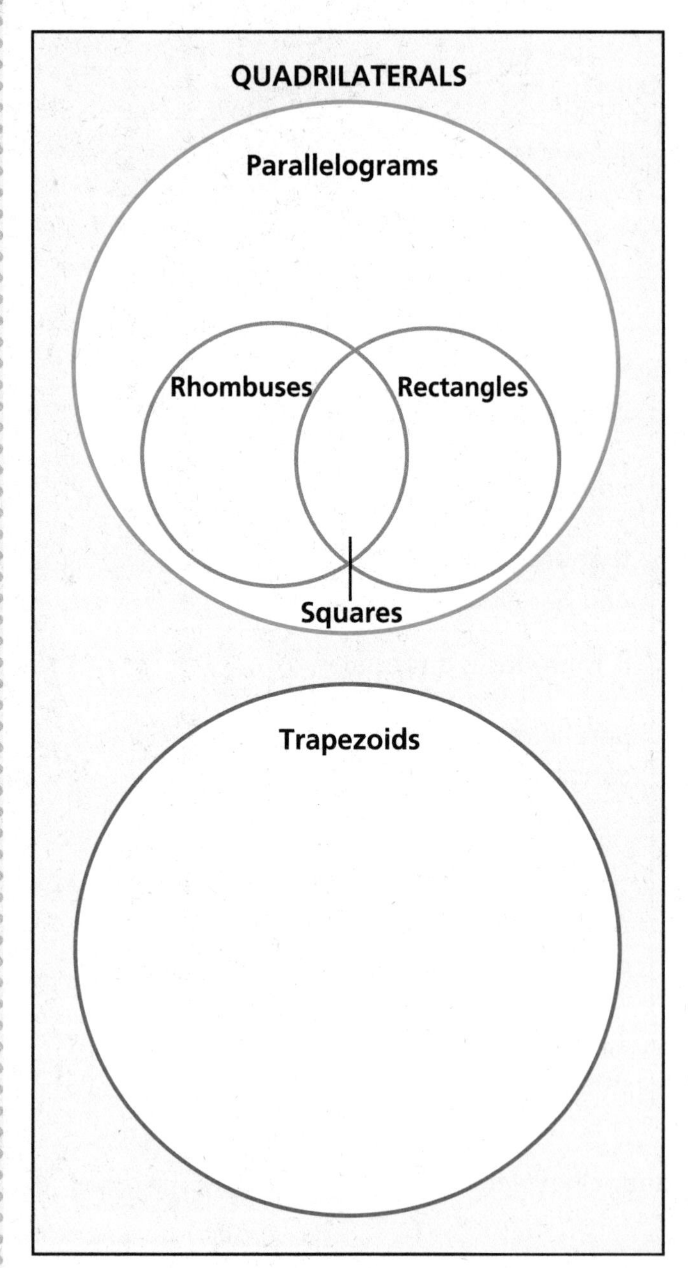

Complete the sentences by writing *always*, *sometimes*, or *never*.

A rhombus is ____________ a square.

A parallelogram is ____________ a rectangle.

A rhombus is ____________ a parallelogram.

A trapezoid is ____________ a parallelogram.

A square is ____________ a rhombus.

1. **Explain** why the circle for parallelograms does not intersect the circle for trapezoids.

____

____

____

2. Draw a quadrilateral with four pairs of perpendicular sides and four congruent sides.

Name ___________________________________

Share and Show

1. Use quadrilateral *ABCD* to answer each question. Complete the sentence.

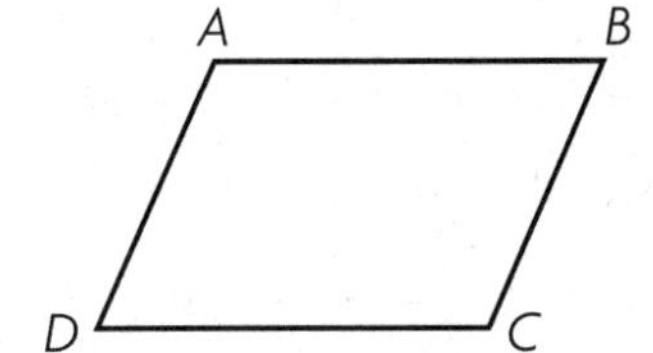

   a. Measure the sides. Are any of the sides congruent? _______
   Mark any congruent sides.

   b. How many right angles, if any, does the quadrilateral have? _______

   c. How many pairs of parallel sides, if any, does the quadrilateral have? _______

   So, quadrilateral *ABCD* is a ________________.

Can the parallel sides of a trapezoid be the same length? Explain your answer.

Classify the quadrilateral in as many ways as possible. Write *quadrilateral, parallelogram, rectangle, rhombus, square,* or *trapezoid.*

 2. 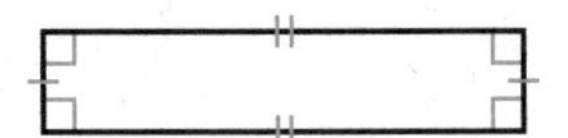

____

 3.

____

Problem Solving

Solve the problems.

4. H.O.T. What's the Error? A quadrilateral has exactly 3 congruent sides. Davis claims that the figure must be a rectangle. Why is his claim incorrect? Use diagrams to explain your answer.

____

____

____

5. H.O.T. Multi-Step I am a figure with four sides. I can be placed in the following categories: quadrilateral, parallelogram, rectangle, rhombus, and square. Draw me. Explain why I fit into each category.

____

____

____

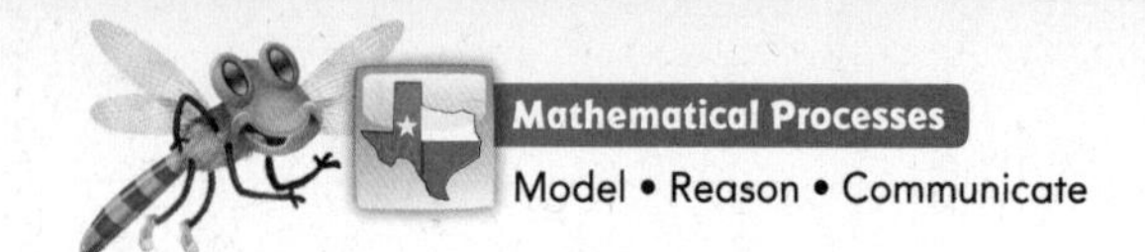

Daily Assessment Task

Fill in the bubble completely to show your answer.

6. Rita only uses parallelograms in her design. Which of the following shapes can she use?

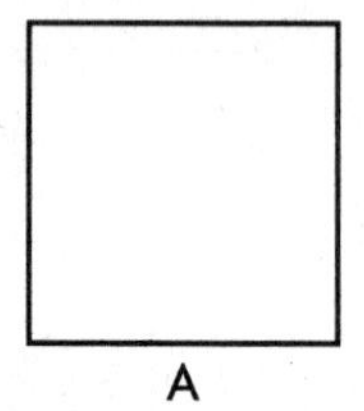

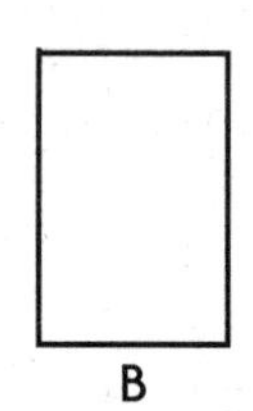

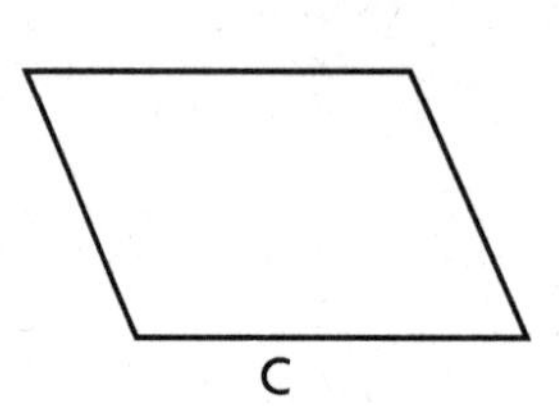

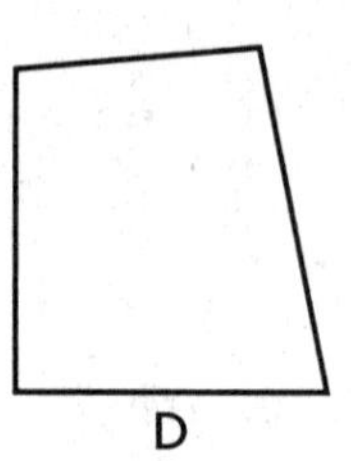

Ⓐ B, C, D only
Ⓑ A, B, C only
Ⓒ A and D only
Ⓓ B and C only

7. Which statement is true about squares and rhombuses?

Ⓐ A square is never a rhombus.
Ⓑ A rhombus is never a square.
Ⓒ A square is always a rhombus.
Ⓓ A rhombus is always a square.

8. **Multi-Step** A quadrilateral has two pairs of parallel sides. It also has four congruent sides. What might the shape be?

Ⓐ square or rhombus
Ⓑ rectangle or trapezoid
Ⓒ square or trapezoid
Ⓓ trapezoid or parallelogram

TEXAS Test Prep

9. A quadrilateral has exactly 1 pair of parallel sides and no congruent sides. What type of quadrilateral is it?

Ⓐ rectangle
Ⓑ rhombus
Ⓒ parallelogram
Ⓓ trapezoid

TEKS Geometry and Measurement—5.5.A
MATHEMATICAL PROCESSES 5.1.E, 5.1.G

Name ____________________

11.3 Quadrilaterals

Classify the quadrilateral in as many ways as possible. Write *quadrilateral, parallelogram, rectangle, rhombus, square,* or *trapezoid.*

1.

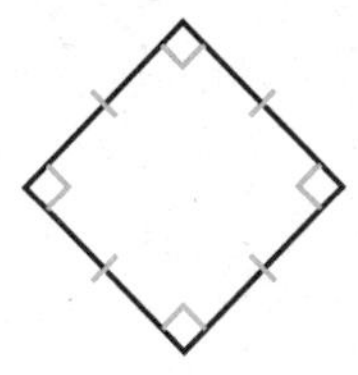

2.

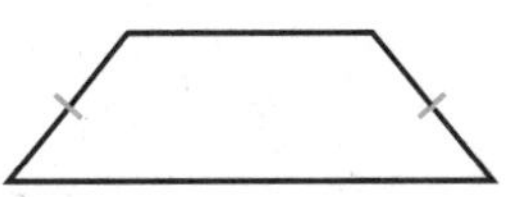

3.

4.

5.

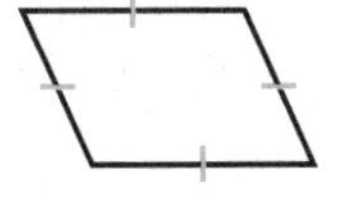

6.

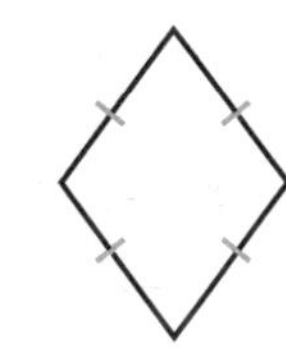

Problem Solving

7. Brooke draws quadrilaterals on a canvas in her art class. Is it possible for Brooke to draw a parallelogram that is not a rectangle? **Explain.**

8. Is it possible for Brooke to draw a square and a rhombus that are congruent? **Explain.**

Lesson Check

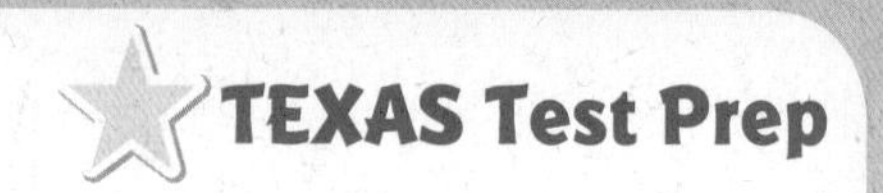

Fill in the bubble completely to show your answer.

9. Which figures have perpendicular sides?

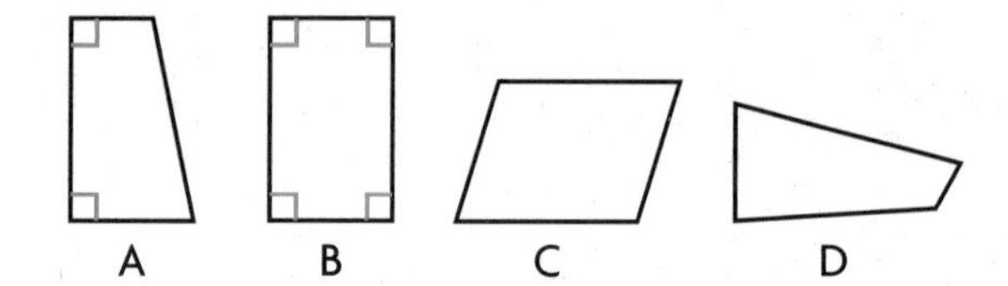

Ⓐ A and B only

Ⓑ A and C only

Ⓒ B and D only

Ⓓ C and D only

10. Which statement is true about the two figures below?

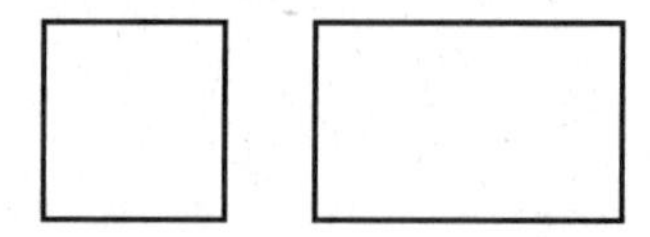

Ⓐ They have a different number of right angles.

Ⓑ They are not congruent.

Ⓒ They are rhombuses.

Ⓓ They are squares.

11. Which of the following is NOT a parallelogram?

Ⓐ rhombus

Ⓑ square

Ⓒ trapezoid

Ⓓ rectangle

12. Which of the following is a regular polygon?

Ⓐ parallelogram

Ⓑ rectangle

Ⓒ rhombus

Ⓓ square

13. **Multi-Step** Becka draws two different quadrilaterals. Both quadrilaterals have two pairs of parallel sides. Only one quadrilateral has four right angles. What might the quadrilaterals be?

Ⓐ square and parallelogram

Ⓑ rectangle and square

Ⓒ rectangle and trapezoid

Ⓓ parallelogram and trapezoid

14. **Multi-Step** Tim cuts out paper quadrilaterals like the one below to use in an art project.

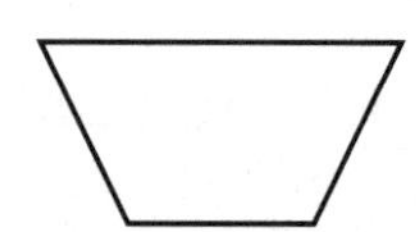

If he cuts the quadrilateral in half, which quadrilaterals result from the cut?

Ⓐ two rhombuses

Ⓑ two parallelograms

Ⓒ two trapezoids

Ⓓ a trapezoid and a parallelogram

Name ____________________

11.4 PROBLEM SOLVING • Properties of Two-Dimensional Figures

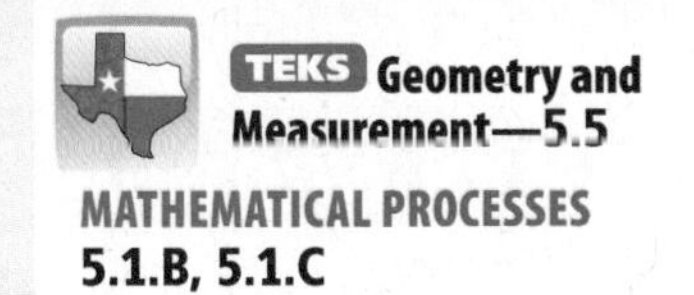

Essential Question

How can you use the strategy *act it out* to approximate whether the sides of a figure are congruent?

Unlock the Problem

Lori has a quadrilateral with vertices *A, B, C,* and *D*. The quadrilateral has four right angles. She wants to show that quadrilateral *ABCD* is a square, but she does not have a ruler to measure the lengths of the sides. How can she show that the quadrilateral has four congruent sides and is a square?

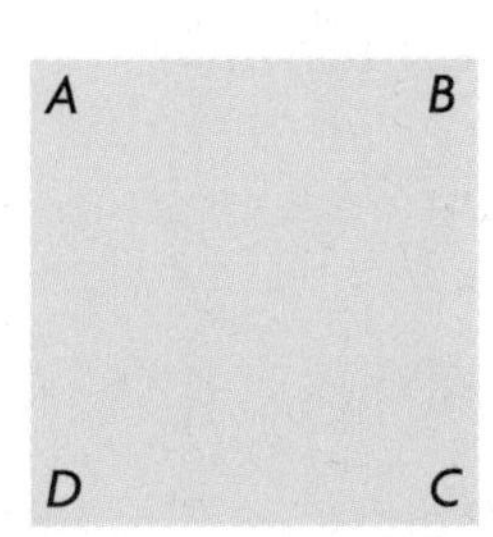

Use the graphic organizer below to help you solve the problem.

Read

What do I need to find?

I need to determine whether the quadrilateral has

4 ____________ sides and is a ____________.

What information am I given?

The quadrilateral has ____________ angles. To be a square, it must also have ____________ sides.

Plan

What is my plan or strategy?

I can trace the figure, cut it out, and then fold it to match each pair of sides to show that sides ____________ are ____________.

Solve

I traced the quadrilateral and cut it out. I used *act it out* by folding to match each pair of sides.

- I folded the quadrilateral to match side *AB* to side *DC*.

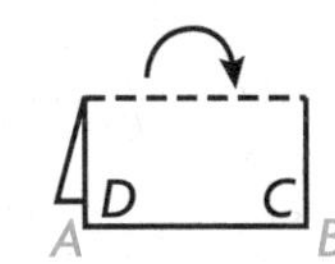

- I folded the quadrilateral to match side *AD* to side *BC*.

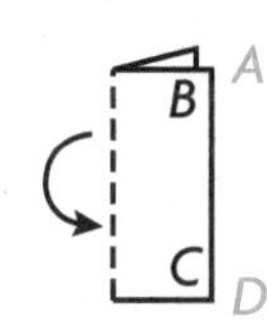

- I folded the quadrilateral diagonally to match side *AD* to side *AB* and side *CD* to side *CB*.

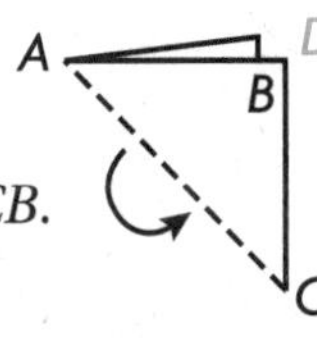

1. What else do you need to do to solve the problem?

____

____

So, quadrilateral *ABCD* ____________ a square.

Try Another Problem

Terrence has drawn a triangle with vertices *E*, *F*, and *G*. The triangle has three congruent angles. He wants to show that triangle *EFG* has three congruent sides, but he does not have a ruler to measure the lengths of the sides. How can he show that the triangle has three congruent sides?

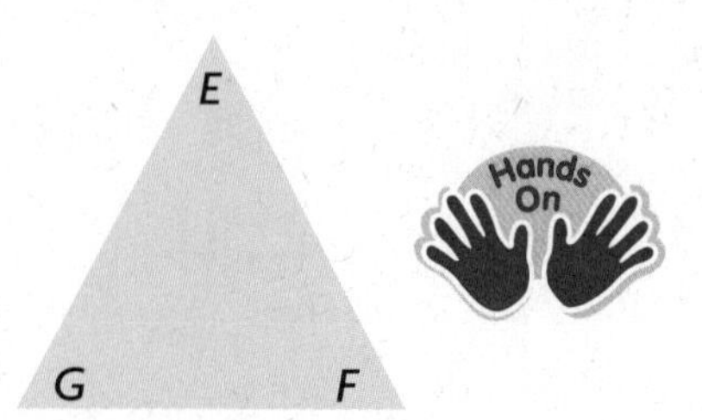

Read	Solve
What do I need to find?	Record your work by drawing your model after each fold. Label each drawing with the sides that you find are congruent.
What information am I given?	
Plan	
What is my plan or strategy?	

2. How can you use reasoning to show that all three sides of the triangle are congruent using just two folds? **Explain**.

Name ______________________

Share and Show

1. Erica thinks that triangle XYZ, at the right, has two congruent sides, but she does not have a ruler to measure the sides. Are two sides congruent?

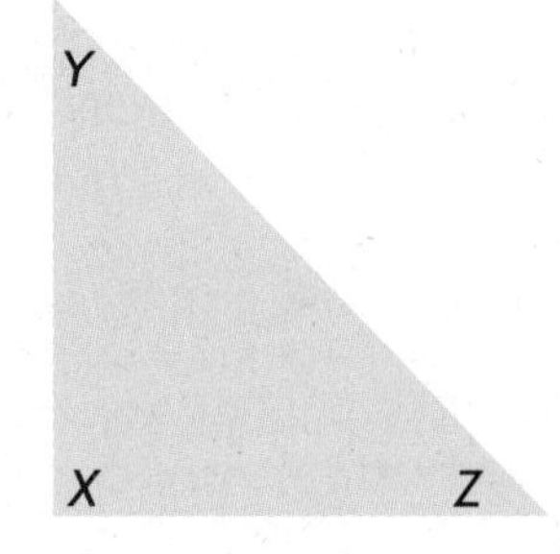

First, trace the triangle and cut out the tracing.

Then, fold the triangle to match each pair of sides to determine if at least two of the sides are congruent. As you test the sides, record or draw the results for each pair to make sure that you have checked all pairs of sides.

Finally, answer the question.

____

____

Math Talk

Mathematical Processes

What if Erica also wants to show, without using a protractor, that the triangle has one right angle and two acute angles? **Explain** how she can show this.

2. December, January, and February were the coldest months in Kristen's town last year. February was the warmest of these months. December was not the coldest. What is the order of these months from coldest to warmest?

____

Problem Solving

3. **H.O.T.** **Multi-Step** Jan enters a 20-foot by 30-foot rectangular room. The long sides face north and south. Jan enters the exact center of the south side and walks 10 feet north. Then she walks 8 feet east. How far is she from the east side of the room?

____

4. **H.O.T.** **Use Diagrams** Max drew a grid to divide a piece of paper into 18 congruent squares. What is the least number of lines Max can draw to divide the grid into 6 congruent rectangles? Use the diagram to show your reasoning.

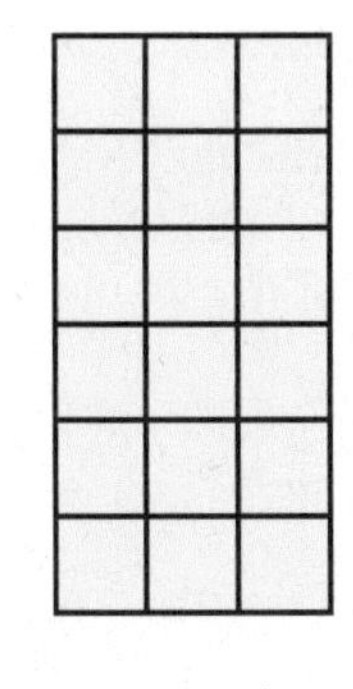

____

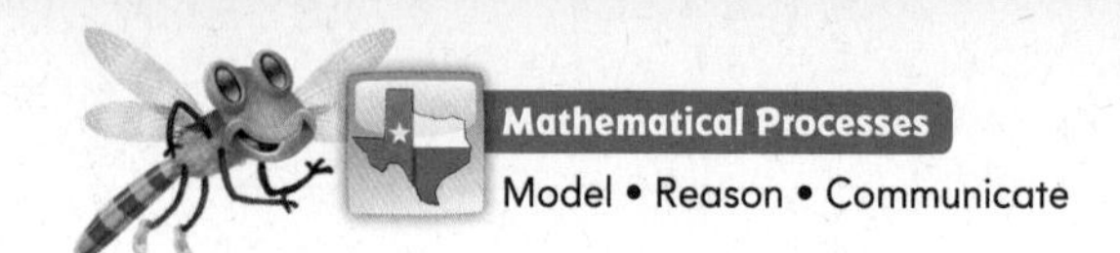

Daily Assessment Task

Fill in the bubble completely to show your answer.

5. Pierre uses a sheet of printer paper for origami. How can he check if the paper is a rectangle?

Ⓐ Use a square corner to see if the paper has four right angles.

Ⓑ Fold the paper in half both ways to see if the opposite sides are congruent.

Ⓒ Both A and B

Ⓓ Neither A nor B

6. **Use Math Language** Meaghan has drawn and cut out triangle *LMN*. She folds side *LM* to side *MN* and they match evenly. She folds side *MN* to side *NL* and they do not match evenly. Which of these describes Meaghan's triangle?

Ⓐ scalene triangle

Ⓑ equilateral triangle

Ⓒ isosceles triangle

Ⓓ right triangle

7. **Multi-Step** Bethany uses six congruent equilateral triangles to create a polygon. Which of the following describes the polygon she creates?

Ⓐ regular pentagon

Ⓑ regular hexagon

Ⓒ square

Ⓓ regular triangle

TEXAS Test Prep

8. Which figure below is a quadrilateral that has opposite sides that are congruent and parallel?

Ⓐ 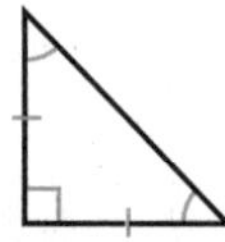

Ⓒ 

Ⓑ 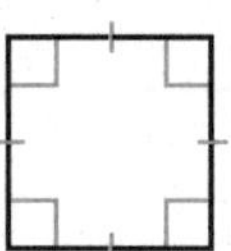

Ⓓ 

Name ______________________

11.4 PROBLEM SOLVING • Properties of Two-Dimensional Figures

1. **Explain** a strategy you can use to draw a figure that is congruent to the figure at the right.

____

____

2. Classify the figure at the right in as many ways as possible. Explain your strategy.

____

____

____

3. Draw two polygons with the same number of sides and angles in each polygon. Make one of the polygons regular and one of the polygons not regular. Are the figures congruent? **Explain**.

____

____

4. Combine the two congruent trapezoids at the right to make new polygons. Draw your new polygons and classify them.

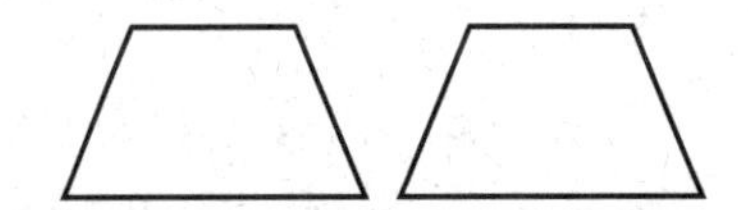

____

Problem Solving (Real World)

5. Shoshanna draws a square. What polygons can she make if she draws a line that cuts the square in half? **Explain**.

____

____

____

Lesson Check

TEXAS Test Prep

Fill in the bubble completely to show your answer.

6. A regular octagon has total perimeter of 24 inches. What is the length of one side of the octagon?

Ⓐ 8 inches

Ⓑ 1 inch

Ⓒ 4 inches

Ⓓ 3 inches

7. Adolfo drew a quadrilateral. He says at least one of the angles is acute. Which polygon could Adolfo have drawn?

Ⓐ parallelogram

Ⓑ square

Ⓒ rectangle

Ⓓ isosceles triangle

8. Classify the polygon named *MNPR* in the figure below

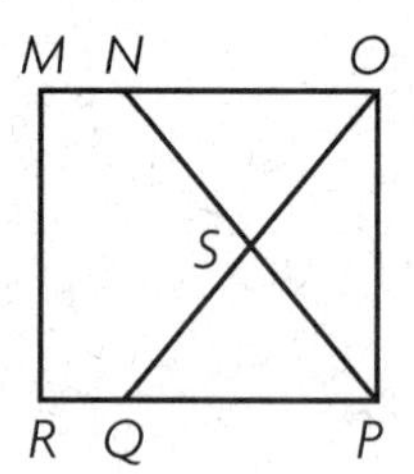

Ⓐ trapezoid

Ⓑ triangle

Ⓒ rectangle

Ⓓ parallelogram

9. Which describes the quadrilateral?

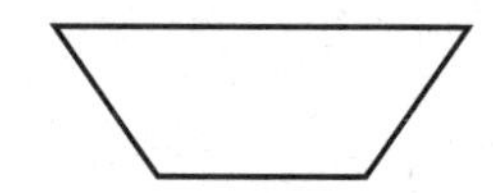

Ⓐ 2 pairs of parallel sides

Ⓑ 2 pairs of perpendicular sides

Ⓒ 1 pair of parallel sides

Ⓓ no pairs of parallel sides

10. **Multi-Step** Veronica folded an equilateral triangle in half and cut along the fold to make two congruent figures. What figures did she make?

Ⓐ two scalene right triangles

Ⓑ a triangle and a trapezoid

Ⓒ two isosceles acute triangles

Ⓓ two equilateral triangles

11. **Multi-Step** Rocco places four congruent squares side by side in a row. The length of one side of a square is 2 cm. What is the perimeter and the area of the larger rectangle Rocco makes?

Ⓐ $P = 32$ cm; $A = 16$ sq cm

Ⓑ $P = 20$ cm; $A = 8$ sq cm

Ⓒ $P = 10$ cm; $A = 4$ sq cm

Ⓓ $P = 20$ cm; $A = 16$ sq cm

Name ______________________________

Module 11 Assessment

Vocabulary

Vocabulary
congruent
nonagon
regular polygon

Choose the best term from the box.

1. A closed plane figure with all sides congruent and all angles congruent is called a ______________. (p. 410)
2. Line segments that have the same length or angles that have the same measure are ______________. (p. 410)

Concepts and Skills

Draw the triangle in the correct group. TEKS 5.5.A

3. All three sides are 2 cm long.
4. Two sides are 2 cm long. The third side is 1 cm long.

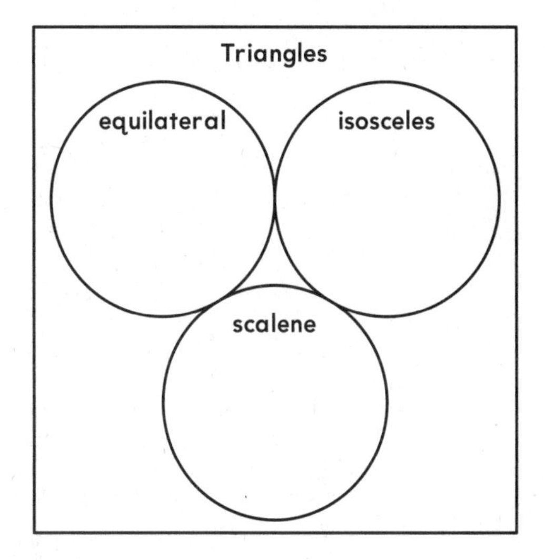

Classify each triangle. Write *isosceles, scalene,* or *equilateral.* Then write *acute, obtuse,* or *right.* TEKS 5.5.A

5. 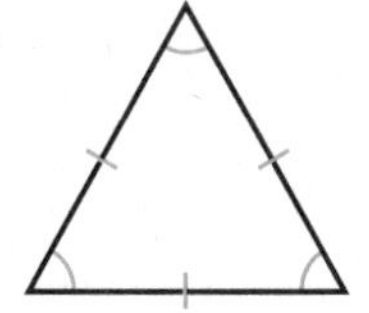

____

____

6. 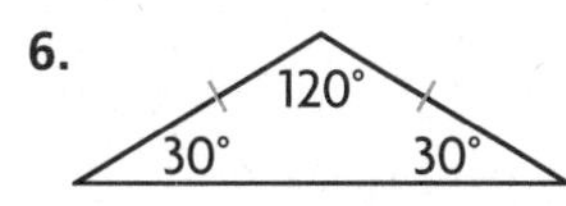

____

____

Classify the quadrilateral in as many ways as possible. Write *quadrilateral, parallelogram, rectangle, rhombus, square,* or *trapezoid.* TEKS 5.5.A

7. 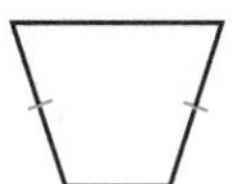

____

____

8. 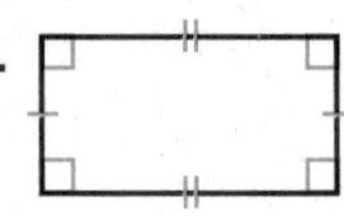

____

____

Fill in the bubble completely to show your answer.

9. What type of triangle is shown below? TEKS 5.5.A

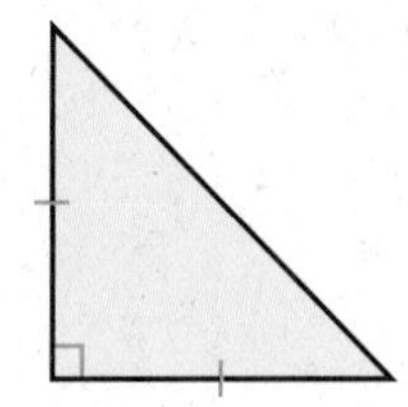

Ⓐ right isosceles

Ⓑ right scalene

Ⓒ equilateral

Ⓓ obtuse scalene

10. Which of the following figures can never be classified as a square? TEKS 5.5.A

Ⓐ rectangle

Ⓑ parallelogram

Ⓒ rhombus

Ⓓ trapezoid

11. Which of the following CANNOT be used for the unknown shape in the graphic organizer? TEKS 5.5.A

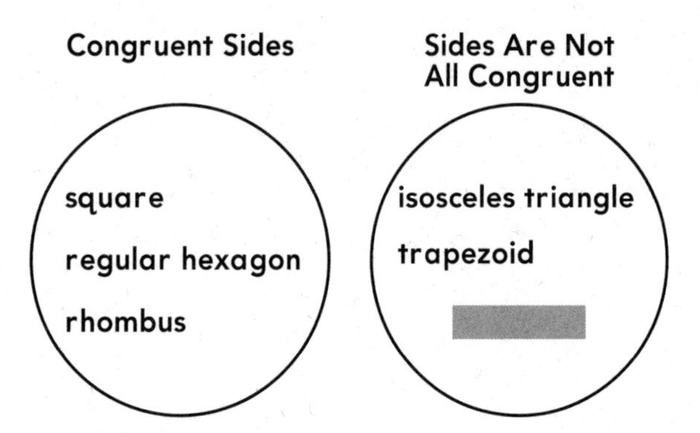

Ⓐ scalene triangle

Ⓑ irregular pentagon

Ⓒ equilateral triangle

Ⓓ irregular nonagon

Name ____________________

12.1 Unit Cubes and Solid Figures

TEKS Geometry and Measurement—5.6.A

MATHEMATICAL PROCESSES 5.1.E, 5.1.F

Essential Question

What is a unit cube and how can you use it to build a solid figure?

Investigate

Hands On

You can build rectangular prisms using unit cubes. How many different rectangular prisms can you build with a given number of unit cubes?

Materials ■ centimeter cubes

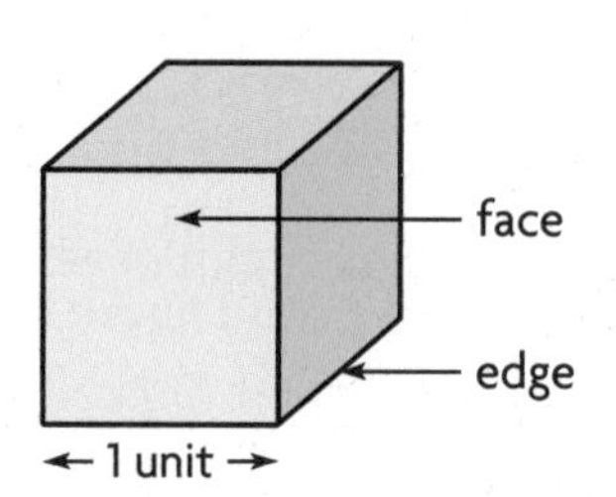

A **unit cube** is a cube that has a length, width, and height of 1 unit. A cube has ______ square faces. All of its faces are congruent. It has ______ edges. The lengths of all its edges are equal.

A. Build a rectangular prism with 2 unit cubes.

Think: When the 2 cubes are pushed together, the faces and edges that are pushed together make 1 face and 1 edge.

- How many faces does the rectangular prism have? ______
- How many edges does the rectangular prism have? ______

B. Build as many different rectangular prisms as you can with 8 unit cubes.

C. Record in units the dimensions of each rectangular prism you built with 8 cubes.

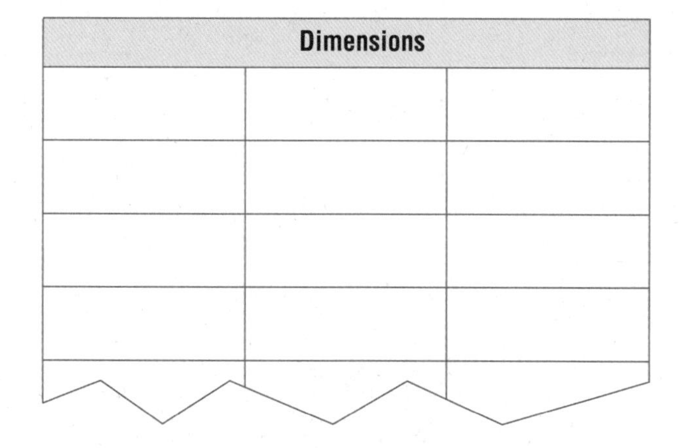

Dimensions		

Math Talk

Mathematical Processes

Describe the different rectangular prisms that you can make with 4 unit cubes.

So, with 8 unit cubes, I can build ______ different rectangular prisms.

Make Connections

You can build other solid figures and compare the solid figures by counting the number of unit cubes.

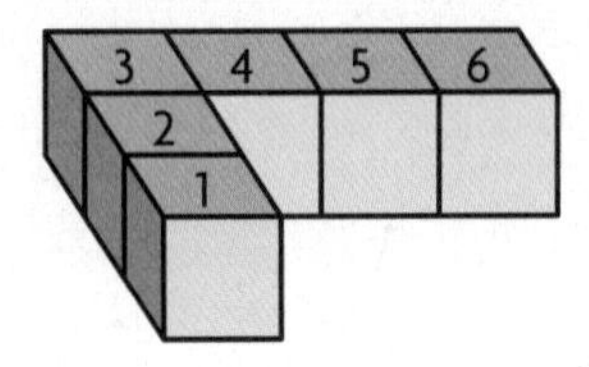

Figure 1

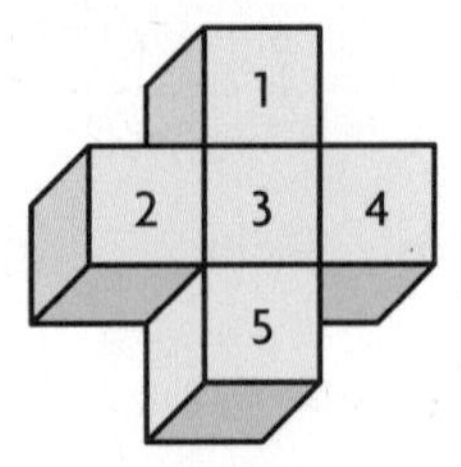

Figure 2

Figure 1 is made up of ______ unit cubes.

Figure 2 is made up of ______ unit cubes.

So, Figure ______ has more unit cubes than Figure ______.

- Use 12 unit cubes to build a solid figure that is not a rectangular prism. Share your model with a partner. Describe how your model is the same and how it is different from your partner's model.

____

____

Share and Show

Count the number of cubes used to build each solid figure.

1. The rectangular prism is made up of ______ unit cubes.

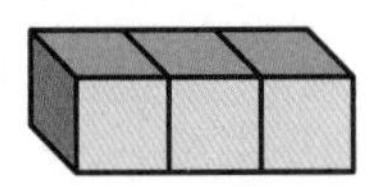

2. 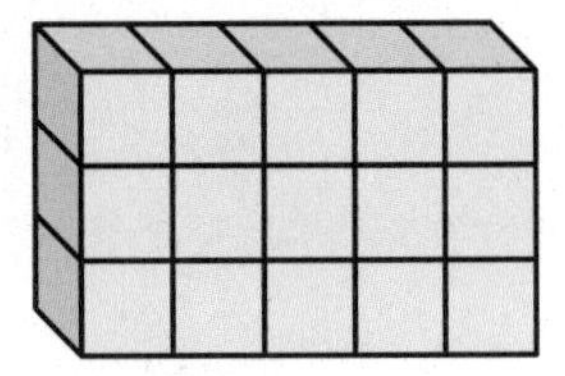

______ unit cubes

3. 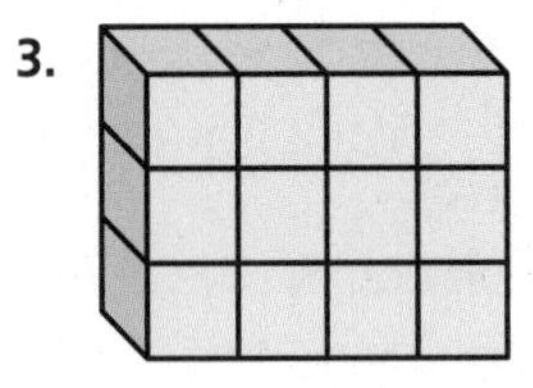

______ unit cubes

 4. 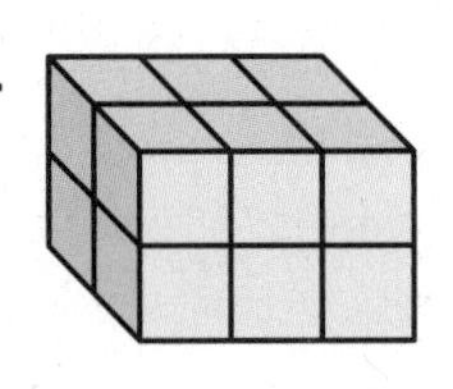

______ unit cubes

5. 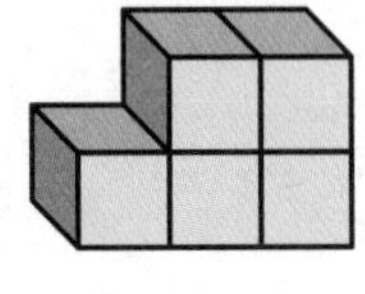

______ unit cubes

6. 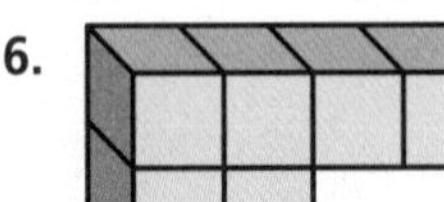

______ unit cubes

 7. 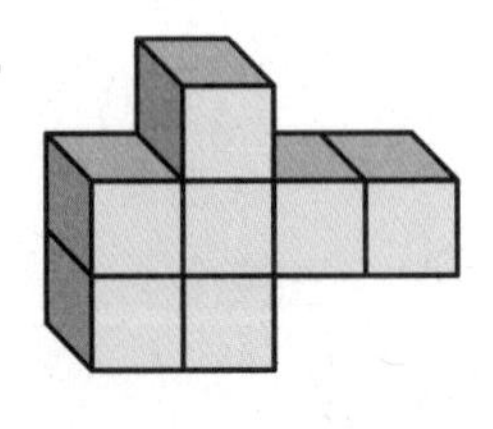

______ unit cubes

Name ______________________________

Problem Solving

8. H.O.T. How are the rectangular prisms in Exercises 3 and 4 related? Is there a different rectangular prism with the same relationship? Use a model or a diagram to show your answer.

____

____

____

9. Write Math ▶ **Explain** why a rectangular prism composed of 2 unit cubes has 6 faces. How do its dimensions compare to a unit cube?

____

____

____

____

10. Write Math ▶ **Explain** how the number of edges for the rectangular prism compares to the number of edges for the unit cube.

____

____

11. H.O.T. **Multi-Step** The Nakagin Capsule Tower has 140 modules, and is 14 stories high. If all of the modules were divided evenly among the number of stories, how many modules would be on each floor? How many different rectangular prisms could be made from that number?

____

12. H.O.T. A cube-shaped house can hold 1,000 unit cubes that are 1 meter by 1 meter by 1 meter. Describe the dimensions of the house using unit cubes.

____

____

Daily Assessment Task

Fill in the bubble completely to show your answer.

13. **Multi-Step** Seth makes 3 more of the figure shown below to build a fort. How many cubes does he use?

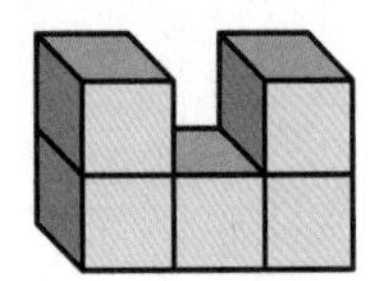

Ⓐ 5 cubes
Ⓑ 25 cubes
Ⓒ 4 cubes
Ⓓ 20 cubes

14. How many cubes were used to make the figure?

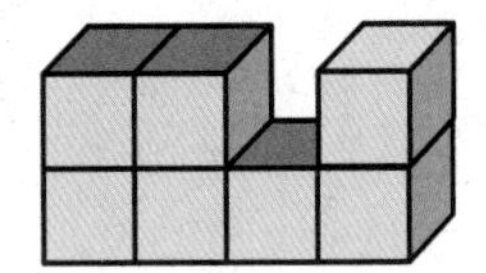

Ⓐ 7 cubes
Ⓑ 9 cubes
Ⓒ 8 cubes
Ⓓ 10 cubes

15. **Multi-Step** Alexandra built these two figures. How many cubes did she use in all?

Ⓐ 9 cubes
Ⓑ 6 cubes
Ⓒ 15 cubes
Ⓓ 30 cubes

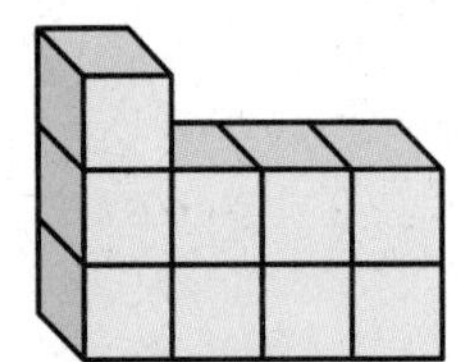

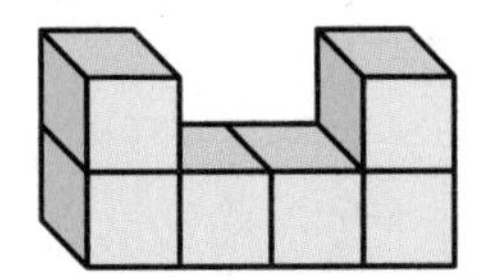

TEXAS Test Prep

16. **Multi-Step** How many more cubes can Marcy use to make the figure below a rectangular prism?

Ⓐ 5 cubes
Ⓑ 13 cubes
Ⓒ 2 cubes
Ⓓ 7 cubes

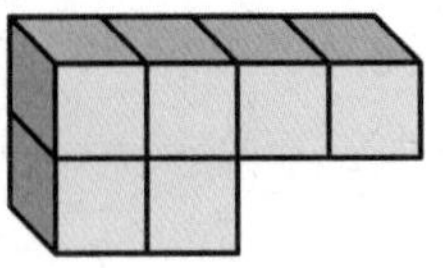

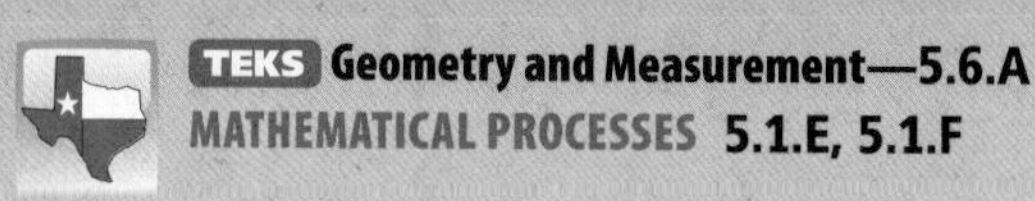

Homework and Practice

Name ____________________

12.1 Unit Cubes and Solid Figures

Count the number of cubes used to build each solid figure.

1. 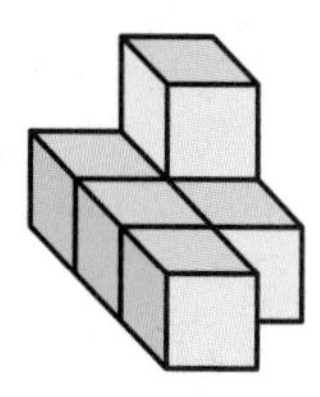

_____ unit cubes

2. 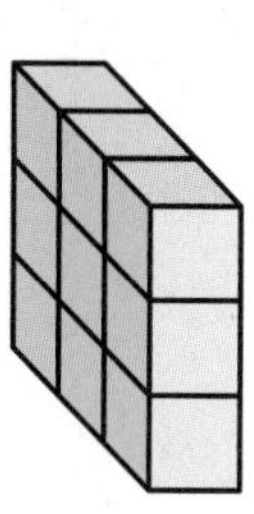

_____ unit cubes

3. 

_____ unit cubes

4. 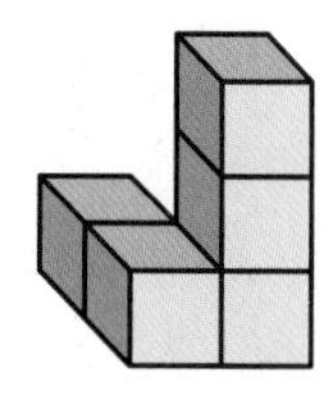

_____ unit cubes

5. 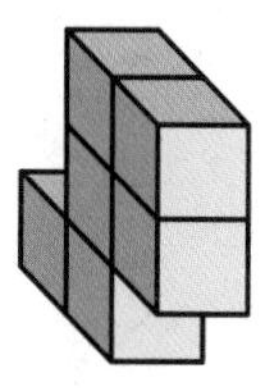

_____ unit cubes

6. 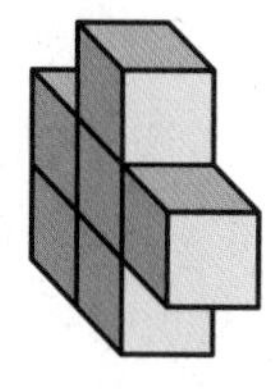

_____ unit cubes

7. 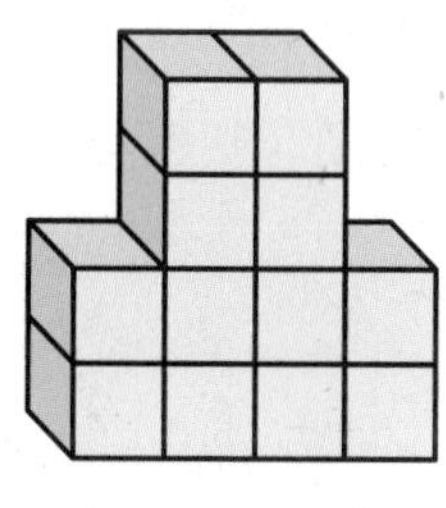

_____ unit cubes

8. 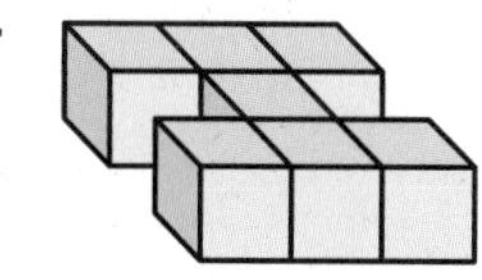

_____ unit cubes

9. 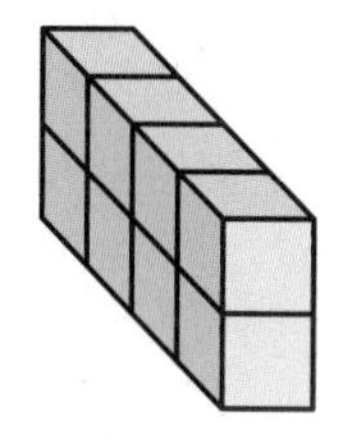

_____ unit cubes

Problem Solving

10. Jen used unit cubes to build a rectangular prism with a length of 4 cubes, a width of 3 cubes, and height of 5 cubes. Ethan built a rectangular prism with a length of 3 cubes, a width of 3 cubes and a height of 6 cubes. Who used more cubes? **Explain.**

____

____

11. Mrs. Hernandez keeps her classroom supply of centimeter cubes in a box that is 20 cm by 6 cm by 3 cm. How many centimeter cubes will fill the box?

____

Lesson Check

★ TEXAS Test Prep

Fill in the bubble completely to show your answer.

12. Blaine makes the figure shown below using unit cubes. How many cubes does Blaine use?

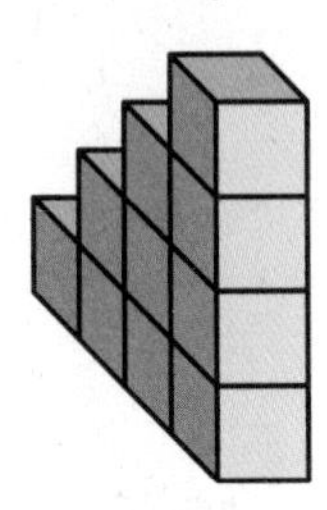

Ⓐ 14 cubes
Ⓑ 20 cubes
Ⓒ 10 cubes
Ⓓ 9 cubes

13. Lucas covers a rectangle with 5 rows of 4 unit cubes. Then he stacks identical layers to make a prism. How many cubes does Lucas use to make 4 layers?

Ⓐ 80 cubes
Ⓑ 20 cubes
Ⓒ 100 cubes
Ⓓ 24 cubes

14. Lola has 30 cubes. She wants to use all the cubes to make a rectangular prism. Which could be the dimensions of her prism?

Ⓐ $5 \times 2 \times 3$
Ⓑ $3 \times 3 \times 3$
Ⓒ $4 \times 5 \times 2$
Ⓓ $3 \times 10 \times 2$

15. **Multi-Step** How many cubes will be in the figure shown below if 12 cubes are added?

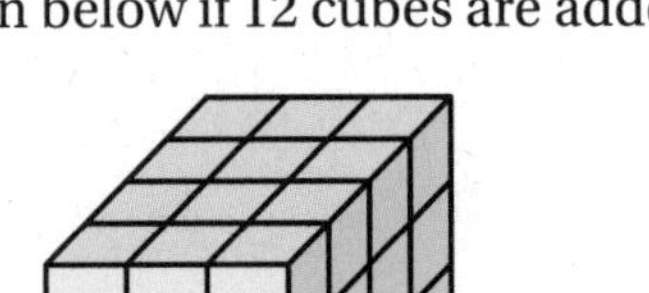

Ⓐ 36 cubes
Ⓑ 24 cubes
Ⓒ 48 cubes
Ⓓ 60 cubes

16. **Multi-Step** Stella built these two figures. How many more cubes did she use in figure A than in figure B?

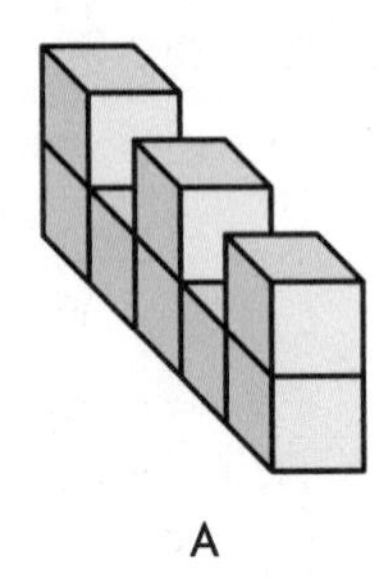

A

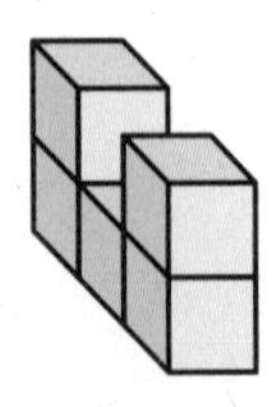

B

Ⓐ 8 cubes
Ⓑ 5 cubes
Ⓒ 3 cubes
Ⓓ 2 cubes

17. **Multi-Step** Owen wants to make a rectangular prism with a length of 6 cubes, a width of 3 cubes, and a height of 4 cubes. He has 54 cubes. How many more cubes does Owen need?

Ⓐ 36 cubes
Ⓑ 42 cubes
Ⓒ 22 cubes
Ⓓ 18 cubes

Name ______________________________

12.2 Understand Volume

TEKS Geometry and Measurement—5.6.A, 5.6.B

MATHEMATICAL PROCESSES 5.1.C, 5.1.D

Essential Question How can you use unit cubes to find the volume of a rectangular prism?

Investigate

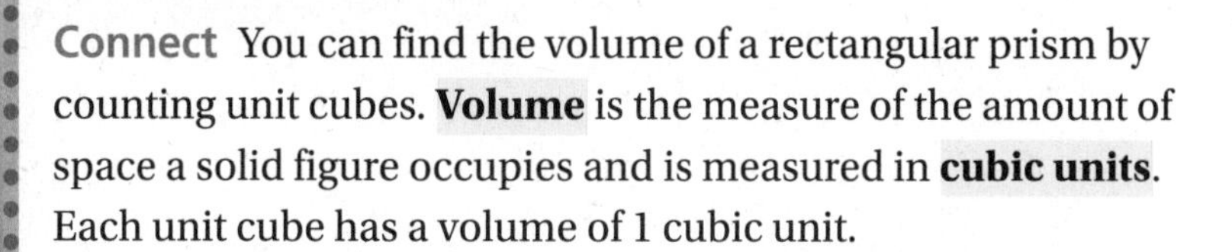

Connect You can find the volume of a rectangular prism by counting unit cubes. **Volume** is the measure of the amount of space a solid figure occupies and is measured in **cubic units**. Each unit cube has a volume of 1 cubic unit.

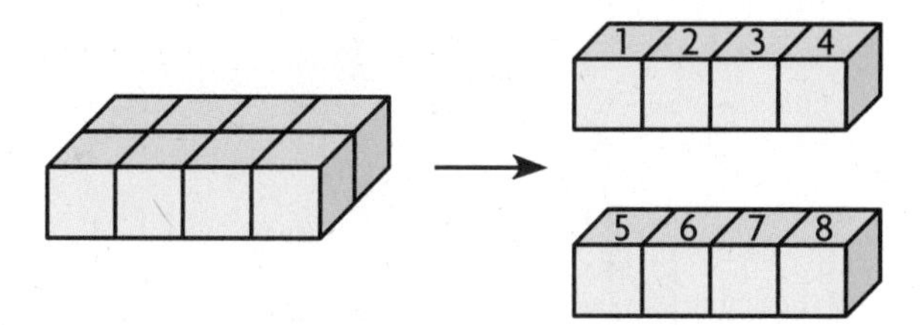

The rectangular prism above is made up of _______ unit cubes

and has a volume of _______ cubic units.

Materials ▪ rectangular prism net A ▪ centimeter cubes

A. Cut out, fold, and tape the net to form a rectangular prism.

B. Use centimeter cubes to fill the base of the rectangular prism without gaps or overlaps. Each centimeter cube has a length, width, and height of 1 centimeter and a volume of 1 cubic centimeter.

- How many centimeter cubes make up the length of the first layer? the width? the height?

  length: _______ width: _______ height: _______

- How many centimeter cubes are used to fill the base? _______

C. Continue filling the rectangular prism, layer by layer. Count the number of centimeter cubes used for each layer.

- How many centimeter cubes are in each layer? _______
- How many layers of cubes fill the rectangular prism? _______
- How many centimeter cubes fill the prism? _______

So, the volume of the rectangular prism is _______ cubic centimeters.

Make Connections

To find the volume of three-dimensional figures, you measure in three directions. For a rectangular prism, you measure its length, width, and height. Volume is measured using cubic units, such as cubic centimeters or cubic inches. You can also write these as cu cm or cu in.

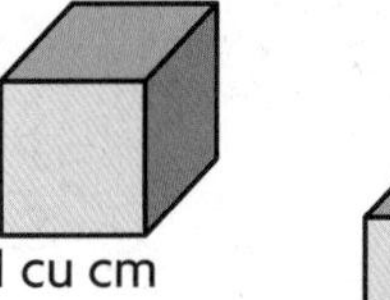

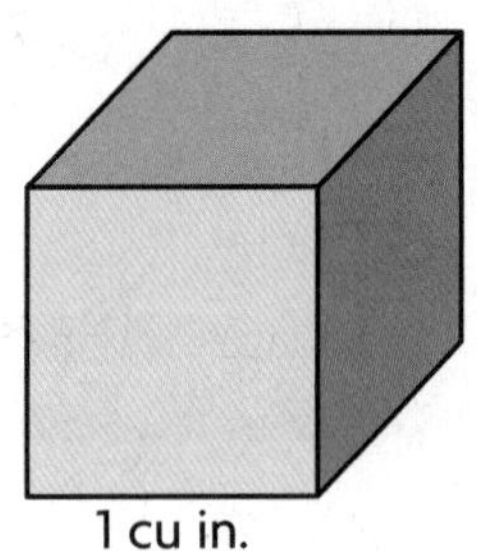

- Which has a greater volume, 1 cu cm or 1 cu in.? **Explain.**

____

____

Find the volume of the prism if each cube represents 1 cu cm, 1 cu in., and 1 cu ft.

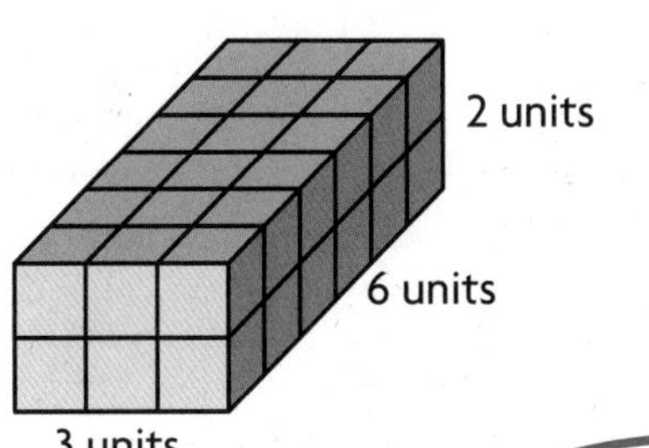

_______ cu cm

_______ cu in.

_______ cu ft

Math Talk — Mathematical Processes

Would the prism above be the same size if it were built with centimeter cubes, inch cubes, or foot cubes? **Explain.**

Share and Show

 **1.**

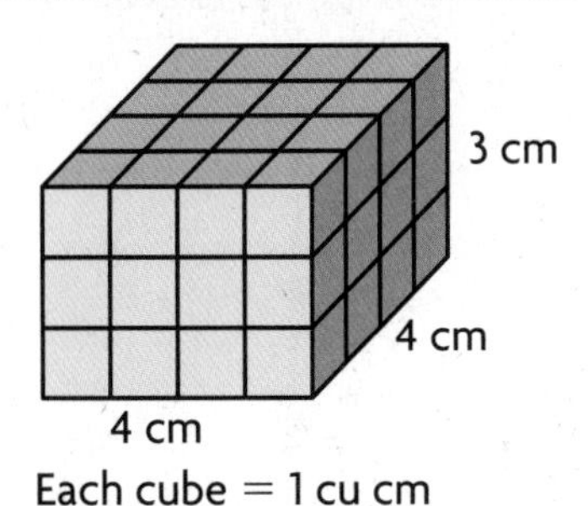

Each cube = 1 cu cm

Volume = _______ cu _______

 **2.**

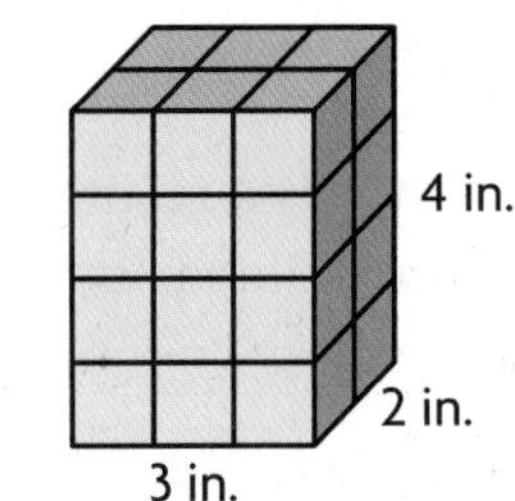

Each cube = 1 cu in.

Volume = _______ cu _______

Compare the volumes. Write <, >, or =.

3.

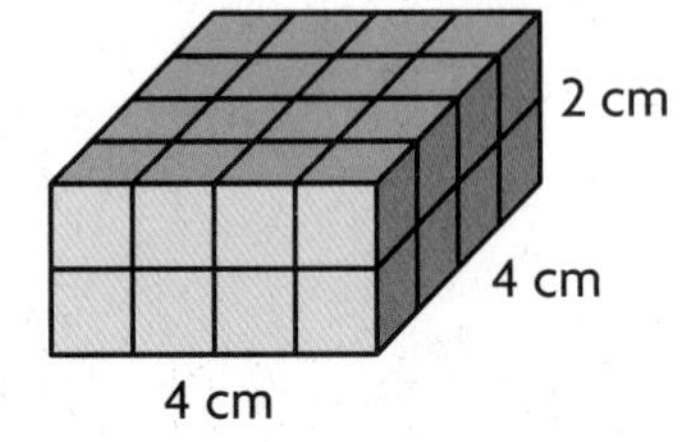

Each cube = 1 cu cm

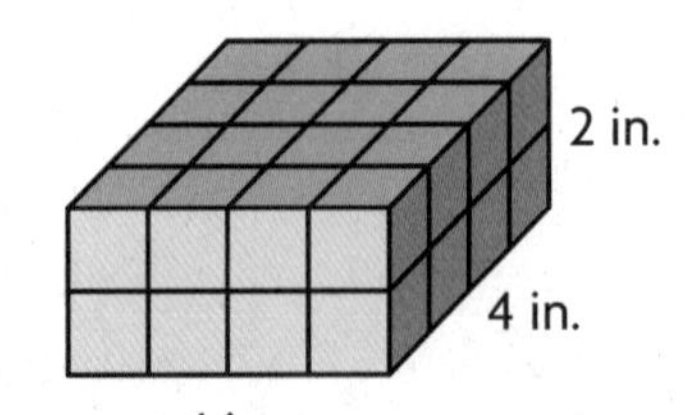

Each cube = 1 cu in.

_______ cu cm ◯ _______ cu in.

Name ______________________________

Problem Solving Real World

4. **H.O.T.** **Connect** What is the relationship among the number of centimeter cubes you used to fill each layer, the number of layers, and the volume of the prism on page 441?

5. **H.O.T.** If you had a rectangular prism that had a length of 3 units, a width of 4 units, and a height of 2 units, how many unit cubes would you need for each layer? How many unit cubes would you need to fill the rectangular prism?

6. **H.O.T.** **What's the Error?** Al says that a cube with edges that measure 10 cm has a volume that is twice as much as a cube with sides that measure 5 cm. **Explain** and correct Al's error.

7. **H.O.T.** Pia built a rectangular prism with cubes. The base of her prism has 12 cm cubes. If the prism was built with 108 cm cubes, what is the height of her prism?

8. **Multi-Step** A packing company makes boxes with edges each measuring 3 feet. What is the volume of a box? If 10 boxes are put in a shipping container and completely fill it with no gaps or overlaps, what is the volume of the shipping container?

Daily Assessment Task

Fill in the bubble completely to show your answer.

9. Nabanita needs 140 cubes to make a model. The figure shows the number of cubes in a box. How many boxes of cubes does Nabanita need to buy so she has enough cubes for her model?

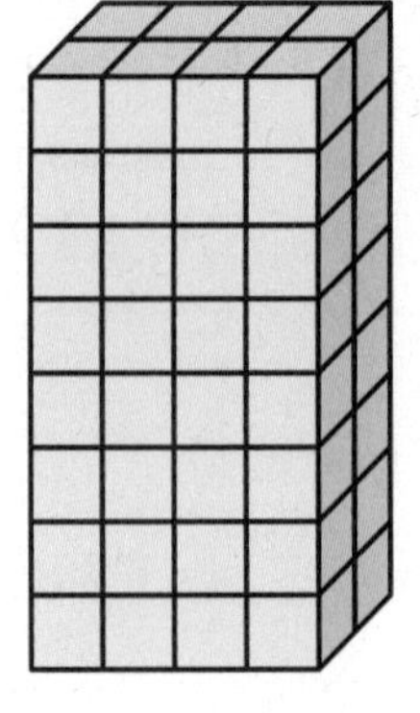

Ⓐ 2 boxes

Ⓑ 3 boxes

Ⓒ 14 boxes

Ⓓ 16 boxes

10. A box is filled with speakers. Each speaker has a volume of 1 cubic foot. Ten speakers can fit in each layer and the height of the box is 4 feet. What is the volume of the box?

Ⓐ 40 cubic feet

Ⓑ 14 cubic feet

Ⓒ 10 cubic feet

Ⓓ 20 cubic feet

11. **Multi-Step** A jewelry box has 3 drawers. Each drawer is 10 inches long, 5 inches wide, and 6 inches tall. Find the combined volume of the drawers.

Ⓐ 11 cu. in.

Ⓑ 300 cu. in.

Ⓒ 33 cu. in.

Ⓓ 900 cu. in.

TEXAS Test Prep

12. Find the volume of the rectangular prism.

Ⓐ 25 cubic feet

Ⓑ 25 cubic meters

Ⓒ 75 cubic meters

Ⓓ 75 cubic centimeters

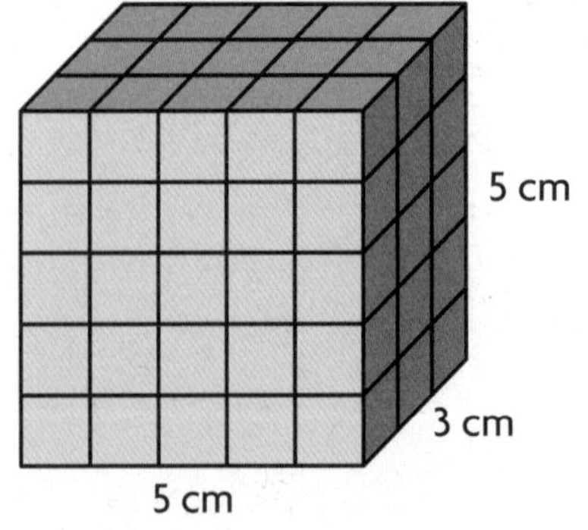

Homework and Practice

TEKS Geometry and Measurement—5.6.A, 5.6.B
MATHEMATICAL PROCESSES 5.1.C, 5.1.D

Name ______________________

12.2 Understand Volume

1.

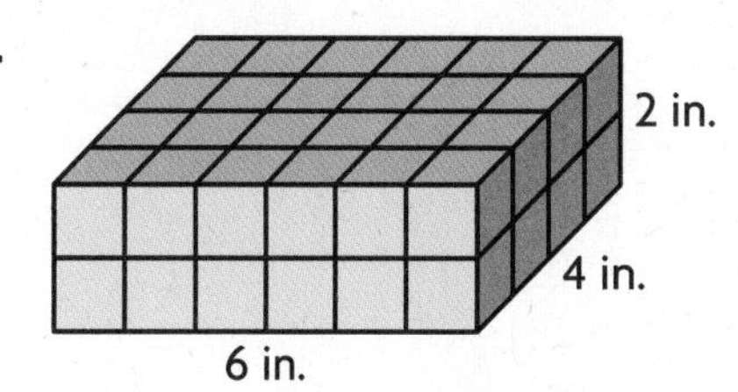

Each cube = 1 cu in.

Volume = ______ cu ______

2.

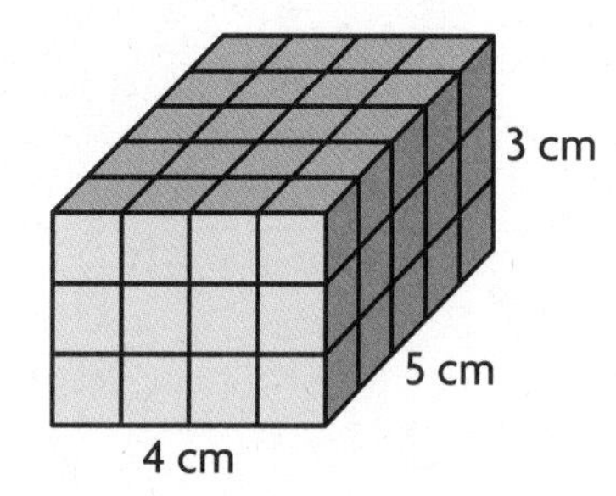

Each cube = 1 cu cm

Volume = ______ cu ______

Compare the volumes. Write <, >, or =.

3.

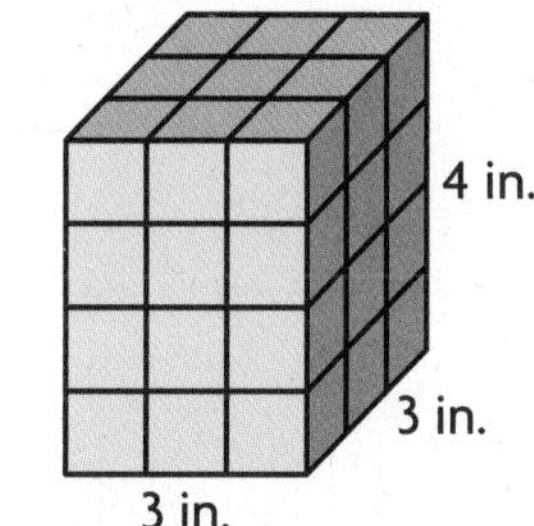

Each cube = 1 cu in.

4 cm
3 cm
3 cm

Each cube = 1 cu cm

______ cu in. ◯ ______ cu cm

Problem Solving

4. Salim built a rectangular prism with a length of 5 inches, a width of 4 inches, and a height of 3 inches. Would the prism Natalie built with a length of 3 inches, a width of 4 inches, and a height of 5 inches have the same volume or a different volume than Salim's prism? **Explain.**

____

____

____

5. Oliver and Layla each built a rectangular prism with centimeter cubes. Both prisms have a volume of 24 cubic centimeters, but they do not look the same. Give possible dimensions for each prism.

____

____

____

____

Lesson Check

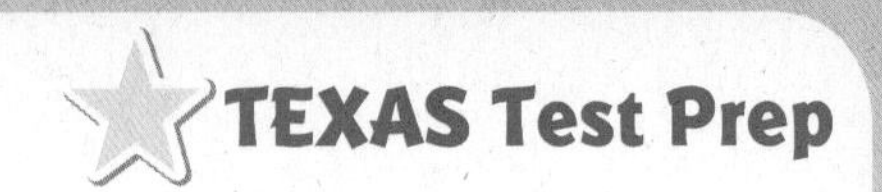

Fill in the bubble completely to show your answer.

6. Find the volume of the rectangular prism.

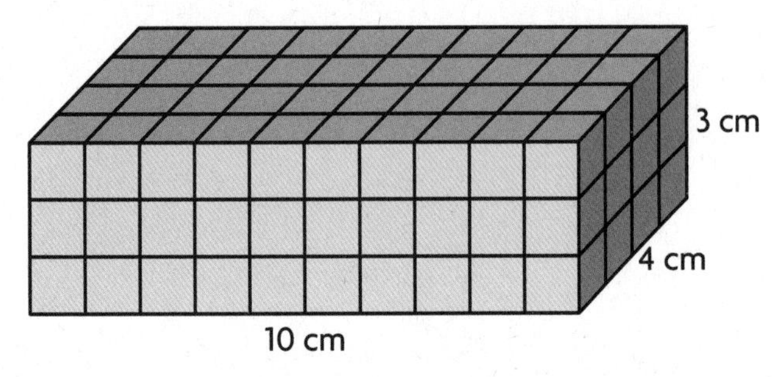

Each cube = 1 cu cm

Ⓐ 120 cubic inches

Ⓑ 120 cubic centimeters

Ⓒ 70 cubic inches

Ⓓ 70 cubic centimeters

7. Mason builds a tower with centimeter cubes for his design project. The figure below shows the part of the tower that he has completed so far.

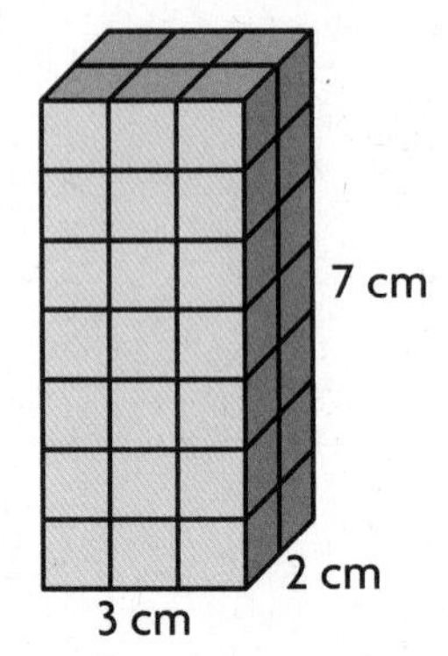

What does Mason need to do for the tower to have a volume of 54 cubic centimeters?

Ⓐ Add one layer of cubes.

Ⓑ Add 33 cubes.

Ⓒ Add 2 cubes.

Ⓓ Add two layers of cubes.

8. A chest is filled with toy blocks. Each block has a volume of 1 cubic foot. Twenty-five blocks fit in the bottom of the chest and the height of the chest is 3 feet. What is the volume of the chest?

Ⓐ 75 cubic feet

Ⓑ 60 cubic feet

Ⓒ 28 cubic feet

Ⓓ 25 cubic feet

9. Which of the measures below represents the greatest volume?

Ⓐ 14 cubic inches

Ⓑ 14 cubic feet

Ⓒ 14 cubic centimeters

Ⓓ 14 cubic meters

10. **Multi-Step** Lily serves 1-inch cheese cubes to her guests on a rectangular tray that is 6 inches long, 4 inches wide, and 2 inches tall. When the tray is only half full, what is the volume of the cheese cubes?

Ⓐ 96 cu in.

Ⓑ 12 cu in.

Ⓒ 48 cu in.

Ⓓ 24 cu in.

11. **Multi-Step** Fernando builds a rectangular prism with centimeter cubes. The length of the prism is 2 centimeters. The width is twice the length and the height is twice the width. What is the volume of Fernando's prism?

Ⓐ 48 cu cm

Ⓑ 16 cu cm

Ⓒ 8 cu cm

Ⓓ 64 cu cm

Name ______________________________

12.3 Volume of Rectangular Prisms

TEKS Geometry and Measurement—5.6.B
Also 5.4.G

MATHEMATICAL PROCESSES
5.1.F, 5.1.G

Essential Question

How can you find the volume of a rectangular prism?

Connect The base of a rectangular prism is a rectangle. You know that area is measured in square units and that the area of a rectangle can be found by multiplying the length and the width.

Volume is measured in cubic units, such as cubic feet or cu ft. When you build a prism and add each layer of cubes, you are adding a third dimension, height.

The area of the base

is ______ sq units.

Unlock the Problem

Sid built the rectangular prism shown at the right, using 1-inch cubes. The prism has a base that is a rectangle and has a height of 4 cubes. What is the volume of the rectangular prism that Sid built?

You can find the volume of a prism in cubic units by multiplying the number of square units in the base shape by the number of layers, or its height.

Each layer of Sid's rectangular prism

is composed of ______ inch cubes.

+12
+12
+12
12

Height (in layers)	1	2	3	4
Volume (in cubic inches)	12	24		

Multiply the height by ______.

1. How does the volume change as each layer is added?

____

____

2. What does the number you multiply the height by represent?

____

____

So, the volume of Sid's rectangular prism is ______ cu in.

Share and Show

Find the volume.

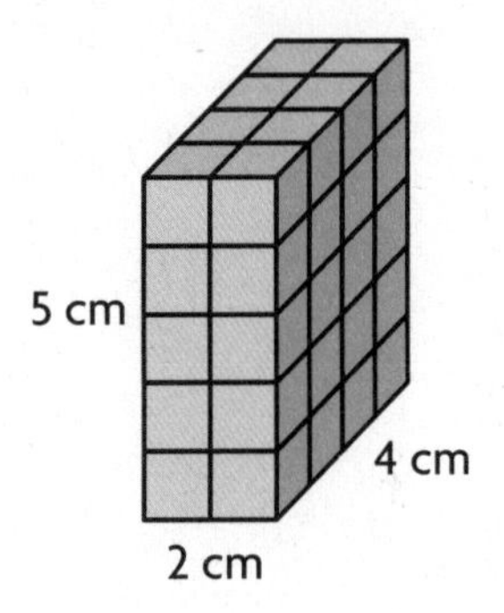

1. The length of the rectangular prism is ___________.

   The width is ___________. So, the area of the base is ___________.

   The height is ___________. So, the volume of the prism is ___________.

2.

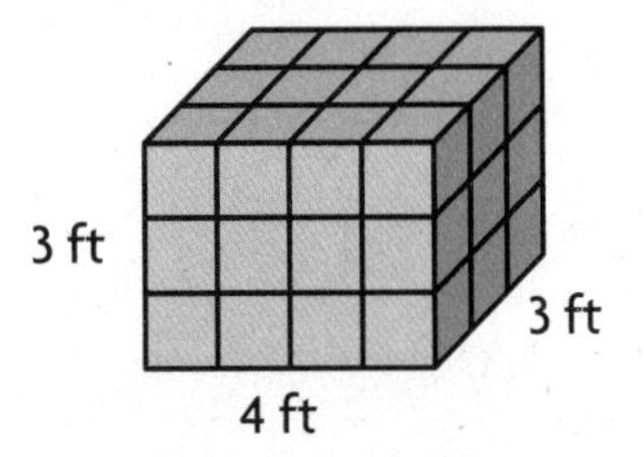

Volume: ___________

3.

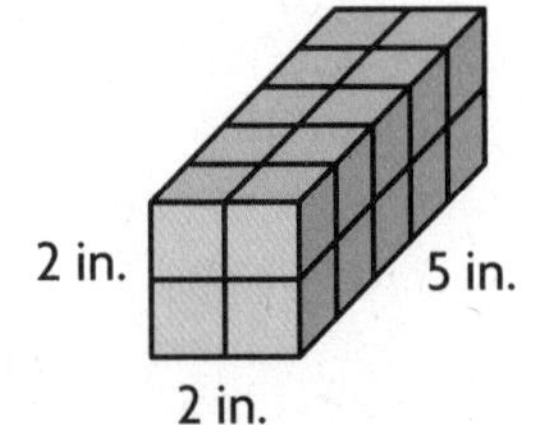

Volume: ___________

Math Talk

How many more layers should be added to the prism in Exercise 3 so that the volume of the prism is 60 cubic inches? **Explain.**

Problem Solving

4. **Explain** what else you need to know to find the volume of a rectangular prism if you know the area of the base.

____

____

5. **H.O.T.** **Reasoning** How can you find the volume of a cube if you know the area of the base is 25 sq cm?

____

____

____

____

6. **H.O.T.** The volume of a rectangular prism is 40 cu ft. The height of the prism is 10 ft. What is the area of the base of the prism? **Explain.**

____

____

Name ______________________________

Problem Solving Real World

7. Kayan is designing a box for sugar cubes. Each sugar cube has a volume of 1 cubic inch. Kayan wants to have 12 cubes in each layer. If he wants to fit 60 cubes in each box, how tall should the box be?

8. H.O.T. **Multi-Step** Golf balls are packed in cardboard boxes that are 2 inches long, 2 inches wide, and 2 inches high. The boxes are then packed into larger containers that are 20 inches long, 30 inches wide, and 20 inches high. How many golf balls can fit in the larger container?

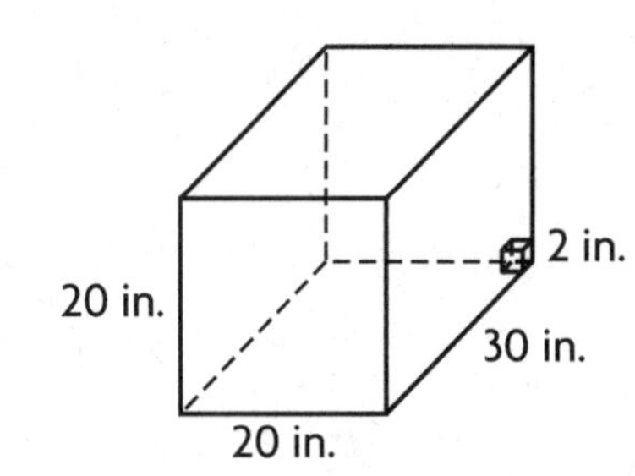

9. **Multi-Step** Yvette uses centimeter cubes to make a bed for her doll. The bed is in the shape of a rectangular prism. She wants the length of the prism to be 15 cm. The width should be 5 cm and the height 5 cm. How many centimeter cubes does Yvette need?

10. H.O.T. **Multi-Step** Cameron uses a rectangular baking pan with a base measuring 12 square inches. Cameron pours batter in the pan so that it is 2 inches deep. The finished cake will be 3 times as tall as the batter. What is the volume of the cake?

Daily Assessment Task

Fill in the bubble completely to show your answer.

11. A cube-shaped block of cheese has side lengths of 6 inches. The block of cheese is cut into smaller pieces. Each piece has a volume of 1 cubic inch. How many pieces of cheese will there be?

Ⓐ 18 pieces

Ⓑ 36 pieces

Ⓒ 216 pieces

Ⓓ 72 pieces

12. Frank is packing cube-shaped containers into large boxes. He can fit 15 containers in each layer. If he stacks 8 layers into one box, what is the volume of the box?

Ⓐ 64 cubes

Ⓑ 120 cubes

Ⓒ 128 cubes

Ⓓ 256 cubes

13. **Multi-Step** A rectangular block of cheese has a length of 8 centimeters, a width of 4 centimeters, and a height of 3 centimeters. If the block is cut into two equal pieces, what will be the volume of each piece?

Ⓐ 15 cubic cm

Ⓑ 28 cubic cm

Ⓒ 48 cubic cm

Ⓓ 96 cubic cm

TEXAS Test Prep

14. What is the volume of the rectangular prism at the right?

Ⓐ 28 sq cm

Ⓑ 140 sq cm

Ⓒ 28 cu cm

Ⓓ 140 cu cm

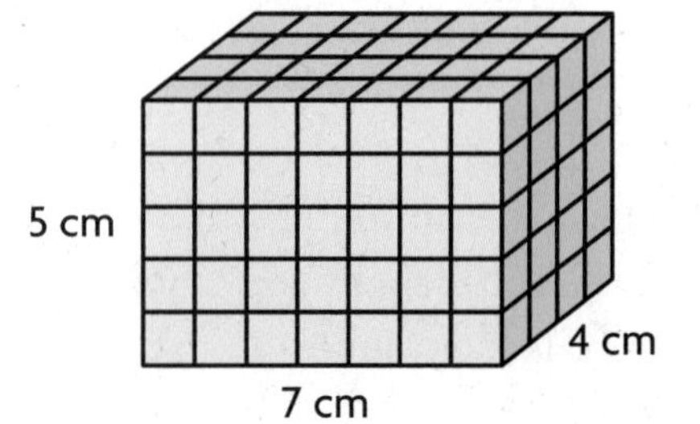

Name ______________________

12.3 Volume of Rectangular Prisms

Find the volume.

1.

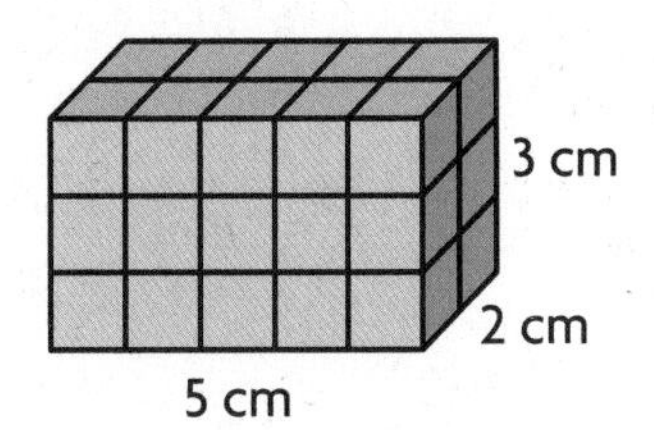

Volume: __________

2.

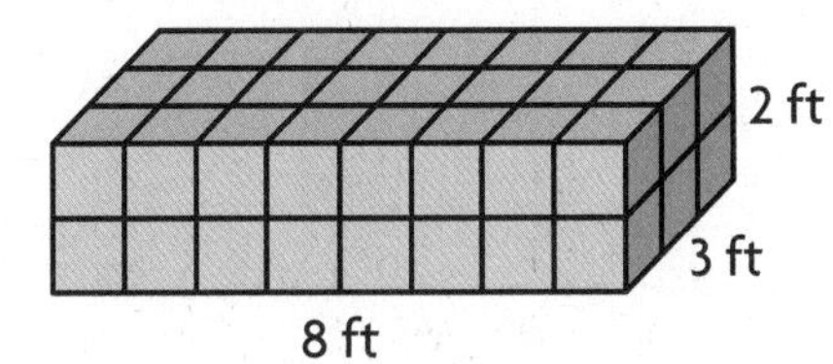

Volume: __________

3.

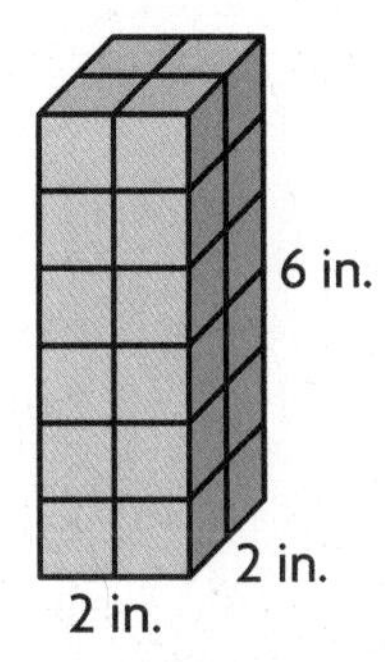

Volume: __________

4.

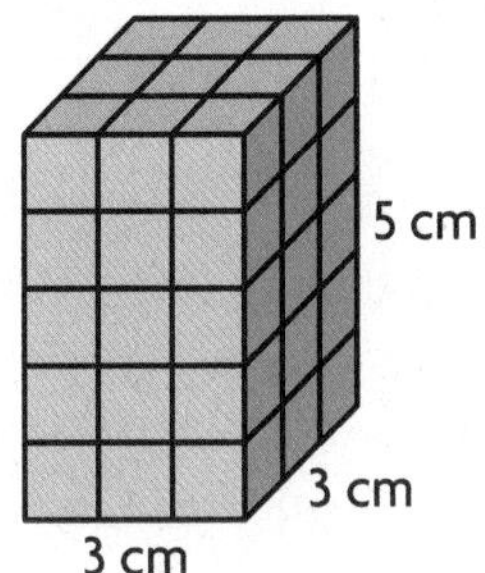

Volume: __________

5.

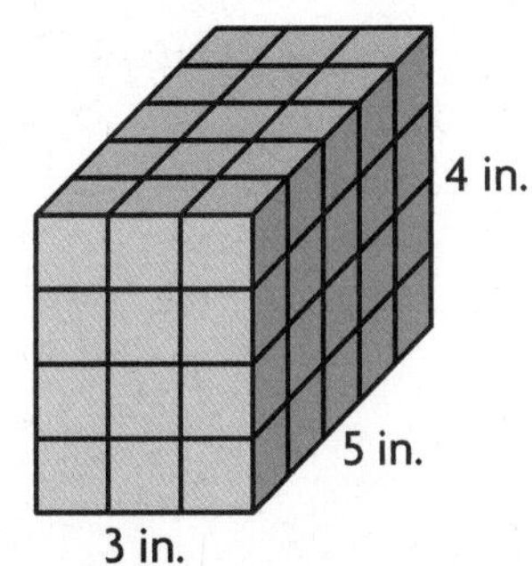

Volume: __________

6.

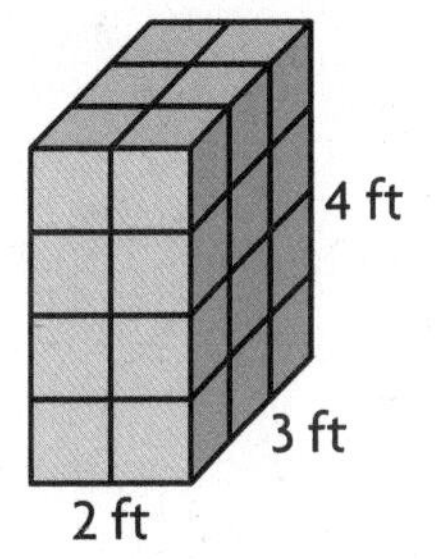

Volume: __________

Problem Solving

7. Vijay has a collection of 50 number cubes that are each 1 cubic inch. He finds a box that is 4 inches high. He fits 12 cubes into the bottom of the box. Can Vijay fit all his number cubes into the box? **Explain.**

____

____

8. Maya wants to use 1-centimeter cubes to make a larger cube with side lengths of 3 centimeters. How many 1-centimeter cubes will Maya need?

____

Lesson Check

TEXAS Test Prep

Fill in the bubble completely to show your answer.

9. What is the volume of the rectangular prism shown below?

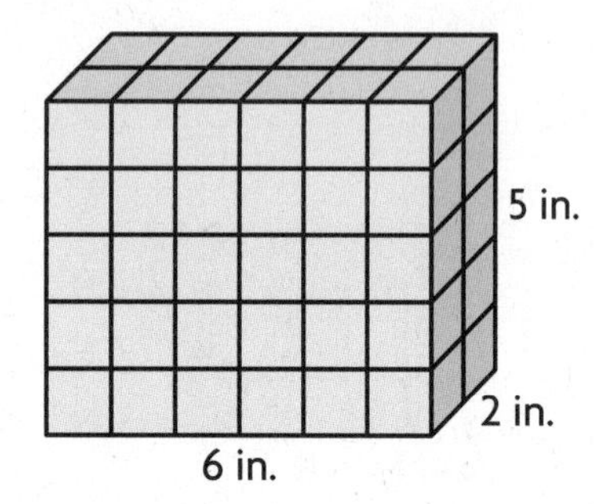

Ⓐ 12 sq in.

Ⓑ 60 sq in.

Ⓒ 12 cu in.

Ⓓ 60 cu in.

10. Miranda packs cube-shaped jewelry boxes into a display box that is a rectangular prism. In the bottom layer, she can fit 4 rows of 7 jewelry boxes. If she stacks 6 layers into the display box, what is the volume of the display box?

Ⓐ 168 cubes

Ⓑ 28 cubes

Ⓒ 196 cubes

Ⓓ 66 cubes

11. Jaden fills a box with 32 cubes. The box is 4 cubes long and 2 cubes wide. How many layers of cubes are in the box?

Ⓐ 3

Ⓑ 4

Ⓒ 8

Ⓓ 5

12. Javier has forty 1-centimeter cubes. He builds a rectangular prism with 6 cubes in the bottom layer. He wants to have the fewest cubes left over. How many layers can Javier make?

Ⓐ 7

Ⓑ 5

Ⓒ 6

Ⓓ 8

13. **Multi-Step** The shipping clerk packs a cube with side lengths of 8 inches into a box with side lengths of 10 inches. What is the volume of the space left in the larger box for packing materials?

Ⓐ 598 cubic inches

Ⓑ 1,000 cubic inches

Ⓒ 512 cubic inches

Ⓓ 488 cubic inches

14. **Multi-Step** The volume of cube *A* is 64 cubic feet. What is the volume of cube *B* if its side lengths are half the length of cube *A*'s sides?

Ⓐ 8 cubic feet

Ⓑ 32 cubic feet

Ⓒ 16 cubic feet

Ⓓ 4 cubic feet

Name ____________________

12.4 Apply Volume Formulas

ALGEBRA

TEKS Geometry and Measurement—5.6.B
Also 5.4.H
MATHEMATICAL PROCESSES
5.1.A

Essential Question

How can you use a formula to find the volume of a rectangular prism?

Connect Both prisms show the same dimensions and have the same volume.

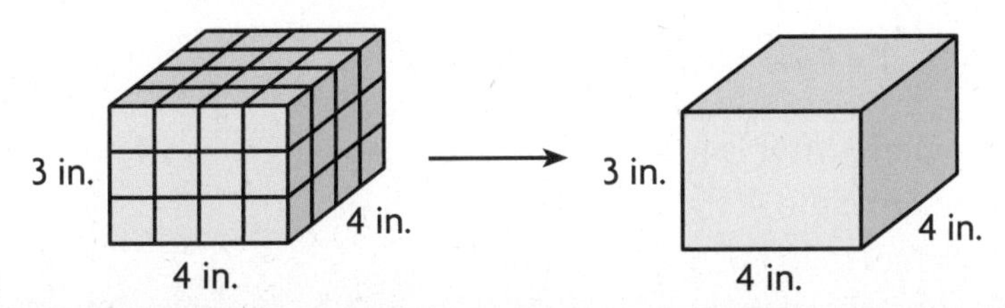

Unlock the Problem

Mike is making a box to hold his favorite DVDs. The length of the box is 7 inches, the width is 5 inches and the height is 3 inches. What is the volume of the box Mike is making?

- Underline what you are asked to find.
- Circle the numbers you need to use to solve the problem.

One Way Use length, width, and height.

You can use a formula to find the volume of a rectangular prism.

Volume = *length* × *width* × *height*

$V = l \times w \times h$

STEP 1 Identify the length, width, and height of the rectangular prism.

length = ______ in.

width = ______ in.

height = ______ in.

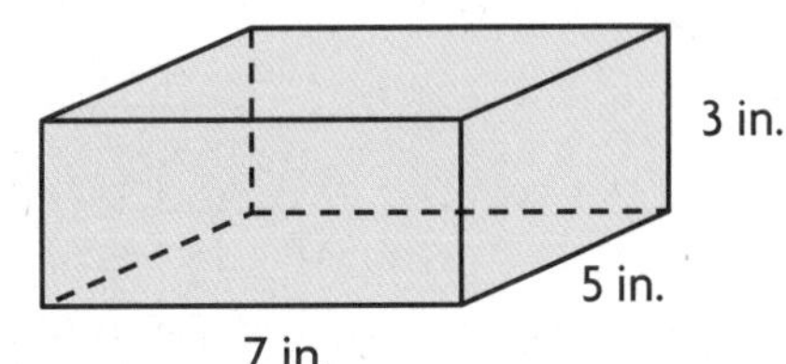

STEP 2 Multiply the length by the width.

______ × ______ = ______

STEP 3 Multiply the product of the length and width by the height.

35 × ______ = ______

So, the volume of Mike's DVD box is ____________ cubic inches.

Math Talk

Mathematical Processes

Explain how you can use the Associative Property to group the part of the formula that represents area.

You have learned one formula for finding the volume of a rectangular prism. You can also use another formula.

Volume = *Base area* × *height*

$V = B \times h$

B = area of the base shape,

h = height of the solid figure.

Another Way Use the area of the base shape and height.

Emilio's family has a sand castle kit. The kit includes molds for several solid figures that can be used to make sand castles. One of the molds is a rectangular prism like the one shown at the right. How much sand will it take to fill the mold?

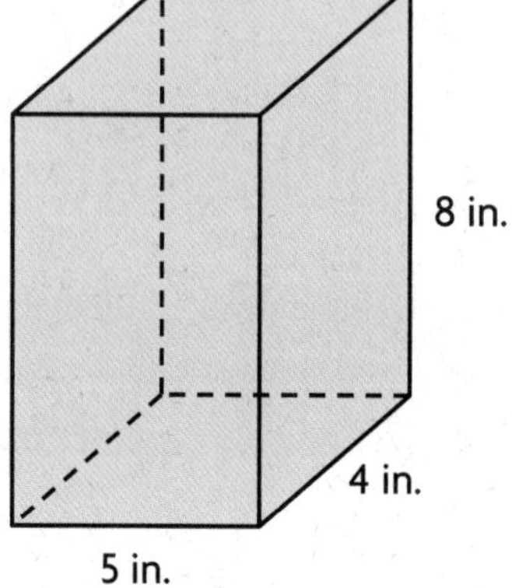

$V = \quad B \quad \times \quad h$ — Replace B with an expression for the area of the base shape. Replace h with the height of the solid figure.

$V = (\_\_\_\_ \times \_\_\_\_) \times \_\_\_\_$ — Multiply.

$V = \_\_\_\_ \times \_\_\_\_$

$V = \_\_\_\_$ cu in.

So, it will take ______ cubic inches of sand to fill the rectangular prism mold.

Share and Show

Find the volume.

 **1.**

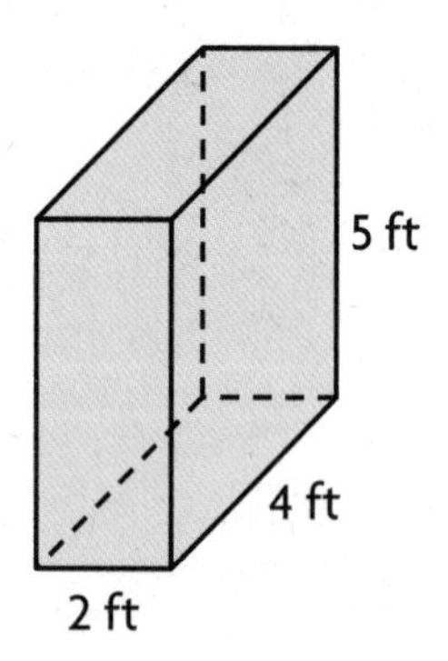

$V =$ ______

 **2.**

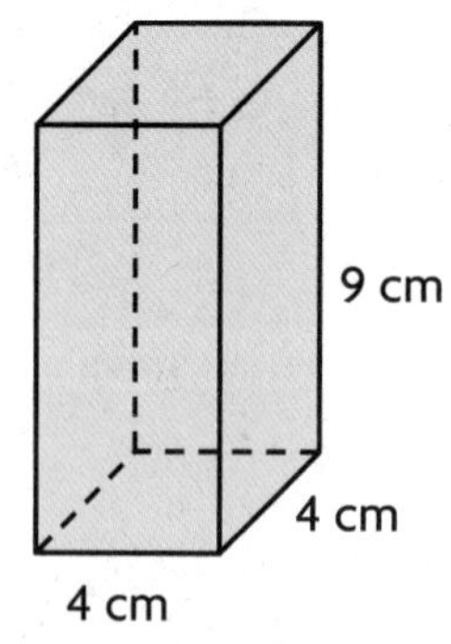

$V =$ ______

Name ____________________

Problem Solving

H.O.T. **Algebra** **Find the unknown measurement.**

3.

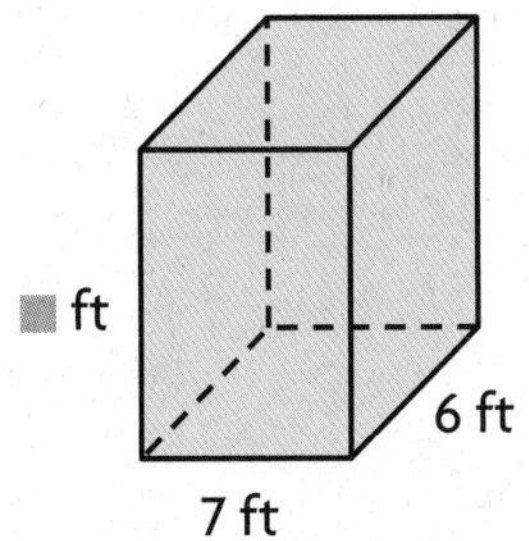

$V = 420$ cu ft ■ = ______ ft

4.

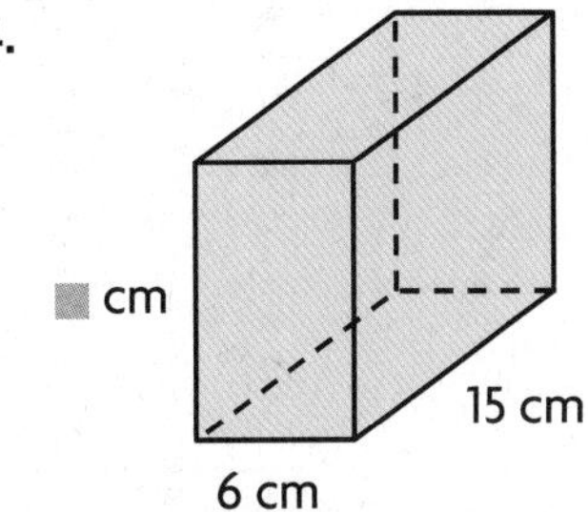

$V = 900$ cu cm ■ = ______ cm

5. **Write Math** ▶ Describe the difference between area and volume.

____

____

Problem Solving

6. **Apply** The Jade Restaurant has a large aquarium on display in its lobby. The base of the aquarium is 5 feet by 2 feet. The height of the aquarium is 4 feet. How many cubic feet of water are needed to completely fill the aquarium?

____

7. **Multi-Step** The Pearl Restaurant put a larger aquarium in its lobby. The base of their aquarium is 6 feet by 3 feet, and the height is 4 feet. How many more cubic feet of water does the Pearl Restaurant's aquarium hold than the Jade Restaurant's aquarium?

____

8. **H.O.T.** Eddie measured his aquarium using a small fish food box. The box has a base area of 6 inches and a height of 4 inches. Eddie found that the volume of his aquarium is 3,456 cubic inches. How many boxes of fish food could fit in the aquarium? **Explain** your answer.

____

____

____

Daily Assessment Task

Fill in the bubble completely to show your answer.

9. A cardboard box has a length of 12 inches, a width of 7 inches, and a height of 4 inches. What is the volume of the box?

   Ⓐ 23 cubic inches
   Ⓒ 46 cubic inches
   Ⓑ 84 cubic inches
   Ⓓ 336 cubic inches

10. Which expression shows how to find the volume of the following prism?

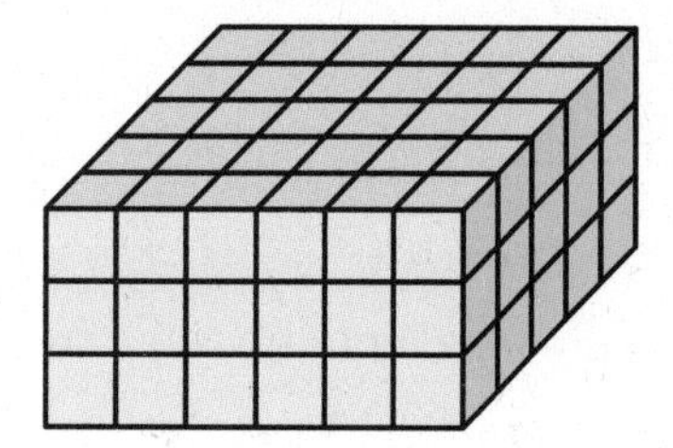

   Ⓐ 30×3
   Ⓒ $6 + 6 + 5 + 5 + 3 + 3$
   Ⓑ $6 \times 5 \times 3 \times 6 \times 5 \times 3$
   Ⓓ 6×5

11. **Multi-Step** Jumana built these prisms out of cube-shaped blocks. How many blocks did she use?

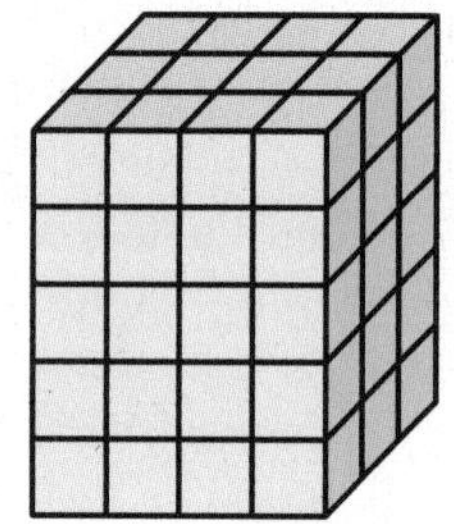

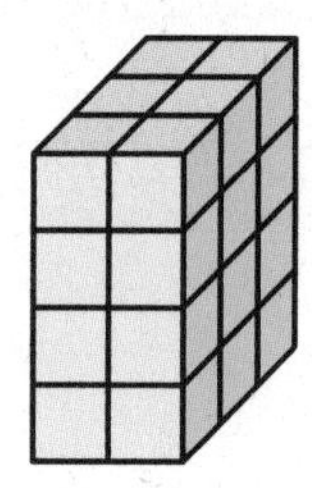

   Ⓐ 120 blocks
   Ⓑ 84 blocks
   Ⓒ 21 blocks
   Ⓓ 1,440 blocks

TEXAS Test Prep

12. Adam stores his favorite CDs in a box like the one shown below. What is the volume of the box?

   Ⓐ 750 cubic centimeters
   Ⓑ 150 cubic centimeters
   Ⓒ 1,050 cubic centimeters
   Ⓓ 1,150 cubic centimeters

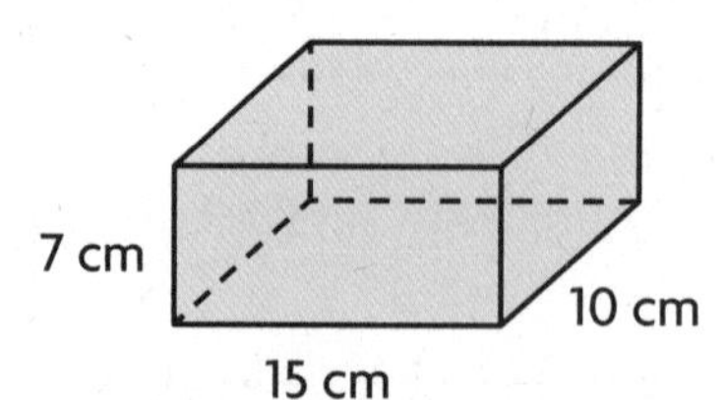

TEKS Geometry and Measurement—5.6.B
Also 5.4.H
MATHEMATICAL PROCESSES 5.1.A

Name ______

12.4 Apply Volume Formulas

Find the unknown measurement.

1.

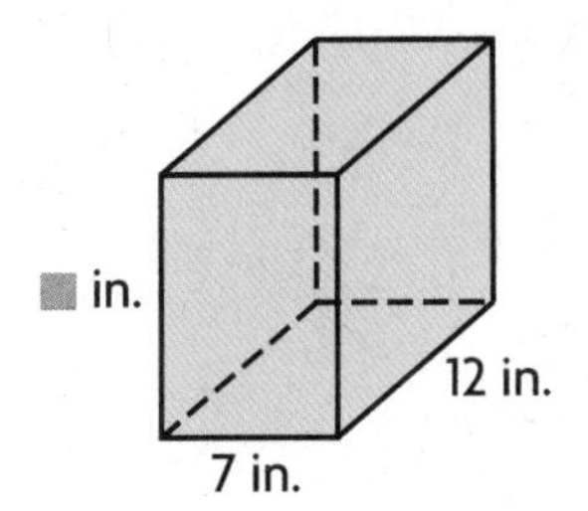

$V = 840$ cu in.

■ = ______ in.

2.

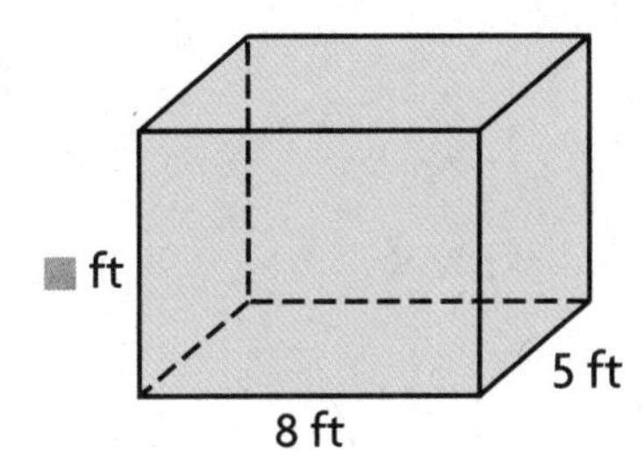

$V = 240$ cu ft

■ = ______ ft

3.

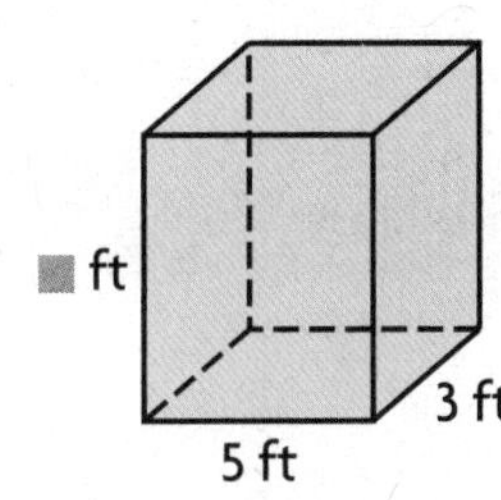

$V = 90$ cu ft

■ = ______ ft

4.

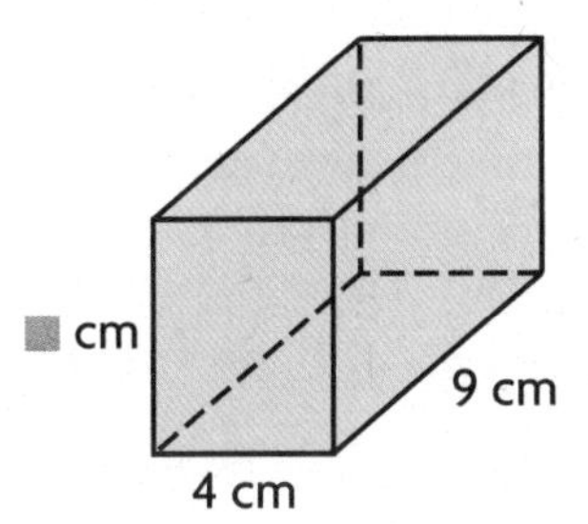

$V = 180$ cu cm

■ = ______ cm

5.

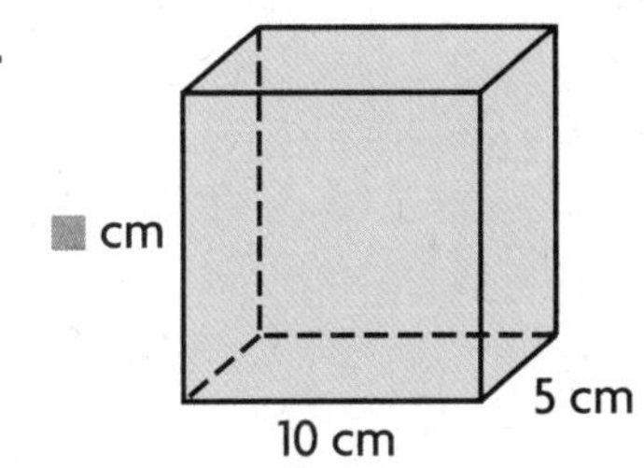

$V = 500$ cu cm

■ = ______ cm

6.

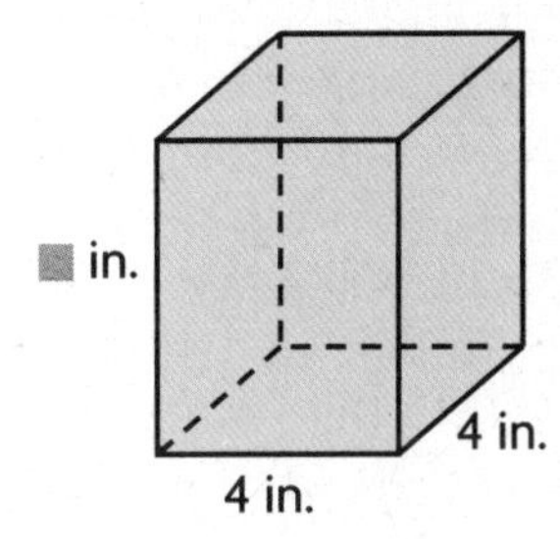

$V = 80$ cu in.

■ = ______ in.

Problem Solving

7. At the community center, athletic gear is stored in a large locker. The locker floor is 10 feet by 9 feet. The height of the locker is 8 feet. How much space is in the locker?

______

8. A storage locker is 15 ft long, 2 ft wide, and 4 ft high. How many boxes that are 3 ft long, 2 ft wide, and 1 ft high can the locker fit?

______

Lesson Check

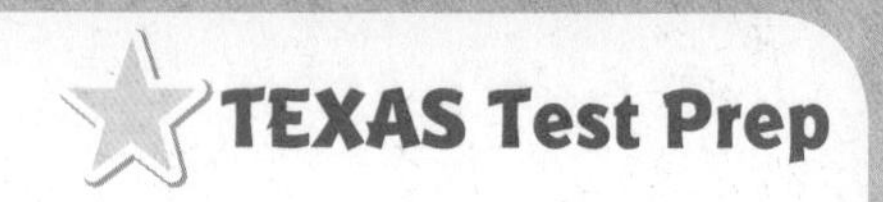

Fill in the bubble completely to show your answer.

9. Which expression shows how to find the volume of the prism shown below?

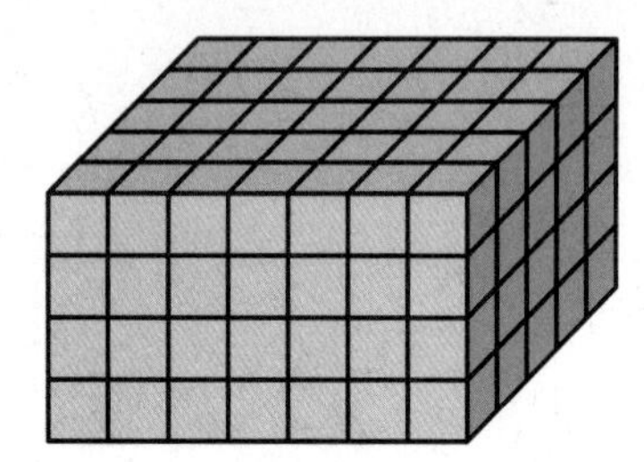

Ⓐ $7 \times 5 + 4$

Ⓑ 35×4

Ⓒ $7 + 7 + 7 + 7 \times 5$

Ⓓ $7 + 5 \times 4$

10. Jack builds a box for a birdhouse like the one shown below.

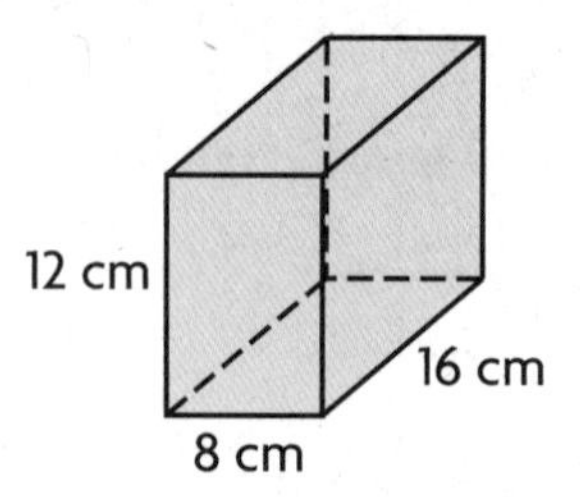

What is the volume of the box?

Ⓐ 1,426 cubic centimeters

Ⓑ 288 cubic centimeters

Ⓒ 1,536 cubic centimeters

Ⓓ 140 cubic centimeters

11. A rectangular cake pan has a length of 13 inches, a width of 9 inches, and a height of 3 inches. What is the volume of the cake pan?

Ⓐ 117 cubic inches

Ⓑ 351 cubic inches

Ⓒ 120 cubic inches

Ⓓ 66 cubic inches

12. Jada stores her winter clothes in a wooden chest with a base area of 8 square feet and a height of 2 feet. How many cubic feet of space does the chest contain?

Ⓐ 128 cubic feet

Ⓑ 10 cubic feet

Ⓒ 32 cubic feet

Ⓓ 16 cubic feet

13. Multi-Step Malaya packs two small suitcases each with a length of 2 feet, a width of 2 feet, and a height of 1 foot. What is the difference between their combined volume and the volume of one large suitcase with a length of 4 feet, a width of 3 feet, and a height of 2 feet?

Ⓐ 20 cubic feet

Ⓑ 16 cubic feet

Ⓒ 19 cubic feet

Ⓓ 14 cubic feet

14. Multi-Step Candace and Trevor built the prisms shown below out of cube-shaped blocks.

How many more blocks were used in the prism with the greater volume?

Ⓐ 24 blocks

Ⓑ 48 blocks

Ⓒ 12 blocks

Ⓓ 36 blocks

Name ______________________________

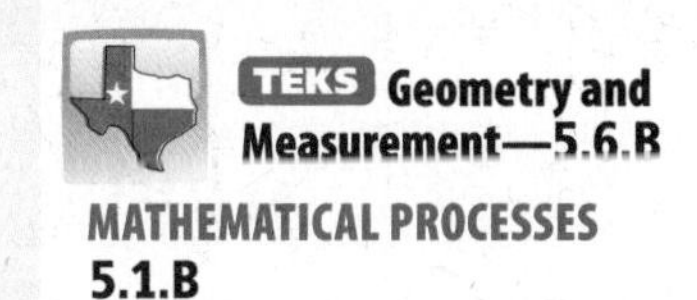

MATHEMATICAL PROCESSES
5.1.B

12.5 PROBLEM SOLVING • Compare Volumes

Essential Question

How can you use the strategy *make a table* to compare different rectangular prisms with the same volume?

Unlock the Problem

Adam has 50 one-inch cubes. The cubes measure 1 inch on each edge. Adam wonders how many rectangular prisms, each with a different-size base, that he could make with all of the one-inch cubes.

Read

What do I need to find?

I need to find the number of ______________,

each with a different-size __________, that have

a volume of ______________.

What information am I given?

I can use the formula ______________

__________ and the factors of __________.

Plan

What is my plan or strategy?

I will use the formula and the factors of

50 in a ______________ that shows all of the possible combinations of dimensions with a

volume of ______________ without repeating the dimensions of the bases.

Solve

Complete the table.

Base (sq in.)	Height (in.)	Volume (cu in.)
(1 × 1)	50	(1 × 1) × 50 = 50
(1 × 2)	25	(1 × 2) × 25 = 50
(1 × 5)	10	(1 × 5) × 10 = 50
(1 × 10)	5	(1 × 10) × 5 = 50
(1 × 25)	2	(1 × 25) × 2 = 50
(1 × 50)	1	(1 × 50) × 1 = 50

1. What else do you need to do to solve the problem? ______________________________

____

2. How many rectangular prisms with different bases can Adam make using fifty one-inch cubes? ______________________________

Try Another Problem

Mrs. Wilton is planning a rectangular flower box for her front window. She wants the flower box to hold exactly 16 cubic feet of soil. How many different flower boxes, all with whole-number dimensions and a different-size base, will hold exactly 16 cubic feet of soil?

Use the graphic organizer below to help you solve the problem.

Read	Solve
What do I need to find?	
What information am I given?	
Plan **What is my plan or strategy?**	

Math Talk
Mathematical Processes

Explain how a flower box with dimensions of $(1 \times 2) \times 8$ is different from a flower box with dimensions of $(2 \times 8) \times 1$.

3. How many flower boxes with different-size bases will hold exactly 16 cubic feet of soil, using whole-number dimensions?

____

Name ______________________________

Share and Show

Unlock the Problem Tips

✓ Circle the question.

✓ Break the problem into easier steps.

1. Mr. Price makes cakes that have a volume of 360 cubic inches. The cakes are 3 inches tall, and have different whole number lengths and widths. No cakes have a length or width of 1 or 2 inches. How many different cakes, each with a different-size base, have a volume of 360 cubic inches?

   First, think about what you need to find and the information you have.

   Next, make a table using the information from problem.

   Finally, use the table to solve the problem.

   ____

   ____

2. H.O.T. **What if** the 360 cubic-inch cakes are 4 inches thick and any whole number length and width are possible? How many different cakes could be made? Suppose that the cost of a cake that size is \$25, plus \$1.99 for every 4 cubic inches of cake. How much would the cake cost?

   ____

   ____

3. One company makes inflatable swimming pools that come in four sizes of rectangular prisms. The length of each pool is twice the width and twice the depth. The depth of the pools are each a whole number from 2 to 5 feet. If the pools are filled all the way to the top, what is the volume of each pool?

   ____

   ____

Problem Solving Real World

4. H.O.T. **Multi-Step** Kathy has ribbons that have lengths of 7 inches, 10 inches, and 12 inches. **Explain** how she can use these ribbons to measure a length of 15 inches.

   ____

   ____

   ____

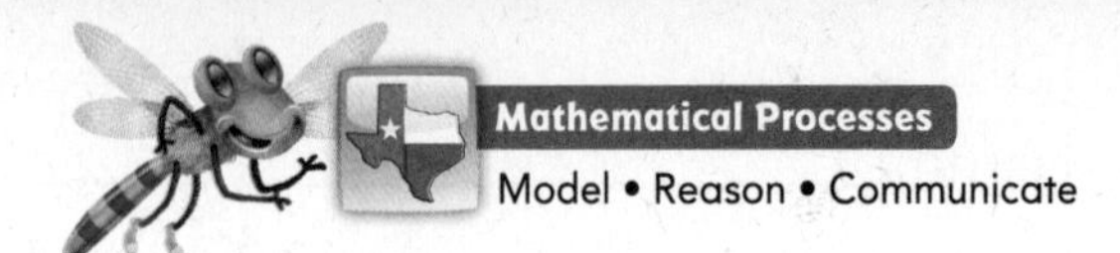

Daily Assessment Task

Fill in the bubble completely to show your answer.

5. **Analyze** Rhoda makes a platform using one-inch cubes. The platform is shaped like a rectangular prism and needs to be 4 inches tall. How many different platforms can Rhoda make using only 16 one-inch cubes?

   Ⓐ 2
   Ⓑ 3
   Ⓒ 4
   Ⓓ 5

6. Selena is building a sculpture using 100 one-inch cubes. She wants the sculpture, which is shaped like a rectangular prism, to be 2 inches tall. Which of the following shows a dimension combination that Selena should NOT use?

   Ⓐ $(25 \times 2) \times 2$
   Ⓑ $(50 \times 1) \times 2$
   Ⓒ $(10 \times 5) \times 2$
   Ⓓ $(10 \times 10) \times 2$

7. **Multi-Step** Jonah has 20 one-inch cubes and uses them all to create a rectangular prism. The height of the prism is 10 inches. Mila uses 20 one-inch cubes to make a rectangular prism that has a height of 2 inches. Which statement is true about the volumes of the two prisms?

   Ⓐ They do not have the same volume.
   Ⓑ The volumes are the same because both prisms are made using 20 one-inch cubes.
   Ⓒ The volumes are the same because Jonah and Mila used 20 cubes for an area of 20 square inches.
   Ⓓ The volume of the first prism is five times the volume of the second prism.

TEXAS Test Prep

8. John is making a chest that will have a volume of 1,200 cubic inches. The length is 20 inches and the width is 12 inches. How many inches tall should his chest be?

   Ⓐ 6 in.
   Ⓑ 5 in.
   Ⓒ 4 in.
   Ⓓ 7 in.

Name ____________________

12.5 PROBLEM SOLVING • Compare Volumes

1. Cole has a rectangular prism that measures 4 inches by 5 inches by 6 inches. He says that by changing one dimension, he can make a prism with a volume of 240 cubic inches. What are the three ways Cole can do this?

____

2. Sydney wants to use centimeter cubes to build a rectangular prism with a length of 8 centimeters, a width of 10 centimeters, and a height of 6 centimeters. If the centimeter cubes come in packages of 100, how many packages does Sydney need to make the prism?

____

3. Rhoda has 27 unit cubes. How many rectangular prisms with different-size bases can she make if she uses all the unit cubes in each prism?

____

____

4. Alejandro has 64 centimeter cubes. He uses them to build cubes with different side lengths. How many different cubes can he make? **Explain.**

____

____

Problem Solving Real World

5. Ava builds a storage box that is 10 cm long, 12 cm wide, and 10 cm tall. She wants to build a second box that is 10 cm long and 20 cm tall. If the volume of both boxes is the same, how wide is the second box?

____

Lesson Check

TEXAS Test Prep

Fill in the bubble completely to show your answer.

6. Dominic builds a rectangular prism using centimeter cubes. The volume of his prism is 60 cubic centimeters. Which of the following is NOT a possible combination of dimensions for the prism?

Ⓐ $(5 \times 6) \times 3$

Ⓑ $(2 \times 15) \times 2$

Ⓒ $(6 \times 10) \times 1$

Ⓓ $(4 \times 5) \times 3$

7. An architect makes a model of a building with a volume of 1,440 cubic centimeters. The length of the model is 15 centimeters and the width is 12 centimeters. How many centimeters tall is the model?

Ⓐ 10 cm

Ⓑ 8 cm

Ⓒ 7 cm

Ⓓ 12 cm

8. Erin designs a trophy stand using one-inch cubes. The stand is shaped like a rectangular prism. How many different stands can Erin design using exactly 12 one-inch cubes?

Ⓐ 8

Ⓑ 3

Ⓒ 5

Ⓓ 2

9. The volume of a rectangular prism is 140 cubic inches. How does that volume compare to the volume of a cube that measures 5 inches on each side?

Ⓐ The rectangular prism's volume is greater than the cube's volume.

Ⓑ The cube's volume is greater than the rectangular prism's volume.

Ⓒ The volumes are equal.

Ⓓ The rectangular prism's volume is less than the cube's volume.

10. **Multi-Step** Three rectangular prisms built using centimeter cubes have the following dimensions: Prism A: $(6 \times 7) \times 5$; Prism B: $(7 \times 4) \times 6$; Prism C: $(6 \times 8) \times 4$. Which lists the prisms in order from greatest to least volume?

Ⓐ *A; B; C*

Ⓑ *B; C; A*

Ⓒ *A; C; B*

Ⓓ *C; A; B*

11. **Multi-Step** Seth builds a rectangular prism with centimeter cubes with a length of 12 centimeters, a width of 6 centimeters, and a height of 4 centimeters. Seth adds more cubes to his prism, so the prism now has a height of 6 centimeters. If the base measurements stay the same, how many more cubes does Seth use?

Ⓐ 72 cubes

Ⓑ 288 cubes

Ⓒ 144 cubes

Ⓓ 78 cubes

Name ______________________________

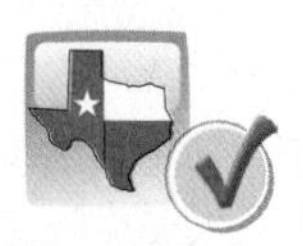

Module 12 Assessment

Vocabulary

Vocabulary
cubic unit
unit cube
rectangular prism

Choose the best term from the box.

1. A ____________ has a length, width, and height of 1 unit. (p. 435)

2. Volume is measured in ____________. (p. 441)

Concepts and Skills

Count the number of cubes used to build each solid figure. TEKS 5.6.A

3. 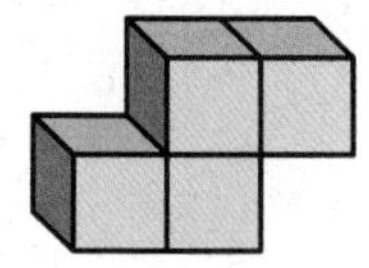

____________ unit cubes

4. 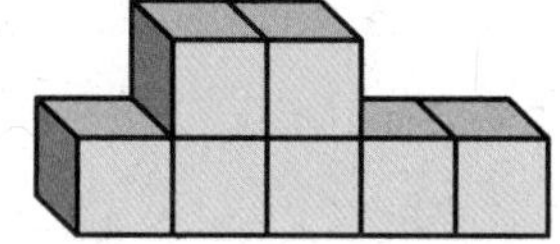

____________ unit cubes

5. 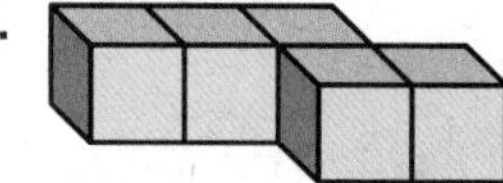

____________ unit cubes

Find the volume. TEKS 5.6.A, 5.6.B

6. 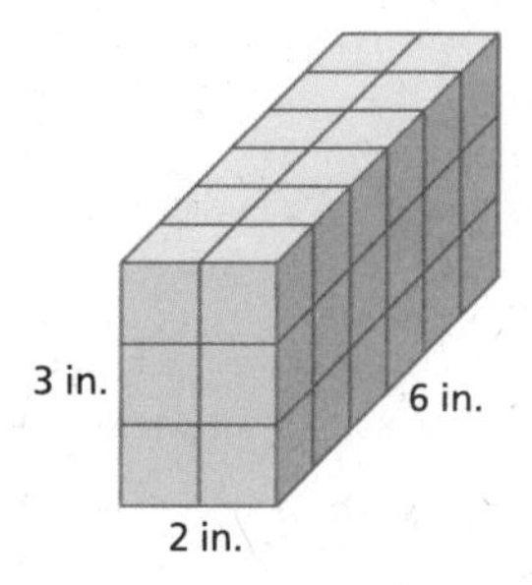

Volume: ____________

7. 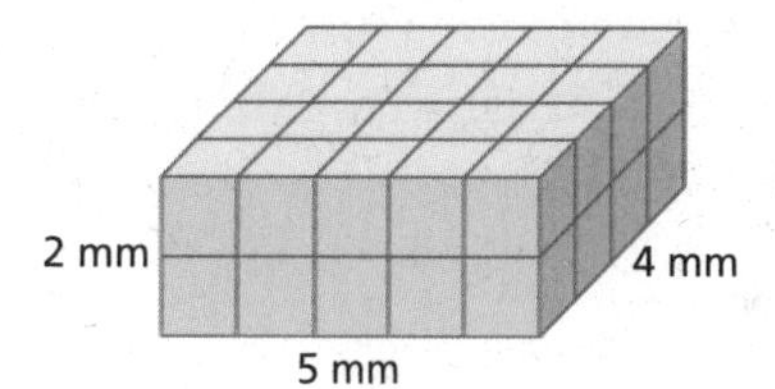

Volume: ____________

8. 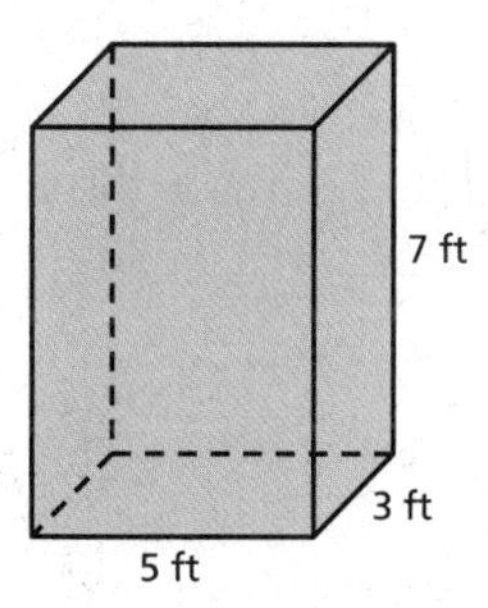

Volume: ____________

9. 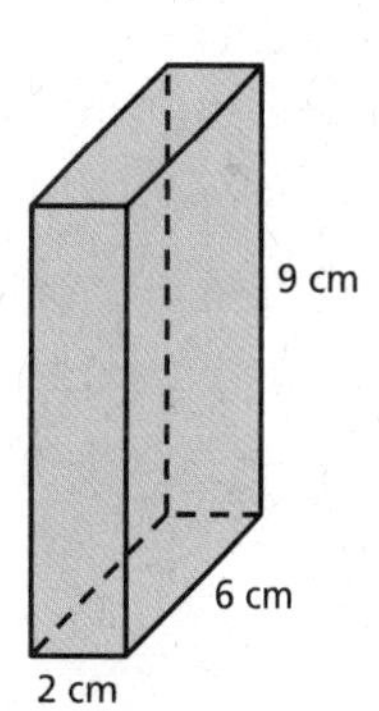

Volume: ____________

Fill in the bubble completely to show your answer.

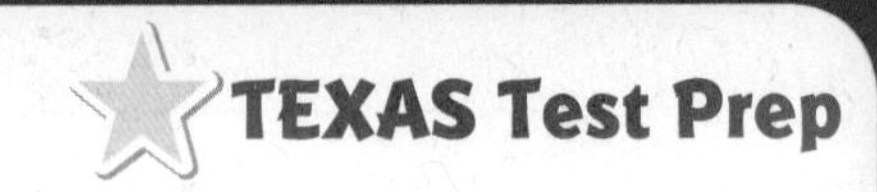

10. Sharri packed away her old summer clothes in a storage tote that had a length of 3 feet, a width of 4 feet, and a height of 3 feet. What was the volume of the tote that Sharri used? TEKS 5.6.B

Ⓐ 36 cu ft

Ⓑ 21 cu ft

Ⓒ 24 cu ft

Ⓓ 10 cu ft

11. A manufacturing company constructs a shipping box to hold its cereal boxes. Each cereal box has a volume of 40 cubic inches. If the shipping box holds 8 layers with 4 cereal boxes in each layer, what is the volume of the shipping box? TEKS 5.6.B

Ⓐ 160 cu in.

Ⓑ 320 cu in.

Ⓒ 480 cu in.

Ⓓ 1,280 cu in.

12. Angela is deciding which of two aquariums to buy. One aquarium has a base that is 18 inches by 14 inches and a height that is 12 inches. The other aquarium has a base that is 25 inches by 9 inches and a height that is 14 inches. What is the difference between volumes of the two aquariums? TEKS 5.6.B

Ⓐ 3,024 cu in.

Ⓑ 3,150 cu in.

Ⓒ 126 cu in.

Ⓓ 150 cu in.

13. Roberto wants to build a wooden box with a volume of 8 cubic feet. How many different boxes, all with whole-number dimensions and a different-size base, will have a volume of 8 cubic feet? TEKS 5.6.B

Record your answer and fill in the bubbles on the grid. Be sure to use the correct place value.

			.		
⓪	⓪	⓪		⓪	⓪
①	①	①		①	①
②	②	②		②	②
③	③	③		③	③
④	④	④		④	④
⑤	⑤	⑤		⑤	⑤
⑥	⑥	⑥		⑥	⑥
⑦	⑦	⑦		⑦	⑦
⑧	⑧	⑧		⑧	⑧
⑨	⑨	⑨		⑨	⑨

Name ____________________

13.1 Appropriate Tools and Units

Essential Question What tools and units would you use to measure length, capacity, and weight or mass?

Unlock the Problem (Real World)

Mr. Lee wants to find Eric's height. What tool and unit should Mr. Lee use to measure Eric's height?

Tell which units are measured by each tool.

Customary Length: Inch, Foot, Yard, and Mile		
ruler ______ yardstick ______ ______	trundle wheel ______ ______	odometer ______

So, Mr. Lee would use a ____________ to measure Eric's height, and the unit he would use is ____________.

Tell which units are measured by each tool.

Customary Capacity: Teaspoon, Tablespoon, Cup, Pint, Quart, and Gallon		
______ ______	______	______

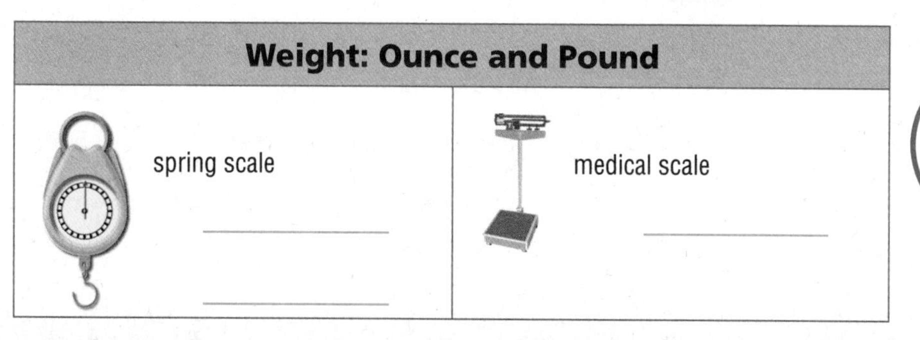

Weight: Ounce and Pound	
spring scale ______ ______	medical scale ______

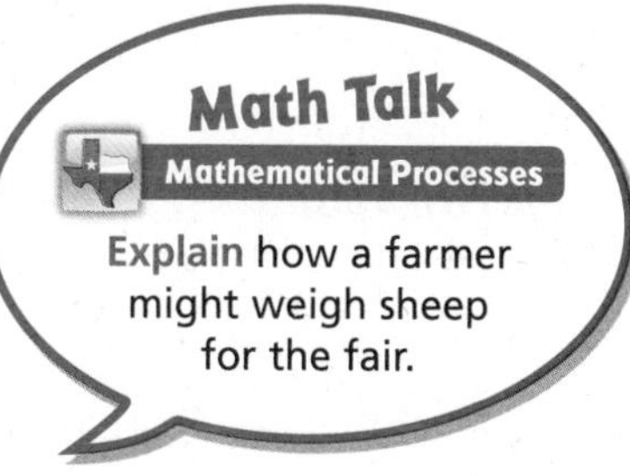

Example

pan balance

large scale

Mr. Wilkins takes his dog to the vet. What tool and unit would the vet use to measure the dog's mass?

Some metric units for measuring mass are grams, kilograms, and milligrams. Some tools that can be used are a pan balance and a large scale.

So, the vet would use a ____________ to measure the dog's

mass, and the unit he would use is ____________.

Try This! **Tell which units are measured by each tool.**

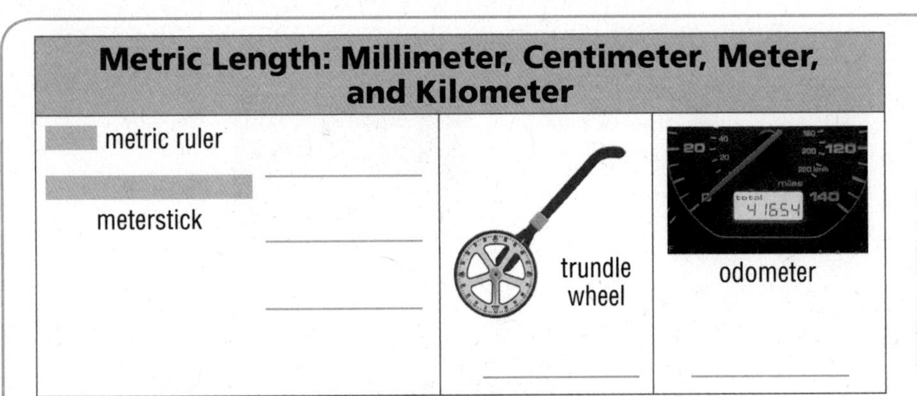

Metric Length: Millimeter, Centimeter, Meter, and Kilometer		
metric ruler ________ meterstick ________ ________	trundle wheel ________	odometer ________

Math Idea

Millimeter (mm), milliliter (mL), and milligram (mg) are very small metric units of length, capacity, and mass.

Metric Capacity: Milliliter and Liter		
 ________	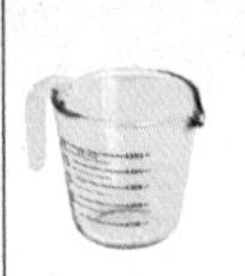 ________	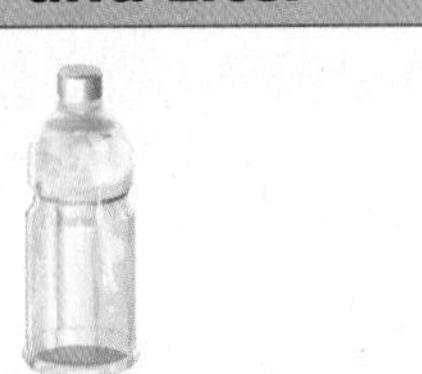 ________

Share and Show

Choose the appropriate metric tool and unit.

1. length of a pencil

________ ________

2. mass of a strawberry

________ ________

3. capacity of a medicine bottle

________ ________

Metric	
Tools	**Units**
metric ruler	millimeter
medicine spoon	meter
measuring cup	kilometer
pan balance	gram
meterstick	kilogram
odometer	liter
trundle wheel	milliliter

Name ___________________________

Problem Solving

4. H.O.T. **Multi-Step** Maria used one customary unit to measure the height of a tomato plant when it was first planted and a different customary unit when it was full grown. She used the same measurement tool both times. What tool did she use? What unit did she use each time?

____

5. Jill wants to know the length of a toy car in metric units. What tool and unit will she use?

____

6. **Use Tools** Glen used ounces to measure the weight of an object. What tool did he use? What could the object be?

____

Problem Solving Real World

7. H.O.T. **Reasoning** Would an inch ruler be a reasonable tool to use to measure the height of a water tower that is more than 68 feet tall? **Explain.**

____

____

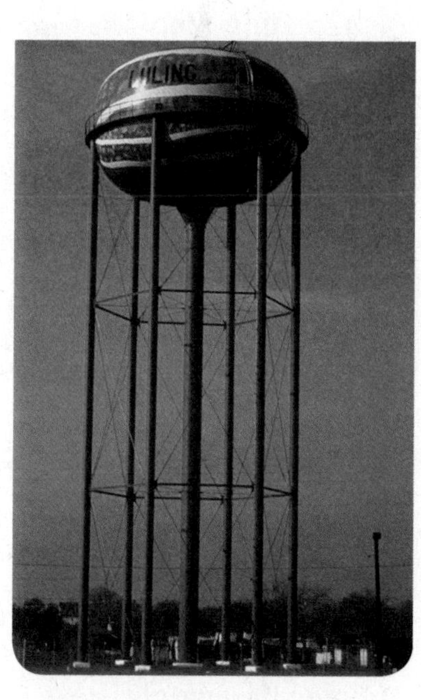

▲ The Luling, Texas, water tower was built and painted to look like a watermelon in honor of the town's annual Watermelon Thump Festival.

8. **Explain** Which customary unit would most likely be used to measure the capacity of a water tower? Why?

____

____

9. H.O.T. **Multi-Step** What tool would you use to find the perimeter of a rectangular patio? What unit would you use?

____

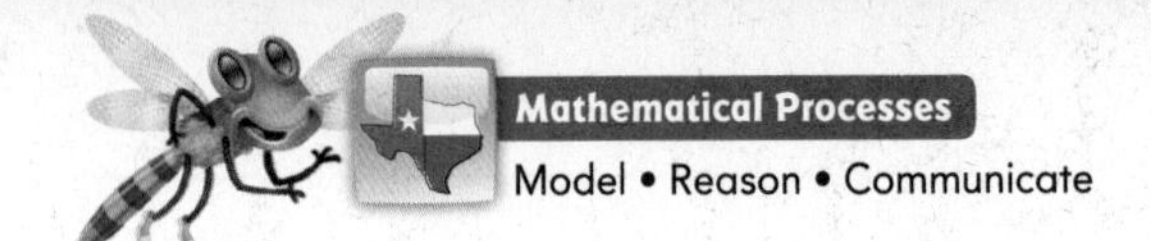

Daily Assessment Task

Fill in the bubble completely to show your answer.

10. Pablo swims 1 length of a swimming pool. What unit would be best for measuring the length of the pool?

Ⓐ inch
Ⓑ centimeter
Ⓒ foot
Ⓓ kilometer

11. Which of the following would you most likely measure in grams?

Ⓐ mass of a berry
Ⓑ mass of a watermelon
Ⓒ length of a berry
Ⓓ height of a watermelon

12. **Multi-Step** Mia used a measuring cup to find a particular measurement. She recorded the measurement as 5 liters. What could Mia have been measuring?

Ⓐ weight of a punch bowl
Ⓑ capacity of a punch bowl
Ⓒ weight of a cereal bowl
Ⓓ capacity of a cereal bowl

TEXAS Test Prep

13. **Use Tools** Which tool would you use to measure the capacity of a coffee mug?

Ⓐ meterstick
Ⓑ spring scale
Ⓒ measuring cup
Ⓓ 1-liter container

Homework and Practice

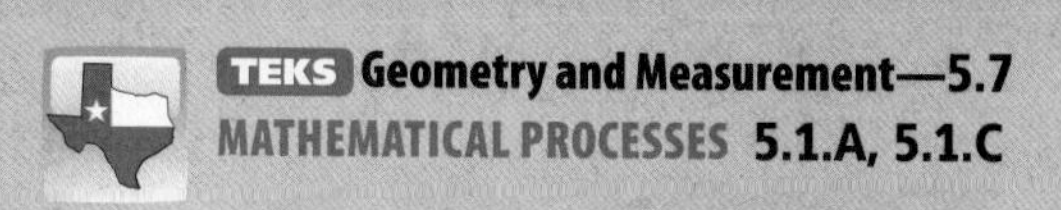

Name ____________________

13.1 Appropriate Tools and Units

Choose the appropriate metric tool and unit.

Metric	
Tools	**Units**
metric ruler	centimeter
medicine spoon	meter
measuring cup	kilometer
pan balance	gram
meterstick	kilogram
odometer	liter
trundle wheel	milliliter

1. height of a soccer trophy

   __________ __________

2. driving distance from home to the soccer field

   __________ __________

3. length of a soccer field

   __________ __________

4. capacity of a bucket

   __________ __________

5. mass of a coin

   __________ __________

6. length of a car

   __________ __________

7. capacity of an eye dropper

   __________ __________

8. mass of an orange

   __________ __________

9. length of school building

   __________ __________

Problem Solving Real World

10. The Guadalupe River is a popular destination for rafters and canoers. Which customary unit would most likely be used to measure the length of a river? Why?

11. Would a yardstick be a reasonable tool to use to measure the length of a canoe paddle? **Explain**.

Lesson Check

TEXAS Test Prep

Fill in the bubble completely to show your answer.

12. Which of the following would you most likely measure in kilograms?

Ⓐ mass of a paper clip
Ⓑ length of a horseshoe
Ⓒ length of a longhorn cow
Ⓓ mass of a longhorn cow

13. Which tool would you use to measure the mass of a mobile phone?

Ⓐ meterstick
Ⓑ trundle wheel
Ⓒ pan balance
Ⓓ odometer

14. Every spring, cyclists participate in a two day fundraising ride from Houston to Austin. Which unit would be best for measuring the distance they ride?

Ⓐ meter
Ⓑ kilometer
Ⓒ foot
Ⓓ yard

15. Kaylee measures honey into a bowl with ingredients for a batch of muffins. Which is the most likely measurement for the honey?

Ⓐ 3 tablespoons
Ⓑ 3 gallons
Ⓒ 3 liters
Ⓓ 3 kilograms

16. Brian serves ice cream to his family. Which is the most likely measurement for the capacity of the ice cream carton?

Ⓐ 1 cup
Ⓑ 1 gallon
Ⓒ 1 teaspoon
Ⓓ 1 milliliter

17. Which container would most likely have a capacity that is measured in liters?

Ⓐ a drinking glass
Ⓑ a watering can
Ⓒ a baby bottle
Ⓓ a soup spoon

18. **Multi-Step** Tristan used a measuring cup to find a particular measurement. He recorded the measurement as 6 cups. What could Tristan have been measuring?

Ⓐ capacity of a mixing bowl
Ⓑ weight of a mixing bowl
Ⓒ capacity of a juice glass
Ⓓ weight of a juice glass

19. **Multi-Step** A scientist measured a museum specimen. She recorded the measurement as 75 centimeters. What could the scientist have been measuring?

Ⓐ length of a dinosaur bone
Ⓑ mass of a dinosaur bone
Ⓒ length of a gem
Ⓓ mass of a gem

Name ___

13.2 Customary Length

TEKS Geometry and Measurement—5.7.A
MATHEMATICAL PROCESSES 5.1.D

Essential Question How can you compare and convert customary units of length?

Unlock the Problem (Real World)

To build a new swing, Mr. Mattson needs 9 feet of rope for each side of the swing and 6 more feet for the monkey bar. The hardware store sells rope by the yard.

- How many feet of rope does Mr. Mattson need for the swing? ___
- How many feet does Mr. Mattson need for the swing and the monkey bar combined? ___

Mr. Mattson needs to find how many yards of rope he needs to buy. He will need to convert 24 feet to yards. How many groups of 3 feet are in 24 feet?

A 12-inch ruler is 1 foot.		

A yardstick is 1 yard.

___ feet = 1 yard

Use a strip diagram to write an equation.

MODEL

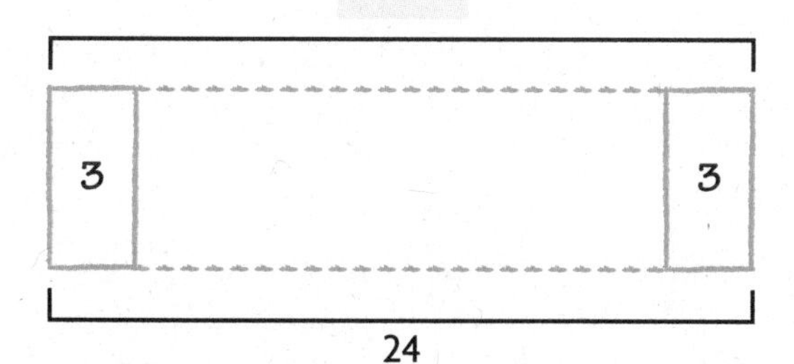

RECORD

total feet → 24 ÷ feet in 1 yard → ___ = total yards → ___

So, Mr. Mattson needs to buy ___ yards of rope.

Math Talk Mathematical Processes

What operation did you use when you found groups of 3 feet in 24 feet? Do you multiply or divide when you convert a smaller unit to a larger unit? **Explain.**

Example

Use the table to find the relationship between miles and feet.

Customary Units of Length
1 foot (ft) = 12 inches (in.)
1 yard (yd) = 3 ft
1 mile (mi) = 5,280 ft
1 mile = 1,760 yd

The distance between the new high school and the football field is 2 miles. How does this distance compare to 10,000 feet?

When you convert larger units to smaller units, you need to multiply.

STEP 1 Convert 2 miles to feet.

Think: 1 mile is equal to 5,280 feet.

I need to ____________ the total number of miles by ____________.

total miles ↓ feet in 1 mile ↓ total feet ↓

2 × ____________ = ____________

2 miles = ____________ feet

STEP 2 Compare. Write <, >, or =.

____________ feet ◯ 10,000 feet

Since ____________ is ____________ than 10,000, the distance between the new high school and the football field is ____________ than 10,000 feet.

- Sometimes you need to convert a single unit of measurement to mixed measures. Convert 62 inches into feet and inches.

Think: 1 foot is equal to 12 inches.

62 ÷ ______ = ______ r ______ or ______ ft ______ in.

Share and Show

Convert.

1. 2 mi = ____________ yd

2. 6 yd = ____________ ft

3. 90 in. = ______ ft ______ in.

Math Talk
Mathematical Processes
Explain how you know when to multiply to convert a measurement.

Name ______________________

Problem Solving

Practice: Copy and Solve **Convert.**

4. 60 in. = ■ ft

5. ■ ft = 7 yd

6. 4 mi = ■ yd

7. 120 in. = ■ ft

8. 46 ft = ■ yd ■ ft

9. 42 yd = ■ ft

Use Symbols **Compare. Write $<$, $>$ or $=$.**

10. 8 ft ○ 3 yd

11. 2 mi ○ 10,500 ft

12. 3 yd 2 ft ○ 132 in.

13. H.O.T. **Representations** Make a table that shows the number of feet and inches in 1, 2, 3, and 4 yards. What do you notice about the relationship between the number of larger units and the number of smaller units as the length increases?

____

____

____

Problem Solving Real World

14. H.O.T. **Multi-Step** Javon is helping his dad build a tree house. He has a piece of trim that is 13 feet long. How many pieces can Javon cut that are 1 yard long? How much of a yard will he have left over?

____

15. H.O.T. **Multi-Step** Patty is building a rope ladder for a tree house. She needs two 5-foot pieces of rope for the sides of the ladder. She needs 7 pieces of rope, each 18 inches long, for the steps. How many feet of rope does Patty need to make the ladder? Write your answer as a mixed number and as a mixed measure in feet and inches.

____

Daily Assessment Task

Fill in the bubble completely to show your answer.

16. Kelly lives 2 miles from school. Harry lives closer to the school than Kelly. Which could be the distance that Harry lives from school?

Ⓐ 3,800 yards

Ⓑ 10,560 feet

Ⓒ 10,600 feet

Ⓓ 3,461 yards

17. Bart measured a piece of wood to be 9 feet long. How could he calculate the length of the wood in inches?

Ⓐ $9 \div 12$

Ⓑ 9×12

Ⓒ $12 + 9$

Ⓓ $12 \div 9$

18. **Multi-Step** Aliesha has a 55-inch rope. Mike has a rope that is 17 inches longer. What is the length of Mike's rope?

Ⓐ 1 yard

Ⓑ 5 feet

Ⓒ 2 yards

Ⓓ 7 feet

TEXAS Test Prep

19. Katy's driveway is 120 feet long. How many yards long is Katy's driveway?

Ⓐ 60 yards

Ⓑ 40 yards

Ⓒ 20 yards

Ⓓ 10 yards

Homework and Practice

Name ________________________

13.2 Customary Length

Convert.

1. 3 mi = ■ yd
2. 72 in. = ■ ft
3. ■ ft = 8 yd
4. 132 in. = ■ ft
5. 36 ft = ■ yd
6. 46 yd = ■ ft
7. 15 ft = ■ in.
8. ■ ft = 24 yd 2 ft
9. ■ ft = 7 mi

Compare. Write <, >, or =.

10. 2 mi ○ 3,526 yd
11. 4 yd ○ 13 ft
12. 5 mi ○ 26,300 ft
13. 90 ft ○ 32 yd
14. 27 ft ○ 324 in.
15. 5 yd 2 ft ○ 200 in.

Problem Solving

16. A prickly pear cactus is 1 yard tall. A yucca plant is 35 inches tall. Which plant is taller? Tell how you know.

____

____

____

17. The length of the Beecher family's driveway is 20 yd. The length of their SUV is one fourth the length of the driveway. How many feet long is the SUV?

____

Lesson Check

TEXAS Test Prep

Fill in the bubble completely to show your answer.

18. The length of a cruise ship is 1,092 feet. How many yards long is the cruise ship?

Ⓐ 3,276 yards

Ⓑ 91 yards

Ⓒ 330 yards

Ⓓ 364 yards

19. Nadia runs 8 miles each weekend. How many yards does Nadia run each weekend?

Ⓐ 14,080 yards

Ⓑ 42,240 yards

Ⓒ 14,960 yards

Ⓓ 220 yards

20. Since the 1980 eruption of Mount St. Helens in Washington state, the elevation of its summit is about 1,300 feet lower. How can you calculate the difference in elevation in inches?

Ⓐ $1,300 \times 12$

Ⓑ $1,300 \div 12$

Ⓒ $1,300 \times 3$

Ⓓ $1,300 - 12$

21. The height of the U.S. Capitol building from the ground to the top of the Statue of Freedom is 96 yards. The height of the Texas State Capitol building is greater than the U.S. Capitol. Which could be the height of the Texas State Capitol?

Ⓐ 310 feet

Ⓑ 288 feet

Ⓒ 3,452 inches

Ⓓ 3,420 inches

22. **Multi-Step** Tyler's older brother Joseph is 5 feet 6 inches tall. Joseph is 16 inches taller than Tyler. How tall is Tyler?

Ⓐ 4 ft 2 in.

Ⓑ 4 ft

Ⓒ 6 ft 10 in.

Ⓓ 6 ft 4 in.

23. **Multi-Step** Calvin fishes from a dock that is 85 inches long. Which of the following is equal to 85 inches?

Ⓐ 2 yd 12 ft 1in.

Ⓑ 2 yd 1 ft 1 in.

Ⓒ 1 yd 3 ft 1 in.

Ⓓ 1 yd 4 ft 3 in.

Name ______________________

13.3 Customary Capacity

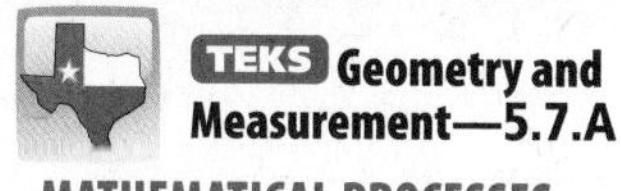

TEKS Geometry and Measurement—5.7.A

MATHEMATICAL PROCESSES
5.1.D, 5.1.G

Essential Question

How can you compare and convert customary units of capacity?

Unlock the Problem

Mara has a can of paint with 3 cups of purple paint in it. She also has a bucket with a capacity of 26 fluid ounces. Will the bucket hold all of the paint Mara has?

The capacity of a container is the amount the container can hold.

1 cup (c) = ______ fluid ounces (fl oz)

- What capacity does Mara need to convert?

____

- After Mara converts the units, what does she need to do next?

____

____

Use a strip diagram to write an equation.

STEP 1 Convert 3 cups to fluid ounces.

MODEL

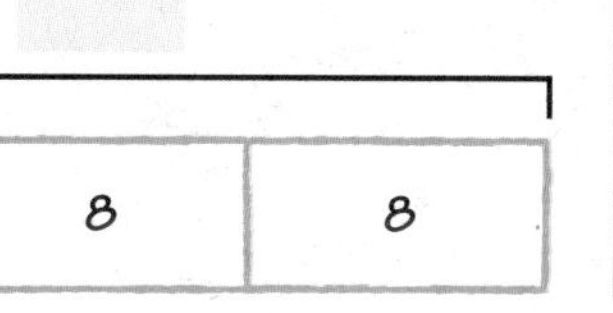

RECORD

total cups		fl oz in 1 cup		total fl oz
↓		↓		↓
3	×	______	=	______

STEP 2 Compare. Write <, >, or =.

______ fl oz ◯ 26 fl oz

Since ______ fluid ounces is ________ than 26 fluid ounces,

Mara's bucket ________ hold all of the paint.

- **What if** Mara has 7 cups of green paint and a container filled with 64 fluid ounces of yellow paint? Which color paint does Mara have more of? **Explain** your reasoning.

____

____

Example

Coral made 32 pints of fruit punch for a party. She needs to transport the punch in 1-gallon containers. How many containers does Coral need?

To convert a smaller unit to a larger unit, you need to divide. Sometimes you may need to convert more than once.

Customary Units of Capacity
1 cup (c) = 8 fluid ounces (fl oz)
1 pint (pt) = 2 cups
1 quart (qt) = 2 pints
1 gallon (gal) = 4 quarts

Convert 32 pints to gallons.

STEP 1 Write an equation to convert pints to quarts.

total pints ↓ 32 ◯ pints in 1 qt ↓ ____ ◯ total quarts ↓ ____

STEP 2 Write an equation to convert quarts to gallons.

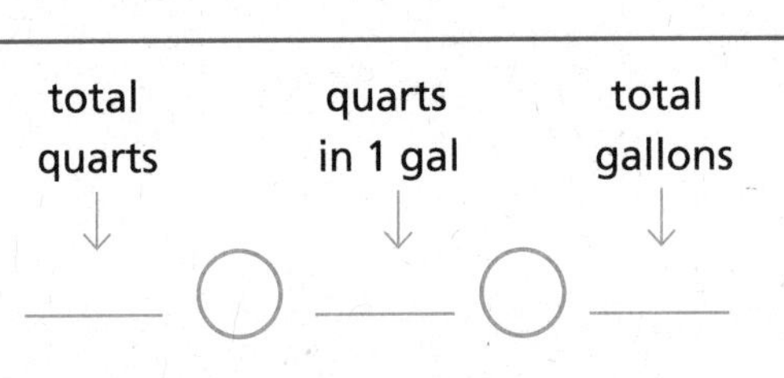

So, Coral needs ______ 1-gallon containers to transport the punch.

Share and Show

1. Use the picture to complete the statements and convert 3 quarts to pints.

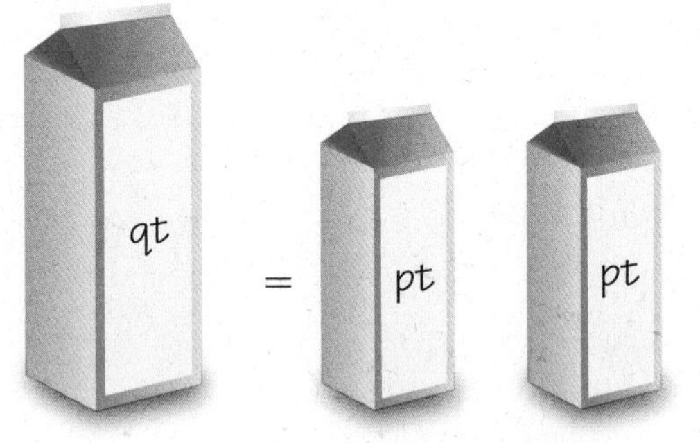

a. 1 quart = ______ pints

b. 1 quart is ________ than 1 pint.

c. 3 qt ◯ ______ pt in 1 qt = ______ pt

Convert.

2. 3 gal = ______ pt

✓ 3. 5 qt = ______ pt

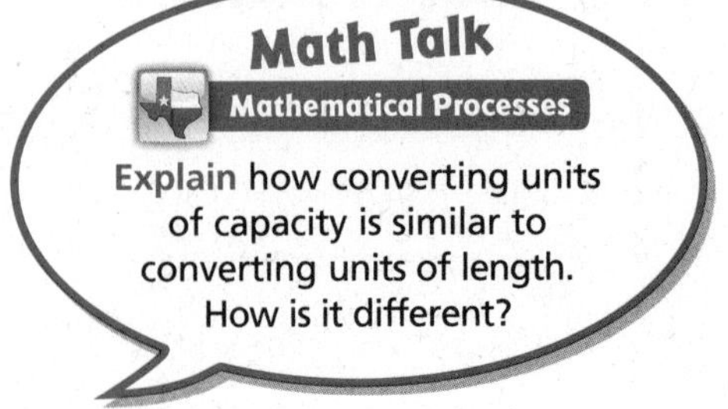

✓ 4. 6 qt = ______ c

Name ___________________________

Problem Solving

Practice: Copy and Solve **Compare. Write <, >, or =.**

5. 28 c ◯ 14 pt

6. 25 pt ◯ 13 qt

7. 20 qt ◯ 80 c

8. **Write Math** ▸ Which of exercises 5–7 could you solve mentally? **Explain** your answer for one exercise.

____

____

Problem Solving Real World

Show your work. For 9–11, use the table.

9. **H.O.T.** **Use Graphs** Complete the table, and make a graph showing the relationship between quarts and pints.

Quarts	0	1	2	3	4
Pints	0				

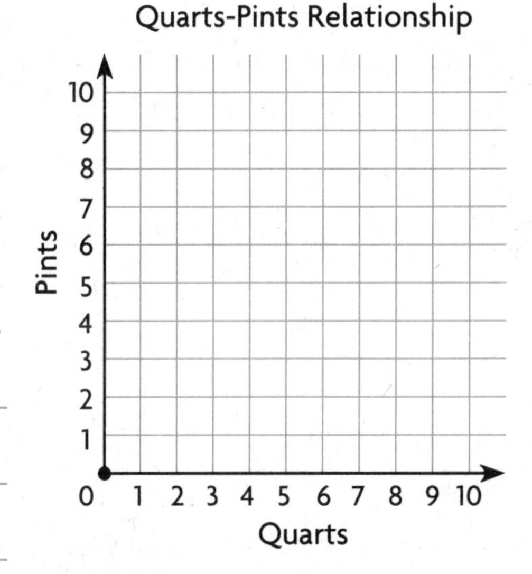

10. **H.O.T.** **Multi-Step** Describe any pattern you notice in the pairs of numbers you graphed. Write a rule to describe the pattern.

____

____

____

11. **H.O.T.** What other pair of customary units of capacity have the same relationship as pints and quarts? **Explain.**

____

____

____

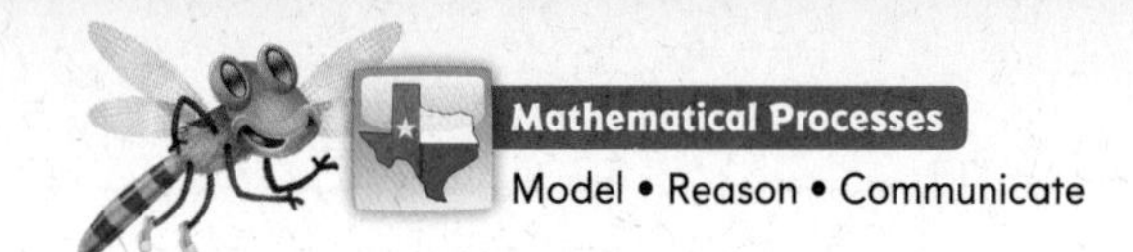

Daily Assessment Task

Fill in the bubble completely to show your answer.

12. Malcolm the Monster needs 3 quarts of fried ant eggs to make his favorite shampoo. How many pints of fried ant eggs does Malcolm need?

Ⓐ 3 pints

Ⓑ $1\frac{1}{2}$ pints

Ⓒ 6 pints

Ⓓ $9\frac{1}{3}$ pints

13. Gina has a container that holds 32 fluid ounces of orange juice. What operation would she use to find how many gallons of orange juice the container holds?

Ⓐ division

Ⓑ addition

Ⓒ multiplication

Ⓓ subtraction

14. **Multi-Step** Marco has 10 quarts of water and 20 cups of milk. How much liquid does he have in all?

Ⓐ 60 cups

Ⓑ 15 cups

Ⓒ 60 quarts

Ⓓ 15 pints

TEXAS Test Prep

15. Shelby made 5 quarts of juice for a picnic. How many cups of juice did Shelby make?

Ⓐ 1 cup

Ⓑ 5 cups

Ⓒ 10 cups

Ⓓ 20 cups

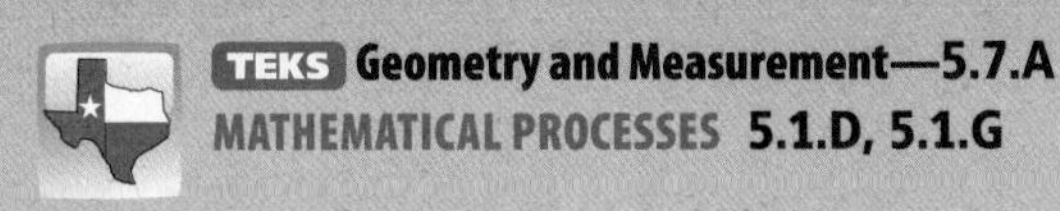

Homework and Practice

Name ______________________

13.3 Customary Capacity

Compare. Write $<$, $>$, or $=$.

1. 12 c ◯ 98 fl oz
2. 34 c ◯ 18 pt
3. 16 pt ◯ 8 qt
4. 22 qt ◯ 90 c
5. 19 pt ◯ 9 qt
6. 20 gal ◯ 75 qt
7. 65 qt ◯ 32 gal
8. 28 c ◯ 6 qt
9. 15 gal ◯ 120 pt

10. **Explain** how you can solve exercise 3 mentally.

____

____

Problem Solving

11. Complete the table and make a graph showing the relationship between gallons and quarts.

Gallons	0	1	2	3	4
Quarts	0				

Gallons-Quarts Relationship

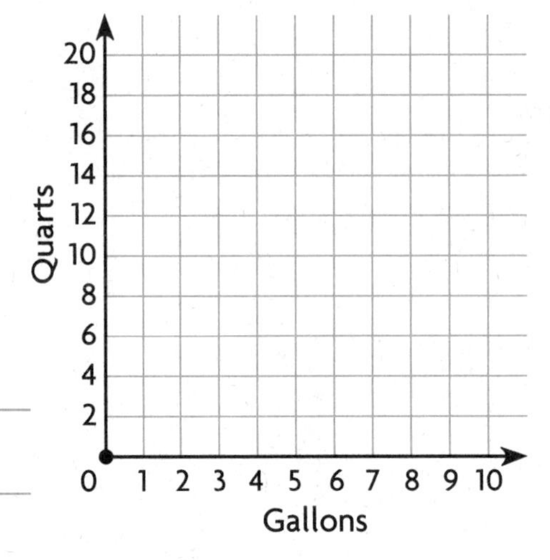

12. Describe any pattern you notice in the pairs of numbers you graphed. Write a rule to describe the pattern.

____

____

Lesson Check

TEXAS Test Prep

Fill in the bubble completely to show your answer.

13. The frozen yogurt shop uses 1 pint of milk in each milkshake. How many milkshakes can be made with 24 quarts of milk?

Ⓐ 96
Ⓑ 12
Ⓒ 6
Ⓓ 48

14. What if the yogurt shop has 8 gallons of milk? How many milkshakes can be made from 8 gallons with 1 pint of milk in each shake?

Ⓐ 64
Ⓑ 32
Ⓒ 128
Ⓓ 16

15. Allan needs 3 quarts of water to fill a pot for soup. How many times will he need to fill an 8-ounce measuring cup to fill the pot?

Ⓐ 16
Ⓑ 12
Ⓒ 24
Ⓓ 4

16. Noriko and her friends made 26 pints of lemonade to sell at the fundraiser. Which operation will Noriko use to find how many cups of lemonade they have to sell?

Ⓐ addition
Ⓑ subtraction
Ⓒ multiplication
Ⓓ division

17. The paint store has 45 gallons of white paint in stock. How many quarts of white paint is this?

Ⓐ 90 quarts
Ⓑ 360 quarts
Ⓒ 9 quarts
Ⓓ 180 quarts

18. Which expression can you use to convert 32 cups to pints?

Ⓐ $32 \div 4$
Ⓑ $32 \div 2$
Ⓒ 32×2
Ⓓ 32×4

19. **Multi-Step** The Holbrooks ordered 25 gallons of orange juice and 16 pints of cranberry juice for their restaurant. How much juice do they have in all?

Ⓐ 57 gallons
Ⓑ 29 gallons
Ⓒ 216 pints
Ⓓ 164 pints

20. **Multi-Step** Mrs. Sullivan calculates that she needs 12 gallons of paint to paint her house. She already has 8 quarts of the paint she needs. How many gallons of paint should she buy?

Ⓐ 10 gallons
Ⓑ 4 gallons
Ⓒ 8 gallons
Ⓓ 6 gallons

Name ________________________________

13.4 Weight

TEKS Geometry and Measurement—5.7.A

MATHEMATICAL PROCESSES 5.1.D, 5.1.E

Essential Question

How can you compare and convert customary units of weight?

Unlock the Problem (Real World)

Hector's school is having a model rocket competition. To qualify, each rocket must weigh 4 pounds or less. Hector's unpainted rocket weighs 62 ounces. What is the weight of the most paint he can use for his model rocket to qualify for entry?

1 pound = ______ ounces

- What weight does Hector need to convert?

  ____

- After Hector converts the weight, what does he need to do next?

  ____

Use a strip diagram to write an equation.

STEP 1 Convert 4 pounds to ounces.

MODEL

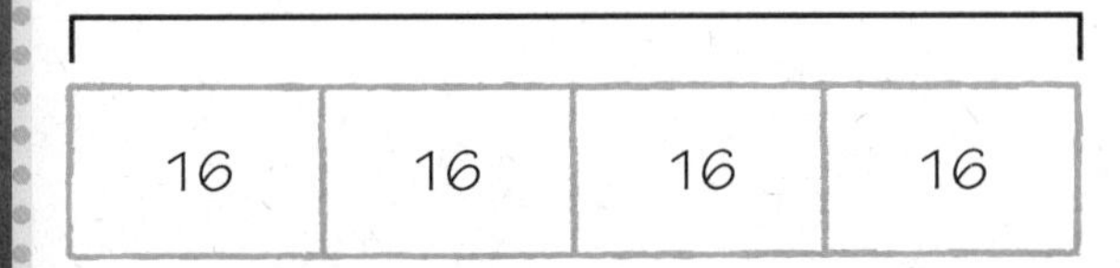

16	16	16	16

RECORD

total lb		oz in 1 lb		total oz
↓		↓		↓
4	◯	______	◯	______

STEP 2 Subtract the rocket's weight from the total ounces a rocket can weigh to qualify.

______ − 62 = ______

So, the weight of the paint can be at most ______ ounces for Hector's model rocket to qualify for entry.

Math Talk
Mathematical Processes

How did you choose which operation to use to change from pounds to ounces? Explain.

Example

The rocket boosters for a U.S. space shuttle weigh 1,292,000 pounds each when the shuttle is launched. How many tons does each rocket booster weigh?

Use mental math to convert pounds to tons.

Units of Weight
1 pound (lb) = 16 ounces (oz)
1 ton (T) = 2,000 lb

STEP 1 Decide which operation to use.

Since pounds are smaller than tons,

I need to ________ the number

of pounds by ________.

STEP 2 Break 2,000 into two factors that are easy to divide by mentally.

$2{,}000 =$ ________ $\times 2$

STEP 3 Divide 1,292,000 by the first factor. Then divide the quotient by the second factor.

$1{,}292{,}000 \div$ ________ $=$ ________

________ $\div 2 =$ ________

So, each rocket booster weighs ________ tons when launched.

Share and Show

1. Use the picture to complete each equation.

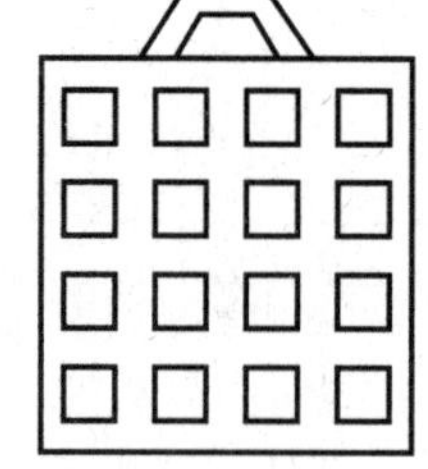

a. 1 pound = ______ ounces

b. 2 pounds = ______ ounces

c. 3 pounds = ______ ounces

d. 4 pounds = ______ ounces

e. 5 pounds = ______ ounces

Convert.

2. 15 lb = ______ oz

3. 3 T = ______ lb

4. 320 oz = ______ lb

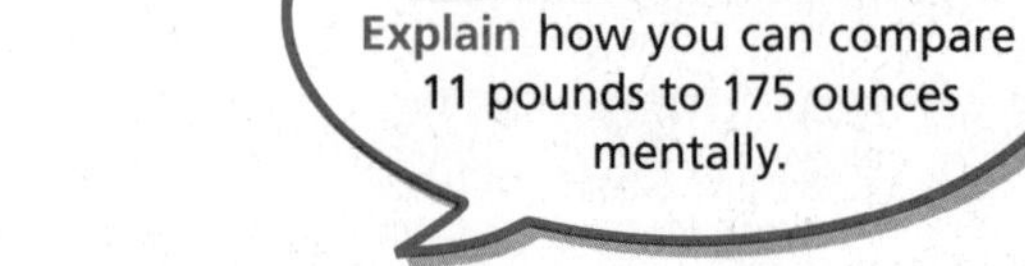

Math Talk

Mathematical Processes

Explain how you can compare 11 pounds to 175 ounces mentally.

Name ______________________________

Problem Solving

Practice: Copy and Solve **Convert.**

5. 23 lb = ■ oz
6. 6 T = ■ lb
7. 144 oz = ■ lb
8. 15 T = ■ lb
9. 352 oz = ■ lb
10. 18 lb = ■ oz

Use Symbols **Compare. Write <, >, or =.**

11. 130 oz ◯ 8 lb
12. 16 T ◯ 32,000 lb
13. 14 lb ◯ 229 oz

14. **Write Math** ▶ **Explain** how you can use mental math to compare 7 pounds to 120 ounces.

____

____

____

____

Problem Solving

15. **H.O.T.** **Multi-Step** Kia wants to have 4 pounds of munchies for her party. She has 36 ounces of popcorn and wants the rest to be pretzel sticks. How many ounces of pretzel sticks does she need to buy?

____

16. **H.O.T.** **Multi-Step** Kevin uses 36 ounces of dried apples and 18 ounces of dried cranberries to make a fruit snack. He plans to sell the snack in $\frac{1}{2}$-pound containers. How may containers will he fill? Will any fruit snack be left over?

____

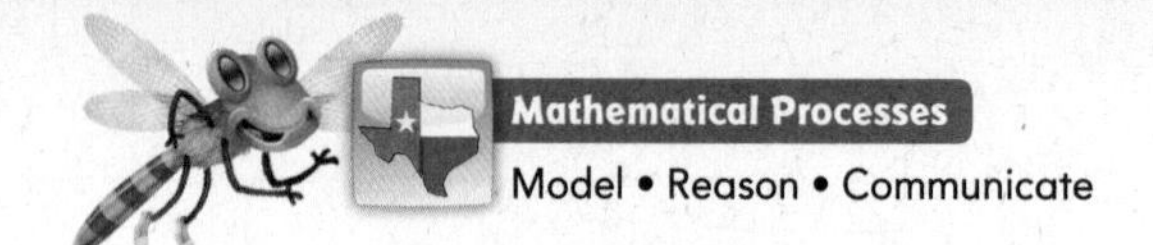

Daily Assessment Task

Fill in the bubble completely to show your answer.

17. An elephant's brain weighs around 11 pounds, while a human's brain weighs about 48 ounces. How many more ounces does an elephant's brain weigh than a human's brain?

Ⓐ 37 ounces

Ⓑ 128 ounces

Ⓒ 4 ounces

Ⓓ 592 ounces

18. **Use Symbols** Which of the following inequalities is correct?

Ⓐ 63 ounces > 4 pounds

Ⓑ 40 pounds < 600 ounces

Ⓒ 3.5 tons > 5,000 pounds

Ⓓ 200 pounds < 3,000 ounces

19. **Multi-Step** A 9-pound block of butter is delivered each morning to a restaurant. A recipe for 1 pot of soup calls for 6 ounces of butter. Using all of the butter, how many pots of soup can the restaurant make each day?

Ⓐ 24 pots of soup

Ⓑ 18 pots of soup

Ⓒ 11 pots of soup

Ⓓ 4 pots of soup

TEXAS Test Prep

20. Carlos used 32 ounces of walnuts in a muffin recipe. How many pounds of walnuts did Carlos use?

Ⓐ 8 pounds

Ⓑ 4 pounds

Ⓒ 2 pounds

Ⓓ 1 pound

Homework and Practice

TEKS Geometry and Measurement—5.7.A
MATHEMATICAL PROCESSES 5.1.D, 5.1.E

Name ______________________

13.4 Weight

Convert.

1. 160 oz = ▢ lb
2. 5 T = ▢ lb
3. 16 lb = ▢ oz
4. 12 T = ▢ lb
5. 128 oz = ▢ lb
6. 26 lb = ▢ oz

Compare. Write <, >, or =.

7. 140 oz ◯ 9 lb
8. 7 T ◯ 15,000 lb
9. 208 oz ◯ 13 lb
10. 23 lb ◯ 365 oz
11. 20 T ◯ 40,000 lb
12. 19 lb ◯ 298 oz
13. **Explain** how you can use mental math to compare 175 ounces to 11 pounds.

____

____

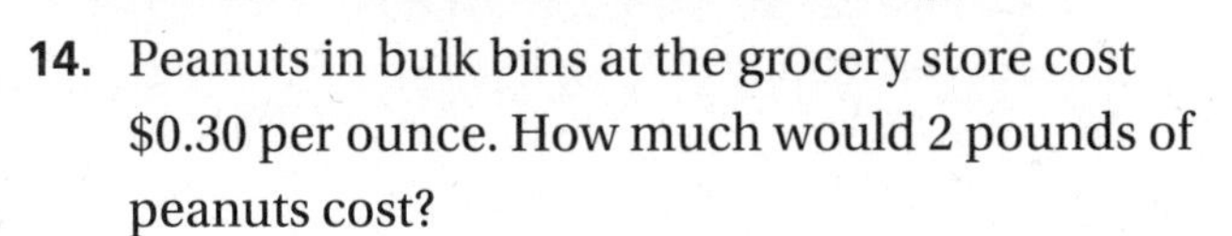

Problem Solving (Real World)

14. Peanuts in bulk bins at the grocery store cost \$0.30 per ounce. How much would 2 pounds of peanuts cost?

____

15. Pecans in bulk bins at the grocery store cost \$0.65 per ounce. How much would you spend if you bought 1 pound 8 ounces of peanuts and 2 pounds of pecans?

____

Lesson Check

TEXAS Test Prep

Fill in the bubble completely to show your answer.

16. Greg's cocker spaniel weighs 32 pounds. His kitten weighs 15 ounces. How many more ounces does the cocker spaniel weigh than the kitten?

(A) 256 ounces

(B) 241 ounces

(C) 497 ounces

(D) 512 ounces

17. The snack machine at the ball park contains 48 ounces of potato chips. How many pounds of chips are in the snack machine?

(A) 4 pounds

(B) 2 pounds

(C) 6 pounds

(D) 3 pounds

18. A bag of corn chips weighs 8 ounces. How many bags of chips weigh 12 pounds?

(A) 24

(B) 6

(C) 16

(D) 48

19. Which expression could be used to convert 86,000 pounds to tons?

(A) $86,000 \div 1,000$

(B) $86,000 \times 1,000$

(C) $86,000 \times 2,000$

(D) $86,000 \div 2,000$

20. Which of the following inequalities is correct?

(A) 12.5 pounds $>$ 200 ounces

(B) 490 ounces $>$ 30 pounds

(C) 6 tons $<$ 10,000 pounds

(D) 8,000 pounds $<$ 4 tons

21. A car weighs 2 tons. How many ounces equal 2 tons?

(A) 64,000

(B) 4,000

(C) 32,000

(D) 6,400

22. **Multi-Step** Eight baseballs weigh 40 ounces. How many pounds do 16 baseballs weigh?

(A) 5 pounds

(B) 4 pounds

(C) 20 pounds

(D) 80 pounds

23. **Multi-Step** A football weighs 14 ounces. A carton of footballs weighs 7 pounds. How many footballs are in a carton?

(A) 12

(B) 8

(C) 7

(D) 4

Name ________________________________

13.5 Multi-Step Measurement Problems

TEKS Geometry and Measurement—5.7.A

MATHEMATICAL PROCESSES 5.1.A

Essential Question

How can you solve multi-step problems that include measurement conversions?

Unlock the Problem

A leaky faucet in Jarod's house drips 2 cups of water each day. After 2 weeks of dripping, the faucet is fixed. If it dripped the same amount each day, how many quarts of water dripped from Jarod's leaky faucet in 2 weeks?

Use the steps to solve the multi-step problem.

STEP 1

Record the information you are given.

The faucet drips ______ cups of water each day.

The faucet drips for ______ weeks.

STEP 2

Find the total amount of water dripped in 2 weeks.

Since you are given the amount of water dripped each day, you must convert 2 weeks into days and multiply.

Think: There are 7 days in 1 week.

cups each day		days in 2 weeks		total cups
↓		↓		↓
2	×	______	=	______

The faucet drips ______ cups in 2 weeks.

STEP 3

Convert from cups to quarts.

Think: There are 2 cups in 1 pint.

There are 2 pints in 1 quart.

______ cups = ______ pints

______ pints = ______ quarts

So, Jarod's leaky faucet drips ______ quarts of water in 2 weeks.

- **What if** the faucet dripped for 4 weeks before it was fixed? How many quarts of water would have leaked?

____

Example

A carton of large, Grade A eggs weighs about 1.5 pounds. If a carton holds a dozen eggs, how many ounces does each egg weigh?

STEP 1

In ounces, find the weight of a carton of eggs.

Think: 1 pound = ______ ounces

Weight of a carton (in ounces):

total lb ↓ oz in 1 lb ↓ total oz ↓

1.5 × ______ = ______

The carton of eggs weighs about ______ ounces.

STEP 2

In ounces, find the weight of each egg in a carton.

Think: 1 carton (dozen eggs) = ______ eggs

Weight of each egg (in ounces):

total oz ↓ eggs in 1 carton ↓ oz of 1 egg ↓

24 ÷ ______ = ______

So, each egg weighs about ______ ounces.

Share and Show

Solve.

1. After each soccer practice, Scott runs 4 sprints of 20 yards each. If he continues his routine, how many practices will it take for Scott to have sprinted a total of 2 miles combined?

Scott sprints ____________ yards each practice.

Since there are ____________ yards in 2 miles, he will need to continue his routine for

____________ practices.

2. A worker at a mill is loading 5-lb bags of flour into boxes to deliver to a local warehouse. Each box holds 12 bags of flour. If the warehouse orders 3 tons of flour, how many boxes are needed to fulfill the order?

____

3. Cory brings five 1-gallon jugs of juice to serve during parent night at his school. If the paper cups he is using for drinks can hold 8 fluid ounces, how many drinks can Cory serve for parent night?

____

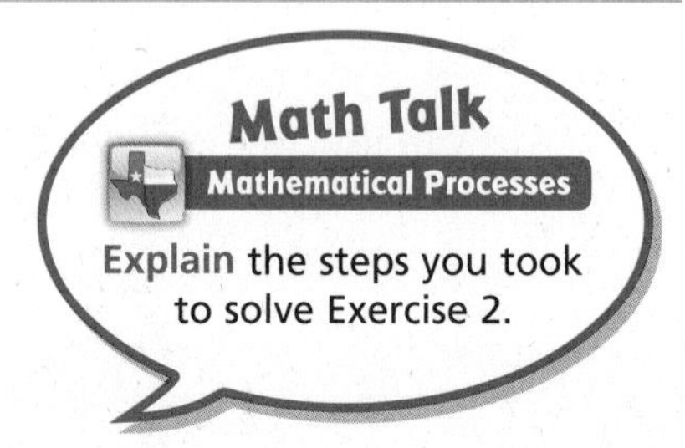

Name ______________________

Problem Solving

Solve.

4. **Apply** A science teacher needs to collect lake water for a lab she is teaching about purifying water. The lab requires each student to use 4 fluid ounces of lake water. If 68 students are participating, how many pints of lake water will the teacher need to collect?

____

5. **H.O.T.** **Use Diagrams** A string of decorative lights is 28 feet long. The first light on the string is 16 inches from the plug. If the lights on the string are spaced 4 inches apart, how many lights are there on the string? Draw a picture to help you solve the problem.

____

6. **Multi-Step** When Jamie's car moves forward such that each tire makes one full rotation, the car has traveled 72 inches. How many full rotations do the tires make when Jamie's car travels 10 yards?

____

7. **Multi-Step** A male African elephant weighs 7 tons. If a male African lion at the local zoo weighs 13,650 pounds less than the male African elephant, how many pounds does the lion weigh?

____

8. **Multi-Step** An office supply company is shipping a case of pencils to a store. There are 64 boxes of pencils in the case. If each box of pencils weighs 2.5 ounces, what is the weight, in pounds, of the case of pencils?

____

9. **H.O.T.** At a local animal shelter there are 12 small-size dogs and 5 medium-size dogs. Every day, the small-size dogs are each given 12.5 ounces of dry food and the medium-size dogs are each given 18 ounces of the same dry food. How many pounds of dry food does the shelter serve in one day?

Math on the Spot

____

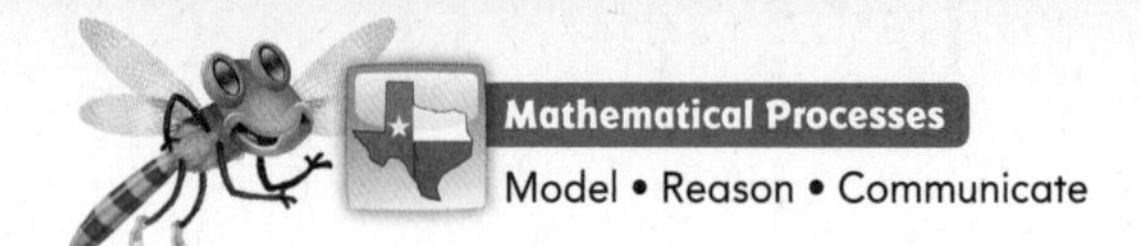

Daily Assessment Task

Fill in the bubble completely to show your answer.

10. **Analyze** A 2.3-ton shark is on one side of a pan balance in a cartoon. Seals are piling up on the other side, trying to "outweigh" the shark. What is the least number of 150-pound seals that would have a combined weight greater than the shark's weight?

Ⓐ 28 seals

Ⓑ 30 seals

Ⓒ 29 seals

Ⓓ 31 seals

11. Sara has 2 pounds of chicken. She uses 5 ounces of chicken while cooking. How can you determine the mass of chicken that she has left?

Ⓐ Divide 2 by 16, and then subtract 5.

Ⓑ Divide 2 by 16, and then add 5.

Ⓒ Multiply 2 by 16, and then subtract 5.

Ⓓ Multiply 2 by 16, and then add 5.

12. **Multi-Step** Leo has three pieces of ribbon. One piece is 4 yards long, another piece is 5 feet long, and the last piece is 10 inches long. How much ribbon does Leo have in all?

Ⓐ 214 inches

Ⓑ 118 inches

Ⓒ 19 inches

Ⓓ 57 inches

TEXAS Test Prep

13. For a class assignment, students are asked to record the total amount of water they drink in one day. Melinda records that she drank four 8-fluid ounce glasses of water and two 1-pint bottles. How many quarts of water did Melinda drink during the day?

Ⓐ 2 quarts

Ⓑ 4 quarts

Ⓒ 3 quarts

Ⓓ 8 quarts

Homework and Practice

Name ____________________

13.5 Multi-Step Measurement Problems

Solve.

1. Diego drinks 16 ounces of his favorite sport drink every day after soccer practice for 2 weeks. How many quarts of the sport drink does Diego consume in 2 weeks?

____

2. A rancher is putting a fence around a square animal pen. The perimeter of the pen is 32 feet. The fence posts will be 16 inches apart. She starts by putting 1 fence post at each corner of the pen. How many fence posts does she use altogether? Draw a picture to model the problem.

____

3. A koala weighs 20 pounds. In her pouch, she carries her joey that weighs 20 ounces. What is the combined weight of the adult koala and her joey in ounces?

____

4. On Friday, 32 students in Mr. Tanika's class are each served 6 ounces of milk for lunch. How many quarts of milk are served to the class on Friday?

____

Problem Solving Real World

5. Vanessa bought 5 feet of ribbon. She cut off 36 inches to wrap a package and 18 inches to decorate her scrapbook. How much ribbon does Vanessa have left?

____

6. Students fill beanbags to play a classroom number game. Each beanbag contains 3 cups of beans. They have a 1-pint container, a 1-quart container, and a 1-gallon container filled with beans to use for the beanbags. What is the greatest number of beanbags they can make?

____

Lesson Check

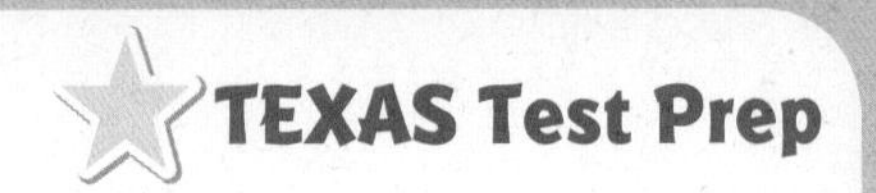

Fill in the bubble completely to show your answer.

7. A large brick weighs 8 pounds. A small brick weighs 52 ounces. How can you determine the difference in weight between the large brick and the small brick?

Ⓐ Divide 16 by 8, and then add 52.

Ⓑ Divide 16 by 8, and then subtract 52.

Ⓒ Multiply 8 by 16, and then add 52.

Ⓓ Multiply 8 by 16, and then subtract 52.

8. Ariel has one gallon container of juice and one quart container of juice. How many 1-cup servings of juice does Ariel have?

Ⓐ 20

Ⓑ 36

Ⓒ 12

Ⓓ 44

9. The veterinarian weighs Jim's two dogs. His collie weighs 37 pounds. His terrier weighs 240 ounces. What is the total weight of Jim's dogs?

Ⓐ 592 ounces

Ⓑ 52 pounds

Ⓒ 53 pounds

Ⓓ 12 pounds

10. An elevator has a maximum weight limit of 1.5 tons. Rozell Company workers load boxes that weigh 150 pounds each into the elevator to transport them to the first floor. What is the greatest number of boxes the elevator can hold?

Ⓐ 16

Ⓑ 13

Ⓒ 10

Ⓓ 20

11. **Multi-Step** An artist painted a rectangular mural on the wall. Two sides are each 26 inches long. The other two sides are each 2 yards long. What is the perimeter of the mural?

Ⓐ 98 inches

Ⓑ 196 inches

Ⓒ 62 inches

Ⓓ 144 inches

12. **Multi-Step** Vince has a rectangular rug in his room with an area of 10 feet. The length of the rug is 18 inches longer than the width. Which could be the dimensions of the rug?

Ⓐ length: 4 feet; width 2.5 feet

Ⓑ length: 2 feet; width 3 feet

Ⓒ length: 5 feet; width 2 feet

Ⓓ length: 2.5; width 4 feet

Name ______________________________

TEKS Geometry and Measurement—5.7.A

MATHEMATICAL PROCESSES 5.1.F

13.6 Metric Measures

Essential Question

How can you compare and convert metric units?

Unlock the Problem

Using a map, Alex estimates the distance between his house and his grandparent's house to be about 15,000 meters. About how many kilometers away from his grandparent's house does Alex live?

- Underline the sentence that tells you what you are trying to find.
- Circle the measurement you need to convert.

The metric system is based on place value. Length, capacity, and mass each have a base unit (meter, liter, or gram) and use prefixes to show the relationship between larger and smaller units.

One Way Convert 15,000 meters to kilometers.

	×10 →	×10 →	×10 →	×10 →	×10 →	×10 →
kilo- (k)	hecto- (h)	deka- (dk)	meter (m) liter (L) gram (g)	deci- (d)	centi- (c)	milli- (m)
	← ÷10	← ÷10	← ÷10	← ÷10	← ÷10	← ÷10

STEP 1 Find the relationship between the units.

There are ______ meters in 1 kilometer.

STEP 2 Determine the operation to be used.

I am converting from a ____________ unit to a ____________ unit, so I will ____________.

STEP 3 Convert.

number of meters		meters in 1 kilometer		number of kilometers
↓		↓		↓
15,000	◯	______	=	______

So, Alex's house is ______ kilometers from his grandparent's house.

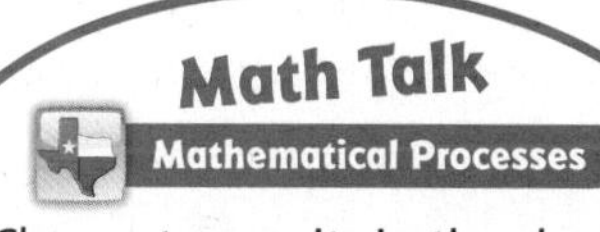

Choose two units in the chart. Explain how the two units are related.

Another Way Use a diagram.

Jamie made a bracelet 1.8 decimeters long. How many millimeters long is Jamie's bracelet?

Convert 1.8 decimeters to millimeters.

				1	8	
kilo-	hecto-	deka-	meter liter gram	deci-	centi-	milli-

STEP 1 Show 1.8 decimeters.

Since the unit is decimeters, place the decimal point so that decimeters are the whole number unit.

STEP 2 Convert.

Cross out the decimal point and rewrite it so that millimeters will be the whole number unit. Write a zero to the left of the decimal point to complete the whole number.

STEP 3 Record the value with the new unit.

1.8 dm = ____________ mm

So, Jamie's bracelet is ____________ millimeters long.

Try This! **Complete the equation to show the conversion.**

A Convert 247 milligrams to centigrams, decigrams, and grams.

Are the units being converted to a larger unit or a smaller unit? ____________

Should you multiply or divide to convert? ____________

247 mg ◯ 10 = ______ cg

247 mg ◯ 100 = ______ dg

247 mg ◯ 1,000 = ______ g

B Convert 3.9 hectoliters to dekaliters, liters, and deciliters.

Are the units being converted to a larger unit or a smaller unit? ____________

Should you multiply or divide to convert? ____________

3.9 hL ◯ 10 = ______ daL

3.9 hL ◯ 100 = ______ L

3.9 hL ◯ 1,000 = ______ dL

Name ____________________

Share and Show

Complete the equation to show the conversion.

1. 8.47 L ◯ 10 = ______ dL

   8.47 L ◯ 100 = ______ cL

   8.47 L ◯ 1,000 = ______ mL

Think: Are the units being converted to a larger unit or a smaller unit?

2. 9,824 dg ◯ 10 = ______ g

   9,824 dg ◯ 100 = ______ dag

   9,824 dg ◯ 1,000 = ______ hg

Convert.

3. 4,250 cm = ______ m

4. 6,000 mL = ______ L

5. 4 dg = ______ cg

Problem Solving

Practice: Copy and Solve **Compare. Write <, >, or =.**

6. 32 hg ◯ 3.2 kg

7. 6 km ◯ 660 m

8. 525 mL ◯ 525 cL

9. **H.O.T.** **Analyze** How can you compare 4.25 decimeters and 4.25 centimeters without converting?

____

____

Problem Solving Real World

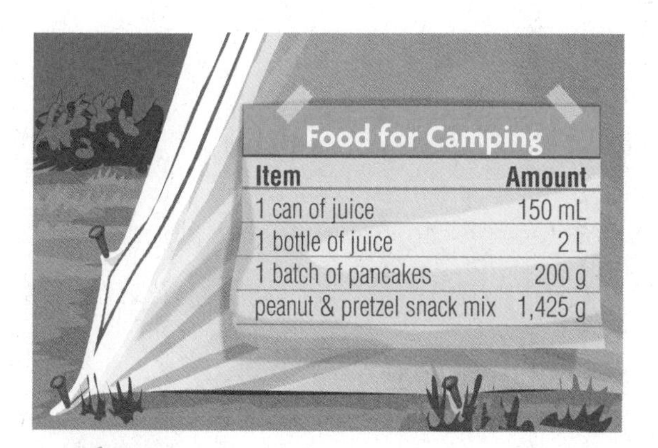

Food for Camping

Item	Amount
1 can of juice	150 mL
1 bottle of juice	2 L
1 batch of pancakes	200 g
peanut & pretzel snack mix	1,425 g

For 10–11, use the table.

10. **Multi-Step** Kelly made one batch of peanut and pretzel snack mix. How many grams does she need to add to the snack mix to make 2 kilograms?

____

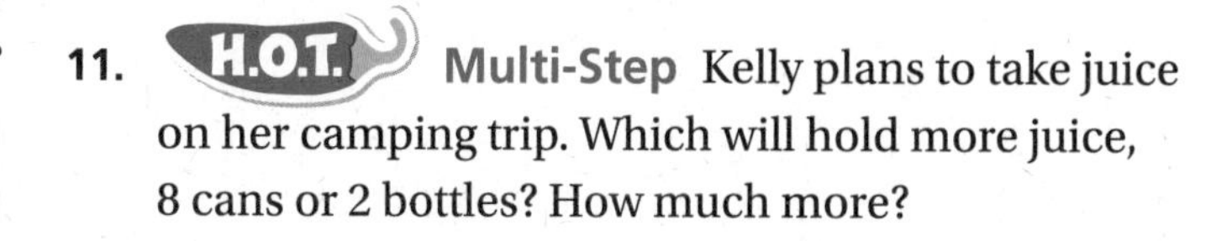

11. **H.O.T.** **Multi-Step** Kelly plans to take juice on her camping trip. Which will hold more juice, 8 cans or 2 bottles? How much more?

____

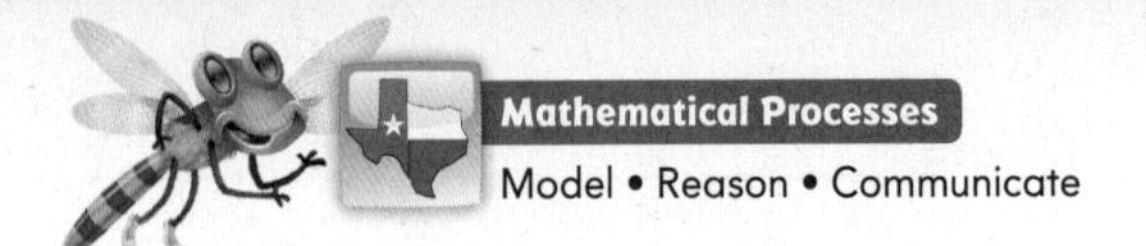

Daily Assessment Task

Fill in the bubble completely to show your answer.

12. **Apply** A snowboard instructor has 4.2 liters of liquid wax for waxing snowboards. If she uses 1 milliliter for each snowboard, how many snowboards can she wax?

Ⓐ 4
Ⓑ 42
Ⓒ 420
Ⓓ 4,200

13. Daija wants to trim 3.5 centimeters from her hair. How should she move the decimal point to convert this number to millimeters?

Ⓐ 1 place to the left
Ⓑ 1 place to the right
Ⓒ 2 places to the left
Ⓓ 2 places to the right

14. **Multi-Step** Vincent mixed 500 grams of raisins, 400 grams of dried cranberries, and 300 grams of almonds to make Trail Mix. How many grams of cashews must he add to make 2 kilograms of Trail Mix?

Ⓐ 140 grams
Ⓑ 200 grams
Ⓒ 800 grams
Ⓓ 1,200 grams

TEXAS Test Prep

15. Monica has 426 millimeters of fabric. How many centimeters of fabric does Monica have?

Ⓐ 4,260 centimeters
Ⓑ 42.6 centimeters
Ⓒ 4.26 centimeters
Ⓓ 0.426 centimeters

Name ______________________

13.6 Metric Measures

Convert.

1. 350 cm = ______ m
2. 4,000 mL = ______ L
3. 62 dg = ______ cg
4. 9 m = ______ mm
5. 150 g = ______ hg
6. 16 L = ______ hL

Compare. Write <, >, or =.

7. 6 km ◯ 54,000 mm
8. 3 kL ◯ 30,000 L
9. 20 g ◯ 0.02 kg
10. 52 L ◯ 5,200 mL
11. 14 m ◯ 140 cm
12. 312 mg ◯ 312 dg

13. Is 25 milligrams lighter or heavier than 25 centigrams? **Explain** how you know.

____

____

Problem Solving Real World

14. Lucy and Donavan measured the length of the school garden. Lucy's measurement is 11.3 meters and Donavan's measurement is 113 centimeters. Could both be correct? **Explain.**

____

____

____

____

15. Shanika makes 2,800 milliliters of chicken soup for a dinner party. She needs 3.5 liters. How many more milliliters does Shanika need to make? How many liters is that?

____

Lesson Check

TEXAS Test Prep

Fill in the bubble completely to show your answer.

16. Jordan has 3.2 liters of paint left after painting the scenery for the school play. How can she convert this number to find how many milliliters of paint she has left?

Ⓐ Multiply by 100.

Ⓑ Multiply by 1,000.

Ⓒ Divide by 100.

Ⓓ Divide by 1,000.

17. Martin needs to ship a box that weighs 12,000 grams. How should he move the decimal point to convert this number to kilograms?

Ⓐ 2 places to the right

Ⓑ 3 places to the right

Ⓒ 2 places to the left

Ⓓ 3 places to the left

18. Akeem has 24 meters of rope. Which of the following lengths is equal to 24 meters?

Ⓐ 0.024 kilometer

Ⓑ 0.24 kilometer

Ⓒ 2.4 kilometers

Ⓓ 240 kilometers

19. A pastry chef bought a 0.26-liter container of vanilla extract for baking. If she uses 1 milliliter of vanilla in each batch of pastries, how many batches can she make?

Ⓐ 2,600

Ⓑ 260

Ⓒ 26

Ⓓ 2.6

20. **Multi-Step** The weight limit for luggage at the airport is 22 kilograms per person. Rico packs two suitcases and finds their weights to be 8,500 grams and 9,200 grams. How many more grams can he pack without going over the weight limit?

Ⓐ 4,300 grams

Ⓑ 5,700 grams

Ⓒ 13,500 grams

Ⓓ 17,700 grams

21. **Multi-Step** The county repairs three sections of a road. The first section is 2.5 kilometers long, the second section is 12 hectometers long, and the third section is 800 meters long. What is the total length of the repaired sections of the road?

Ⓐ 3.5 kilometers

Ⓑ 4.0 kilometers

Ⓒ 4.5 kilometers

Ⓓ 0.5 kilometer

Name ____________________

13.7 PROBLEM SOLVING • Customary and Metric Conversions

TEKS Geometry and Measurement—5.7.A
MATHEMATICAL PROCESSES 5.1.A, 5.1.B

Essential Question How can you use the strategy *make a table* to help you solve problems about customary and metric conversions?

Unlock the Problem Real World

Aaron is making fruit punch for a family reunion. He needs to make 120 cups of punch. If he wants to store the fruit punch in gallon containers, how many gallon containers will Aaron need?

Use the graphic organizer below to help you solve the problem.

Conversion Table

	gal	qt	pt	c
1 gal	1	4	8	16
1 qt	$\frac{1}{4}$	1	2	4
1 pt	$\frac{1}{8}$	$\frac{1}{2}$	1	2
1 c	$\frac{1}{16}$	$\frac{1}{4}$	$\frac{1}{2}$	1

Read

What do I need to find?

I need to find ____________________

____

____

____________________.

What information am I given?

I am given ____________________

____

____________________.

Plan

What is my plan or strategy?

I will make a table to show the relationship between the number of ____________ and the number of ____________.

Solve

There are ______ cups in 1 gallon. So, each cup is ______ of a gallon. Complete the table below.

c	1	2	3	4	120
gal	$\frac{1}{16}$	$\frac{1}{8}$	$\frac{3}{16}$	$\frac{1}{4}$	

Multiply by ______.

So, Aaron needs ______ gallon containers to store the punch.

- Will all of the gallon containers Aaron uses be filled to capacity? **Explain.** ____________________

____

Try Another Problem

Sharon is working on a project for art class. She needs to cut strips of wood that are each 1 decimeter long to complete the project. If Sharon has 7 strips of wood that are each 1 meter long, how many 1-decimeter strips can she cut?

Conversion Table

	m	dm	cm	mm
1 m	1	10	100	1,000
1 dm	$\frac{1}{10}$	1	10	100
1 cm	$\frac{1}{100}$	$\frac{1}{10}$	1	10
1 mm	$\frac{1}{1,000}$	$\frac{1}{100}$	$\frac{1}{10}$	1

Read

What do I need to find?

What information am I given?

Plan

What is my plan or strategy?

Solve

So, Sharon can cut _______ 1-decimeter lengths to complete her project.

- What relationship did the table you made show? ______________________________

____

Math Talk
Mathematical Processes
Explain how you could use another strategy to solve this problem.

Name ______________________________

Share and Show

1. Edgardo has a drink cooler that holds 10 gallons of water. He is filling the cooler with a 1-quart container. How many times will he have to fill the quart container?

First, make a table to show the relationship between gallons and quarts. →

gal	1	2	3	4	10
qt	4				

Then, look for a rule to help you complete your table. → number of gallons × ______ = number of quarts

Finally, use the table to solve the problem. → Edgardo will need to fill the quart container ______ times.

2. **What if** Edgardo only uses 32 quarts of water to fill the cooler. How many gallons of water does he use?

____

3. If Edgardo uses a 1-cup container to fill the cooler, how many times will he fill the 1-cup container?

____

Problem Solving

Write Math ▸ Show Your Work

4. **Multi-Step** Jane is making 13 leather belts. Each belt is 6.4 decimeters long. How many meters of leather does she use?

____

5. **H.O.T.** **Evaluate** Carl is packing sports equipment in a box that can hold 22 kilograms. He packed equipment with a mass of 220 dekagrams and says the box can't hold any more. Is Carl right? **Explain.**

____

____

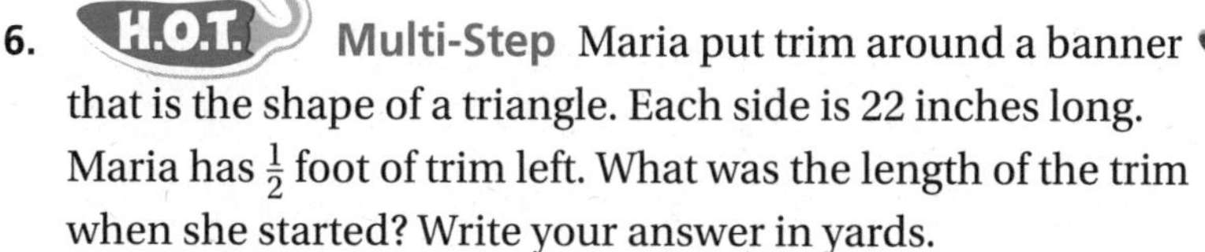

6. **H.O.T.** **Multi-Step** Maria put trim around a banner that is the shape of a triangle. Each side is 22 inches long. Maria has $\frac{1}{2}$ foot of trim left. What was the length of the trim when she started? Write your answer in yards.

____

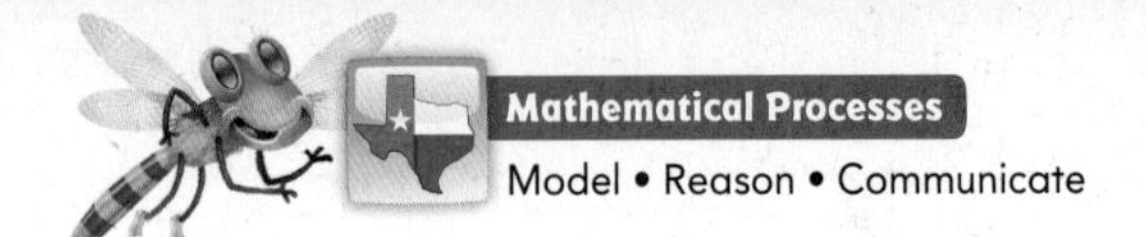

Daily Assessment Task

Fill in the bubble completely to show your answer.

7. **Representations** Three lizards ran across a patch of grass. Larry ran 3.6 meters, Lou ran 2,600 millimeters, and Lola ran 310 centimeters. Which statement correctly compares the distances the lizards ran?

   Ⓐ Larry ran the farthest.

   Ⓑ Lou ran farther than Lola.

   Ⓒ Lola ran farther than Larry.

   Ⓓ Lola ran the shortest distance.

8. Miranda is making lemonade from a powdered mix. She needs to add 3 cups of powdered mix to a large pitcher of water, but she only has a scoop that holds 2 ounces. How many 2-ounce scoops will she use?

   Ⓐ 4 scoops

   Ⓑ 8 scoops

   Ⓒ 10 scoops

   Ⓓ 12 scoops

9. **Multi-Step** Mrs. Gonzalez is adding a border to her bulletin board. She has a strip of green border that is 8 feet long. How many 16-inch pieces can she cut from the strip?

   Ⓐ 4 pieces

   Ⓑ 6 pieces

   Ⓒ 8 pieces

   Ⓓ 12 pieces

TEXAS Test Prep

10. Tony needs 16-inch-long pieces of gold chain to make each of 3 necklaces. He has a piece of chain that is 4 feet 6 inches long. How much chain will he have left after making the necklaces?

    Ⓐ 6 inches

    Ⓑ 12 inches

    Ⓒ 18 inches

    Ⓓ 24 inches

Name ____________________

13.7 Customary and Metric Conversions

1. Jeremy walks through a maze. He begins by walking 25 feet, turning right, and walking 6 yards. Then he walks 32 more feet. He has 13 more yards to walk to complete the maze. What is the length of the maze? Write your answer in yards.

____

2. Randy uses a pedometer to keep track of the distances he walks each day. He discovers that the trip to his mailbox and back is 300 meters. How many kilometers does Randy walk to his mailbox and back if he collects his mail 6 days a week for 4 weeks?

____

3. Team members are participating in a scavenger hunt. They meet at the starting point and ride their bikes 2 kilometers. They find the first clue that says the second clue is 10 hectometers away. When they reach the second clue, they are told to go back 300 dekameters. Will the team members reach the point where they started after they follow the instructions for the second clue? **Explain.**

____

____

____

Problem Solving Real World

4. Mrs. Arnold is serving hamburgers to her family of 6 tonight for dinner. She uses $\frac{1}{2}$ pound of ground meat for each hamburger patty. She buys a package of meat that weighs 50 ounces. Will Mrs. Arnold have enough meat? **Explain.**

____

____

Lesson Check

TEXAS Test Prep

Fill in the bubble completely to show your answer.

5. The lengths of three snakes exhibited in the zoo's reptile house are labeled. The king snake is 65 inches. The eastern diamondback rattlesnake is 2 yards. The ridge-nosed rattlesnake is 4 feet. Which statement correctly compares the lengths of the snakes?

Ⓐ The king snake is the longest snake.

Ⓑ The ridge-nosed rattlesnake is longer than the eastern diamondback rattlesnake.

Ⓒ The eastern diamondback rattlesnake is the longest snake.

Ⓓ The eastern diamondback rattlesnake is shorter than the king snake.

6. Mr. Martinez has 2.5 kilograms of colored sand for his art students to use on their sand art project. He packages the sand into individual bags with 125 grams in each bag. How many bags of sand can Mr. Martinez make?

Ⓐ 2.5

Ⓑ 16

Ⓒ 20

Ⓓ 200

7. A baker needs 6 quarts of milk for a cupcake frosting recipe. He only has an 8-ounce measuring cup to measure the milk into the bowl. How many cups of milk will he use?

Ⓐ 16 cups

Ⓑ 24 cups

Ⓒ 20 cups

Ⓓ 32 cups

8. When Rosa makes lemonade, she uses 500 milliliters of lemon juice for every liter of water. If she made 12 liters of lemonade, how much lemon juice did she use?

Ⓐ 4,000 milliliters

Ⓑ 6,000 milliliters

Ⓒ 8,000 milliliters

Ⓓ 2,000 milliliters

9. **Multi-Step** A Komodo dragon is 3 meters long. A dwarf gecko is 15 millimeters long. How many dwarf geckos lined up end-to-end would match the length of the Komodo dragon?

Ⓐ 200

Ⓑ 100

Ⓒ 150

Ⓓ 300

10. **Multi-Step** Campers use a roll of string that is 250 yards long to make kites. Each kite will have 50 feet of kite line. How many kite lines can they cut from the roll of string?

Ⓐ 5

Ⓑ 50

Ⓒ 150

Ⓓ 15

Name ____

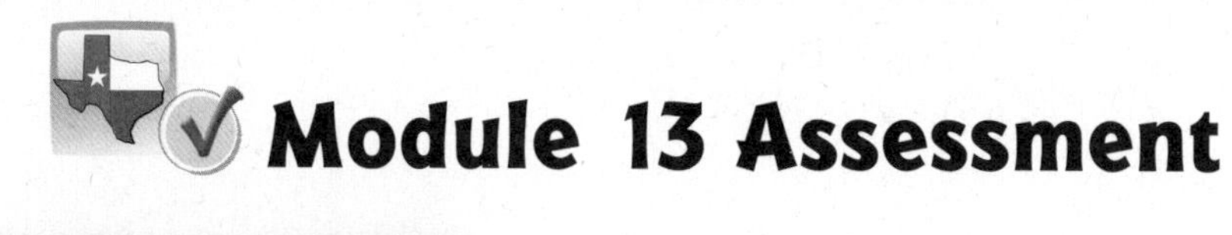

Module 13 Assessment

Concepts and Skills

Convert. TEKS 5.7.A

1. 5 mi = __________ yd
2. 48 qt = __________ gal
3. 9 T = __________ lb
4. 5 kg = __________ g
5. 12 ft = ______ yd
6. 8,000 mm = __________ m

Compare. Write <, >, or =. TEKS 5.7.A

7. 96 fl oz ◯ 13 c
8. 4 L ◯ 4,000 mL
9. 8 yd ◯ 288 in.

Solve. TEKS 5.7.A

10. A large freight elevator can carry a maximum of 9,800 pounds. Movers loaded equipment on the elevator that weighs 4 tons. How many more pounds of equipment can the elevator carry?

____

11. A standard coffee mug has a capacity of 16 fluid ounces. If Annie needs to fill 26 mugs with coffee, how many total quarts of coffee does she need?

____

Fill in the bubble completely to show your answer.

12. Howard cuts 80 centimeters off a 1.5-meter board. How much of the board does Howard have left? TEKS 5.7.A

Ⓐ 230 centimeters

Ⓑ 70 centimeters

Ⓒ 20 centimeters

Ⓓ 1,420 centimeters

13. Mr. Carter fills a tub with water so he can give his dog a bath. Which is the most appropriate unit for measuring the capacity of a tub? TEKS 5.7

Ⓐ fluid ounce

Ⓑ pound

Ⓒ pint

Ⓓ gallon

14. Milton purchases a 5-gallon aquarium for his bedroom. To fill the aquarium with water, he uses a container with a capacity of 1 quart. How many times will Milton fill and empty the container before the aquarium is full? TEKS 5.7.A

Ⓐ 10 Ⓑ 15 Ⓒ 20 Ⓓ 25

15. Alfred uses the same tool to measure the distance across a sidewalk and the distance across town. Which tool does he use? TEKS 5.7

Ⓐ odometer

Ⓑ metric ruler

Ⓒ medical scale

Ⓓ trundle wheel

16. A girl walks 5,000 meters in one hour. If the girl walks at the same speed for 4 hours, how many kilometers will she walk? TEKS 5.7.A

Record your answer and fill in the bubbles on the grid. Be sure to use the correct place value.

			.		
⓪	⓪	⓪		⓪	⓪
①	①	①		①	①
②	②	②		②	②
③	③	③		③	③
④	④	④		④	④
⑤	⑤	⑤		⑤	⑤
⑥	⑥	⑥		⑥	⑥
⑦	⑦	⑦		⑦	⑦
⑧	⑧	⑧		⑧	⑧
⑨	⑨	⑨		⑨	⑨

Name ________________________________

14.1 Ordered Pairs

Essential Question

How can you identify and plot points in a coordinate grid?

Connect Locating a point on a coordinate grid is similar to describing directions using North-South and West-East. The horizontal number line on the grid is the ***x*-axis**. The vertical number line on the grid is the ***y*-axis**.

Each point on the coordinate grid can be described by an **ordered pair** of numbers. The ***x*-coordinate**, the first number in the ordered pair, is the horizontal location, or the distance the point is from 0 in the direction of the *x*-axis. The ***y*-coordinate**, the second number in the ordered pair, is the vertical location, or the distance the point is from 0 in the direction of the *y*-axis.

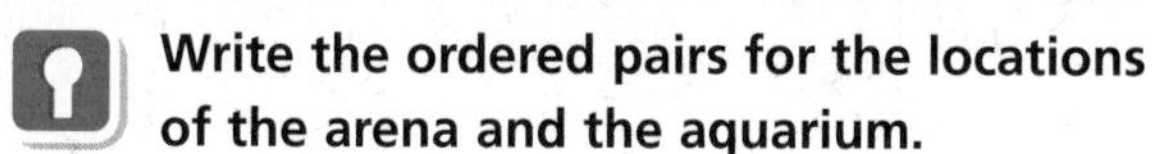

The *x*-axis and the *y*-axis intersect at the point (0, 0), called the **origin**.

Unlock the Problem

Real World

Write the ordered pairs for the locations of the arena and the aquarium.

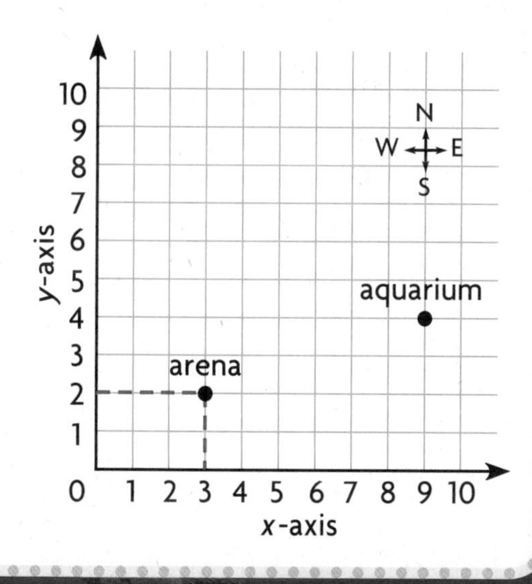

Locate the point for which you want to write an ordered pair.

Look below at the *x*-axis to identify the point's horizontal distance from 0, which is its *x*-coordinate.

Look to the left at the *y*-axis to identify the point's vertical distance from 0, which is its *y*-coordinate.

So, the ordered pair for the arena is (3, 2) and the ordered pair for the aquarium

is (_______, _______).

- Describe the path you would take to get from the origin to the aquarium, using horizontal, then vertical movements.

____

____

Example Use the graph.

A point in a coordinate grid can be labeled with an ordered pair, a letter, or both.

A **Plot the point (5, 7) and label it *J*.**

From the origin, move right 5 units and then up 7 units.

Plot and label the point.

B **Plot the point (8, 0) and label it *S*.**

From the origin, move right ________ units and

then up ________ units.

Plot and label the point.

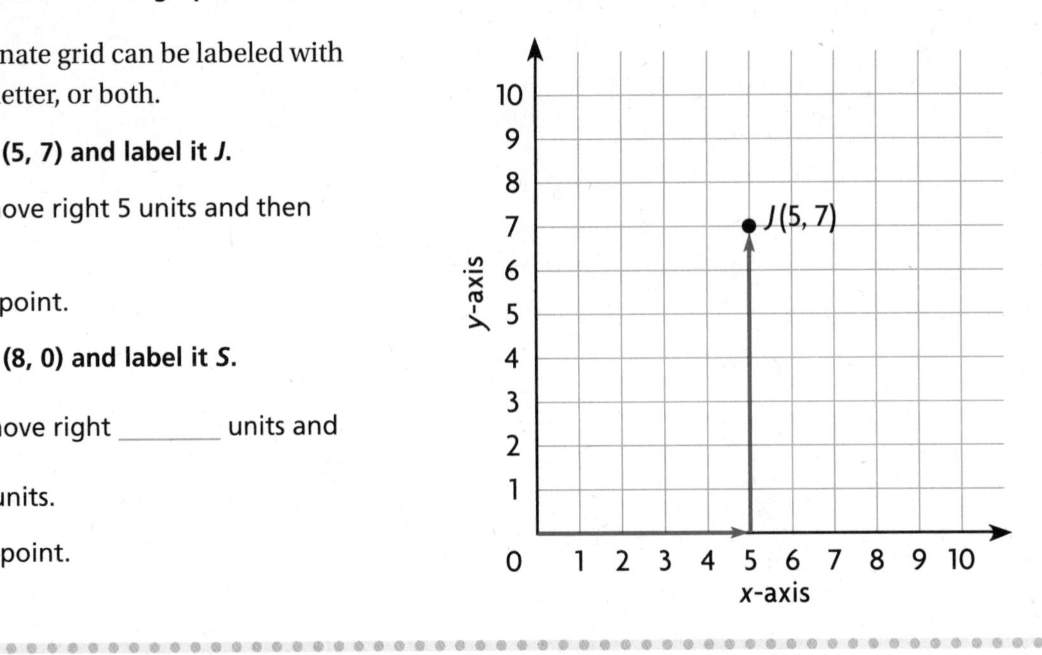

Share and Show

Use Coordinate Grid A to write an ordered pair for the given point.

1. C ____________

2. D ____________

3. E ____________

4. F ____________

Plot and label the points in Coordinate Grid A.

5. $M(0, 9)$

6. $H(8, 6)$

7. $K(10, 4)$

8. $T(4, 5)$

9. $W(5, 10)$

10. $R(1, 3)$

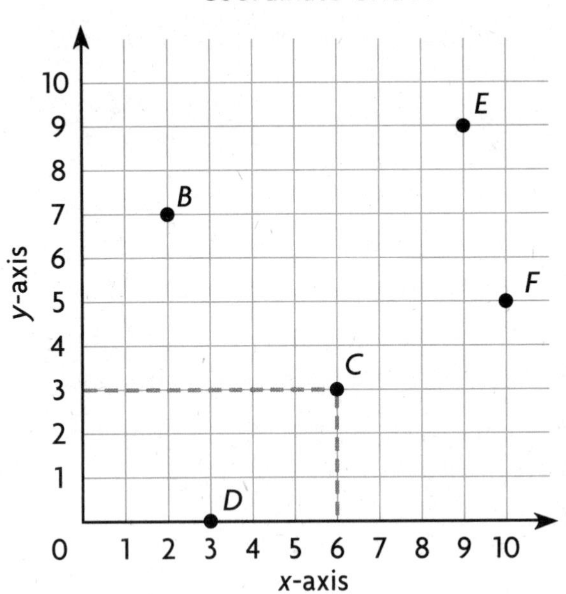

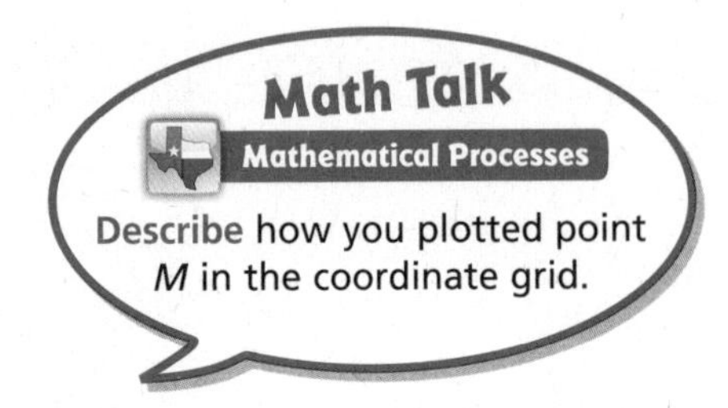

Name ________________________________

Problem Solving

11. Write Math ▶ Write directions for plotting a point to represent the ordered pair (4, 6).

____

12. H.O.T. If the *y*-coordinate for a point is zero, on which axis will the point lie? **Explain.**

____

____

Problem Solving Real World

Nathan and his friends are planning a trip to New York City. Use the map for 13–15. Each unit represents 1 city block.

13. H.O.T. **What's the Error?** Nathan says that Madison Square Garden is located at (0, 3) on the map. Is his ordered pair correct? **Explain.**

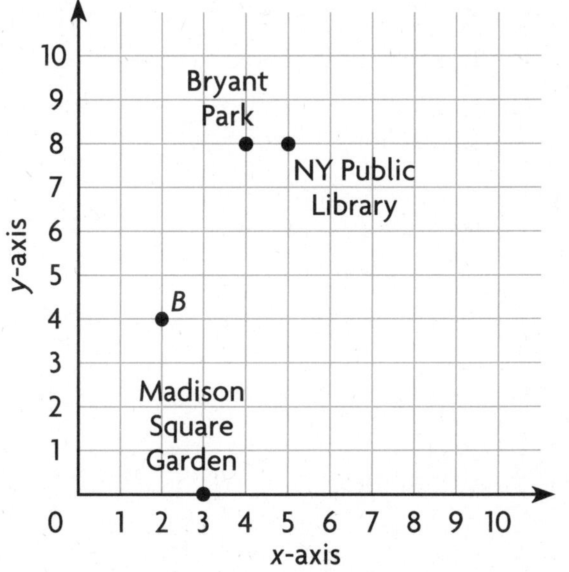

____

____

____

14. **Use Graphs** The Empire State Building is located 5 blocks right and 1 block up from (0, 0). Write the ordered pair for this location. Plot and label a point for the Empire State Building.

____

15. H.O.T. **Multi-Step** Paulo walks from point *B* to Bryant Park. Raul walks from point *B* to Madison Square Garden. If they only walk along the grid lines, who walks farther? **Explain.**

____

____

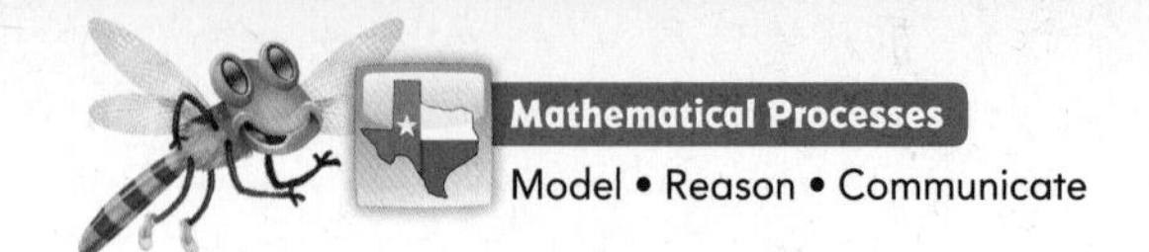

Daily Assessment Task

Fill in the bubble completely to show your answer.
Use the map for 16–17.

State Capitol
Governor's Mansion
Austin History Center
O.Henry Museum
Austin Children's Museum
Congress Avenue Bridge
y-axis
x-axis
0 1 2 3 4 5 6 7 8 9 10

16. Austin has the largest bat colony of any North American city. In the evening, the bats fly out from under the Congress Avenue Bridge. Which ordered pair shows the Congress Avenue Bridge?

Ⓐ (6, 6)

Ⓑ (6, 0)

Ⓒ (0, 6)

Ⓓ (0, 0)

17. You are standing very close to the O. Henry Museum. Where might you be standing?

Ⓐ (3, 9) Ⓒ (9, 2)

Ⓑ (2, 9) Ⓓ (0, 10)

18. Multi-Step Look at the map. Today you went shopping at (0, 4) and had lunch at (8, 2). Which locations did you visit?

Ⓐ J and K

Ⓑ J and M

Ⓒ K and L

Ⓓ K and M

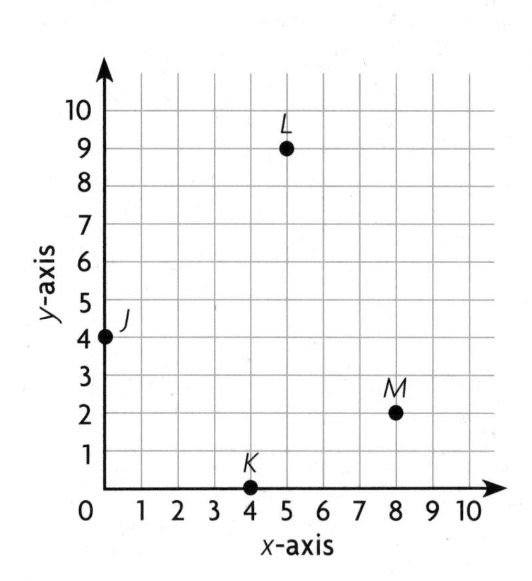

TEXAS Test Prep

19. Point R is 6 units to the right and 1 unit up from the origin. What ordered pair describes point R?

Ⓐ (1, 6) Ⓒ (6, 1)

Ⓑ (6, 0) Ⓓ (1, 1)

Homework and Practice

TEKS Geometry and Measurement—5.8.A, 5.8.B Also 5.8.C
MATHEMATICAL PROCESSES 5.1.D, 5.1.E

Name ______________________

14.1 Ordered Pairs

Use Coordinate Grid M to write an ordered pair for the given point.

1. N __________
2. O __________
3. P __________
4. Q __________

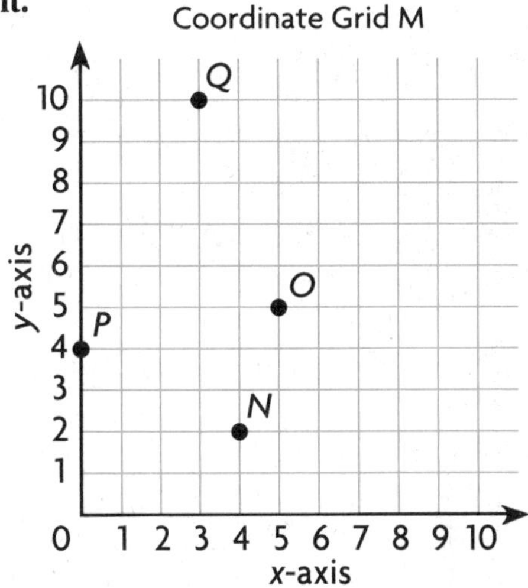

Plot and label the points in Coordinate Grid M.

5. $R(2, 8)$
6. $S(6, 0)$
7. $T(8, 7)$
8. $U(10, 8)$

9. Is the ordered pair (4, 5) the same as the ordered pair (5, 4)? **Explain.**

____

____

Problem Solving Real World

The Alvarez family is spending the afternoon at the outdoor shopping center. Use the map for 10–11. Each unit represents 1 block.

10. The toy store is located 1 block right and 8 blocks up from (0, 0). Write the ordered pair for this location. Plot and label a point for the toy store.

____

11. As Alma leaves the shoe store, it begins to rain. She runs to the closest store. How many blocks is it to the closest store? **Explain.**

____

____

____

Lesson Check

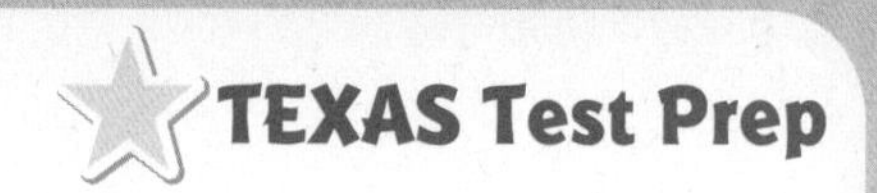

Fill in the bubble completely to show your answer.

12. The instructions for plotting a point in the coordinate grid read, "Start at the origin. Move right 6 units and then up 3 units." What is the ordered pair for the point?

Ⓐ (6, 9)

Ⓑ (6, 3)

Ⓒ (3, 6)

Ⓓ (5, 2)

13. If you start at the origin, which of the following shows how to plot the point (2,5) in the coordinate grid?

Ⓐ Move up 5 units and then up 2 units.

Ⓑ Move right 2 units and then right 5 units.

Ⓒ Move right 2 units and then up 5 units.

Ⓓ Move right 5 units and then up 2 units.

Use the map of the garden center for 14–15.

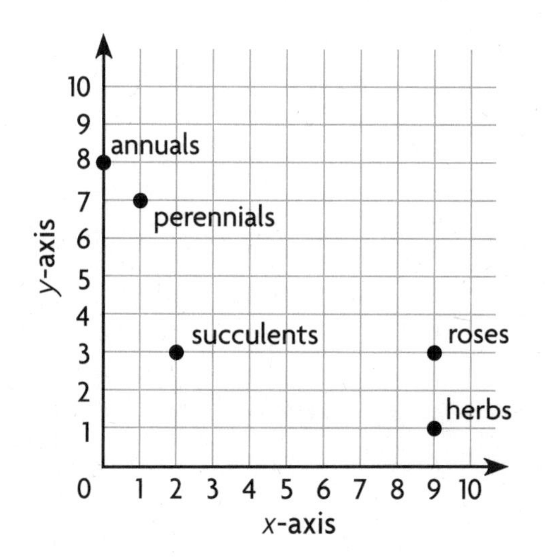

14. Which ordered pair shows the location of the annuals?

Ⓐ (0, 8)

Ⓑ (8, 0)

Ⓒ (8, 8)

Ⓓ (0, 0)

15. Which type of plants would you find at (9, 1)?

Ⓐ perennials

Ⓑ succulents

Ⓒ roses

Ⓓ herbs

16. Multi-Step Look at the map. Which are the correct ordered pairs for points *A* and *B*?

Ⓐ (1, 6) and (0, 7)

Ⓑ (0, 7) and (6, 1)

Ⓒ (7, 0) and (1, 6)

Ⓓ (6, 1) and (7, 0)

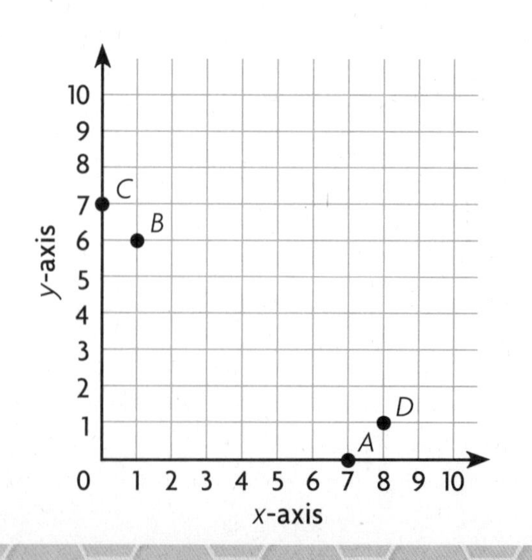

Name ______________________

MATHEMATICAL PROCESSES
5.1.F, 5.1.G

14.2 Graph Data

Essential Question How can you use a coordinate grid to display data collected in an experiment?

Investigate

Hands On

Materials ■ paper cup ■ water ■ Fahrenheit thermometer ■ ice cubes ■ stopwatch

When data is collected, it can be organized in a table.

A. Fill the paper cup more than halfway with room-temperature water.

B. Place the Fahrenheit thermometer in the water and find its beginning temperature before adding any ice. Record this temperature in the table at 0 seconds.

C. Place three cubes of ice in the water and start the stopwatch. Find the temperature every 10 seconds for 60 seconds. Record the temperatures in the table.

Water Temperature

Time (in seconds)	Temperature (in °F)
0	
10	
20	
30	
40	
50	
60	

Make Connections

You can use a coordinate grid to graph and analyze the data you collected in the experiment.

STEP 1 Write the related pairs of data as ordered pairs.

(0, ______) (30, ______) (50, ______)
(10, ______) (40, ______) (60, ______)
(20, ______)

STEP 2 Construct a coordinate grid and write a title for it. Label each axis.

STEP 3 Plot a point for each ordered pair.

Water Temperature

y-axis: Temperature (in °F): 5, 10, 15, 20, 25, 30, 35, 40, 45, 50, 55, 60, 65, 70, 75

x-axis: Time (in seconds): 0, 10, 20, 30, 40, 50, 60

Math Talk

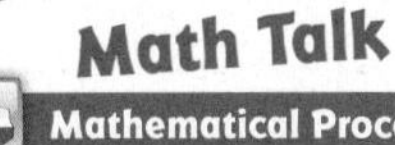

Analyze your observations about the temperature of the water during the 60 seconds.

Share and Show

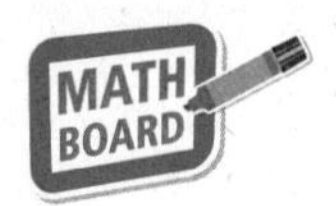

Graph the data in the coordinate grid.

1.

Ryan's Height					
Age (in years)	1	2	3	4	5
Height (in inches)	30	35	38	41	44

Ordered pairs: ______________________

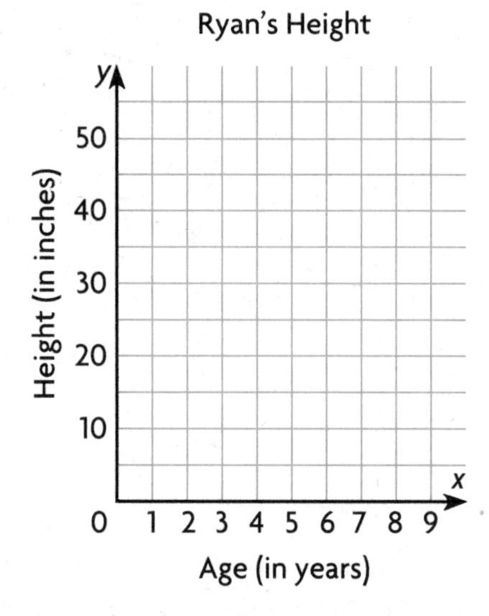

2.

Plant Height					
Day	5	10	15	20	25
Height (in cm)	1	3	8	12	16

Ordered pairs: ______________________

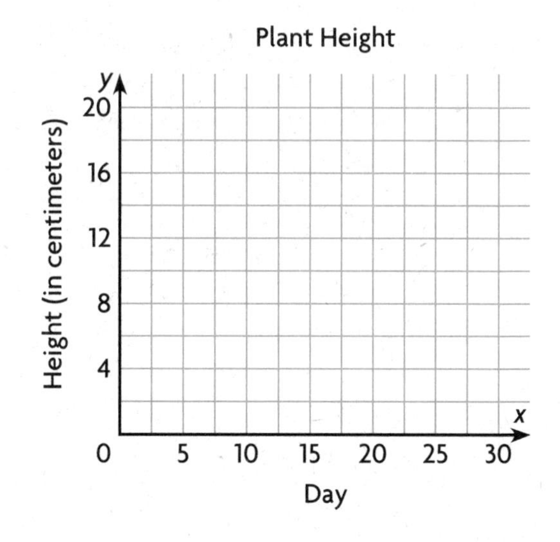

Problem Solving Real World

Use the table at the right for 3–4.

Weight of a Bird				
Month	1	2	3	4
Weight (in grams)	4	7	9	10

3. **Multi-Step** Write ordered pairs to show the relationship between the month and the weight of a bird. Plot each point in the coordinate grid.

____

4. **H.O.T. Analyze** What do you think would happen to the bird's weight over the next four months?

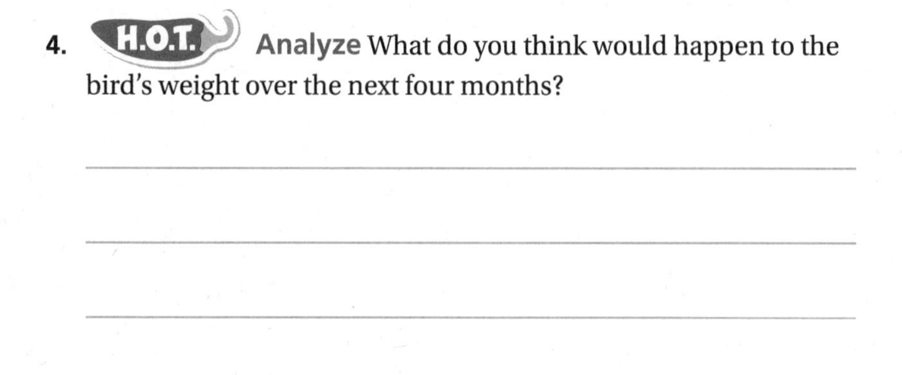

____

____

____

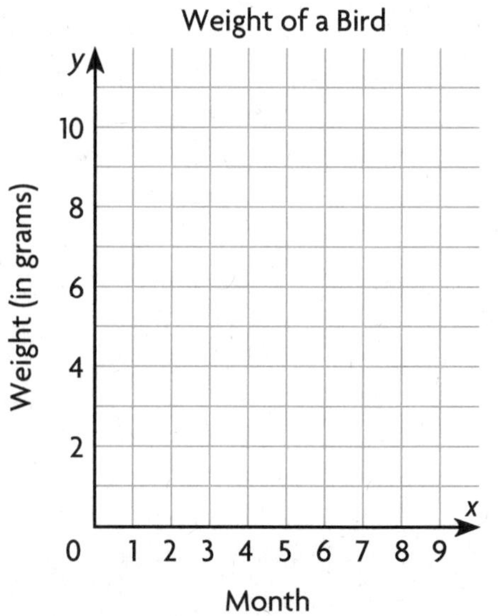

Name ______________________________

What's the Error?

5. Mary places a miniature car onto a track with launchers. The speed of the car is recorded every foot. Some of the data is shown in the table. Mary graphs the data in the coordinate grid below.

Miniature Car's Speed	
Distance (in feet)	Speed (in miles per hour)
0	0
1	4
2	8
3	6
4	3

Look at Mary's graphed data. Find her error.

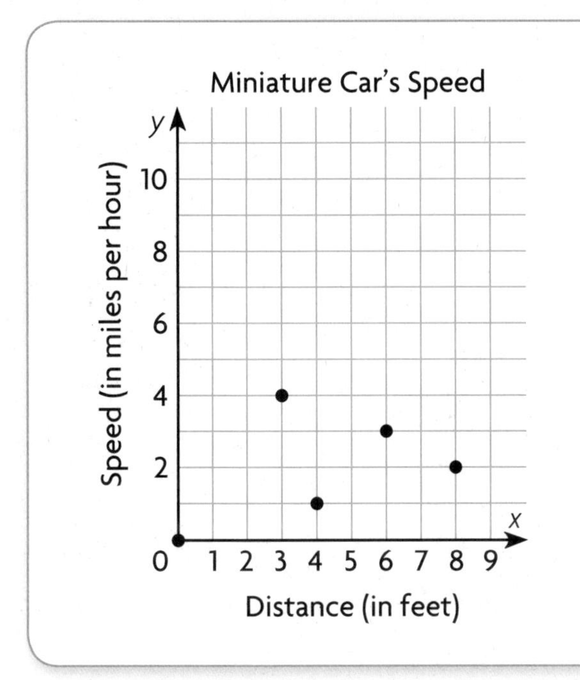

Graph the data and correct the error.

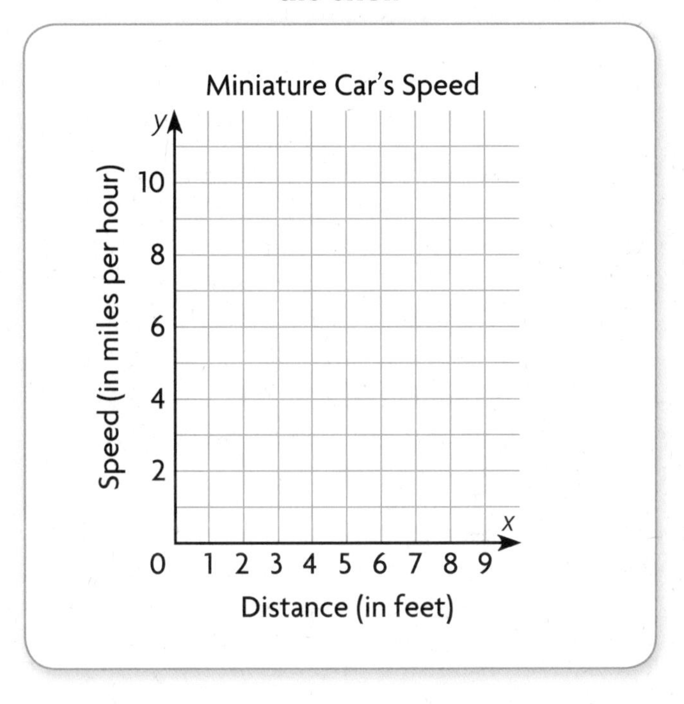

6. **Communicate** Describe the error Mary made.

____

____

7. **Reasoning** Where do you think the miniature car will stop? Write the ordered pair. **Explain.**

____

____

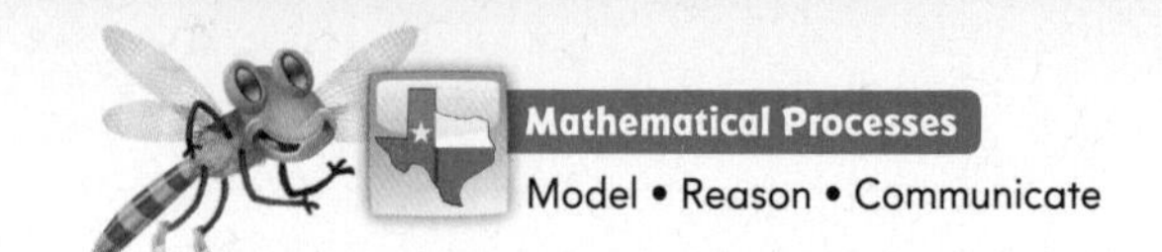

Daily Assessment Task

Fill in the bubble completely to show your answer.

8. The graph shows the relationship between the length of an eruption of Old Faithful, *x*, and the length of time until the next eruption, *y*. Which of these ordered pairs is on the graph?

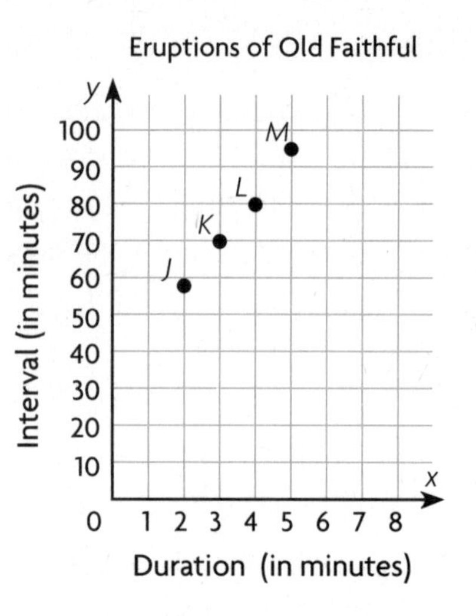

Ⓐ (95, 5) Ⓒ (70, 3)

Ⓑ (2, 50) Ⓓ (4, 80)

9. Which set of ordered pairs shows the data in the table?

Ⓐ (1, 2), (3, 4), (5, 3), (9, 13), (17, 20)

Ⓑ (1, 3), (2, 9), (3, 13), (4, 17), (5, 20)

Ⓒ (20, 5), (17, 4), (13, 3), (9, 2), (3, 3)

Ⓓ (1, 3), (9, 2), (13, 3), (4, 17), (20, 5)

Weight of Alisha's Puppy

Age (months)	1	2	3	4	5
Weight (pounds)	3	9	13	17	20

10. **Multi-Step** Sean is growing a plant in a jar. He makes a graph to show the days since he put the seed in the jar, and the length of the longest root (in centimeters). He first sees the root in 4 days, and he writes the ordered pair (4, 2). Three days later, the root measures 18 cm. Five days later, it has grown another 25 cm. What ordered pairs does Sean add to his graph?

Ⓐ (7, 18), (12, 43) Ⓒ (3, 18), (5, 25)

Ⓑ (18, 3), (25, 5) Ⓓ (18, 7), (43, 12)

TEXAS Test Prep

11. Marie was in fifth grade when she began to record her baby sister's height and her own height in inches every six months for 3 years. She plots the data on a graph where the *x*-coordinate represents her sister's height and the *y*-coordinate represents Marie's height. Which ordered pair could NOT be on the graph?

Ⓐ (24, 51) Ⓒ (55, 30)

Ⓑ (33, 60) Ⓓ (28, 52)

Name ________________

14.2 Graph Data

Graph the data in the coordinate grid.

1.

Outside Temperature					
Hour	1	2	3	4	5
Temperature (in °C)	8	10	11	12	16

Ordered pairs: ________________

____

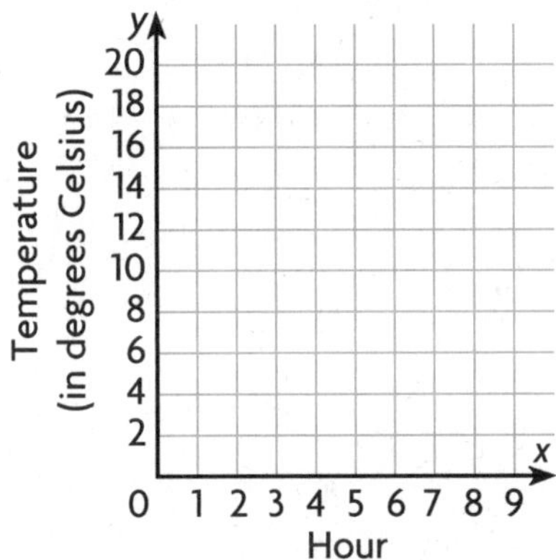

2.

Henry's Video Game Score					
Time (in seconds)	10	20	30	40	50
Points Scored	15	25	35	40	45

Ordered pairs: ________________

____

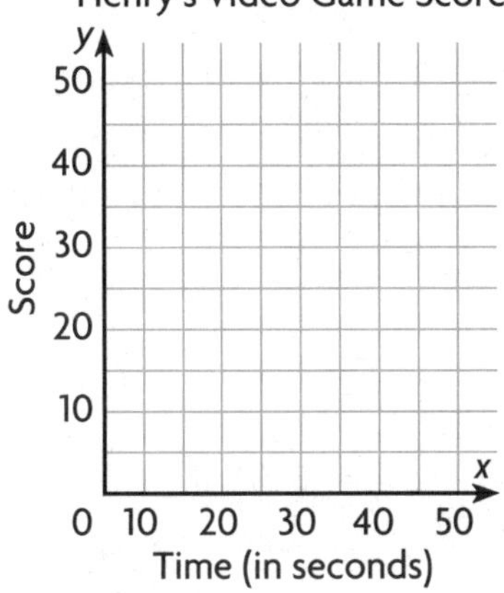

Problem Solving

Use the table at the right for 3–4.

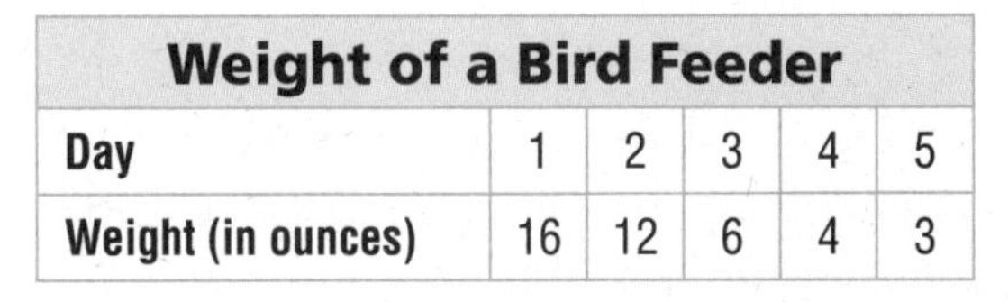

Weight of a Bird Feeder					
Day	1	2	3	4	5
Weight (in ounces)	16	12	6	4	3

3. Write ordered pairs to show the relationship between the day and the weight of the bird feeder. Plot each point in the coordinate grid.

____

4. Do you think the weight of the bird feeder will be 10 ounces on day 6? **Explain.**

____

____

____

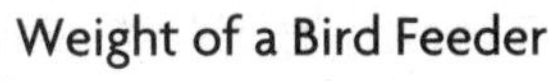

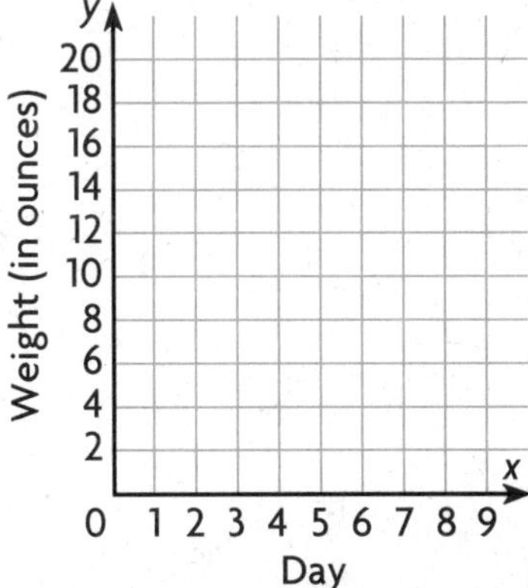

Lesson Check

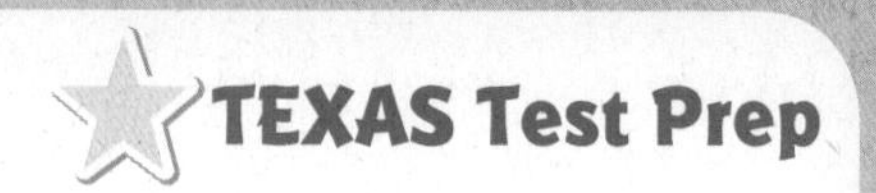

Fill in the bubble completely to show your answer.
Use the graph for 5–6.

5. The graph shows the relationship between the length of time and the number of kernels popped. Which of these ordered pairs is on the graph?

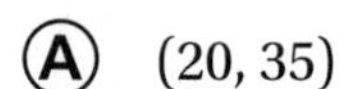
Ⓐ (20, 35)

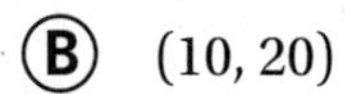
Ⓑ (10, 20)

Ⓒ (85, 40)

Ⓓ (90, 50)

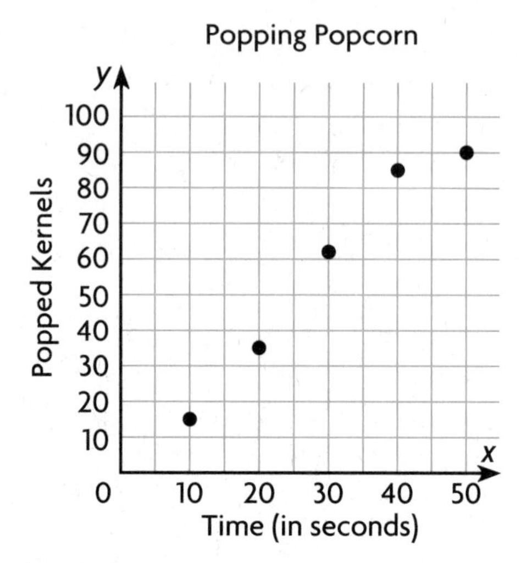

6. The number of popped kernels stays the same after 50 seconds. Which ordered pair can you plot to show the number of popped kernels after 60 seconds?

Ⓐ (50, 90)

Ⓑ (90, 50)

Ⓒ (60, 90)

Ⓓ (90, 60)

7. Marc plots the point (1, 20) in a coordinate grid to show the number of minutes it takes him to walk 1 mile. Which ordered pair might Marc use to show how many minutes it takes him to walk 3 miles?

Ⓐ (3, 3)

Ⓑ (60, 3)

Ⓒ (30, 3)

Ⓓ (3, 60)

8. **Multi-Step** Which set of ordered pairs shows the data in the table?

Weight of Monroe's Kitten					
Age (months)	1	2	3	4	5
Weight (pounds)	2	3	5	7	8

Ⓐ (1, 2), (3, 4), (5, 2), (3, 5), (7, 8)

Ⓑ (8, 5), (7, 4), (5, 3), (3, 2), (1, 1)

Ⓒ (1, 2), (3, 2), (5, 3), (7, 4), (8, 5)

Ⓓ (1, 2), (2, 3), (3, 5), (4, 7), (5, 8)

9. **Multi-Step** Jo measures a puddle as it evaporates. After the first hour, the puddle is 10 cm long. She plots the point (1, 10) in a coordinate grid. After 2 hours, the puddle is 5 cm long. After 3 hours, the puddle is 2 cm long. Which ordered pairs should Jo plot to show the data?

Ⓐ (2, 5), (3, 2)

Ⓑ (5, 2), (2, 3)

Ⓒ (1, 5), (2, 2)

Ⓓ (2, 15), (3, 7)

Name ________________

14.3 Graph Number Patterns

ALGEBRA

TEKS Geometry and Measurement—5.8.C
Also 5.4.C
MATHEMATICAL PROCESSES
5.1.A, 5.1.C, 5.1.D

Essential Question

How can you display number patterns in the coordinate grid?

Unlock the Problem

When Alice completes each level in her favorite video game, she wins 2 extra lives. Use a graph. How many extra lives will Alice have after 4 levels?

STEP 1 Make an input/output table.

Input	Completed Level	1	2	3	4
Output	Extra Lives	2			

STEP 2 Write the related pairs of data as ordered pairs.
The input is the *x*-coordinate and the output is the *y*-coordinate.

Level 1: (1, 2)   Level 3: ________

Level 2: ________   Level 4: ________

STEP 3 Plot the ordered pairs in the coordinate grid.

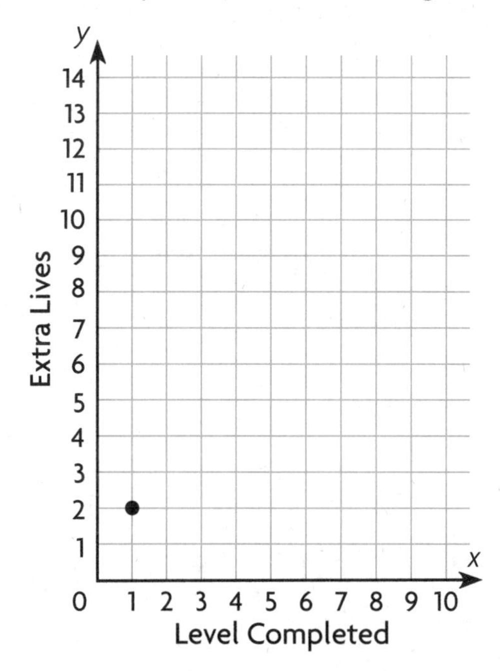

Math Talk Mathematical Processes

Describe the number pattern for extra lives.

So, Alice will have ______ extra lives after completing 4 levels.

Example

The pattern below follows the rule $y = x + 3$, where y is the number of squares and x is the figure number. Use the pattern to find how many squares will be in Figure 5. Display the pattern in the coordinate grid.

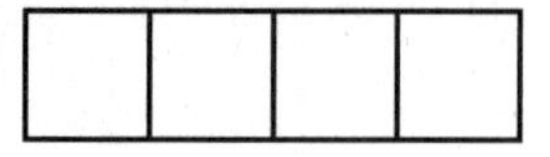
Figure 1

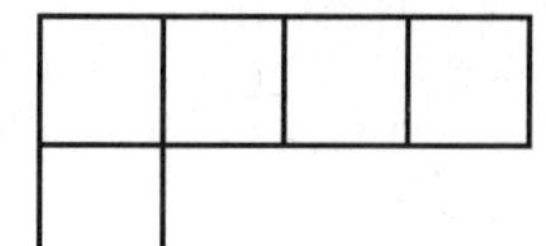
Figure 2

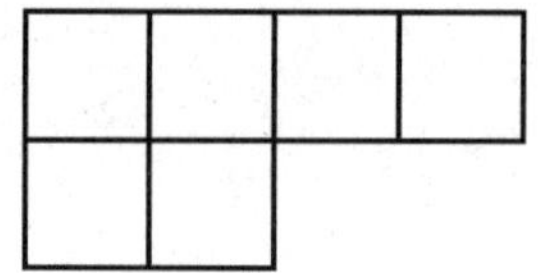
Figure 3

STEP 1 The pattern in the number of squares is 4, 5, 6, ______, ______.

STEP 2 Write ordered pairs using the figure number and the number of squares.

(1, 4) (2, 5) (______, ______) (______, ______) (______, ______)

STEP 3 Plot the ordered pairs in the graph.

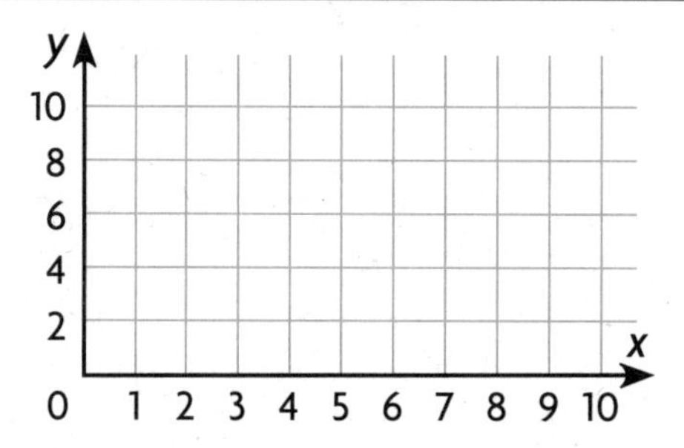

Share and Show

Use the given rules to complete the pattern. Display the pattern in the coordinate grid.

1. Multiply the number of nickels by 5 to find the number of pennies that equal the value.

Input	Nickels	1	2	3	4
Output	Pennies	5	10		

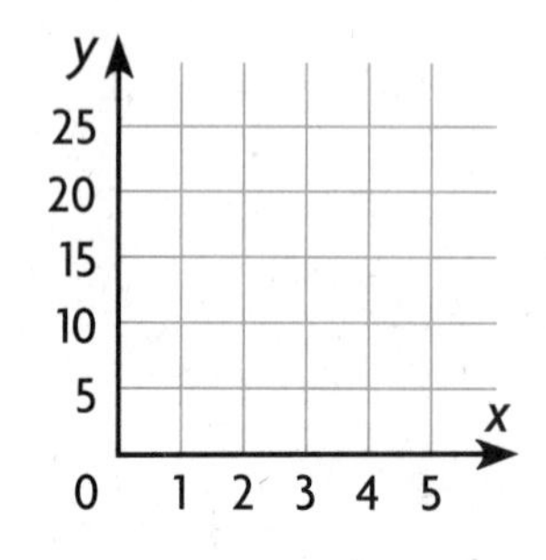

2. Add 5 to the input.

Input	Output
1	
2	
3	
4	

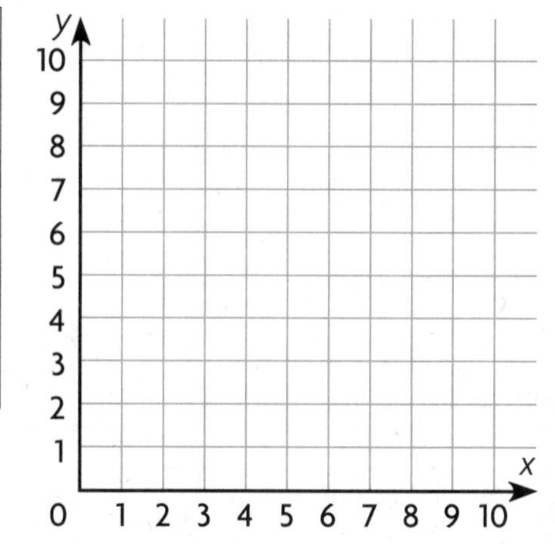

Name ___________________________

Problem Solving

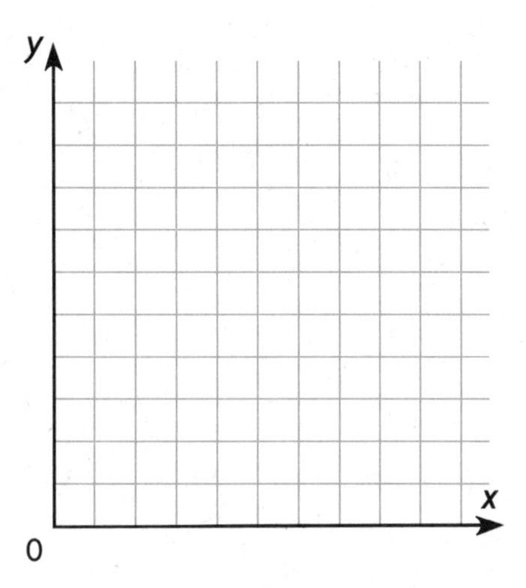

3. **H.O.T.** **Write Math** ▶ The rule for a pattern is *add 4 to the input.* **Explain** how you can use the rule to write ordered pairs that represent the pattern.

____

____

____

4. Write five ordered pairs that represent the pattern rule *multiply input by 3.* **Display** the pattern in the coordinate grid to the right.

____

Problem Solving Real World

Use the coordinate plane for 5–7.

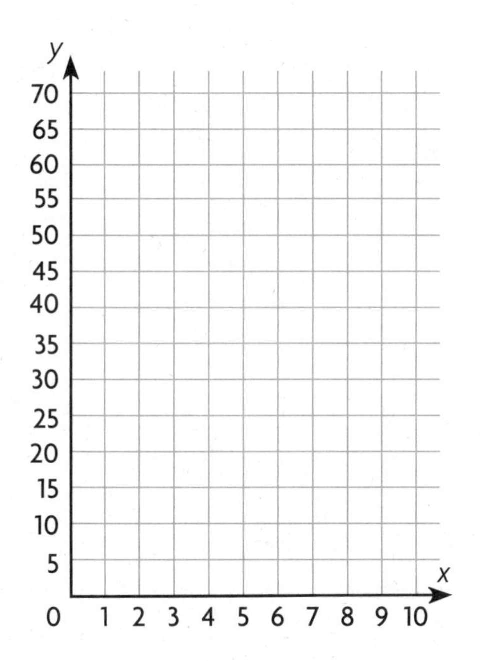

5. **Multi-Step** Emily has a road map with a key that shows an inch on the map equals 5 miles of actual distance. Use the table and the coordinate grid to show the pattern.

Input	Distance on the Map (in.)	1	2	3	4	5
Output	Actual Distance (mi)					

6. **Use Graphs** What is the actual distance if the distance on the map is 6 inches? Write the ordered pair. Plot a point in the coordinate grid to show the appropriate ordered pair.

____

7. **H.O.T.** What is the distance on the map if the actual distance is 45 miles? Plot a point in the coordinate grid to show the appropriate ordered pair.

____

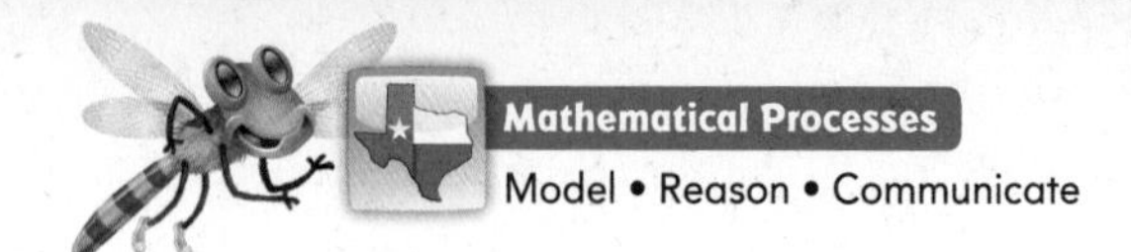

Daily Assessment Task

Fill in the bubble completely to show your answer.

8. Ted gets a $10 allowance every week and saves $6 of it. He makes a graph to show his savings, where the *x*-coordinate represents the number of weeks and the *y*-coordinate represents the number of dollars saved. Which of the following ordered pairs could be on the graph?

   Ⓐ (6, 60) Ⓒ (1, 60)

   Ⓑ (36, 6) Ⓓ (6, 36)

9. Tina owns a flower shop. The table shows the prices for different numbers of flowers. She makes a graph that compares number of flowers to total price. Which ordered pair should NOT be on the graph?

Input	Number of Flowers	2	4	6	8	10
Output	Price (in dollars)	3	6	9		

   Ⓐ (8, 12) Ⓒ (6, 9)

   Ⓑ (6, 4) Ⓓ (10, 15)

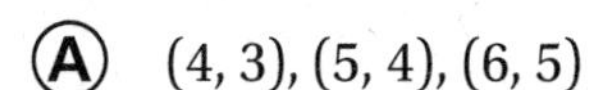

10. **Multi-Step** Steve mixes 4 cups grape juice with 3 cups ginger ale to make a punch. Steve makes a graph to compare the amounts of juice needed for several batches. Which ordered pairs could be on the graph?

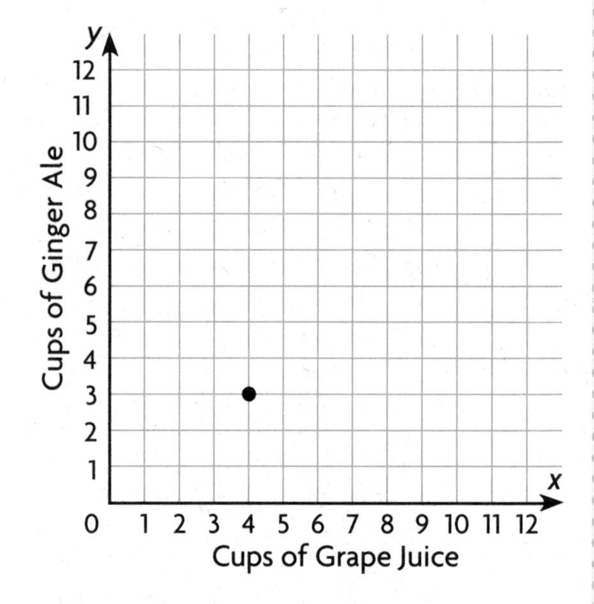

   Ⓐ (4, 3), (5, 4), (6, 5)

   Ⓑ (3, 4), (5, 6), (6, 7)

   Ⓒ (4, 3), (8, 6), (12, 9)

   Ⓓ (3, 4), (8, 6), (12, 9)

TEXAS Test Prep

11. Rob is making a fruit punch for a party. He adds 4 cups of pineapple juice for every cup of orange juice. Which ordered pair shows how many cups of pineapple juice he needs for 3 cups of orange juice?

Orange Juice (c)	*x*	1	2	3
Pineapple Juice (c)	*y*	4	8	

   Ⓐ (4, 8) Ⓒ (3, 12)

   Ⓑ (1, 2) Ⓓ (3, 4)

Name ____________________

14.3 Graph Number Patterns

ALGEBRA

Use the given rules to complete the pattern. Display the pattern in the coordinate grid.

1. Multiply the number of cans by 3 to find the number of tennis balls.

Input	Cans	1	2	3	4
Output	Balls	3	6		

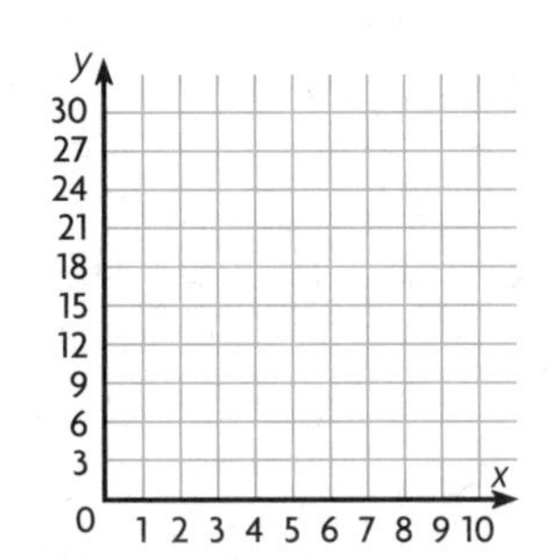

2. Add 2 to the input.

Input	1	2	3	4	5
Output					

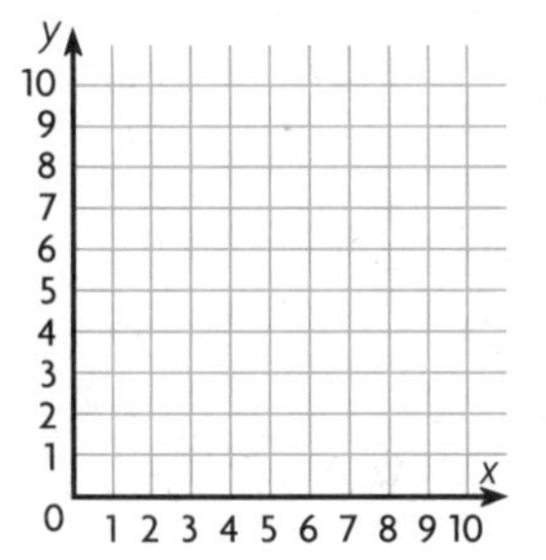

3. Write four ordered pairs that represent the pattern rule *multiply input by 4.* Display the pattern in the coordinate grid to the right.

____

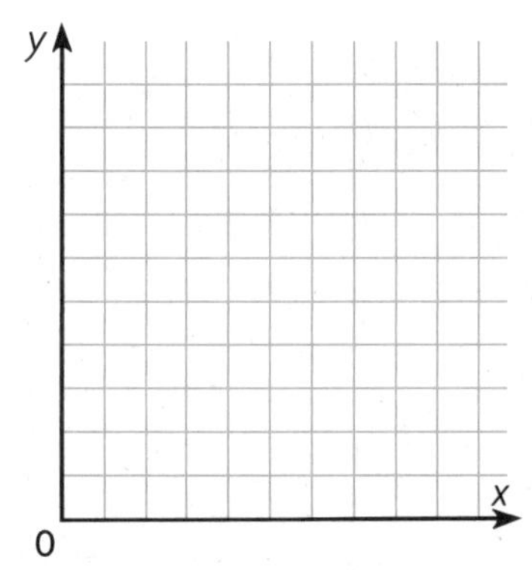

Problem Solving Real World

Use the coordinate grid for 4–5.

4. An architect makes a drawing of a building. One inch in the drawing equals 10 feet in actual measurement. Use the table and the coordinate grid to show the pattern.

Input	Drawing (in.)	1	2	3	4	5
Output	Actual Measurement (ft)					

5. What is the actual measurement if the length in the graph drawing is 7 units? Plot a point in the coordinate grid to show the ordered pair. ____________________

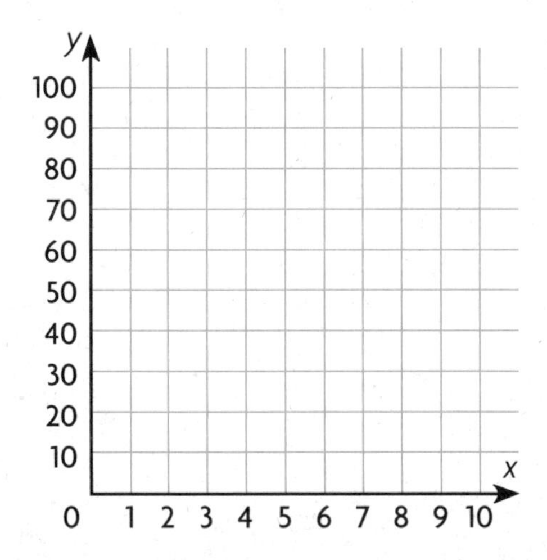

Lesson Check

TEXAS Test Prep

Fill in the bubble completely to show your answer.

6. Carson purchases tulip bulbs for his garden. Each package contains 6 bulbs. Which ordered pair shows the number of bulbs in 4 packages?

Input	Packages	1	2	3	4
Output	Bulbs	6	12		

Ⓐ (4, 24) Ⓒ (3, 16)
Ⓑ (4, 18) Ⓓ (18, 24)

7. For every $1 the students raise for the new playground equipment fund, the parents association donates $10 to the fund. If the x-coordinate is the amount the students raise and the y-coordinate is the amount the parents donate, which ordered pair could be on the graph?

Ⓐ (20, 30) Ⓒ (20, 200)
Ⓑ (20, 10) Ⓓ (20, 2,000)

8. **Multi-Step** Shakira saves $2 for every $3 she spends. She makes a graph that compares the amount she spends to the amount she saves. Which ordered pairs could be on Shakira's graph?

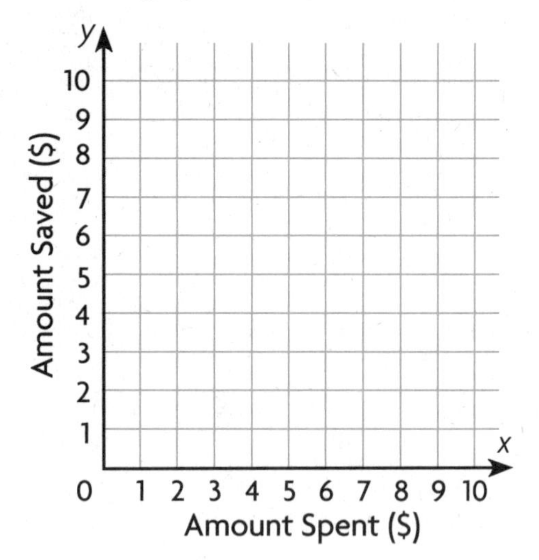

Ⓐ (6, 9), (8, 12)
Ⓑ (2, 3), (4, 6)
Ⓒ (3, 6), (6, 12)
Ⓓ (9, 6), (12, 8)

9. **Multi-Step** When the cook at Barney's Restaurant makes chili, he adds 3 cups of water for every 2 cups of tomato sauce. If you make a graph to compare the amounts of tomato sauce needed for several batches of chili, which ordered pairs could be on the graph?

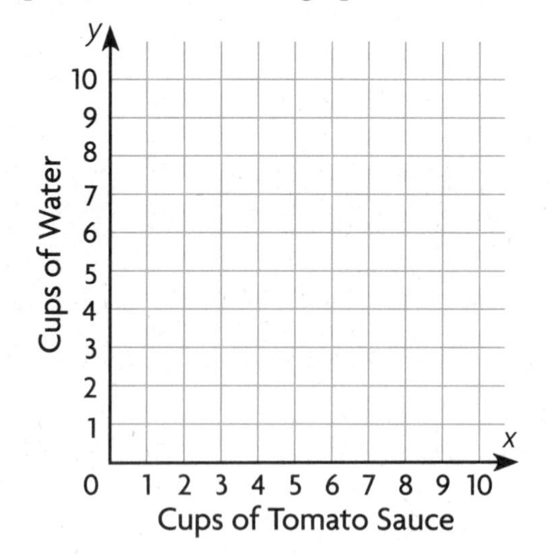

Ⓐ (3, 2), (6, 4), (9, 6)
Ⓑ (2, 3), (3, 4), (5, 6)
Ⓒ (3, 2), (5, 5), (7, 10)
Ⓓ (2, 3), (4, 6), (6, 9)

Name ______________________________

14.4 Graph and Analyze Relationships

MATHEMATICAL PROCESSES
5.1.A, 5.1.B, 5.1.D

Essential Question

How can you write and graph ordered pairs in a coordinate grid using number patterns?

Unlock the Problem

Sasha is making hot cocoa for a party. For each mug of cocoa, he uses 3 tablespoons of cocoa mix. If Sasha makes 9 mugs of cocoa, how many tablespoons of the cocoa mix will he use?

STEP 1 Use the rule to make an input/output table.

Input	Mug(s)	1	2	3	4
Output	Cocoa Mix (tbsp)	3			

STEP 2 Write the related pairs of data as ordered pairs.

(1, 3) ________ ________ ________

STEP 3 Plot and label the ordered pairs in the coordinate grid. Use the pattern to write an ordered pair for the number of tablespoons of the cocoa mix needed for 9 mugs of cocoa. Plot the point in the coordinate grid.

____

So, Sasha will need ______ tablespoons of the cocoa mix to make 9 mugs of cocoa.

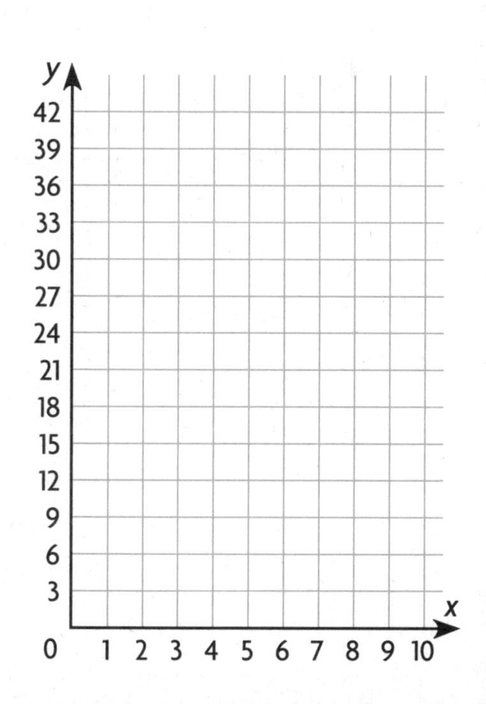

- How can you use the pattern in the coordinate grid to decide if your answer is reasonable?

____

____

Share and Show

Complete the input/output tables. Write ordered pairs and plot them in the coordinate grid.

1. Multiply the number of tablespoons by 2 to find the weight in ounces.

Input	Butter (tbsp)	1	2	3	4	5
Output	Weight (oz)	2				

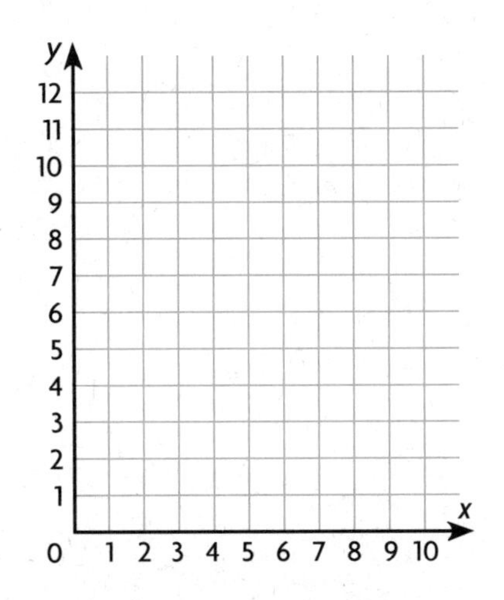

2. Multiply the number of hours by 3 to find the distance in miles.

Input	Time (hr)	1	2	3	4
Output	Distance walked (mi)	3			

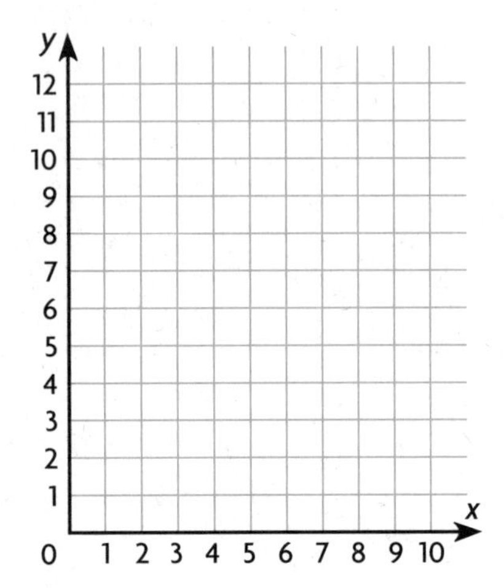

Problem Solving

Use the graph for 3–4.

3. H.O.T. Multi-Step The rule for the pattern is *multiply the input by 5*. Which ordered pair on the graph does not follow the pattern? Explain.

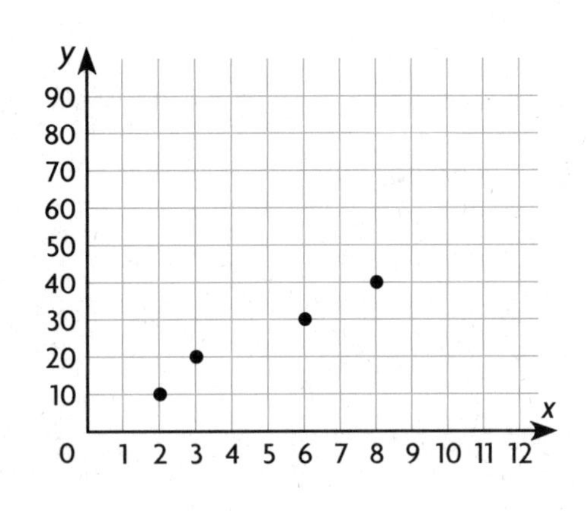

4. H.O.T. Communicate If the input is 12, would the output be greater or less than 40? Write the ordered pair and plot it on the graph.

Name ______________________________

Problem Solving Real World

Use the coordinate grid for 5-6. Complete the table for each recipe and plot the points. Use different colors to plot each person's pattern.

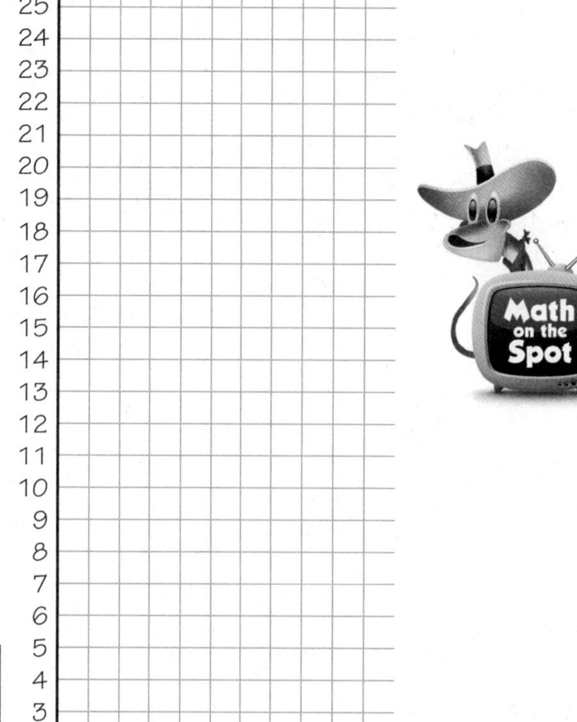

5. Lou and George are making chili for the Annual Firefighter's Ball.

Lou uses 2 teaspoons of hot sauce for every 2 cups of chili.

Input	Lou's chili (cups)	2	4	6	8
Output	Hot sauce (tsp)				

George uses 3 teaspoons of the same hot sauce for every cup of chili.

Input	George's chili (cups)	2	4	6	8
Output	Hot sauce (tsp)				

6. H.O.T. **Sense or Nonsense?** Elsa said that George's chili was hotter than Lou's, because the graph showed that the amount of hot sauce in George's chili was always 3 times as great as the amount of hot sauce in Lou's chili. Does Elsa's answer make sense, or is it nonsense? **Explain.**

____

____

____

____

7. H.O.T. **Multi-Step** If you mix 10 cups of George's chili with 10 cups of Lou's chili, how many teaspoons of hot sauce will there be in that 20 cups of chili?

____

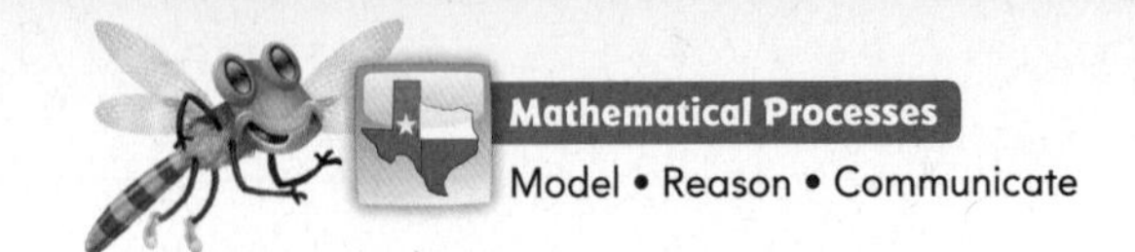

Daily Assessment Task

Fill in the bubble completely to show your answer.

8. The table compares distance on a map to real-life distance. How many miles does a map distance of 6 inches represent?

Input	Number of Inches	1	2	3	4
Output	Number of Miles	6	12	18	24

Ⓐ 24 miles
Ⓑ 30 miles
Ⓒ 36 miles
Ⓓ 6 miles

Use the graph for 9–10.

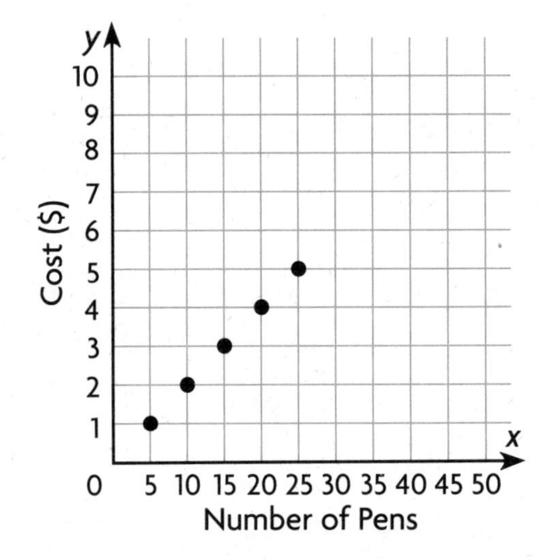

9. Which statement about the data is correct?

Ⓐ One pen costs $5.
Ⓑ Four pens cost $20.
Ⓒ Two pens cost $5.
Ⓓ Five pens cost $1.

10. **Multi-Step** Suppose Jake buys 30 pens. He also buys a notebook for $3. How much does Jake spend in all?

Ⓐ $6
Ⓑ $9
Ⓒ $33
Ⓓ $30

TEXAS Test Prep

11. Duber plots a pattern showing the number of pentagons and the total number of sides for that many pentagons. If the x-coordinate, the number of pentagons, is 8, which ordered pair shows the pattern?

Ⓐ (8, 5)
Ⓑ (5, 8)
Ⓒ (40, 8)
Ⓓ (8, 40)

Homework and Practice

TEKS Geometry and Measurement—5.8.C
Also 5.4.C
MATHEMATICAL PROCESSES 5.1.A, 5.1.B, 5.1.D

Name ________________________________

14.4 Graph and Analyze Relationships

Complete the input/output tables. Write ordered pairs and plot them in the coordinate grid.

1. Multiply the number of days by 5 to find the number of hours worked.

Input	Days	1	2	3	4
Output	Hours worked	5			

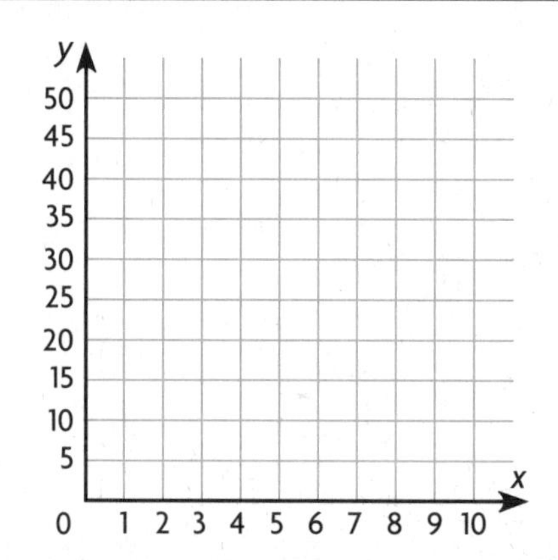

2. Multiply the number of gallons by 4 to find the number of quarts.

Input	Gallons	1	2	3	4	5
Output	Quarts	4				

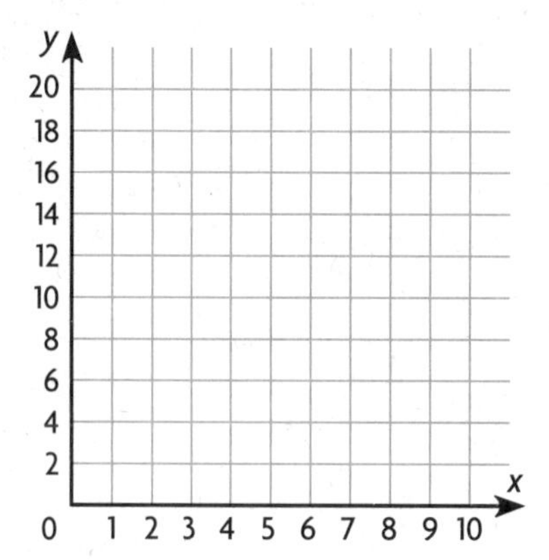

Problem Solving

Use the coordinate grid for 3-4. Complete the table for each person and plot the points. Use different colors to plot each person's pattern.

3. Marion uses 2 buttons for each doll.

Input	Marion's Dolls	1	2	3	4
Output	Number of buttons				

Nola uses 4 buttons for each doll.

Input	Nola's Dolls	1	2	3	4
Output	Number of buttons				

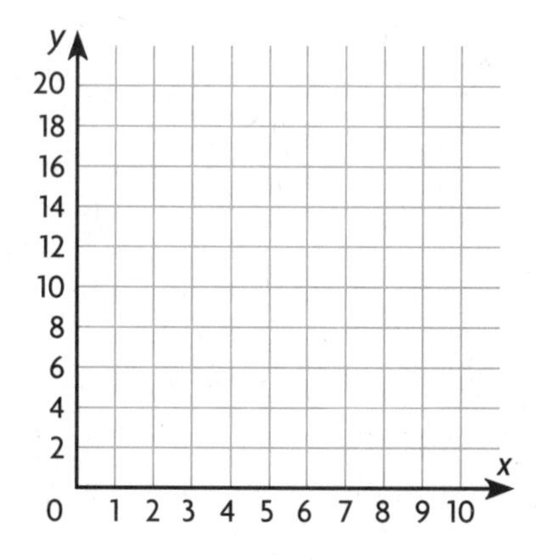

4. How many buttons do Marion and Nola use altogether if they each make 5 dolls?

____

Lesson Check

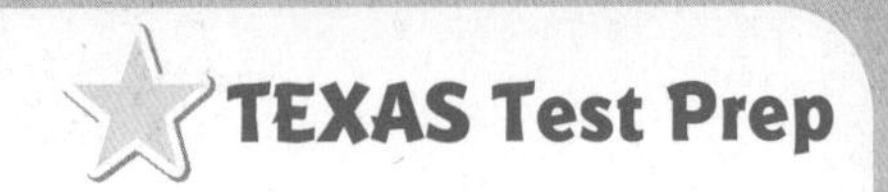

Fill in the bubble completely to show your answer.

5. Shane plots a pattern on a graph that shows the relationship for length of one side of a square and the area of the square. If the x-coordinate, the length of one side of a square, is 6 inches, which ordered pair will Shane plot?

Ⓐ (6, 24)

Ⓑ (6, 36)

Ⓒ (36, 6)

Ⓓ (6, 6)

6. The table compares distance on a map to actual distance. How many kilometers does a map distance of 8 centimeters represent?

Number of Centimeters	1	2	3	4
Number of Kilometers	10	20	30	40

Ⓐ 50 kilometers

Ⓑ 8 kilometers

Ⓒ 40 kilometers

Ⓓ 80 kilometers

Use the graph for 7–9.

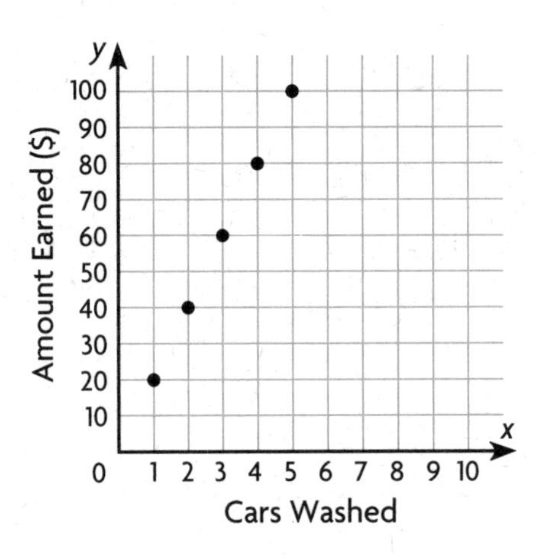

7. Which statement about the data is correct?

Ⓐ The amount earned for washing one car is $10.

Ⓑ The amount earned for washing 20 cars is one dollar per car.

Ⓒ The amount earned for washing one car is $20.

Ⓓ The amount earned for washing 10 cars is $50.

8. **Multi-Step** Suppose LeAnn washes 2 cars on Friday and 3 cars on Saturday. How much does she earn?

Ⓐ $40

Ⓑ $60

Ⓒ $50

Ⓓ $100

9. **Multi-Step** Kyle washes 4 cars. Erin washes 5 cars. Both plan to donate the amount earned to charity. How much more money do they need if they want to contribute $200 to charity?

Ⓐ $20

Ⓑ $180

Ⓒ $40

Ⓓ $100

Name ______________________________

Module 14 Assessment

Vocabulary

Choose the best term from the box.

Vocabulary
ordered pair
origin
x-axis
x-coordinate
y-axis
y-coordinate

1. The ______________ is the point where the x-axis and y-axis meet. Its ______________ is 0, and its ______________ is 0. (p. 511)

2. The horizontal number line in a coordinate grid is called the ______________. (p. 511)

Concepts and Skills

Use the table for 3–4. TEKS 5.8.C

Height of Seedling					
Input	**Weeks**	1	2	3	4
Output	**Height (in cm)**	2	6	14	16

3. Write ordered pairs to show the relationship between the week and the height.

____

4. Graph the data in a coordinate grid.

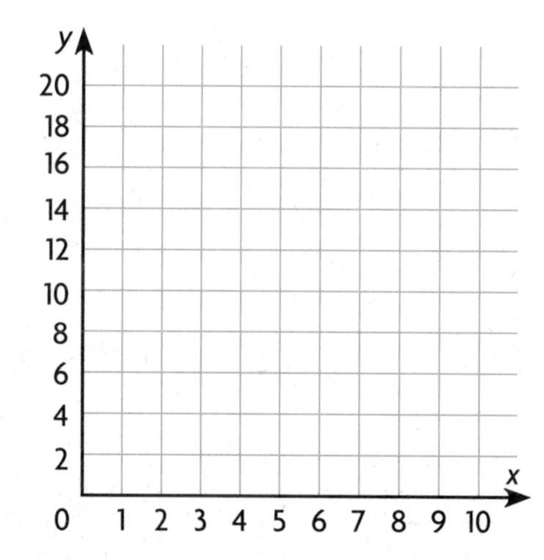

Fill in the bubble completely to show your answer.

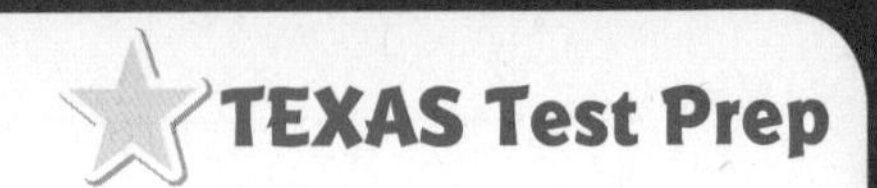

5. Point A is 2 units to the right and 4 units up from the origin. What ordered pair describes point A? TEKS 5.8.A, 5.8.B

Ⓐ (2, 0)

Ⓑ (2, 4)

Ⓒ (4, 2)

Ⓓ (0, 4)

6. The input/output table shows Tori's savings.

Input	Weeks	1	2	3	4	10
Output	Amount Saved (dollars)	20	40	60	80	■

If the x-coordinate is the number of weeks and the y-coordinate is the amount saved, which ordered pair represents the point showing the amount saved in 10 weeks? TEKS 5.8.C

Ⓐ (10, 100)

Ⓑ (100, 10)

Ⓒ (200, 10)

Ⓓ (10, 200)

7. The rule for a pattern is $y = 2x$. Which point in the coordinate plane does NOT represent the pattern rule? TEKS 5.8.C

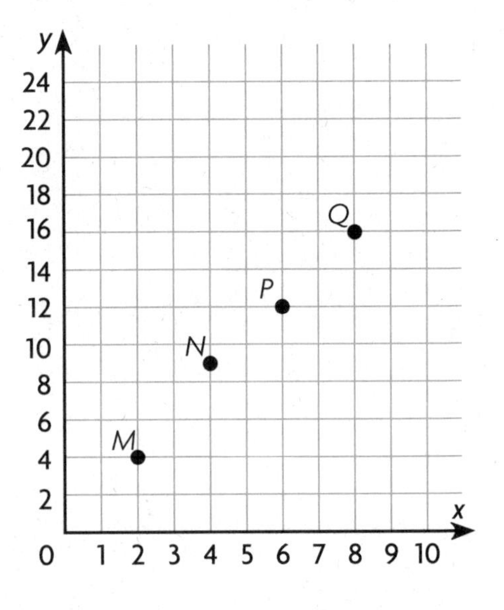

Ⓐ M

Ⓑ N

Ⓒ Q

Ⓓ P

8. In an ordered pair, the x-coordinate represents the number of hexagons, and the y-coordinate represents the total number of sides. If the x-coordinate is 7, what is the y-coordinate? TEKS 5.8.C

Record your answer and fill in the bubbles on the grid. Be sure to use the correct place value.

			.		
⓪	⓪	⓪		⓪	⓪
①	①	①		①	①
②	②	②		②	②
③	③	③		③	③
④	④	④		④	④
⑤	⑤	⑤		⑤	⑤
⑥	⑥	⑥		⑥	⑥
⑦	⑦	⑦		⑦	⑦
⑧	⑧	⑧		⑧	⑧
⑨	⑨	⑨		⑨	⑨

Name ______________________________

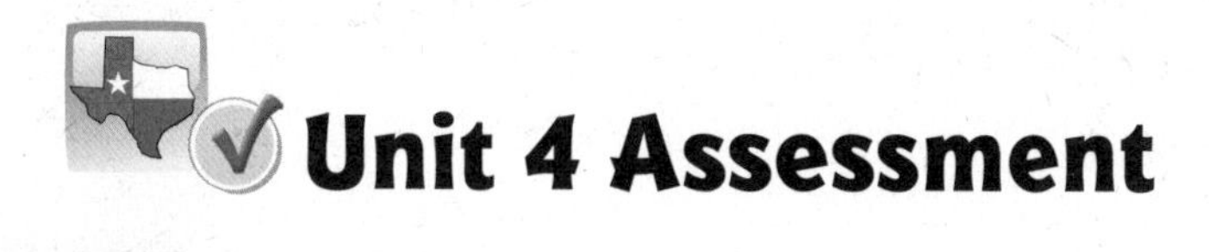

Unit 4 Assessment

Vocabulary

Choose the best term from the box.

Vocabulary
heptagon
nonagon
x-axis
y-axis

1. A ____________ is a polygon with nine sides and nine angles. (p. 409)
2. The vertical number line on a coordinate grid is the ____________. (p. 511)

Concepts and Skills

Convert. TEKS 5.7.A

3. 5 kg = ______ g
4. 65 yd 2 ft = ______ ft
5. 500 min = ______ hr ______ min

Classify each figure in as many ways as possible. TEKS 5.5.A

6. 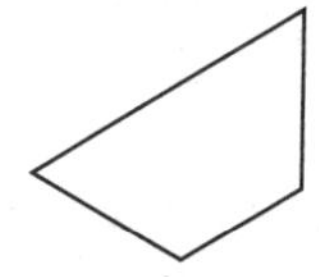

____

____

7. 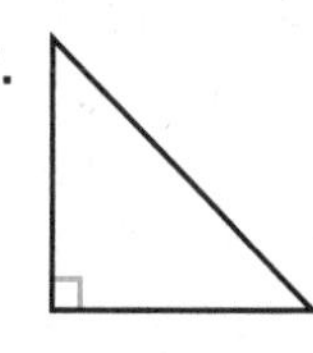

____

____

Use the table for 8–9. TEKS 5.8.C

8. The rule for the pattern is $y = x + 4$. Complete the table and write related number pairs of data as ordered pairs.

Input (x)	1	2	3	4
Output (y)				

____

9. Graph the data in a coordinate grid.

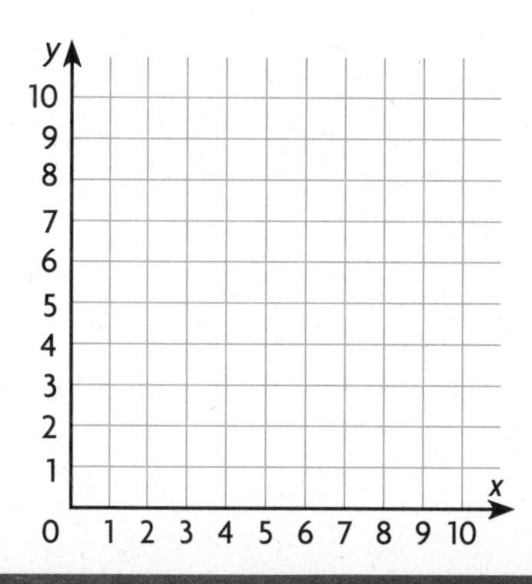

Fill in the bubble completely to show your answer.

10. Sam needs to order a container that can hold 5,200 milliliters of molasses. Which of the following containers is NOT large enough to hold the molasses? TEKS 5.7.A

Ⓐ a 10-liter barrel
Ⓑ a 5-liter barrel
Ⓒ a 50-liter barrel
Ⓓ a 6-liter barrel

11. A shipping container is 20 meters long, 10 meters wide, and 8 meters high. What is the greatest number of cartons that can fit in the container if each carton has a volume of 1 cubic meter? TEKS 5.6.A

Ⓐ Not here
Ⓑ 16,000
Ⓒ 1,600
Ⓓ 2,000

12. Which of the following can be used for the unknown shape in the graphic organizer? TEKS 5.5.A

All Congruent Sides

square

equilateral triangle

Sides Are Not All Congruent

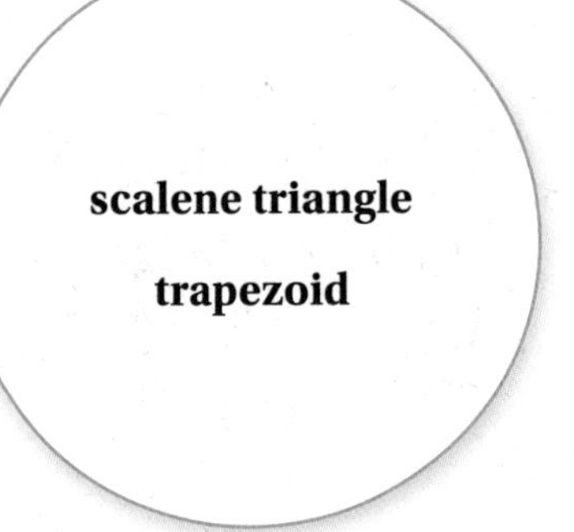

Ⓐ isosceles triangle
Ⓑ rhombus
Ⓒ right triangle
Ⓓ irregular pentagon

13. Leah uses the rule $y = 8x$ to determine the number of legs spiders have. If the number of spiders is the x-coordinate and the total number of legs is the y-coordinate, which ordered pair can Leah use to show the number of legs for 8 spiders? TEKS 5.8.C

Spiders	2	4	6	8
Legs	16	32	48	■

Ⓐ (8, 8)
Ⓑ (64, 8)
Ⓒ (8, 60)
Ⓓ (8, 64)

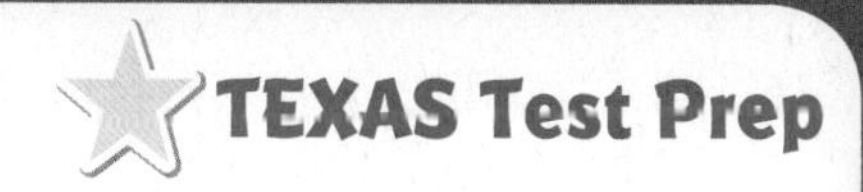

14. Delia has a 2 gallon container filled with fruit punch. How many 8 fluid ounce glasses of punch can she serve from her container? TEKS 5.7.A

Ⓐ 22
Ⓑ 32
Ⓒ 16
Ⓓ 44

15. A large wooden crate is used to store glass blocks used for making special glass walls. Each block is a one-inch cube. If 256 blocks fit in the bottom layer of the crate and the crate is 12 inches tall, what is the volume of the wooden crate? TEKS 5.6.B

Ⓐ 3,072 cubic inches
Ⓑ 192 cubic inches
Ⓒ 64 cubic inches
Ⓓ 768 cubic inches

16. Mayang has 2 pounds of beef. She uses 18 ounces to make a stew. How much more beef should she buy if she needs 2 pounds to make burgers? TEKS 5.7.A

Ⓐ 1 lb
Ⓑ 16 oz
Ⓒ 1 lb 2 oz
Ⓓ 1 lb 14 oz

17. Amy's design features a polygon with congruent sides. All of the angles are obtuse. Which of the following polygons could be in Amy's design? TEKS 5.5.A

Ⓐ equilateral triangle
Ⓑ square
Ⓒ regular pentagon
Ⓓ trapezoid

18. The points on the coordinate grid represent the locations of the first four holes on a golf course.

Which ordered pair describes the location of the hole labeled T? TEKS 5.8.C

Ⓐ (0, 7)
Ⓑ (1, 7)
Ⓒ (7, 0)
Ⓓ (7, 1)

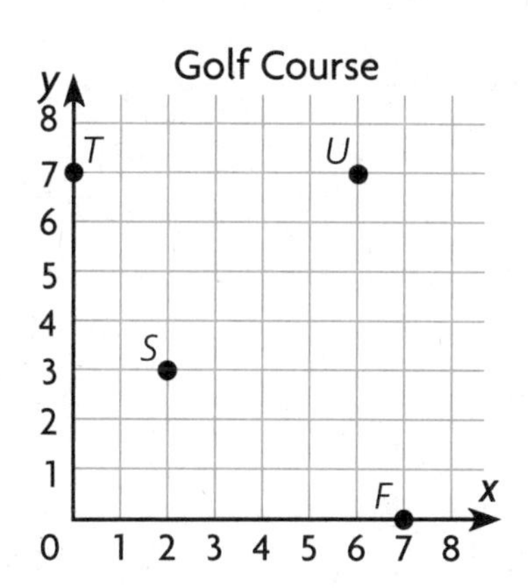

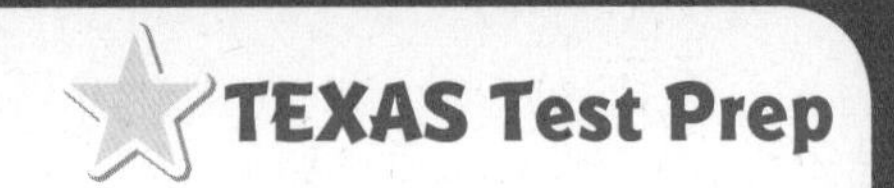

19. Raul builds these models using centimeter cubes. What is the difference in volume between the two models? TEKS 5.6.A

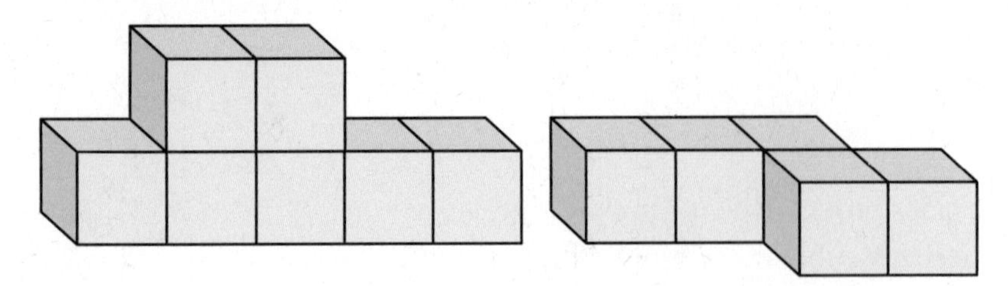

Ⓐ 48 cubic centimeters

Ⓑ 2 cubic centimeters

Ⓒ 3 cubic centimeters

Ⓓ 140 cubic centimeters

20. A scientist is measuring the length of insects. One kind of insect is 1.25 decimeters long. What is its length in millimeters? TEKS 5.7.A

Ⓐ 0.0125 mm

Ⓑ 12.5 mm

Ⓒ 125 mm

Ⓓ 0.125 mm

21. Point *W* is 5 units to the right and 3 units up from the origin. What ordered pair describes point *W*? TEKS 5.8.A, 5.8.B

Ⓐ (5, 0)

Ⓑ (5, 3)

Ⓒ (3, 5)

Ⓓ (0, 5)

22. Parker makes 5 liters of iced tea for a party. He pours the tea into smaller bottles for the guests. If each bottle contains 250 milliliters, how many bottles can Parker fill? TEKS 5.7.A

Ⓐ 5

Ⓑ 20

Ⓒ 10

Ⓓ 4

23. Celeste's card tells her to draw a triangle with two right angles. Can it be drawn? If so, draw the figure. If not, explain why it cannot be drawn. TEKS 5.5

____

____

____

Unit 5

Data Analysis

Show What You Know

Check your understanding of important skills.

Name ______________________________

Read Bar Graphs **Use the graph to answer the questions.**

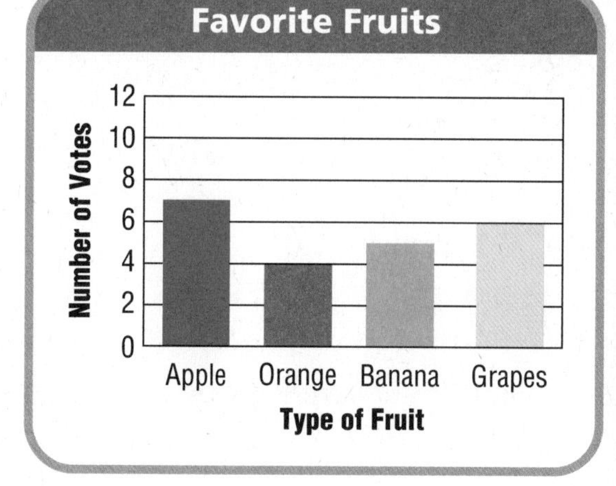

1. Which fruit received the most votes? __________

2. Which fruit received 5 votes? __________

3. There were __________ votes in all.

Subtract Decimals **Estimate. Then find the difference.**

4. Estimate:

$$\begin{array}{r} 6.79 \\ -\ 4.21 \\ \hline \end{array}$$

5. Estimate:

$$\begin{array}{r} 11.82 \\ -\ 2.31 \\ \hline \end{array}$$

Place Value Within 1,000,000 **Show 582,649 in the place-value chart. Write the value of the digits.**

Thousands			Ones		
Hundreds	Tens	Ones	Hundreds	Tens	Ones
		2,			9

6. The value of the 8 is __________.

7. The value of the 4 is __________.

8. The value of the 5 is __________.

GO DIGITAL Assessment Options: Soar to Success Math

Vocabulary Builder

▶ Visualize It

Use the checked words to complete the tree map.

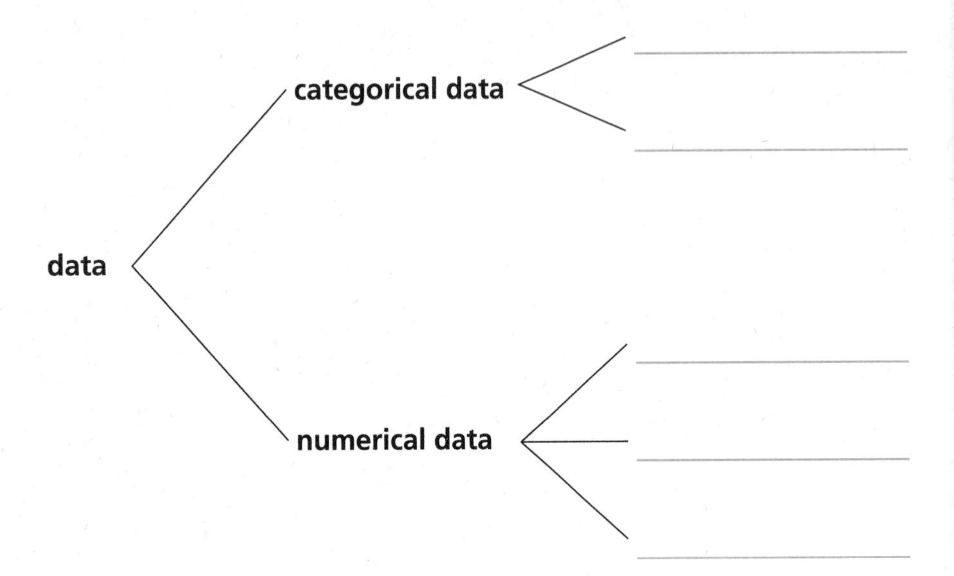

Review Words
data
x-axis
x-coordinate
y-axis
y-coordinate

Preview Words
✓ bar graph
✓ dot plot
frequency
✓ frequency table
prediction
range
✓ stem-and-leaf plot
✓ scatter plot

▶ Understand Vocabulary

Complete the sentences using the preview words.

1. ____________ is the number of times an event occurs.

2. A ____________ would be the best graph to show how many of each of the five types of animals are at the farm.

3. ____________ is the difference between the greatest and least numbers in a group.

4. A graph that shows frequency of data along a number line is a ____________.

5. You can use data to make a ____________.

6. A ____________ shows the relationship between two sets of data.

• Interactive Student Edition
• Multimedia eGlossary

Name ___________________________

Vocabulary

Pictographs and bar graphs are two ways to display data. Each kind of display shows information in a slightly different way.

Look at the data in the table below. Decide whether it would be better to use a pictograph or a bar graph to display the data. Would you need a key? What information would you include in the key? Then make, label, and graph the data set.

Hours Spent Reading	
Time	Number of People
1 Hour	3
2 Hours	7
3 Hours	8
More than 3 Hours	8

Writing For one week, record how much time you spend reading. Write the time you begin and the time you end each day. Then make a bar graph to show the data.

Reading Look for *Holes* by Louis Sachar in your library.

Penny Drop

Object of the Game Partners can play this game and then make a bar graph to compare their scores.

Materials

- 5 pennies
- *Penny Drop* Target
- *Penny Drop* Score Card (one for each player)
- Bar Graph Pattern

Set Up

Give each player one score card.

Number of Players 2

How to Play

1. Place the target on the floor. Decide who will go first.

2. Players stand face to face with their toes just touching one long edge of the target. Players take turns dropping 5 pennies onto the target.

3. When a player has dropped all 5 pennies, he or she adds up their score and records it on the score card.
   - A penny will score 0, 2, 5, or 10 points.
   - If a penny lands on the border between two areas of the target, it will score the lesser of the two values.

4. Repeat Steps 2 and 3. Players add the score to their score from the previous round. The player who has the highest score after 10 rounds wins.

Share Your Thinking Make a bar graph showing your total score for rounds 1 to 10. What information about the game can you get from the graph?

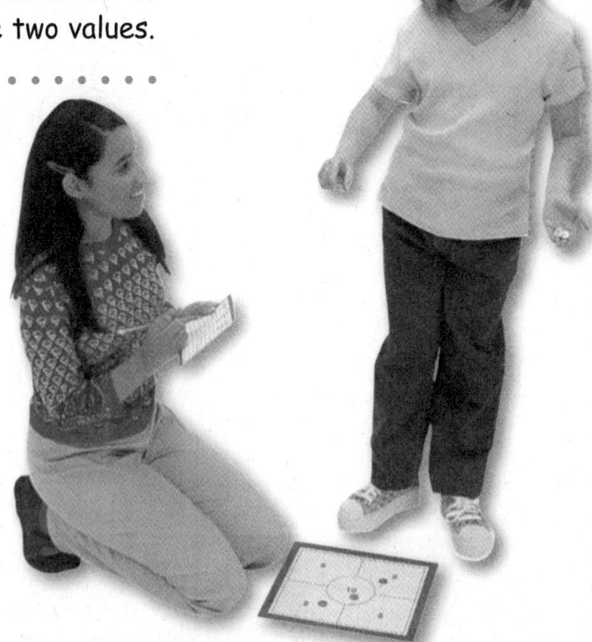

Name ______________________________

TEKS Data Analysis—5.9.A

MATHEMATICAL PROCESSES 5.1.B, 5.1.E

15.1 Make Frequency Tables

Essential Question How can you display data in a frequency table?

Frequency is the number of times an event occurs. A **frequency table** is a table that uses numbers to record data about how often something happens.

Unlock the Problem

Bart kept a record of the sizes of bags of peanuts he sold at a baseball game.

Bags of Peanuts Sold (Sizes)						
M	S	XL	M	XL	S	L
S	S	L	XL	XL	L	XL
XL	XL	S	M	L	L	S
S	XL	L	S	XL	M	M

Make a frequency table of the data.

STEP 1: Write the title at the top of the frequency table.

____

STEP 2: List the sizes of bags of peanuts in the first column.

____

STEP 3: Record the frequency of each size of bag of peanuts sold in the frequency column.

Size	**Frequency**

- If you want to know quickly how many large bags of peanuts Bart sold, would you use his record or would you use the frequency table? **Explain.**

____

____

Try This! **Make a frequency table.**

A librarian records the types of books students checked out one morning. Make a frequency table of the data.

- Write a title for the frequency table.
- List the types of books in the first column.
- Record the frequency of each type of book in the second column.

Books Checked Out			
adventure	mystery	adventure	biography
adventure	mystery	adventure	biography
biography	adventure	mystery	adventure
mystery	adventure	biography	adventure

Types of Books	**Frequency**

Share and Show

Len records the methods of transportation his classmates take to school. Use the data for 1–2.

Transportation to School		
bus	walk	car
walk	walk	bus
bus	bus	walk
car	bus	car
walk	bus	bus
bus	car	walk
car	walk	bus

1. What is a good title for a frequency table of the data?

____

What will be in the first column of the frequency table?

____

What will be in the second column of the frequency table?

____

2. Make a frequency table.

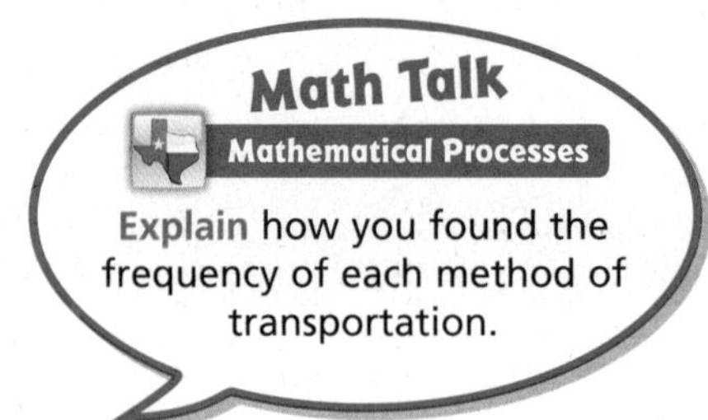

Name ______________________

Problem Solving

A swimming coach records the events swimmers on a team are competing in. Use the data for 3–4.

Swimming Events		
freestyle	backstroke	butterfly
backstroke	breaststroke	freestyle
freestyle	backstroke	freestyle
breaststroke	butterfly	backstroke
backstroke	freestyle	butterfly
freestyle	backstroke	butterfly

3. Make a frequency table of the data. **Explain** how you determine what to put in the first column of the table.

____

____

4. **Multi-Step** How can you prove that the total number of frequencies in your table is correct?

____

____

____

Problem Solving Real World

A restaurant owner recorded salsa flavors that customers asked for at dinner. Use the data for 5–7.

Salsa Flavors									
hot	mild	chunky	hot	mild	mild	spicy	hot	hot	spicy
spicy	chunky	spicy	chunky	chunky	spicy	hot	spicy	hot	hot

Write Math ▶ Show Your Work

5. **Representations** Make a frequency table of the data.

6. H.O.T. **Describe** how the frequency table will change if 4 customers switch from chunky salsa to spicy salsa and 3 customers switch from mild salsa to hot salsa.

____

____

7. H.O.T. **Multi-Step** Think of a topic for a frequency table. Record a set of data for the topic. Use the data to make a frequency table.

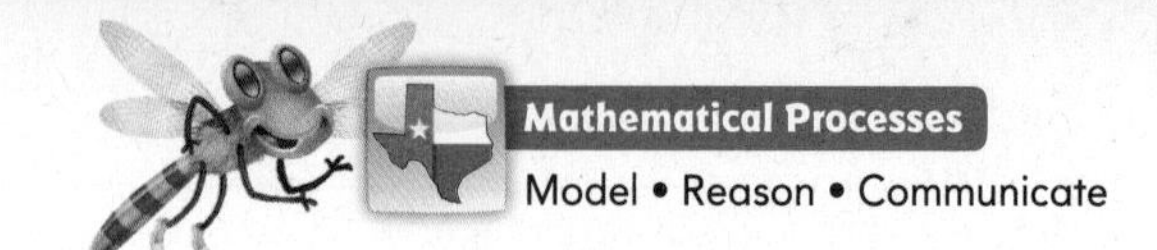

Daily Assessment Task

Fill in the bubble completely to show your answer.

8. Marsha records the breeds of dogs in a dog show. Then she makes a frequency table to show the data. How many different breeds of dogs will be in the frequency table?

Breeds of Dogs			
beagle	pug	bulldog	pug
beagle	bulldog	poodle	bulldog
bulldog	poodle	beagle	bulldog

Ⓐ 2
Ⓑ 12
Ⓒ 3
Ⓓ 4

Students place an order for different sizes of school sweatshirts. They make a frequency table to show the data. Use the frequency table for 9–10.

9. Students order sizes large, small, large, large, medium, small, large, small, large, medium, and small. What frequency should be in the row for medium in the frequency table?

Sweatshirt Order	
Size	**Frequency**
Small	?
Medium	?
Large	?

Ⓐ 5
Ⓑ 2
Ⓒ 4
Ⓓ 3

10. **Multi-Step** Students pay $14 for size small sweatshirts and $16 for size large. How much do they pay for the size small and large sweatshirts they order?

Ⓐ $56
Ⓑ $136
Ⓒ $80
Ⓓ $30

TEXAS Test Prep

11. Paula recorded the colors of all her shoes.

Shoe Colors				
blue	black	red	blue	blue
black	blue	white	red	black
red	purple	white	blue	red

She makes a frequency table of the data. What is the frequency of red shoes?

Ⓐ 3
Ⓑ 4
Ⓒ 15
Ⓓ 2

Name ____________________

15.1 Make Frequency Tables

Patricia records the types of penguins she sees in the Antarctic exhibit at the zoo. Use the data for 1–2.

Antarctic Penguins		
King	Chinstrap	Gentoo
Chinstrap	King	Macaroni
Rockhopper	Chinstrap	King
Gentoo	Gentoo	Gentoo
Macaroni	King	Chinstrap
Rockhopper	Rockhopper	Chinstrap

1. What is a good title for a frequency table of the data?

   ____

   What will be in the first column of the frequency table?

   ____

   What will be in the second column of the frequency table? ____________________

2. Complete the frequency table at the right.

Problem Solving Real World

Mr. Rexford's students recorded the polygons in a sculpture at the modern art museum. Use the data for 3–4.

Polygons				
triangle	rectangle	hexagon	rectangle	rectangle
hexagon	hexagon	pentagon	hexagon	triangle
hexagon	triangle	pentagon	rectangle	rectangle

3. Complete the frequency table of the data.

4. Which polygon had the greatest frequency? Which polygon had the least frequency?

   ____

   ____

Lesson Check

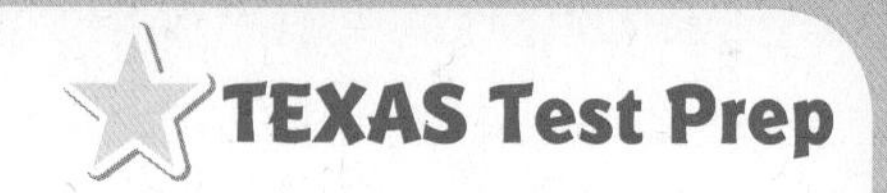

Fill in the bubble completely to show your answer.

5. Milo records the types of shells he collects on the Texas coast. Then he makes a frequency table to show the data. How many different types of shells will be in the frequency table?

   Ⓐ 20
   Ⓑ 4
   Ⓒ 5
   Ⓓ 3

Shells Collected			
clam	clam	conch	whelk
cockle	cockle	clam	scallop
cockle	clam	conch	scallop
scallop	cockle	clam	scallop
clam	scallop	whelk	conch

6. Carmen recorded the types of vehicles she saw while looking out the window of her father's car. She makes a frequency table of the data. What is the frequency of motorcycles?

   Ⓐ 5
   Ⓑ 6
   Ⓒ 7
   Ⓓ 3

Vehicles		
motorcycle	truck	sports car
truck	motorcycle	truck
sports car	motorcycle	SUV
motorcycle	truck	SUV
SUV	SUV	sports car
SUV	truck	motorcycle
motorcycle	truck	SUV

Josef has a pottery booth at the craft fair. He makes a frequency table to record the types of pottery sold one day. Use the frequency table for 7–8.

Pottery Sold	
Type	**Frequency**
Bowl	12
Mug	?
Plate	5
Vase	8

7. **Multi-Step** The number of mugs Josef sold is one fourth of the combined number of bowls and vases sold. What frequency should be in the row for mug in the frequency table?

   Ⓐ 3
   Ⓑ 5
   Ⓒ 2
   Ⓓ 80

8. **Multi-Step** The price of a plate is \$6 and the price of a mug is \$5. How much did Josef collect from the plates and the mugs he sold?

   Ⓐ \$55
   Ⓑ \$25
   Ⓒ \$30
   Ⓓ \$11

Name ________________________________

15.2 Analyze Frequency Tables

TEKS Data Analysis—5.9.C
MATHEMATICAL PROCESSES 5.1.A, 5.1.F

Essential Question

How can you analyze data displayed in a frequency table?

Unlock the Problem

You can solve problems by analyzing data in frequency tables.

Example 1

Students vote for the country they would most like to visit. They record the results in a frequency table.

Countries to Visit

Country	Frequency
England	9
China	24
Italy	17
Canada	15
Iceland	6

Which two countries have the greatest frequency of votes?

The greatest frequencies are ______ and ______.

The countries with the greatest frequencies are ____________ and ____________.

Students who vote for the two countries with the greatest frequency of votes will plan a festival about the countries. How many students will plan the festival?

Add the two greatest frequencies.

______ + ______ = ______

So, ______ students will plan the festival.

Math Talk
Mathematical Processes
Explain how you could use the frequency table to find the total number of students who voted.

Example 2 Solve a multi-step problem.

Jason uses a frequency table to keep track of the posters he sells at his online store. He sells movie posters for $12 each and sports posters for $15 each. How much was Jason paid for the movie posters and sports posters he sold in January?

Posters Sold in January	
Types of Posters	**Frequency**
Animal	13
Sports	13
Rock Star	8
Movie	12

STEP 1: Use the frequency table to find the number of movie posters and sports posters Jason sold in January.

movie posters: ______ sports posters: ______

STEP 2: Multiply to find how much Jason was paid for each type of poster.

movie posters: ______ × $______ = $______

sports posters: ______ × $______ = $______

STEP 3: Add to find the total amount.

$______ + $______ = $______

Jason was paid $______ for movie posters and sports posters in January.

Share and Show

Students vote for their favorite rides at a water park. They record the results in a frequency table. Use the frequency table for 1–3.

Favorite Water Park Rides	
Rides	**Frequency**
River Rapids	15
The Wave	15
Jungle Slide	21
Splashers	9
Mountain Slide	18
Cave Dive	15

1. What is the difference between the frequency of votes for Jungle Slide and Splashers?

   Jungle Slide: ______votes Splashers: ______votes

   ______ − ______ = ______

   The difference is ______ votes.

2. Which rides received an equal number of votes?

   ____

3. How many students voted for Mountain Slide and Cave Dive combined? ______

Name ________________

Problem Solving

Sandy recorded the fruit snacks she ate each day last month in a frequency table. Use the frequency table for 4–5.

Fruit Snacks	
Type of Fruit	**Frequency**
Apple	8
Orange	4
Banana	11
Peach	9
Pear	3

4. **Multi-Step** Sandy circled the fruits that she had fewer than 5 times last month. She decided to eat them 3 times as often next month. How many times will she eat each of those fruits?

5. **H.O.T.** **Multi-Step** Corrie ate fruit as often as Sandy last month and he ate the same types of fruit. But Corrie ate each type of fruit an equal number of times. How many times did Corrie eat each type of fruit? **Describe** the steps you follow to solve the problem.

Problem Solving Real World

Pedro conducts a survey about students' favorite websites. He records the results in a frequency table. Use the data for 6–7.

Favorite Websites	
Type of Websites	**Frequency**
Games	32
Music	20
Videos	41
Sports	18
News	9

6. How many students are in the survey? **Explain** how to use mental math to find the answer.

7. **H.O.T.** **Multi-Step** Which two types of websites combined received the same number of votes as the type of website with the greatest number of votes? **Explain.**

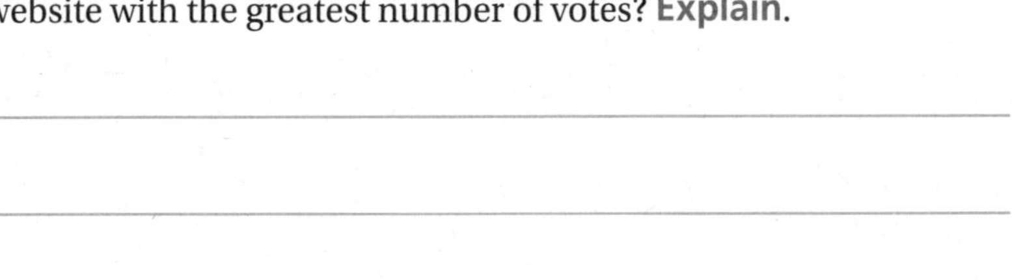

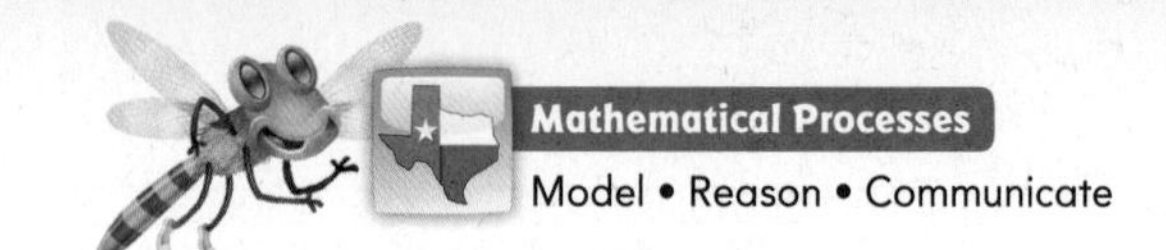

Daily Assessment Task

Fill in the bubble completely to show your answer.

8. **Analyze** Hector has a collection of postcards. The frequency table shows the number of postcards he has from each country. The number of postcards from the United States is 3 times the number he has from which country?

Ⓐ Japan
Ⓑ France
Ⓒ Norway
Ⓓ Canada

Postcard Collection	
Country	**Frequency**
United States	54
Japan	27
France	16
Norway	24
Canada	18

Use the frequency table for 9 and 10.

9. The table shows the types of sandwiches sold at a deli yesterday. How many more chicken than tuna salad sandwiches were sold?

Ⓐ 12
Ⓑ 7
Ⓒ 13
Ⓓ 19

Sandwiches Sold	
Types of Sandwiches	**Frequency**
Tuna Salad	12
Peanut Butter	8
Chicken	19
Grilled Cheese	6

10. **Multi-Step** One customer bought half the peanut butter sandwiches and half the grilled cheese sandwiches that were sold. Each sandwich cost $6. How much did the customer pay?

Ⓐ $24
Ⓑ $18
Ⓒ $84
Ⓓ $42

TEXAS Test Prep

11. Students vote for their favorite hobby and record the results in a frequency table.

Favorite Hobby	
Type of Hobby	**Frequency**
Scrapbooking	13
Collecting Coins	22
Making Videos	7
Sewing	18

How many students voted for the two most popular hobbies?

Ⓐ 35
Ⓑ 40
Ⓒ 4
Ⓓ 30

Name ______________________

15.2 Analyze Frequency Tables

Coach Michaels plans the annual school field day. Students vote for their favorite event and he records the results in a frequency table. Use the frequency table for 1–4.

Field Day Events	
Events	**Frequency**
Scooter race	62
Relay race	11
Cone toss	13
Obstacle course	52
Water balloon toss	26

1. Which event received half the number of votes as water balloon toss? Which event received twice as many votes as water balloon toss?

____

2. Which two events combined received fewer votes than water balloon toss?

____

3. Which three events combined received fewer votes than scooter race?

____

4. Which event do you think Coach Michaels should plan to include in field day? Which event should he consider eliminating? **Explain.**

____

____

Problem Solving Real World

A travel website conducts a survey about Texans' favorite bordering state to visit. Monday's results are posted in a frequency table. Use the data for 5–6.

Favorite State to Visit	
States	**Frequency**
Arkansas	67
Louisiana	89
Oklahoma	78
New Mexico	95

5. **Multi-Step** How many more people prefer to visit Louisiana or New Mexico than Arkansas or Oklahoma?

____

6. **Multi-Step** If 256 more people respond to the survey on Tuesday, how many people have responded to the survey so far? Describe the steps you follow to solve the problem.

____

____

Lesson Check

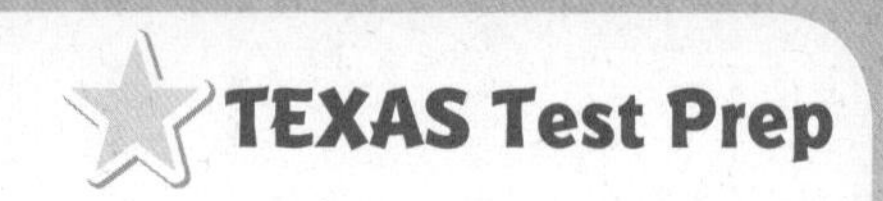

Fill in the bubble completely to show your answer.

7. Students vote for their favorite type of craft project and record the results in a frequency table. What is the difference in frequency between the least favorite craft and the craft with the most votes?

Ⓐ 9 Ⓒ 37

Ⓑ 1 Ⓓ 8

Favorite Craft Project	
Types of Crafts	**Frequency**
Mosaic	23
3-D Mobile	19
Origami	22
Collage	15
Paper Mask	14

8. Students vote for their favorite location for a field trip. Which two locations have the least difference in the frequency?

Ⓐ Aquarium and Zoo

Ⓑ Zoo and Science Museum

Ⓒ Theater and Art Museum

Ⓓ Aquarium and Theater

Favorite Field Trip	
Locations	**Frequency**
Aquarium	27
Zoo	33
Art Museum	19
Science Museum	38
Theater	25

The table shows the types of bagels sold at the bagel shop on Friday. Use the frequency table for 9–11.

9. One eighth of the number of raisin bagels sold on Friday were sold on Saturday. How many raisin bagels were sold on Saturday?

Ⓐ 8 Ⓒ 2

Ⓑ 4 Ⓓ 6

Bagels Sold	
Types of Bagels	**Frequency**
Plain	16
Chocolate Chip	28
Blueberry	36
Raisin	32

10. **Multi-Step** Sasha buys bagels for her garage sale customers. She buys all the chocolate chip bagels and half the plain bagels. Each bagel costs $2.50. How much does Sasha spend on bagels?

Ⓐ $70 Ⓒ $90

Ⓑ $20 Ⓓ $110

11. **Multi-Step** If the total number of bagels sold on Friday was double the number of bagels sold on Saturday, how many bagels were sold on Saturday?

Ⓐ 112 Ⓒ 56

Ⓑ 51 Ⓓ 224

Name ______________________________

15.3 Make Bar Graphs

Essential Question How can you display data on a bar graph?

Investigate

Materials ■ bar graph pattern

Ms. Lyon's class took a survey of their favorite sport to watch. They recorded their results in the table below. Use the data in the table to make a **bar graph** of their favorite sport to watch.

Favorite Sport to Watch				
Sport	Football	Baseball	Soccer	Other
Number of Votes	12	4	6	2

A. Start by labeling the bar graph with important information. What will the title of your bar graph be?

____

Where will you write the label *Sport*?
Where will you write the scale label *Number of Votes*?

____

What labels will the bars of the bar graph have?

____

The scale for all graphs begins with ______. Since this data set is all even numbers, a scale of ______ is appropriate for this graph.

B. Graph the number of students who voted for each sport by drawing and labeling a bar for each survey answer choice.

The bar labeled *Football* will end at ______.

The bar labeled *Baseball* will end at ______.

The bar labeled *Soccer* will end at ______.

The bar labeled *Other* will end at ______.

Draw Conclusions

Use the bar graph you made on the previous page for 1–2.

1. Why might you use a scale of 2 instead of a scale of 1 for this bar graph?

____

____

2. **Explain** how using a scale of 4 would change the bar graph.

____

____

Share and Show

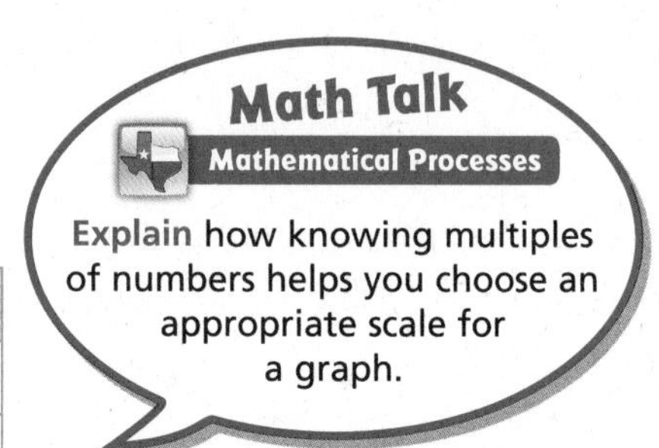

Use the tables for 1–3.

Number of Rainy Days			
Month	April	May	June
Number of Days	20	8	4

Number of Sunny Days			
Month	April	May	June
Number of Days	5	10	15

1. A scale of 5 would be more appropriate for a bar graph of the data in the table titled ______________________.

2. A scale of 4 would be more appropriate for a bar graph of the data in the table titled ______________________.

3. Make bar graphs to display the data in each table.

Name ______________________________

Problem Solving (Real World)

Use the table and bar graph for 4–6.

Preferred Field Trip	
Location	**Number of Votes**
Apple Orchard	6
Museum	2
Planetarium	11
Zoo	4

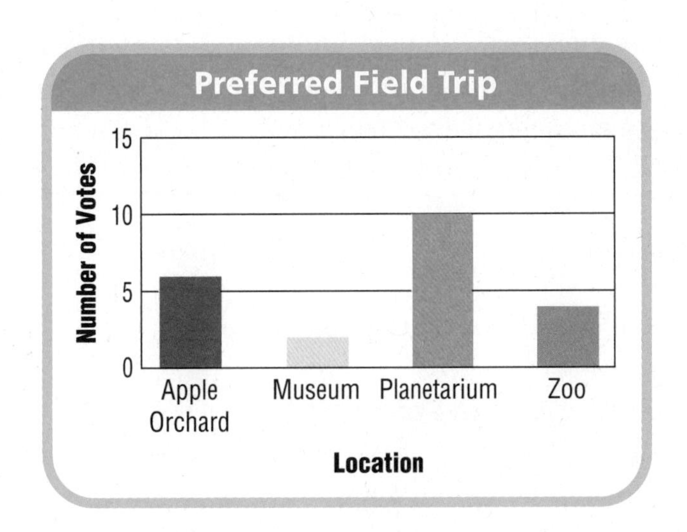

4. **H.O.T.** **What's the Error?** Students in Mr. Tran's class were surveyed about which of four field trip locations they would prefer to visit: an apple orchard, a museum, a planetarium, or a zoo. The results of the survey are shown in the table.

   Tori made a graph of the data. What error did she make? How can she correct the error?

   ____

   ____

5. **H.O.T.** What scale could Tori have used to make reading the values of the bars easier? **Explain.**

   ____

   ____

   ____

6. **Multi-Step** Exactly how many more students voted for the zoo than the museum? Which data display is easier to use to find the answer? **Explain.**

   ____

   ____

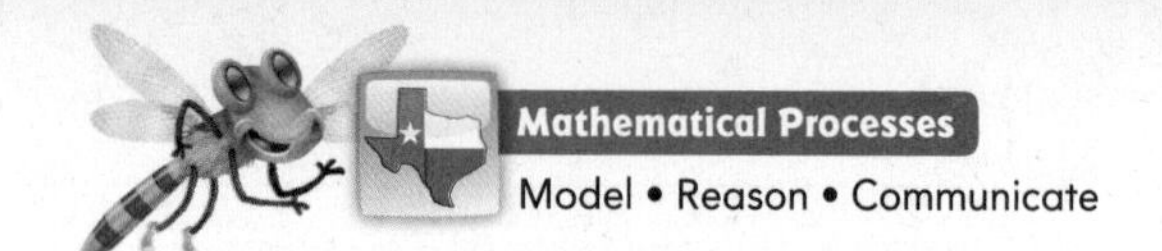

Daily Assessment Task

Fill in the bubble completely to show your answer.

7. Trevor recorded the skateboards that were sold last month in a frequency table. He will display the data in a bar graph. How many bars will the graph have?

Skateboards Sold Last Month			
Style	A	B	C
Number	8	10	4

Ⓐ 3 bars
Ⓑ 4 bars
Ⓒ 10 bars
Ⓓ 8 bars

Use the table and incomplete graph for 8 and 9.

Shirts Sold			
Color	Red	Black	Blue
Number	5	10	7

8. **Analyze** Suppose you are completing the bar graph. Which scale is best?

Ⓐ 1
Ⓑ 2
Ⓒ 12
Ⓓ 10

9. **Multi-Step** Brandy graphed the data correctly. Which statement about the graph is true?

Ⓐ The bar for black is twice as tall as the bar for blue.
Ⓑ The bar for black is twice as tall as the bar for red.
Ⓒ The bar for blue is the tallest bar.
Ⓓ The bar for blue is the shortest bar.

TEXAS Test Prep

10. Marcy is making a bar graph of the data in the frequency table. What scale should she use?

Favorite Lunch			
Item	Soup	Salad	Sandwich
Number of Votes	20	35	15

Ⓐ 2
Ⓑ 25
Ⓒ 5
Ⓓ 1

TEKS Data Analysis—5.9.A
MATHEMATICAL PROCESSES 5.1.A, 5.1.D, 5.1.E

Name ______________________________

15.3 Make Bar Graphs

Use the tables for 1–3.

Number of Races Won			
Team	A	B	C
Number of Races	4	8	5

Number of Points Scored			
Team	A	B	C
Number of Points	20	40	25

1. A scale of 10 would be more appropriate for a bar graph of the data in the table titled ______________________.

2. A scale of 2 would be more appropriate for a bar graph of the data in the table titled ______________________.

3. Make bar graphs below to display the data in each table.

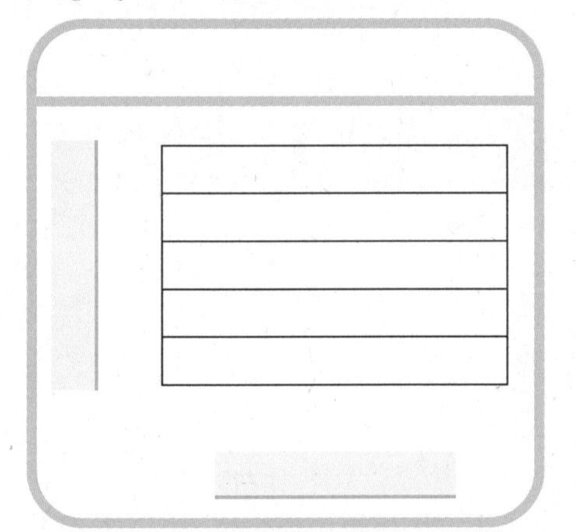

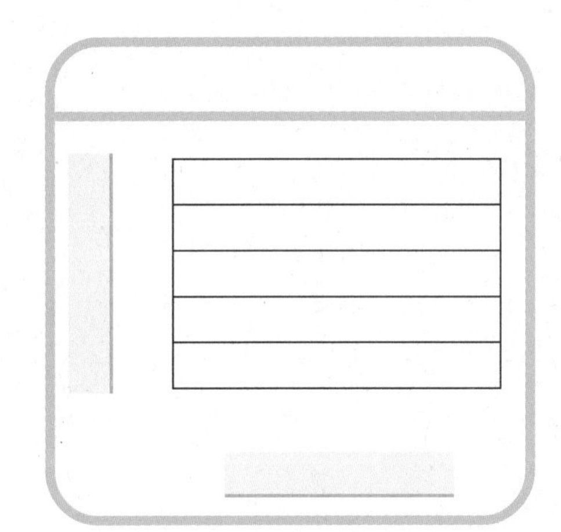

Problem Solving Real World

A pastry chef surveyed her customers to find out which type of berry is their favorite. The results of the survey are shown in the table and bar graph. Use the table and bar graph for 4–5.

Favorite Berry	
Type of Berry	Number of Votes
Blackberry	4
Blueberry	8
Raspberry	20
Strawberry	16

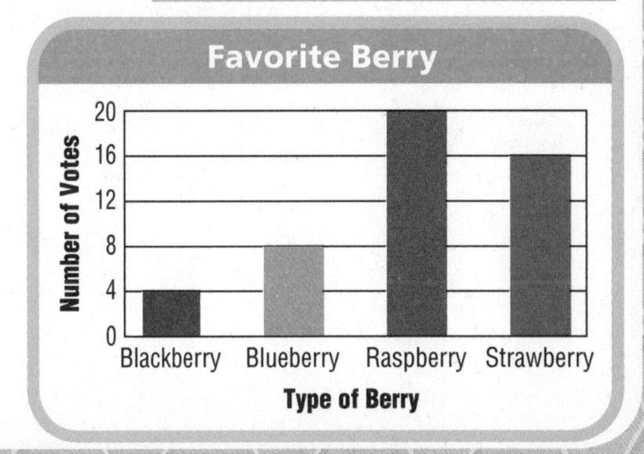

4. What scale was used to make the bar graph? **Explain.**

____

5. Which berry got the most votes? Which data display did you use to find the answer? **Explain.**

____

____

Lesson Check

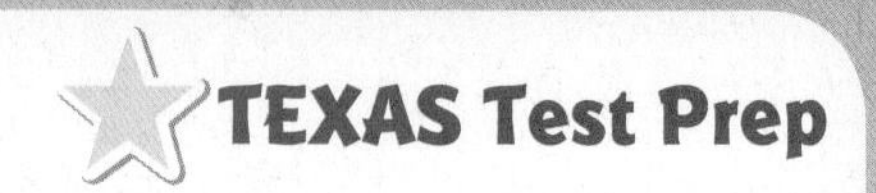

Fill in the bubble completely to show your answer.

6. Leon makes a bar graph of the favorite cheese data in the frequency table. How many bars will the graph have?

Favorite Cheese	
Type of Cheese	**Number of Votes**
Cheddar	12
Monterrey Jack	6
Mozzarella	10
Swiss	5

Ⓐ 12 bars Ⓒ 3 bars

Ⓑ 4 bars Ⓓ 2 bars

7. Felicia makes a bar graph of the favorite citrus fruit data in the frequency table. Where will the bar for tangerine end?

Favorite Citrus Fruit			
Fruit	Grapefruit	Orange	Tangerine
Number of Votes	12	15	18

Ⓐ 12 Ⓒ 20

Ⓑ 18 Ⓓ 3

Use the table and incomplete graph for 8–10.

Bookstore Sales			
Type of Book	New	Used	E-book
Number Sold	35	60	25

Bookstore Sales

Number Sold

Type of Book

8. Which scale is the best choice for completing the graph?

Ⓐ 5

Ⓑ 2

Ⓒ 4

Ⓓ 1

9. **Multi-Step** The number of books the bookstore donates to a library is one fourth the total number of books sold. How many books are donated to a library?

Ⓐ 95

Ⓑ 120

Ⓒ 30

Ⓓ 40

10. **Multi-Step** If the data are graphed correctly, which statement is true?

Ⓐ The bar for new books is the shortest bar.

Ⓑ The bar for e-books is taller than the bar for new books.

Ⓒ The bar for used books is twice as tall as the bar for new books.

Ⓓ The bar for used books is more than twice as tall as the bar for e-books.

Name ___

15.4 Analyze Bar Graphs

TEKS Data Analysis—5.9.C
MATHEMATICAL PROCESSES 5.1.A, 5.1.F

Essential Question How can you analyze data displayed on a bar graph?

Unlock the Problem (Real World)

A bar graph is useful for comparing and analyzing data.

Sometimes you can make a **prediction** based on data. A prediction is a reasonable guess about what may happen, and may end up being true or false.

Example 1

Mrs. Marzipan sold pretzels in a snack bar in a city park. She recorded the number of pretzels sold each day for 5 days.

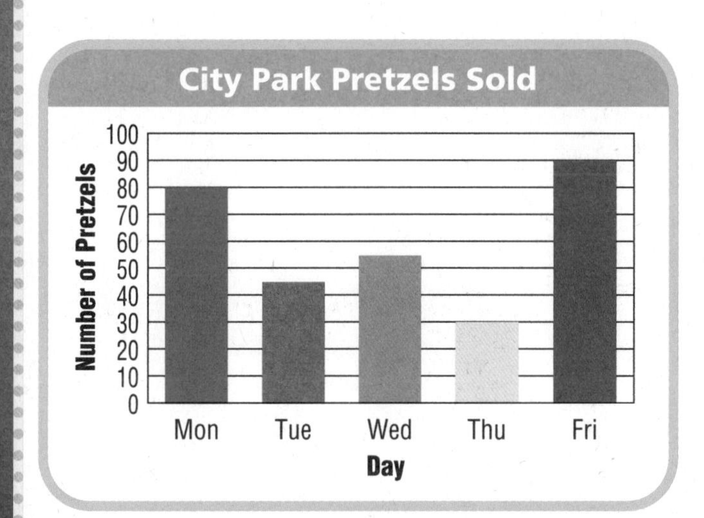

- For how many days did Mrs. Marzipan record the number of pretzels she sold?

___

- What is being compared in this bar graph?

___

___

A Draw a conclusion.

On which day was the greatest number of pretzels sold?

Conclusion: The greatest number of pretzels was sold on ___.

B Make a prediction.

On which day next week will Mrs. Marzipan sell the most pretzels?

Prediction: Next week, Mrs. Marzipan will sell the most pretzels on ___.

Example 2 Solve a multi-step problem.

Students earn $3 for every magazine subscription they sell. How much more money does Aaron earn than Carla?

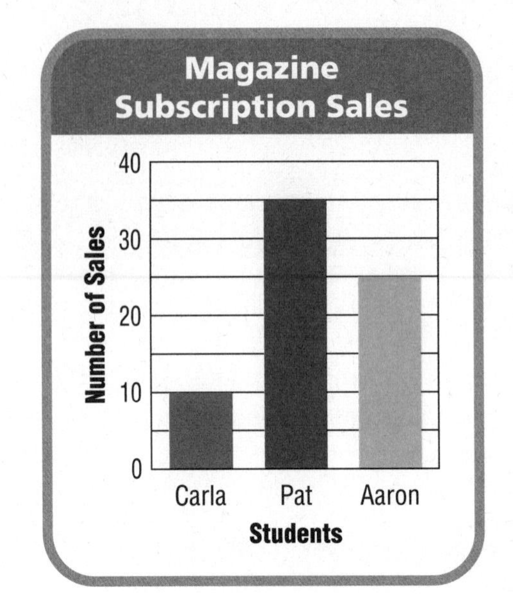

STEP 1 Use the graph to find the number of subscriptions Aaron and Carla each sell.

Aaron: ______ subscriptions

Carla: ______ subscriptions

STEP 2 Multiply to find the amount of money they each earn.

Aaron: ______ × $3 = $______

Carla: ______ × $3 = $______

STEP 3 Subtract to find the difference.

$______ − $______ = $______

So, Aaron earns $______ more selling magazine subscriptions than Carla.

Share and Show

Use the bar graph for 1–2.

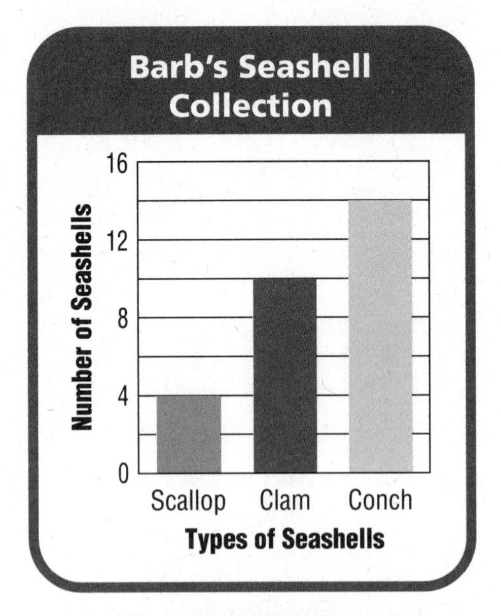

1. How many more clamshells than scallop shells does Barb have?

   number of clamshells: ______

   number of scallop shells: ______

   ______ − ______ = ______

   ______ clamshells

2. What is the total number of seashells in Barb's collection?

   ______

Math Talk

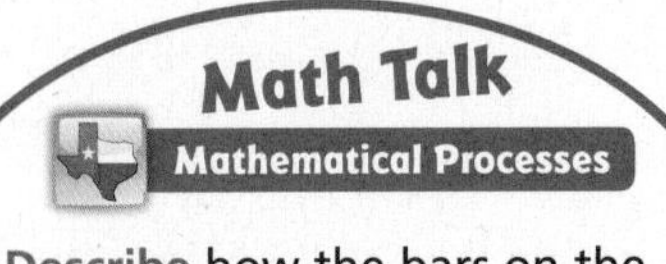

Describe how the bars on the graph would look if Barb had 2 times as many conch shells as clamshells.

Name ___

Problem Solving

The marbles in a bag are red, blue, yellow, and green. Albert draws 20 marbles from the bag and records the results in a bar graph. Use the bar graph for 3–4.

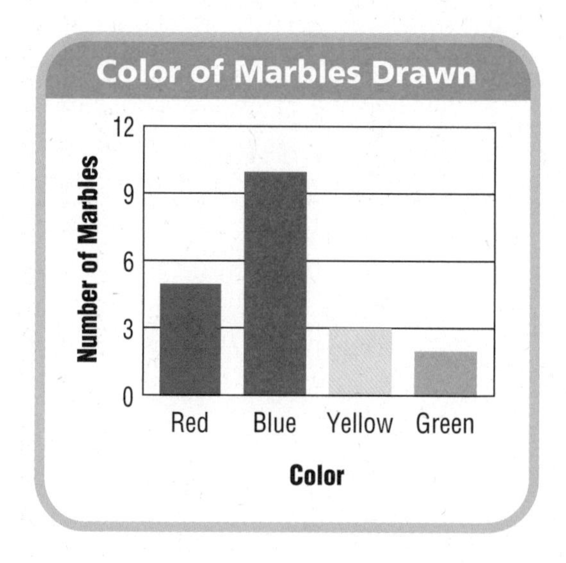

3. **Connect** When you combine the number of two colors of marbles that Albert draws, it is equal to the total number of another color of marbles he draws. Write an equation using color words to represent this relationship.

___

4. 

What color in the bag most likely outnumbers any other color in the bag? **Justify** your answer.

___

___

Problem Solving Real World

Use the graph for 5–6.

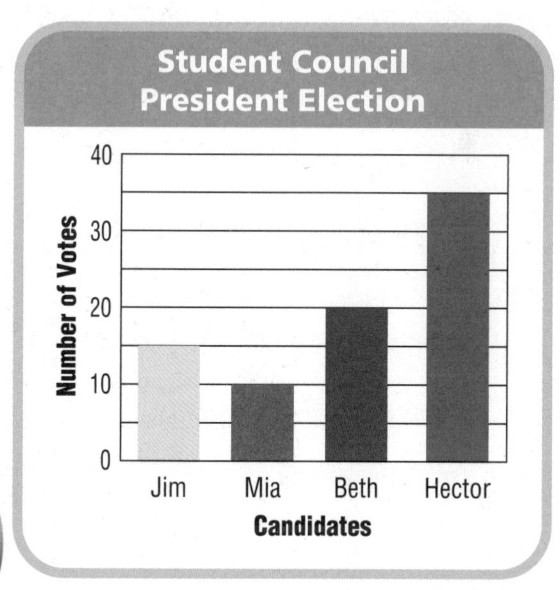

5. **Multi-Step** An article in the school newspaper states that Hector received more than half the votes in the election. Is this statement correct? **Explain.**

___

___

6. H.O.T. **Analyze** Twenty students did not vote in the election. If these students had voted for candidates other than Hector, how might the results of the election be different? Give three different possibilities.

___

___

___

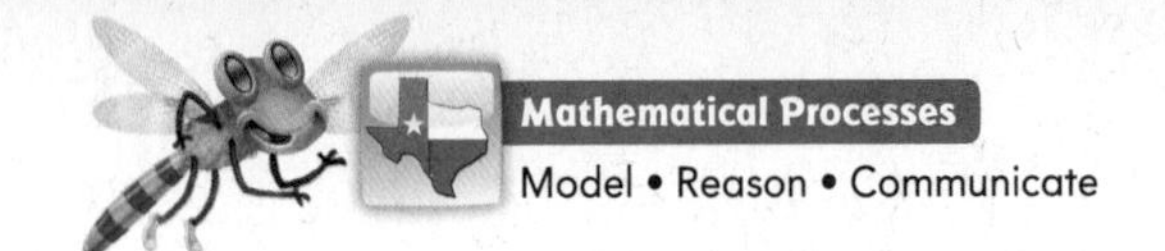

Daily Assessment Task

Use the bar graph for 7–9. Fill in the bubble completely to show your answer.

Amounts of Sauce

Cups of Sauce: 0, 2, 4, 6, 8

Teacher: Steve, Ana, Earl, Jaime

7. The teachers at Marty's school are in a pasta-cooking contest. The bar graph shows the amounts of sauce they use in their recipes. What is the difference between the greatest and least amounts of sauce?

   Ⓐ 7 cups

   Ⓑ 2 cups

   Ⓒ 1 cup

   Ⓓ 6 cups

8. **Analyze** Who could fill more than one 1-quart container with their sauce? Hint: 1 quart = 4 cups

   Ⓐ Steve Ⓒ Earl

   Ⓑ Ana Ⓓ Jaime

9. How much sauce do all the teachers use in their recipes?

   Ⓐ 5 cups Ⓒ 15 cups

   Ⓑ 7 cups Ⓓ 14 cups

TEXAS Test Prep

10. The bar graph shows the number of animals on a farm. The animals eat hay every day. Each horse eats 15 pounds; each cow eats 30 pounds; and each pig eats 1 pound. How much hay do all the farm animals eat in 1 day?

    Ⓐ 46 pounds

    Ⓑ 636 pounds

    Ⓒ 591 pounds

    Ⓓ 33 pounds

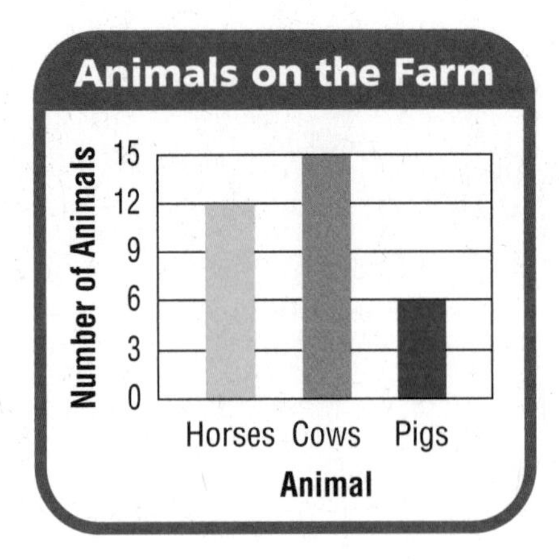

Name ______________________

15.4 Analyze Bar Graphs

A football team uses a bar graph to record and compare the scores for the first four games. Use the bar graph for 1–3.

1. How many more points did the team score in game 4 than in game 2? ____________
2. How many points did the team score in the first three games? ____________
3. What is the total number of points the team scored? ____________

Problem Solving Real World

Students participate in a park clean-up event on Saturday. The principal records the attendance in a bar graph. Use the graph for 4–5.

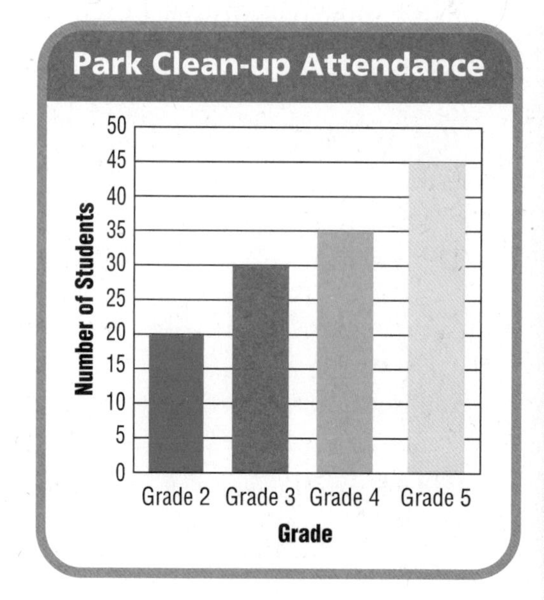

4. Tyler says the fifth graders have more than twice as many participants as the second graders. Is Tyler correct? **Explain.**

____

____

____

5. What if 27 more third graders arrive after lunch to help with the clean up? What is the difference between the number of students in the grade with the greatest attendance and the number of students in the grade with the least attendance? **Explain.**

____

____

____

____

Lesson Check

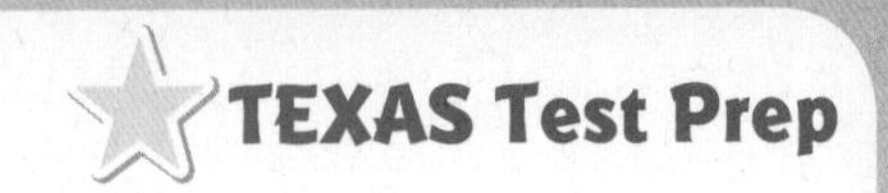

Fill in the bubble completely to show your answer.

6. The bar graph shows the number of hours each person worked at the movie theater on Friday. Al earns $8 an hour, Bob earns $10 an hour, and Elena earns $9.50 an hour. How much will the theater owner pay all three workers on Friday?

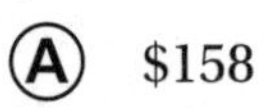

Ⓐ $158

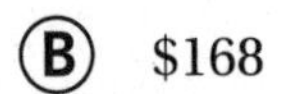

Ⓑ $168

Ⓒ $171

Ⓓ $181

A kennel cares for dogs while their owners are on vacation. The graph shows the amount of food each dog receives each day based on his weight and activity level. Use the graph for 7–9.

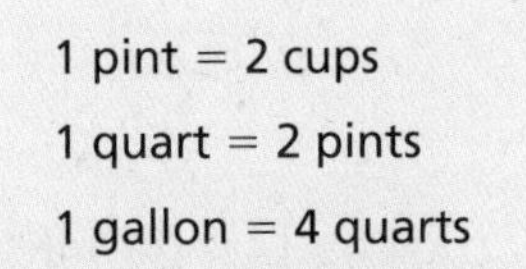

7. Which dog is fed more than 1 quart but less than $\frac{1}{2}$ gallon of food each day?

Ⓐ Buster

Ⓑ Abe

Ⓒ Pepper

Ⓓ Benji

8. **Multi-Step** How much food is Pepper fed in one week?

Ⓐ 7 pints

Ⓑ 7 quarts

Ⓒ 25 cups

Ⓓ 7 gallons

9. **Multi-Step** Which of the following is equivalent to the total amount of dog food all four dogs are fed in one day?

Ⓐ 1 gallon and 1 pint

Ⓑ 8 pints

Ⓒ 3 gallons

Ⓓ 2 quarts and 2 pints

Name ______________________

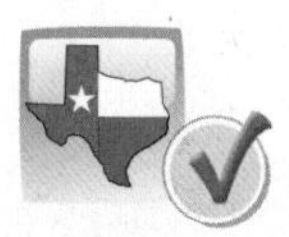

Module 15 Assessment

Vocabulary

Choose the best term from the box.

Vocabulary
frequency table
bar graph
frequency
prediction

1. A ______________ is a graph that uses horizontal or vertical bars to display countable data. (p. 557)

2. A ______________ is a reasonable guess about what may happen, and may end up being true or false. (p. 563)

3. A ______________ is a table that uses numbers to record data about how often something happens. (p. 545)

Concepts and Skills

4. Harry recorded the types of cars in the school parking lot. Make a frequency table of the data. TEKS 5.9.A

Cars in School Parking Lot		
sports car	SUV	sports car
minivan	minivan	SUV
sports car	SUV	minivan
SUV	compact	minivan
compact	minivan	compact

5. Barb conducted a survey of students' favorite breakfast food. She recorded the results in a frequency table. Make a bar graph of the data. TEKS 5.9.A

Favorite Breakfast Food	
Type of Food	Number of Votes
Yogurt	15
Cereal	35
Fruit	20

Fill in the bubble completely to show your answer.

Use the frequency table for 6–7.

Home Runs	
Player	**Frequency**
Chen	4
Pam	2
Dave	5
Rosa	8

6. How many more home runs did Rosa hit than Pam? TEKS 5.9.C

Ⓐ 8 Ⓒ 4

Ⓑ 2 Ⓓ 6

7. Ryan hit 2 times as many home runs as Dave and Chen combined. How many home runs did Ryan hit? TEKS 5.9.C

Ⓐ 10 Ⓒ 18

Ⓑ 8 Ⓓ 9

Use the bar graph for 8–9.

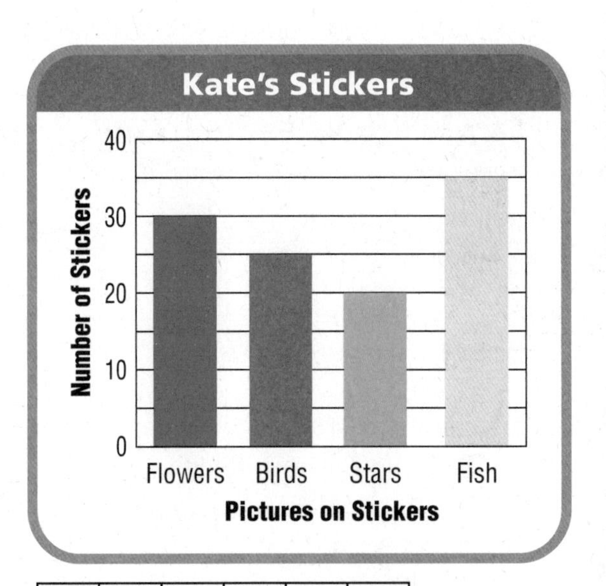

8. Kate puts 5 stickers on each page of a sticker book. How many pages can she fill with fish stickers? TEKS 5.9.C

Ⓐ 5

Ⓑ 4

Ⓒ 7

Ⓓ 6

9. Kate uses half of her flower stickers and half of her star stickers to decorate for a party. How many stickers does she have left in her collection? TEKS 5.9.C

Record your answer and fill in the bubbles on the grid. Be sure to use the correct place value.

			.		
⓪	⓪	⓪		⓪	⓪
①	①	①		①	①
②	②	②		②	②
③	③	③		③	③
④	④	④		④	④
⑤	⑤	⑤		⑤	⑤
⑥	⑥	⑥		⑥	⑥
⑦	⑦	⑦		⑦	⑦
⑧	⑧	⑧		⑧	⑧
⑨	⑨	⑨		⑨	⑨

Name ____________________

16.1 Make Dot Plots

TEKS Data Analysis—5.9.A
MATHEMATICAL PROCESSES
5.1.A, 5.1.D, 5.1.E

Essential Question How can you display data on a dot plot?

A **dot plot** is a graph that shows frequency of data along a number line.

Unlock the Problem

Mia recorded the weight of each bag of apples people picked at an apple orchard.

Weights of Bags of Apples (lb)				
$2\frac{1}{2}$	3	$2\frac{1}{2}$	3	$1\frac{1}{2}$
1	$2\frac{1}{2}$	3	1	$2\frac{1}{2}$

Make a dot plot of the data.

STEP 1 List the data in order from least to greatest.

____

STEP 2 Draw a number line that includes all the numbers on your list.

STEP 3 Mark a dot above each number as many times at it occurs on your list. The number 1 occurs 2 times, so mark 2 dots above 1.

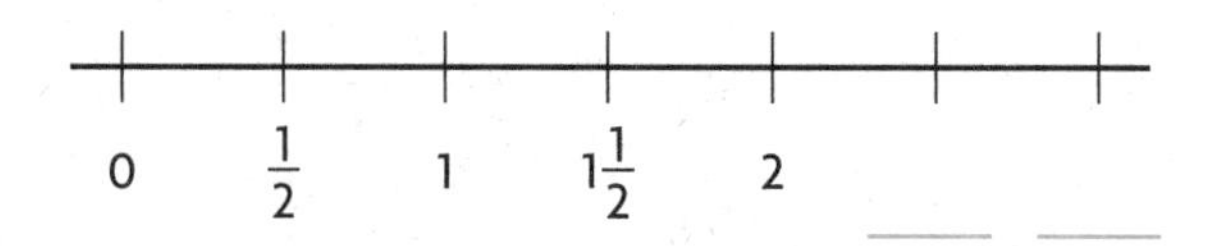

Weights of Bags of Apples (lb)

Math Talk

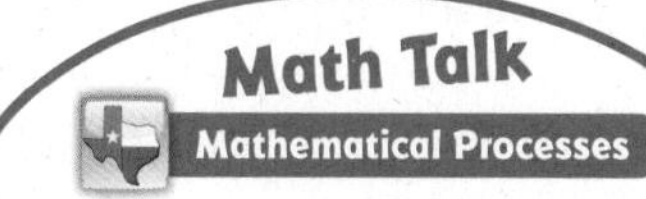

Describe what you observe about the data more easily in the dot plot than in Mia's record.

Try This! **Make a dot plot using decimal data.**

Mike is practicing for a swim meet. His practice times in seconds are 62.5, 63.0, 62.75, 63.0, 63.0, 62.5, 62.5, 62.75, 63.0, 62.0, 62.75, 62.5, 63.0, and 62.5. Make a dot plot of the data.

- List the data in order from least to greatest.

____

____

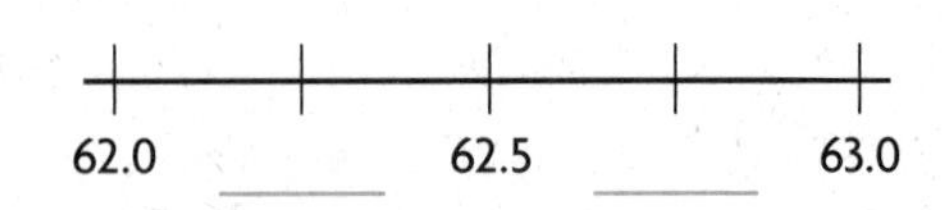

Mike's Practice Times (sec)

- Draw a number line that includes all the numbers on your list.
- Plot the data.

- **Explain** how you can determine if the dot plot correctly shows the data.

____

____

Share and Show

Ana measures the heights of sunflowers in her garden. Use the data for 1–2.

1. Write the data in order from least to greatest.

____

What number will the number line in a dot plot of the data begin with? ______

What number will it end with? ______

How many dots will be on the dot plot? ______

Heights of Sunflowers (ft)			
5	3	5	3
2	6	3	2
6	3	2	6
5	3	2	5

2. Complete the dot plot of the data.

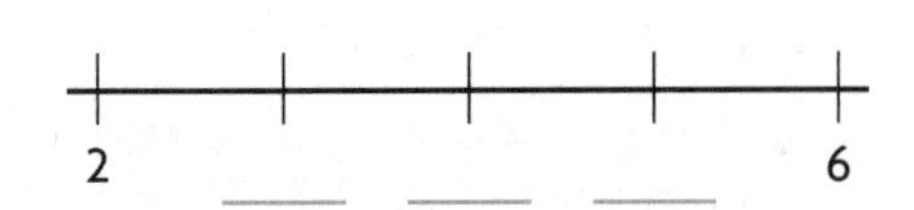

Heights of Sunflowers (ft)

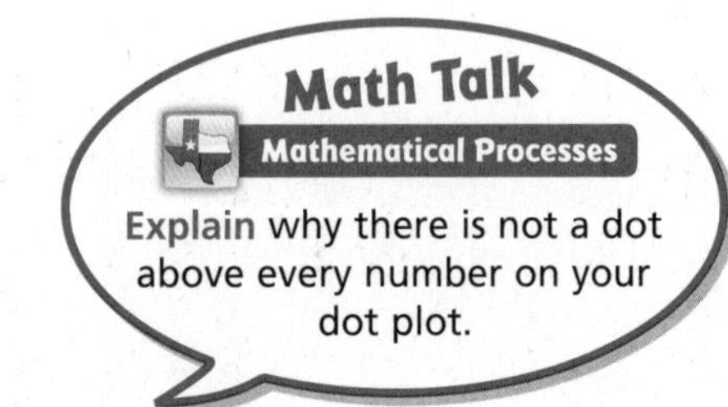

Name ________________________________

Problem Solving

Lily is making a beaded necklace. She makes a list of beads she needs and the mass of each bead. Use the list for 3–4.

Mass of Beads (g)			
$\frac{2}{5}$ g	$\frac{1}{5}$ g	$\frac{3}{5}$ g	$\frac{3}{5}$ g
$\frac{2}{5}$ g	$\frac{2}{5}$ g	$\frac{4}{5}$ g	$\frac{3}{5}$ g
$\frac{4}{5}$ g	$\frac{1}{5}$ g	$\frac{1}{5}$ g	$\frac{2}{5}$ g

3. **Explain** how to determine what numbers to put on the number line for a dot plot of the data.

____

____

____

4. **Multi-Step** Make a dot plot of the data.

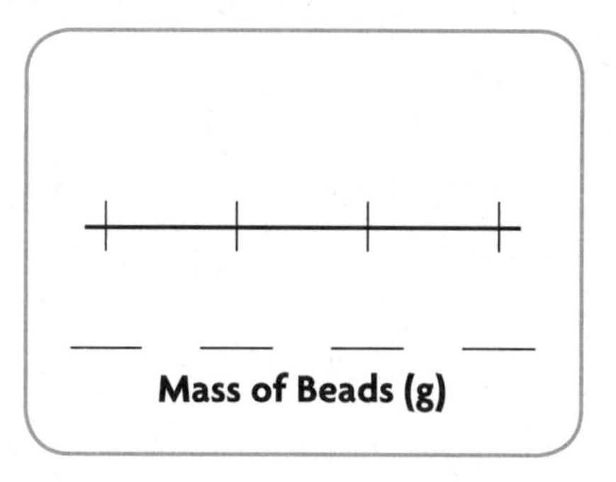

Problem Solving 

Jeanette kept a record of the distances she jumped practicing the long jump. She made a dot plot of the data. Use the record and the dot plot for 5–6.

5. **H.O.T. Multi-Step** Jeanette made more than one error on the dot plot. Describe and correct the errors.

____

____

____

____

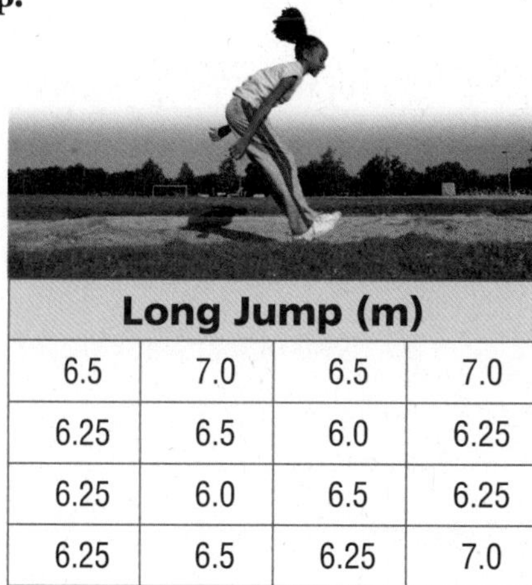

Long Jump (m)			
6.5	7.0	6.5	7.0
6.25	6.5	6.0	6.25
6.25	6.0	6.5	6.25
6.25	6.5	6.25	7.0

6.0 6.25 6.5 6.75

Long Jump (m)

6. **H.O.T. Reasoning** If Jeanette jumped each distance shown on the number line an equal number of times, what would the dot plot look like?

____

____

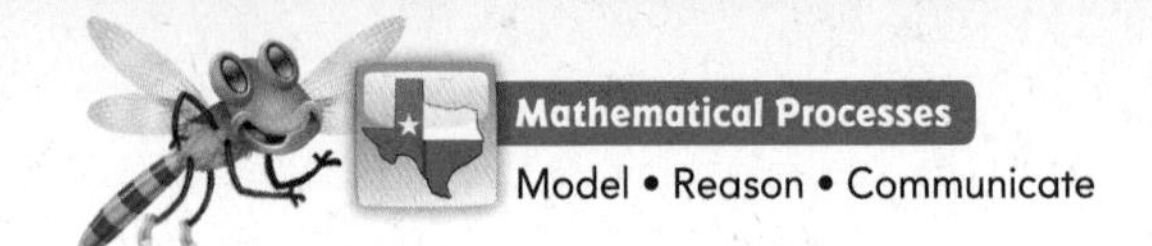

Daily Assessment Task

The table shows the speeds of ants that competed in a go-cart race. Use the data for 7–9. Fill in the bubble completely to show your answer.

Speeds (Miles per Hour)					
6.8	7.1	6.9	6.8	7.1	7.1
6.6	6.8	7.0	6.6	6.8	6.8

7. You are making a dot plot to show the data. Which numbers will you put on the number line for the dot plot?

Ⓐ 6.5, 6.6, 6.7, 6.9, 7.0, 7.1

Ⓑ 6.7, 6.8, 6.9, 7.0, 7.1, 7.2

Ⓒ 6.6, 6.7, 6.8, 6.9, 7.0, 7.1

Ⓓ 6.5, 6.6, 6.7, 6.8, 6.9, 7.0

8. How many dots will you mark above 7.1?

Ⓐ 4

Ⓑ 2

Ⓒ 3

Ⓓ 1

9. **Multi-Step** The go-cart race officials realize that 3 ants in the race should be disqualified. What happens to the dot plot if 3 of the ants with a time of 6.8 miles per hour are removed?

Ⓐ The tallest stack of dots will be above 7.1.

Ⓑ The tallest stack of dots will be above 6.6.

Ⓒ The number of speeds plotted on the dot plot will change to 15.

Ⓓ The dot plot remains the same.

TEXAS Test Prep

10. Sandy has 12 recipes for trail mix. The amount of peanuts in each recipe in cups is $\frac{5}{8}, \frac{3}{8}, \frac{3}{8}, \frac{7}{8}, \frac{7}{8}, \frac{5}{8}, \frac{3}{8}, \frac{3}{8}, \frac{7}{8}, \frac{7}{8}, \frac{5}{8}$, and $\frac{5}{8}$. Sandy makes a dot plot of the data. Which numbers will she put on the number line?

Ⓐ $\frac{3}{8}, \frac{4}{8}, \frac{5}{8}, \frac{6}{8}$

Ⓑ $\frac{3}{8}, \frac{4}{8}, \frac{6}{8}, \frac{7}{8}$

Ⓒ $\frac{4}{8}, \frac{5}{8}, \frac{6}{8}, \frac{7}{8}$

Ⓓ $\frac{3}{8}, \frac{4}{8}, \frac{5}{8}, \frac{6}{8}, \frac{7}{8}$

Name ______________________

16.1 Make Dot Plots

Mrs. O'Malley makes a list to show the miles each dance student travels to the practice center. Use the list for 1–2.

Distance (miles)			
1	2	3	$2\frac{1}{2}$
$2\frac{1}{2}$	$1\frac{1}{2}$	$1\frac{1}{2}$	$2\frac{1}{2}$
$2\frac{1}{2}$	2	3	$1\frac{1}{2}$

1. What is the least distance traveled? What is the greatest distance traveled?

____

2. Make a dot plot of the data.

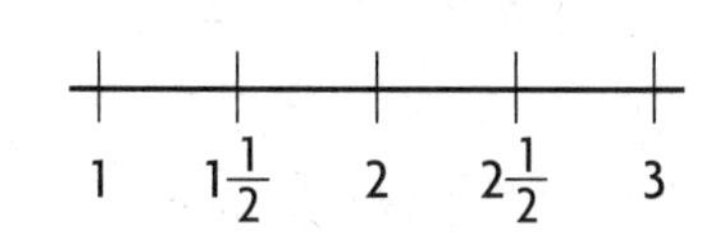

Problem Solving Real World

Colton has a list of the length of each song in his favorites playlist. He makes a dot plot of the data. Use the list and the dot plot for 3–4.

Length of Songs (minutes)			
4.0	2.5	2.5	3.0
4.0	3.5	3.0	2.5
3.0	3.5	4.0	3.5
3.5	3.0	3.5	4.0

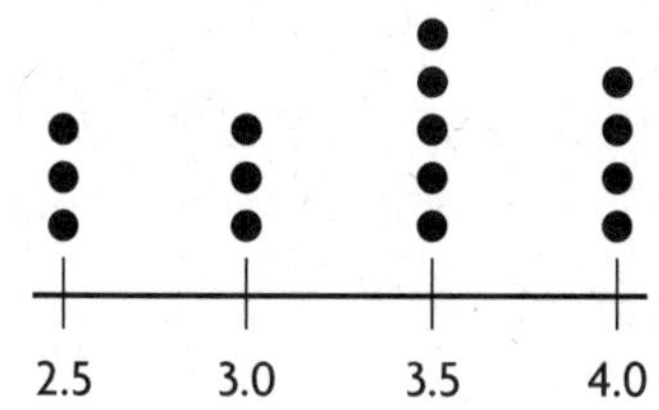

3. Colton counts the number of dots in his dot plot and the data in his list and finds that the numbers are not equal. Explain Colton's error and how he can fix it.

____

____

____

____

4. Colton deletes one song with a length of 3.5 minutes from his playlist and adds one song with a length of 4.0 minutes. How will the dot plot of the data change?

____

____

Lesson Check

TEXAS Test Prep

Fill in the bubble completely to show your answer.

5. The heights of the girls in Leila's class to the nearest $\frac{1}{2}$ inch are: $56\frac{1}{2}$, 57, $56\frac{1}{2}$, 58, 58, $57\frac{1}{2}$, $57\frac{1}{2}$, 57, $58\frac{1}{2}$, and 57. Leila makes a dot plot of the data. How many different heights will be included on the number line?

Ⓐ 10
Ⓑ 5
Ⓒ 3
Ⓓ 9

6. A geologist measures the mass of some rocks to the nearest tenth of a gram and makes a dot plot of the data. The masses are: 5.3, 5.5, 5.6, 5.4, 5.4, 5.3, 5.8, 5.7, 5.8, 5.5, 5.5, and 5.3 grams. She lists two numbers on the number line. How many more numbers will she put on the number line?

Ⓐ 2
Ⓑ 3
Ⓒ 4
Ⓓ 5

A paleontologist measures the lengths of several fossils. The table shows the lengths to the nearest tenth of a centimeter. Use the data for 7–10.

Lengths (cm)				
7.9	7.8	8.1	8.2	7.8
7.8	7.9	8.1	7.8	7.9
7.9	8.1	7.9	7.8	7.9

7. Which numbers will you put on the number line for the dot plot?

Ⓐ 7.8, 7.9, 8.0, 8.1, 8.2
Ⓑ 7.9, 7.8, 8.1, 8.2, 7.8
Ⓒ 7.9, 8.1, 8.2, 8.3, 8.4
Ⓓ 7.8, 7.9, 8.1, 8.2, 8.3

8. Which number will not have any dots marked above?

Ⓐ 7.8
Ⓑ 8.0
Ⓒ 8.1
Ⓓ 8.2

9. **Multi-Step** What is the difference between the total number of dots and the number of dots above the number with the most dots?

Ⓐ 10
Ⓑ 9
Ⓒ 8
Ⓓ 14

10. **Multi-Step** The paleontologist measures the fossils again and finds two errors. Two fossils with a length of 7.9 centimeters instead measure 8.1 and 8.2 centimeters. Which two numbers will have the same number of dots?

Ⓐ 7.8 and 7.9
Ⓑ 8.0 and 8.2
Ⓒ 7.8 and 8.1
Ⓓ 7.9 and 8.1

Name ______________________________

16.2 Analyze Dot Plots

TEKS Data Analysis—5.9.C

MATHEMATICAL PROCESSES 5.1.A, 5.1.B, 5.1.F

Essential Question How can you analyze data displayed on a dot plot?

Unlock the Problem

You can identify the greatest and least numbers in a set of data on a dot plot.

Example 1

Members of a hiking club made a dot plot of the distances they hiked. What is the greatest distance they hiked? What is the least distance?

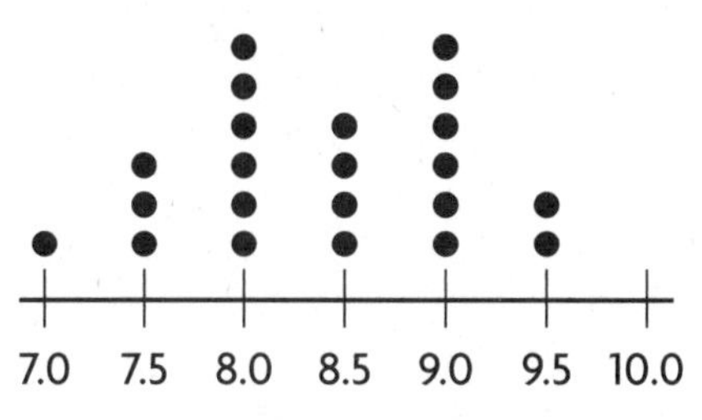

The greatest number on the number line that has a dot above it is ______.

So, the greatest distance they hiked is ______ kilometers.

The least number on the number line that has a dot above it is ______.

So, the least distance they hiked is ______ kilometers.

The difference between the greatest and least numbers in a group is the **range**. What is the range of distances the hiking club hiked?

Subtract the least distance from the greatest distance.

______ km − ______ km = ______ km

The difference between the greatest and least distances is ______ kilometers.

So, the range is ______ kilometers.

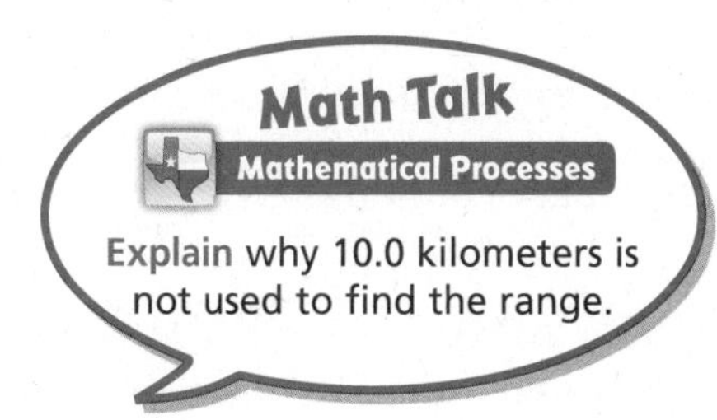

Example 2 Solve a multi-step problem.

A breakfast chef uses three different amounts of milk when making pancakes, depending on the number of pancakes ordered. The dot plot shows customers' orders for pancakes one morning. How much milk does the chef need to make all the pancakes?

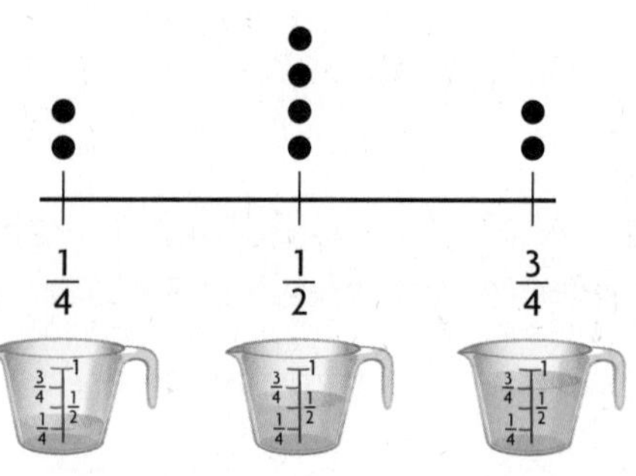

Milk in Pancake Orders (cups)

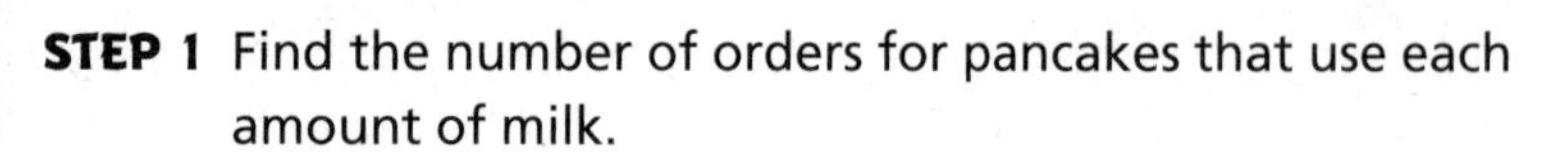

STEP 1 Find the number of orders for pancakes that use each amount of milk.

_____ dots above $\frac{1}{4}$: _____ orders that use $\frac{1}{4}$ cup of milk

_____ dots above $\frac{1}{2}$: _____ orders that use $\frac{1}{2}$ cup of milk

_____ dots above $\frac{3}{4}$: _____ orders that use $\frac{3}{4}$ cup of milk

STEP 2 Find the amount of milk needed for the orders that use each amount of milk.

$\frac{1}{4} \times$ _____ = _____ cup

$\frac{1}{2} \times$ _____ = _____ cups

$\frac{3}{4} \times$ _____ = _____ cups

STEP 3 Add to find the total amount of milk.

_____ cup + _____ cups + _____ cups = _____ cups

So, the chef needs _____ cups of milk to make all the pancakes.

Share and Show

Ana made a dot plot to show the ages of students in the science club. Use the dot plot for 1–3.

8 9 10 11 12

Ages of Students in Science Club (Years)

1. How many more students are 10 years old than 12 years old?

   number of dots above 10: _____

   number of dots above 12: _____

   _____ − _____ = _____

2. The same number of students are what two ages?

   _____

3. What is the range of ages of students in the science club?

   _____

Name ______________________________

Problem Solving

Use the dot plot for 4–5.

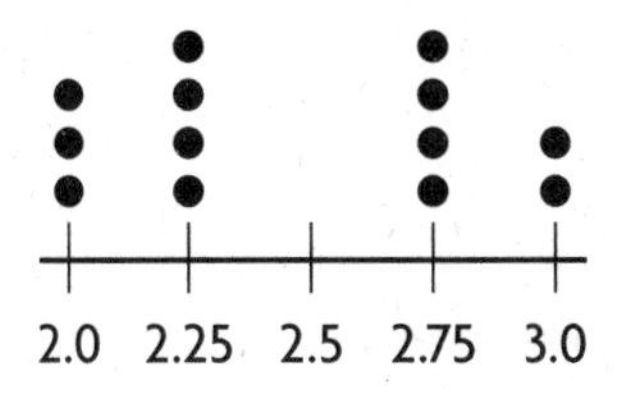

4. **H.O.T.** **Communicate** Describe a situation that could be represented by this dot plot. Give the dot plot a title.

____

____

____

5. **Multi-Step** Write and solve a problem that uses data from the dot plot.

____

____

Unlock the Problem

6. **H.O.T.** **Multi-Step** For 10 straight days, Samantha measured the amount of food that her cat Dewey ate, recording the results on a dot plot. What is the total amount of food that Dewey ate?

a. What do you need to know? _______________________

____

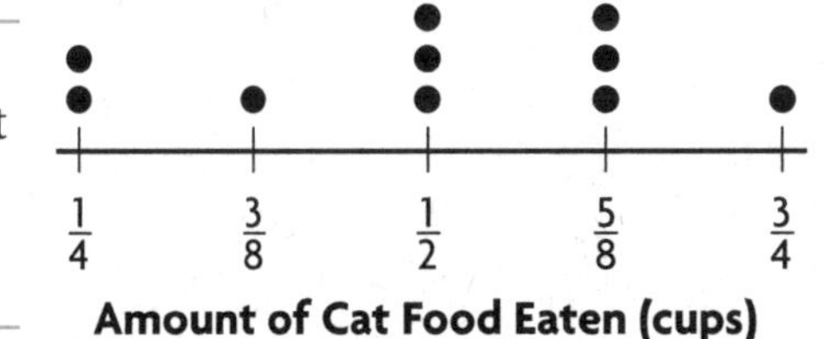

b. What steps could you use to find the total amount of food that Dewey ate?

____

____

c. Fill in the blanks for the totals of each amount measured.

$\frac{1}{4}$ cup: ______ $\frac{5}{8}$ cup: ______

$\frac{3}{8}$ cup: ______ $\frac{3}{4}$ cup: ______

$\frac{1}{2}$ cup: ______

d. Find the total amount of cat food eaten over 10 days.

______ + ______ + ______ + ______ +

______ = ______

So, Dewey ate ______ of cat food.

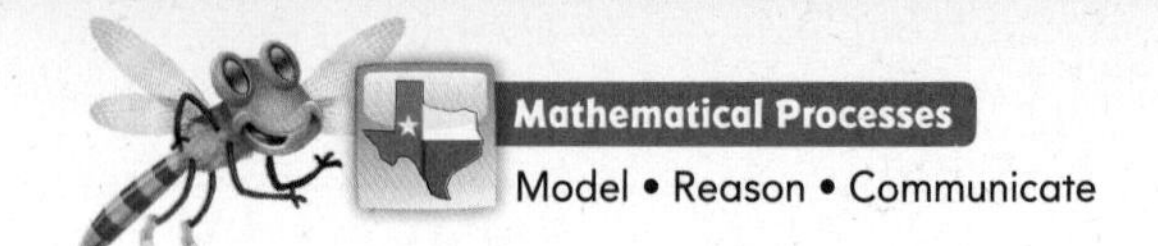

Daily Assessment Task

Fill in the bubble completely to show your answer.

7. **Communicate** Allison is comparing prices of different cell phones. She made a dot plot to show the prices. How can she find the most common price?

   Ⓐ Find the dot all the way to the right.

   Ⓑ Find the dot all the way to the left.

   Ⓒ Find the shortest stack of dots.

   Ⓓ Find the tallest stack of dots.

Use the dot plot for 8–9.

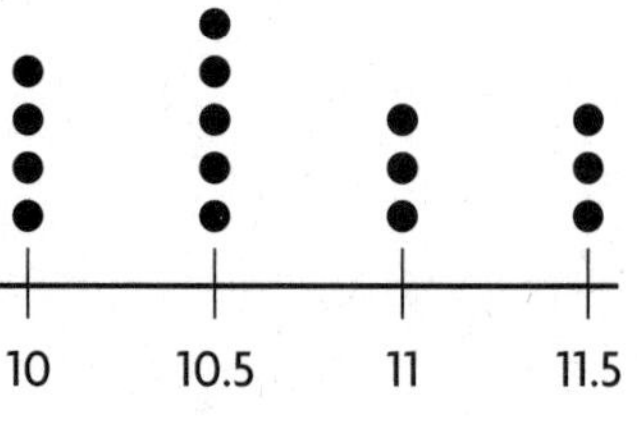

8. How much do the greatest number of pumpkins weigh?

   Ⓐ 11 lb　　Ⓒ 11.5 lb

   Ⓑ 10.5 lb　　Ⓓ 10 lb

9. **Multi-Step** Jane bought all the pumpkins that weigh 10 pounds and 10.5 pounds. What is the total weight of the pumpkins she bought?

   Ⓐ 52.5 lb　　Ⓒ 92.5 lb

   Ⓑ 40 lb　　Ⓓ 81 lb

TEXAS Test Prep

10. The dot plot shows the heights of cornstalks at a farm. The same number of cornstalks are which two heights?

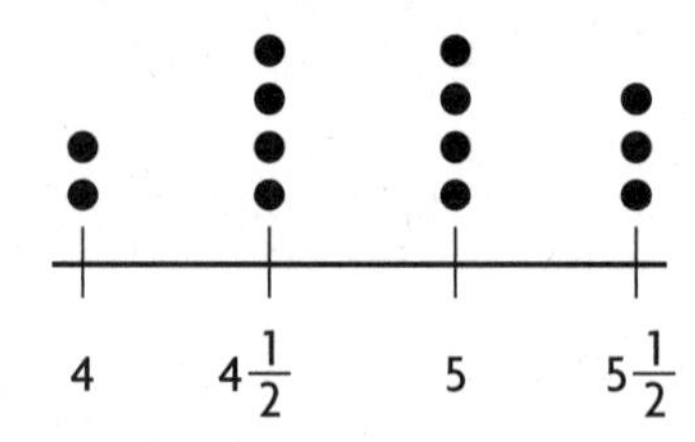

   Ⓐ 5 ft and $5\frac{1}{2}$ ft　　Ⓒ 4 ft and $4\frac{1}{2}$ ft

   Ⓑ $4\frac{1}{2}$ ft and 5 ft　　Ⓓ 4 ft and $5\frac{1}{2}$ ft

Name ______________________

16.2 Analyze Dot Plots

Students in Tony's class made a dot plot of the number of letters in their first name. Use the dot plot for 1–3.

3 4 5 6 7 8

Number of Letters in First Name

1. Write an equation to show how many students have 3, 4, or 5 letters in their name.

____

2. Do more students have first names with fewer than 5 letters or first names with more than 5 letters? **Explain.**

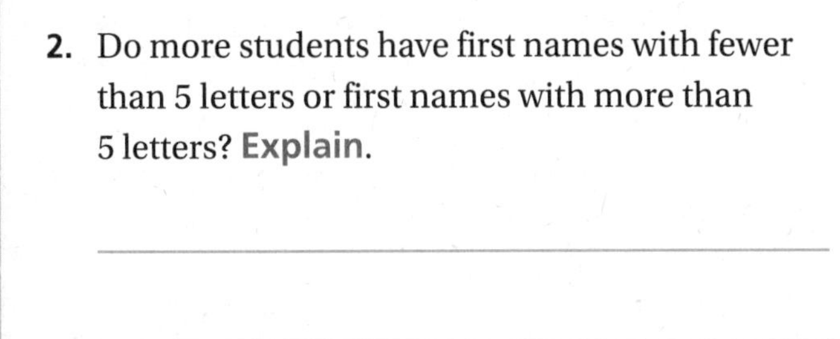

____

3. What is the range of the number of letters in the students' first names? Show how you found your answer.

____

Problem Solving Real World

Use the dot plot for 4–5.

4. Describe a real-world situation that could be represented by the dot plot. Write a title below the dot plot.

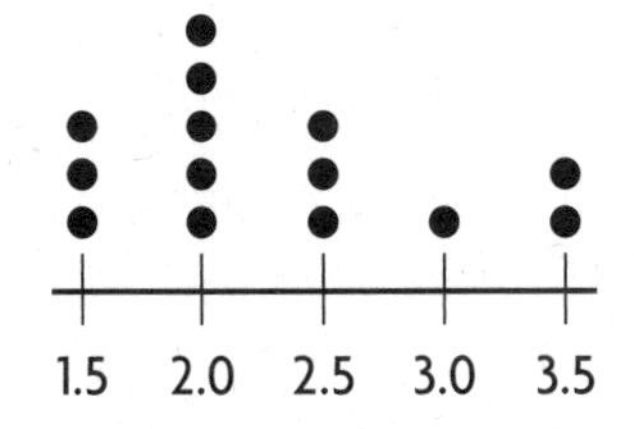

____

5. Write and solve a problem that uses data from the dot plot.

____

Lesson Check

TEXAS Test Prep

Fill in the bubble completely to show your answer.

6. How long was the greatest number of phone calls?

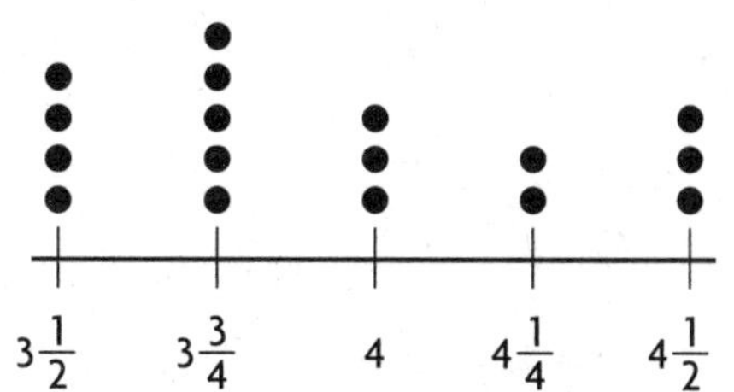

Ⓐ $3\frac{1}{2}$ min

Ⓑ $3\frac{3}{4}$ min

Ⓒ 4 min

Ⓓ $4\frac{1}{2}$ min

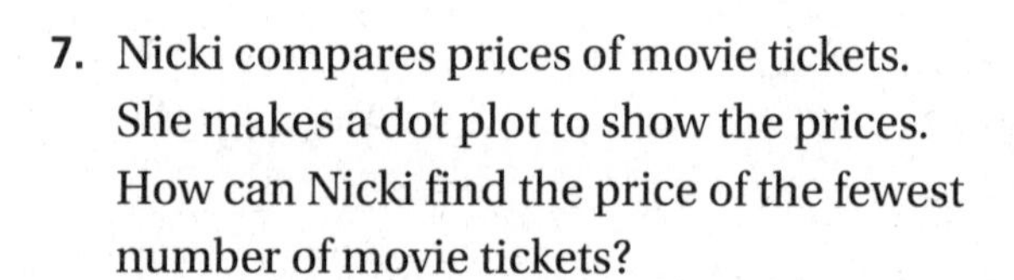

7. Nicki compares prices of movie tickets. She makes a dot plot to show the prices. How can Nicki find the price of the fewest number of movie tickets?

Ⓐ Find the shortest stack of dots.

Ⓑ Find the tallest stack of dots.

Ⓒ Find the difference between the most expensive price and the least expensive price.

Ⓓ Find the dot farthest to the left.

Salads from the restaurant salad bar are sold by the ounce. A restaurant employee made a dot plot to show the weights of salads sold at lunchtime. Use the dot plot for 8–11.

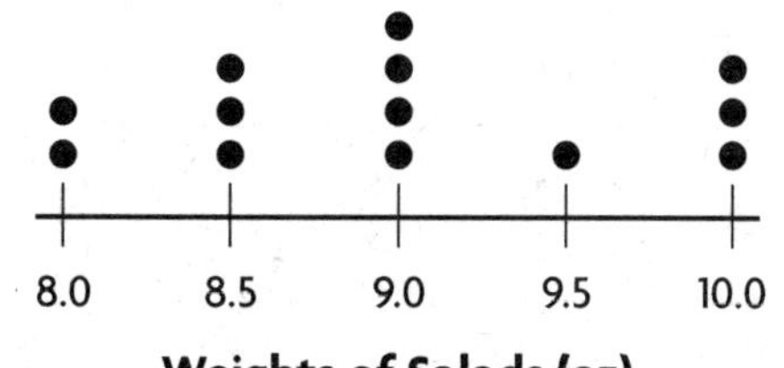

8. How many salads with a weight greater than 8.0 ounces were sold?

Ⓐ 4

Ⓑ 2

Ⓒ 13

Ⓓ 11

9. A total of five salads were sold at which two weights?

Ⓐ 8.0 oz and 8.5 oz

Ⓑ 8.0 oz and 9.0 oz

Ⓒ 8.5 oz and 10 oz

Ⓓ 9.5 oz and 10 oz

10. **Multi-Step** The Ortega family bought all the salads that weigh 9.5 ounces and 10 ounces. What is the total weight of salads they bought?

Ⓐ 30 oz

Ⓑ 19.5 oz

Ⓒ 39.5 oz

Ⓓ 78 oz

11. **Multi-Step** The cost of salad per ounce is $0.50. How much did the restaurant collect for all the salads they sold that weighed 9.0 ounces?

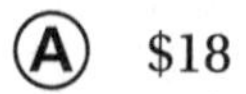

Ⓐ $18

Ⓑ $36

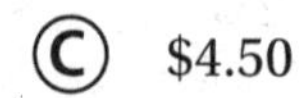

Ⓒ $4.50

Ⓓ $9.50

Name ______________________

16.3 Make Stem-and-Leaf Plots

TEKS Data Analysis—5.9.A

MATHEMATICAL PROCESSES 5.1.D, 5.1.E, 5.1.G

Essential Question How can you display data on a stem-and-leaf plot?

A **stem-and-leaf plot** shows groups of data arranged by place value.

Unlock the Problem (Real World)

Jeremy plays miniature golf every chance he gets. He keeps a record of his scores.

Make a stem-and-leaf plot of the data.

Miniature Golf Scores				
78	67	81	72	62
60	76	65	67	97
80	53	69	82	67

STEP 1 Write a title for the stem-and-leaf plot.

____

STEP 2 Use the tens digits for the stems. Write the tens digits in order from least to greatest.

____

STEP 3 Use the ones digits for the leaves. Write the ones digits for each stem in order from least to greatest.

____

STEP 4 Make a key.

____

Stem	Leaves
5	3
6	0 2 ______
7	2 ______
___	______
___	______

5|3 represents ______.

- **Describe** how the number 80 is shown on the stem-and-leaf plot.

____

- **Explain** how the number that occurs most often in Jeremy's record is shown on the stem-and-leaf plot. What is the number?

____

Try This! **Make a stem-and-leaf plot with hundreds data.**

A group of students do push-ups every morning before school. The number of push-ups they did for the past 12 mornings are 123, 141, 126, 120, 135, 136, 147, 129, 120, 130, 148, and 147. Make a stem-and-leaf plot of the data.

- Write a title.
- Use the hundreds and tens digits to write the stems in order from least to greatest.
- Use the ones digits to write the leaves for each stem in order from least to greatest.

______

Stem	Leaves
12	0 ______
______	______
______	______

12|0 represents ______.

- **Explain** how making a stem-and-leaf plot with hundreds data is similar to making a stem-and-leaf plot with tens data. Explain how it is different.

______

______

______

Share and Show

Ben keeps a record of the heights of his favorite basketball players. Use the data for 1–2.

Heights of Basketball Players (in.)			
82	72	80	78
81	76	69	76
79	70	79	82
74	82	84	79

1. What digits would you use for the stems in a stem-and-leaf plot of the data?

   ______

   How many leaves would a stem-and-leaf plot of the data have? ______

2. Make a stem-and-leaf plot of the data.

______

Stem	Leaves
______	______
______	______
______	______

6|9 represents ______.

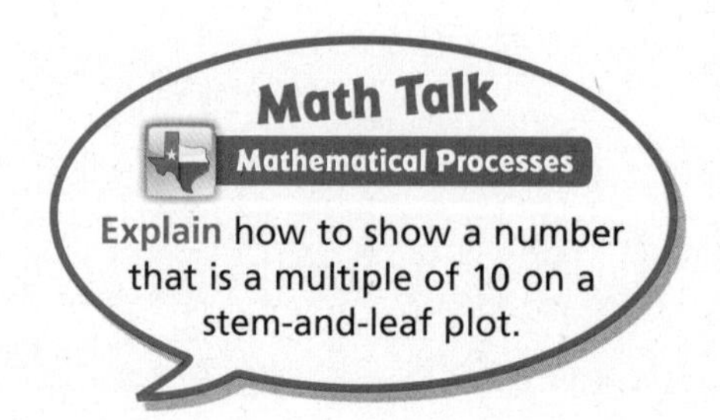

Name ______________________

Problem Solving

3. **H.O.T.** **Representations** Marco made a stem-and-leaf plot titled Game Scores. Each stem has at least 1 leaf. Ten numbers on the stem-and-leaf plot are less than 18 and 8 numbers are 18 or more. The number 10 occurs most often. Draw Marco's stem-and-leaf plot.

Game Scores

Stem	Leaves
0	
1	
2	
3	

____ | ____ represents ____ .

4. **Communicate** How is a number less than 10 shown on a stem-and-leaf plot?

____

Problem Solving

Students were asked how many minutes it took them to get to school. Their responses in minutes were 25, 15, 29, 12, 30, 7, 26, 15, 23, 15, 21, 5, 27, 34, and 32. Use the data for 5–6.

Stem	Leaves

____ | ____ represents ____ .

5. **Representations** Make a stem-and-leaf plot of the data.

6. **Multi-Step** If 5 and 7 minutes are changed to 45 and 47 minutes, how will the stem-and-leaf plot change?

____

____

A salesperson earns a different amount of money each day. The amounts she earns in dollars are 325, 326, 311, 329, 325, 310, 301, 319, 329, 311, 304, 322, 311, 301, and 328. Use the data for 7–8.

Stem	Leaves

____ | ____ represents ____ .

7. **Explain** how to determine what digits to use for stems in a stem-and-leaf plot of the data.

____

____

8. **H.O.T.** **Multi-Step** Make a stem-and-leaf plot of the data.

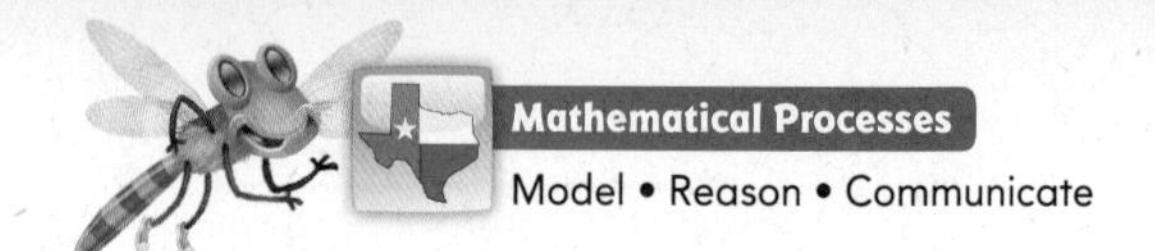

Daily Assessment Task

Fill in the bubble completely to show your answer.

9. Mark visits several bakeries. At each bakery, he asks how many cranberries they use to make a dozen cranberry muffins. Mark wants to use a stem-and-leaf plot to show the data. What are the leaves for the stem of 7?

Number of Cranberries in a Dozen Muffins						
52	58	71	70	68	66	54
57	61	73	70	62	55	80

Ⓐ 0, 0, 1, 3, 5

Ⓑ 0, 1, 3, 5

Ⓒ 0, 1, 3

Ⓓ 0, 0, 1, 3

Use the table for 10 and 11.

Ages of People at Peach Festival							
9	18	20	35	1	14	22	6
16	8	10	26	33	2	18	5

10. Pam is making a stem-and-leaf plot to show the peach festival data. What is the fewest number of stems that she needs?

Ⓐ 3　　Ⓒ 4

Ⓑ 2　　Ⓓ 5

11. **Multi-Step** How many more leaves will be on the stem of 1 than the stem of 3?

Ⓐ 2　　Ⓒ 4

Ⓑ 1　　Ⓓ 3

TEXAS Test Prep

12. Mavis has 19 crossword puzzle books. The number of puzzles in each book is 42, 17, 20, 25, 43, 36, 42, 30, 29, 19, 22, 28, 47, 35, 42, 18, 20, 45, and 31. She makes a stem-and-leaf plot of the data. Which stem will have 4 leaves?

Ⓐ stem 3

Ⓑ stem 1

Ⓒ stem 2

Ⓓ stem 4

TEKS Data Analysis—5.9.A
MATHEMATICAL PROCESSES 5.1.D, 5.1.E, 5.1.G

Name ______________________

16.3 Make Stem-and-Leaf Plots

The number of points scored by the members of a basketball team are recorded. Use the data for 1–2.

Points Scored			
12	24	28	26
32	8	15	16
20	34	26	34

1. What digits would you use for the stems in a stem-and-leaf plot of the data? ____________

   How many leaves would a stem-and-leaf plot of the data have? ____________

2. Make a stem-and-leaf plot of the data.

Stem	Leaves

0|8 represents ____.

3. Explain the difference between stems and leaves on a stem-and-leaf plot.

____

____

____

Problem Solving Real World

Bird watchers were asked how many different species of birds they identified on a recent trip. Their responses were 15, 20, 30, 32, 21, 33, 18, 19, 29, 27, 29, 25, 21, and 26. Use the data for 4–5.

4. Make a stem-and-leaf plot of the data.

Stem	Leaves

1|5 represents ____.

5. If two more bird watchers identify 9 species and 41 species, how will the stem-and-leaf plot change?

____

____

Lesson Check

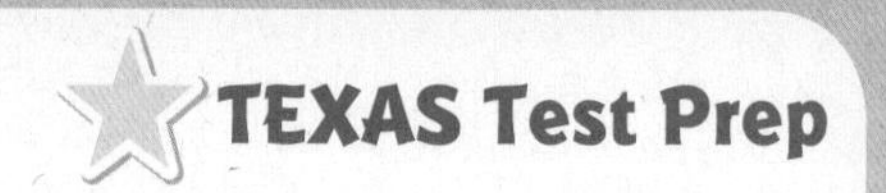

Fill in the bubble completely to show your answer.

6. Maxwell has 14 books in the same mystery series. The number of pages in each book are 112, 108, 95, 88, 96, 105, 115, 114, 85, 87, 90, 96, 116, and 98. Maxwell makes a stem-and-leaf plot of the data. Which stem has the most leaves?

   Ⓐ 9

   Ⓑ 11

   Ⓒ 10

   Ⓓ 8

7. Zara counts the number of raisins in several boxes of raisins. She wants to make a stem-and-leaf plot to show the data.

Number of Raisins in a Box					
72	80	88	95	98	75
90	86	91	95	74	88

   What are the leaves for the stem 9?

   Ⓐ 0, 1, 5, 8

   Ⓑ 0, 1, 5, 5, 8

   Ⓒ 1, 5, 8

   Ⓓ 1, 5, 5, 8

Lincoln Heights Elementary held a student council election. The data show the number of votes each candidate received. Wesley makes a stem-and-leaf plot of the data. Use the table for 8–11.

Number of Votes				
41	30	47	44	50
43	32	52	60	64
45	53	44	34	35

8. What is the number of stems that Wesley needs?

   Ⓐ 15

   Ⓑ 5

   Ⓒ 4

   Ⓓ 3

9. Which statement about the stem-and-leaf plot is true?

   Ⓐ There will be more stems than leaves.

   Ⓑ The stem 6 will have only 1 leaf.

   Ⓒ There will be 15 leaves.

   Ⓓ The number that occurs most often is 4.

10. **Multi-Step** How many more leaves will be on the stem of 4 than the stem of 3?

   Ⓐ 1

   Ⓑ 6

   Ⓒ 4

   Ⓓ 2

11. **Multi-Step** How many stems will have more than 3 leaves?

   Ⓐ 2

   Ⓑ 1

   Ⓒ 3

   Ⓓ 4

Name ___________________________

16.4 Analyze Stem-and-Leaf Plots

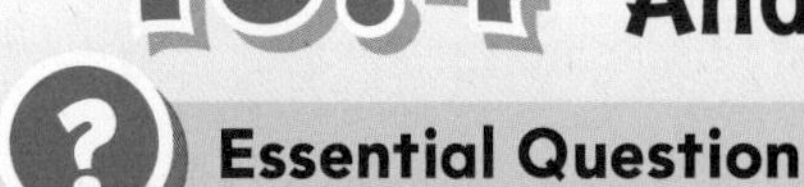

How can you analyze data displayed on a stem-and-leaf plot?

Unlock the Problem (Real World)

A stem-and-leaf plot is useful when you need to see every item in a data set to solve a problem.

Example 1

The stem-and-leaf plot shows the points scored by hockey players this season. The average number of points scored last season was 35. How many players' scores are greater than last year's average? What are the scores?

Points Scored by Hockey Players

Stem	Leaves
2	6 8
3	0 1 2 4 5 6 6 7
4	3 7 9 9 9
5	0 1

2|6 represents 26.

- Locate 35 on the stem-and-leaf plot.

  stem: _______ leaf: _______

- Count the numbers greater than 35.

  There are _______ numbers greater than 35.

So, _______ players' scores are greater than last year's average.

The scores are ____.

Math Talk

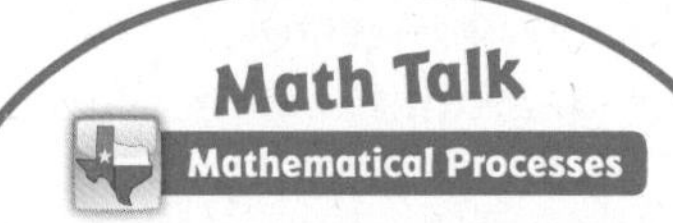

Describe another conclusion you can draw about the data in the stem-and-leaf plot.

- How many points did the greatest number of players score? Explain.

____

____

Example 2 Solve a multi-step problem.

The stem-and-leaf plot shows the amounts of money the first 32 customers spent at the opening of an electronics store. Customers who spent $50 or more received a $12 coupon. Customers who spent less than $50 received a $7 coupon. What is the total value of the coupons the customers received?

STEP 1 Find the number of customers who spent $50 or more. Multiply the number by $12.

_____ × $12 = $_____

STEP 2 Find the number of customers who spent less than $50. Multiply the number by $7.

_____ × $7 = $_____

STEP 3 Add to find the total value of the coupons.

$_____ + $_____ = $_____

So, the total value of the coupons is $_____.

Money Spent by Customers ($)

Stem	Leaves
3	3 4 6 7 9
4	1 2 3 4 5 6 7 8
5	0 5 5 6
6	2 6 6 8
7	0 2 3 4 5
8	4 6 7 7 7 9

3|3 represents 33.

Share and Show

Students made a stem-and-leaf plot to show daily high temperatures. Use the stem-and-leaf plot for 1–3.

1. What is the range of temperatures?

greatest temperature: _____ °F

least temperature: _____ °F

_____ − _____ = _____

The range is _____ °F.

Daily High Temperatures (°F)

Stem	Leaves
6	4 8 8
7	4 5
8	0 0 7 7 7 8 8 9 9 9
9	1 2 3 3 4 5 8

6|4 represents 64.

2. On how many more days was the high temperature in the 80s than the 90s?

_____

3. What were the temperatures on the days when it was less than 80°F?

_____

Name ____________________

Problem Solving

4. H.O.T. **What's the Error?** Jenny made this stem-and-leaf plot. She says that on the days when she did homework for less than 50 minutes, she spent a total of 5 hours doing homework. What's the error?

Daily Homework Time (min)

Stem	Leaves
3	1 2 3 5 6
4	0 3 3 7
5	5 6 7 7 9 9
6	0 0 2
7	4 6 6 7

3|1 represents 31.

5. H.O.T. **Multi-Step** Pablo started to make a stem-and-leaf plot. He wrote the stems for the data: 1, 2, 3, 4, 5, and 6. He also wrote this key: 2|4 = 24. What is the least possible range of the data? What is the greatest possible range? **Explain.**

Problem Solving Real World

The stem-and-leaf plot shows the number of text messages Chester received each day for 24 days. Use the stem-and-leaf plot for 6–7.

6. H.O.T. **Multi-Step** On the days that Chester received more than 50 text messages, he responded to only $\frac{1}{3}$ of the messages. How many text messages did Chester respond to?

Text Messages

Stem	Leaves
2	4 5 7
3	0 2 5 5 6 6 6 7 8 8
4	0 0 3 4 9
5	0 1
6	2 2 4 4

2|4 represents 24.

7. Write Math **Explain** how you can use the stem-and-leaf plot to make a reasonable prediction about the number of text messages Chester will receive each day next week.

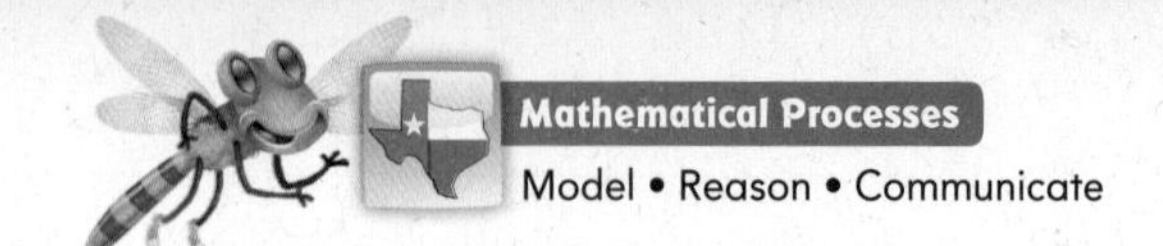

Daily Assessment Task

Fill in the bubble completely to show your answer.

Use the stem-and-leaf plot for 8–10.

Amounts of Money Found (¢)

Stem	Leaves
4	5 6
5	2 2 7 8
6	3 4 9
7	0 0 1
8	3 7

5|2 represents 52.

8. Tom asked people in a survey how much money they could find under their sofa cushions. The stem-and-leaf plot shows the amounts of money. What is the least amount of money a person said they could find?

Ⓐ 4¢
Ⓑ 45¢
Ⓒ 46¢
Ⓓ 456¢

9. Which statement about the data is true?

Ⓐ Two people each found 70¢.
Ⓑ Two people each found 7¢.
Ⓒ One person found 56¢.
Ⓓ Eight people found 37¢.

10. **Multi-Step** Suppose Tom gives two concert tickets to everyone who participates in the sofa cushion survey. How many tickets does he give away?

Ⓐ 10 tickets
Ⓑ 14 tickets
Ⓒ 28 tickets
Ⓓ 38 tickets

TEXAS Test Prep

11. How many people live less than 40 miles from work?

Ⓐ 4
Ⓑ 10
Ⓒ 9
Ⓓ 11

Distance to Work (mi)

Stem	Leaves
2	1 2 3 7 8 9
3	0 1 4
4	7 8 8 9
5	3 3 3 4 7 9

2|4 represents 24.

TEKS Data Analysis—5.9.C
MATHEMATICAL PROCESSES 5.1.A, 5.1.D, 5.1.F

Name ________________________

16.4 Analyze Stem-and-Leaf Plots

Students made a stem-and-leaf plot to show daily low temperatures. Use the stem-and-leaf plot for 1–3.

Daily Low Temperatures (°F)

Stem	Leaves
2	8 9
3	0 0 1 2 6
4	2 4 5 6 6 6 7 9
5	1 3 5

2 | 8 represents 28.

1. What is the range of temperatures? Write an equation to show how you found your answer.

   ____

2. On how many days was the low temperature in the 20s or the 30s?

   ____

3. What were the temperatures on the days when the low temperature was greater than 45°F?

   ____

Problem Solving Real World

Alexandra posted a video on the Internet of her dog performing a trick. The stem-and-leaf plot shows the number of times Alexandra's video was viewed each minute during a 20-minute period. Use the stem-and-leaf plot for 4–5.

Number of Video Views Each Minute

Stem	Leaves
4	0 2
5	1 1 2
6	0 0 8
7	2 3 4 4 5 9
8	2 2 3 4 4 5

4 | 0 represents 40.

4. The average number of views per minute for a video on a pet owner's website is 60. How many times was the number of views of Alexandra's video less than the average? ________________________

5. Alexandra collects data for the next 5 minutes and finds that the number of views each minute are 88, 86, 95, 87, and 99. Explain how you can use the stem-and-leaf plot to make a reasonable prediction about the popularity of her video.

   ____

   ____

Lesson Check

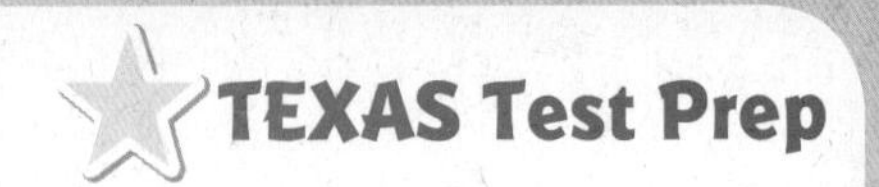

Fill in the bubble completely to show your answer.

6. How many scores are greater than 20?

Ⓐ 9
Ⓑ 3
Ⓒ 7
Ⓓ 5

Points Scored in Carnival Game

Stem	Leaves
0	6 7 7
1	0 1 1 2
2	2 4
3	0 2 2

0 | 6 represents 6

7. **Multi-Step** Half the number of guesses are less than what number?

Ⓐ 83
Ⓑ 73
Ⓒ 74
Ⓓ 79

Guesses for Number of Marbles in a Jar

Stem	Leaves
6	5 5 6 8 9 9
7	2 3 3 8 8 9
8	3 5
9	1 2 3 6

6 | 5 represents 65

The stem-and-leaf plot shows the number of carnival tickets sold each day. Use the stem-and-leaf plot for 8–11.

Carnival Tickets Sold Per Day

Stem	Leaves
3	4 7 7
4	0 1 2 3 4 4
5	2 2 5 6 7 8 9
6	5 6 9
7	0 1 2 3 3

3 | 4 represents 34

8. Ticket sales for the next two days are 55 tickets and 68 tickets. Which statement about the data is true?

Ⓐ The range stays the same.
Ⓑ The range increases by two.
Ⓒ The range decreases.
Ⓓ The range doubles.

9. How many days were carnival tickets sold?

Ⓐ 24 days
Ⓑ 29 days
Ⓒ 20 days
Ⓓ 39 days

10. **Multi-Step** On any day that the number of tickets sold is greater than 70, twice that number of tickets is donated to a children's hospital. How many tickets are donated to the hospital?

Ⓐ 289
Ⓑ 718
Ⓒ 432
Ⓓ 578

11. How many days are the number of tickets sold greater than 40 but less than 55?

Ⓐ 5 days
Ⓑ 7 days
Ⓒ 6 days
Ⓓ 9 days

Name ___________________________

MATHEMATICAL PROCESSES
5.1.A, 5.1.E, 5.1.G

16.5 Make Scatter Plots

Essential Question How can you display data on a scatter plot?

A **scatter plot** is a graph that shows a relationship between two sets of data.

Unlock the Problem Real World

Samantha interviewed shoppers at a mall. She asked them how many hours they had been at the mall and how much money they spent. She recorded their responses in the table.

Spending at the Mall										
Amount of Time (hr)	2	6	3	1	2	2	5	4	1	3
Amount of Money ($)	10	35	17	10	15	18	25	20	5	15

Make a scatter plot to show the relationship between time at the mall and money spent.

STEP 1: Write a title above the graph.

STEP 2: Write ordered pairs that relate the amount of time to the amount of money.

(2, ______), (6, ______), (3, ______), (1, ______), (2, ______),

(2, ______), (5, ______), (4, ______), (1, ______), (3, ______)

STEP 3: Choose a scale that is appropriate for the data on each axis. Then label each axis.

Since the data for the *x*-coordinates are all less than 10, use ______ for the *x*-axis.

Since most of the data for the *y*-coordinates are multiples of 5, use ______ for the *y*-axis.

STEP 4: Graph the ordered pairs.

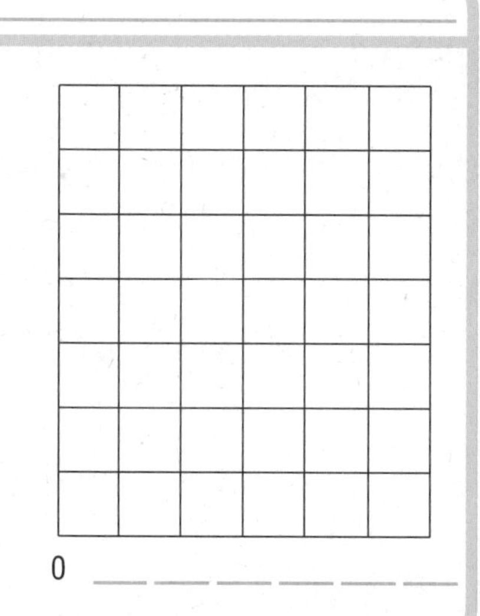

Share and Show

Use the table for 1–2.

1. Write ordered pairs that relate the low daily temperature to the number of coats sold.

   (12, ______), (19, ______), (8, ______), (17, ______), (9, ______),

   (26, ______), (15, ______), (28, ______)

   Choose a scale for the data on each axis of a scatter plot.

   Use ______ for the x-axis. Use ______ for the y-axis.

Shopping in Winter	
Low Daily Temperature (°F)	Number of Coats Sold
12	38
19	31
8	54
17	35
9	49
26	16
15	32
28	11

2. Make a scatter plot of the data.

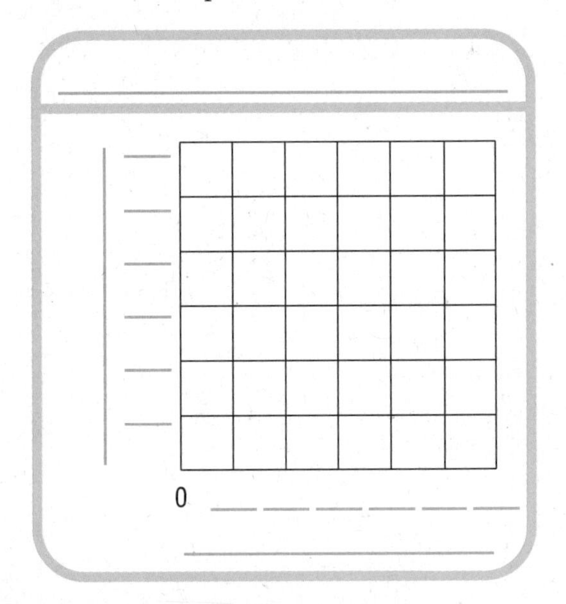

Math Talk

Explain how to use the scatter plot to find the low temperature on the day that 49 coats were sold.

Problem Solving

Jessie recorded the number of students washing cars at a school car wash and the time it took to wash each car. Use the table for 3–4.

Car Wash	
Number of Students	Time (min)
8	4
6	5
5	7
2	10
5	8
1	10

3. What scales would you use for the x- and y-axes of a scatter plot of the data? Explain.

4. H.O.T. What's the Error? Jessie made a scatter plot of the data by plotting points at (8, 4), (6, 5), (5, 7), (10, 2), (5, 8), and (1, 10). What is his error?

Name ______________________________

Problem Solving Real World

Use the table for 5–7.

Age (yr)	Price ($)
6	4,000
3	8,000
5	5,000
9	1,000
8	2,000
4	7,000
7	3,000
2	11,000
10	500
1	18,000

Used Car Sales

5. **Multi-Step** Mrs. Harper is buying a used car. She researched the prices of a particular model of car when it is 1–10 years old and recorded the data in a table. Make a scatter plot of the data.

Price ($)

0

Age (yr)

6. **H.O.T.** Mrs. Harper's friend is also buying a used car. But she is only interested in a car that is more than 5 years old. Would you use the same scales on a scatter plot that shows the prices of the car when it is more than 5 years old? **Explain.**

____

____

____

____

____

7. **Representations** Make a scatter plot showing the data that Mrs. Harper's friend would be interested in. Remember to use scales appropriate for the data.

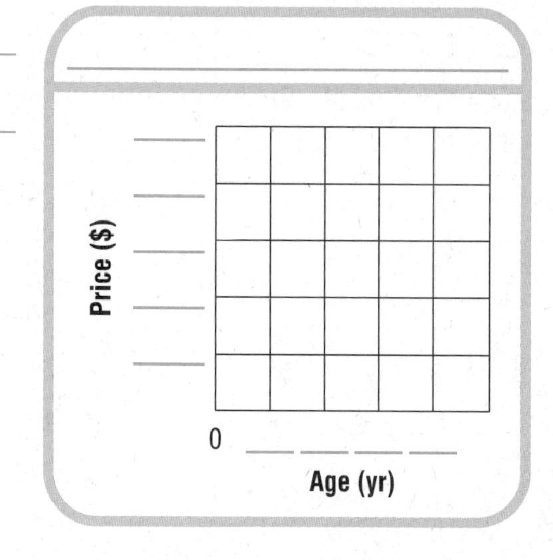

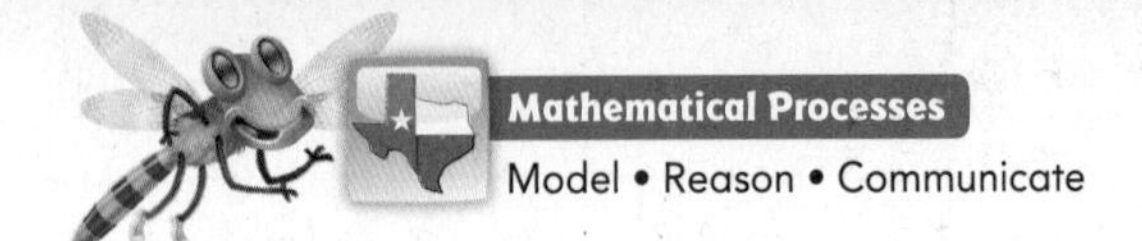

Daily Assessment Task

Fill in the bubble completely to show your answer.

8. A student wants to find the perfect popping time for popcorn. Each time he pops a bag of popcorn, he records the length of time in the microwave and the number of unpopped kernels. He makes a scatter plot of the data. He puts time in seconds on one axis. Which data should be on the other axis?

Ⓐ price of bag of popcorn
Ⓑ number of unpopped kernels
Ⓒ store where bag was bought
Ⓓ amount of popcorn eaten

The scatter plot shows the relationship between the temperature and the number of water bottles sold at a soccer game. Use the scatter plot for 9 and 10.

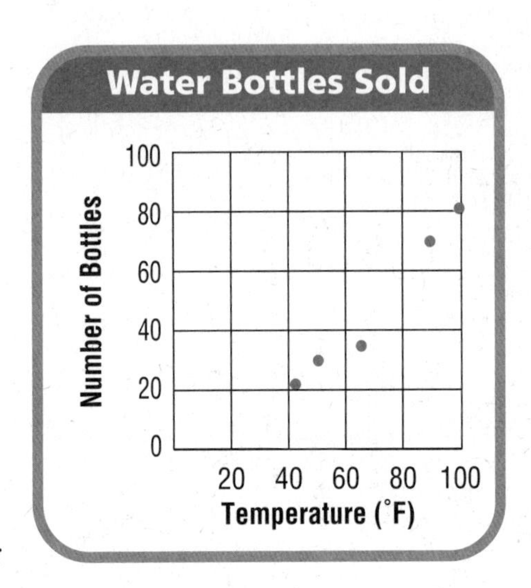

9. You want to add a point on the scatter plot to show that 10 bottles of water were sold when the temperature was 38°F. Where would you add this point to the scatter plot?

Ⓐ bottom right
Ⓑ top right
Ⓒ top left
Ⓓ bottom left

10. **Multi-Step** Suppose one bottle of water costs $1.50. When the temperature was 89°, how much money did people pay for water bottles?

Ⓐ $123
Ⓑ $87
Ⓒ $105
Ⓓ $70

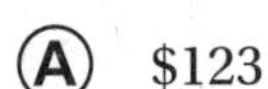

TEXAS Test Prep

11. A storekeeper recorded the number of snow shovels sold during weeks when it snowed.

Which ordered pair would be plotted on a scatter plot of the data?

Snow Shovel Sales						
Weekly Snowfall (in.)	8	2	11	15	3	5
Snow Shovels Sold	16	5	19	25	6	10

Ⓐ (2, 6)
Ⓑ (11, 19)
Ⓒ (5, 25)
Ⓓ (9, 12)

TEKS Data Analysis—5.9.B
MATHEMATICAL PROCESSES 5.1.A, 5.1.E, 5.1.G

Name ____________________

16.5 Make Scatter Plots

Use the table for 1–3.

Quiz Scores								
Hours Studied	1	4	5	2	7	3	4	6
Number of Correct Answers	10	15	25	12	32	14	25	30

1. Write the ordered pairs that relate the number of hours studied to the number of correct answers.

(1, 10), ____________________

____

2. Why is a scale of 1 appropriate for the x-axis? Why is a scale of 5 appropriate for the y-axis?

____

____

____

____

____

3. Make a scatter plot of the data. Remember to use scales appropriate for the data.

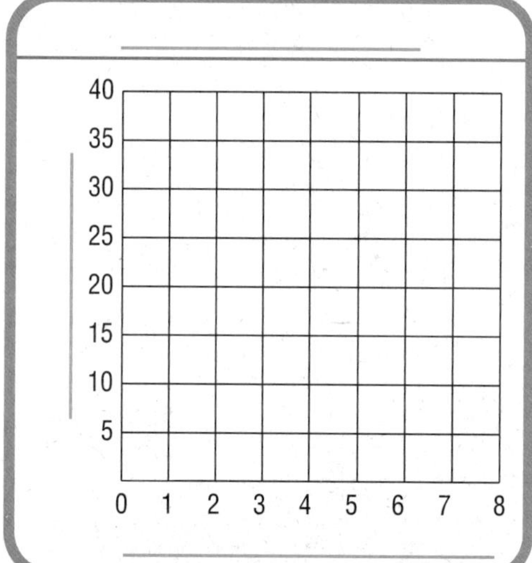

Problem Solving Real World

Use the table for 4–5.

4. Mr. Benson records the gallons of gasoline he has left as he drives his car to Austin. Make a scatter plot of the data.

Gasoline Usage	
Miles Driven	Gas Remaining (gal)
30	15
60	14
90	12
120	10
150	9

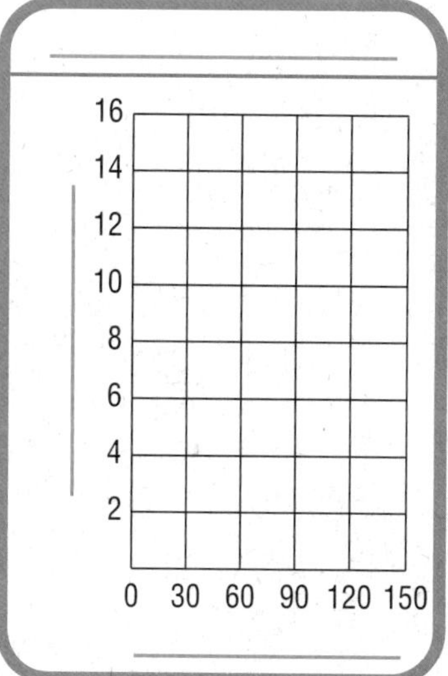

5. If Mr. Benson drives slower on his next trip so he drives more miles on each gallon of gas, should he use the same scales on a scatter plot of the data? **Explain.** ____________________

____

Lesson Check

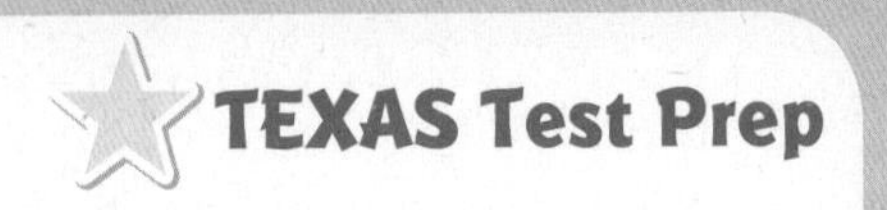

Fill in the bubble completely to show your answer.

6. Sharmeen wants to find the least crowded time to visit the skating rink. She records the temperature outside and the number of skaters at the rink at that time. She makes a scatter plot of the data. She labels one axis "Number of Skaters." Which data should be on the other axis?

   Ⓐ time of day

   Ⓑ number of skaters

   Ⓒ temperature outside

   Ⓓ location of the rink

7. The swim team coach recorded the number of hours each team member practiced each week and the number of ribbons the team member won at the swim meet.

Ribbons Won at Swim Meet					
Time Practiced (hr)	10	14	15	8	12
Ribbons	2	5	5	1	4

Which ordered pair would you plot on a scatter plot of the data?

   Ⓐ (10, 14)   Ⓒ (8, 1)

   Ⓑ (2, 5)   Ⓓ (9, 3)

The scatter plot shows the relationship between the number of hours a waiter worked and the amount of tips received. Use the scatter plot for 8–10.

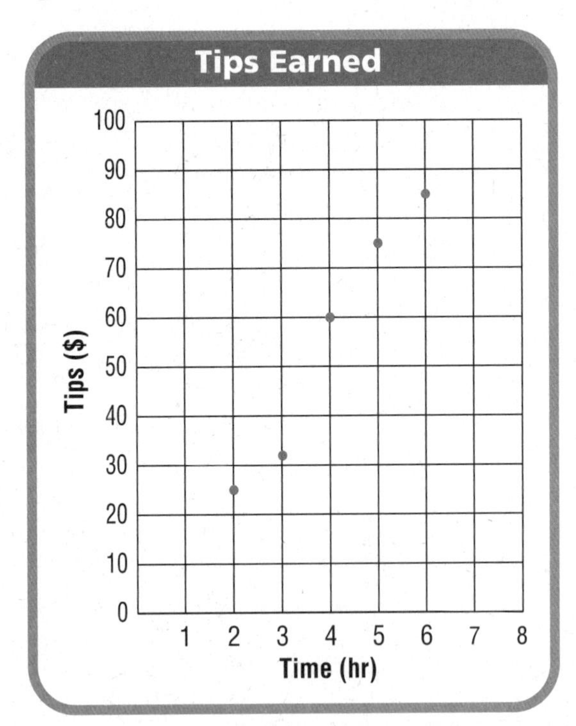

8. You want to add a point on the scatter plot to show that a waiter earned $90 in tips when he worked 7 hours. Where would you add this point on the scatter plot?

   Ⓐ top left

   Ⓑ top right

   Ⓒ bottom left

   Ⓓ bottom right

9. **Multi-Step** A waiter worked 4 hours and earned $8 an hour plus tips. How much did the waiter earn including tips?

   Ⓐ $92   Ⓒ $32

   Ⓑ $68   Ⓓ $60

10. **Multi-Step** A waiter that worked 2 hours and a waiter that worked 5 hours combine their tip money for the day to buy a meal for their coworkers. How much money do they have to spend on the meal?

   Ⓐ $75   Ⓒ $25

   Ⓑ $110   Ⓓ $100

Name ______________________________

TEKS Data Analysis—5.9.C
MATHEMATICAL PROCESSES 5.1.C, 5.1.D, 5.1.F

16.6 Analyze Scatter Plots

Essential Question How can you analyze data displayed on a scatter plot?

Unlock the Problem

You can use a scatter plot to analyze the relationship between two sets of data.

Example 1

Students conducted an experiment about the relationship between the wingspans of paper airplanes and the distances they fly. How far did the paper airplane with a wingspan of 3 inches fly?

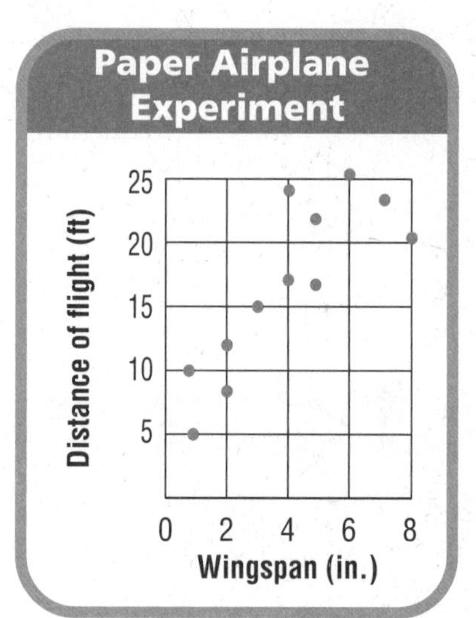

The point with x-coordinate 3 has y-coordinate ______.

So, the paper airplane with a wingspan of 3 inches flew ______ feet.

You can use scatter plots to make generalizations about data.

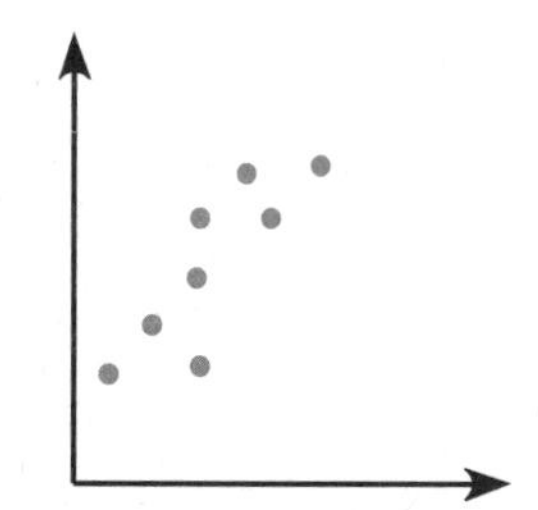

As x-values increase, y-values increase.

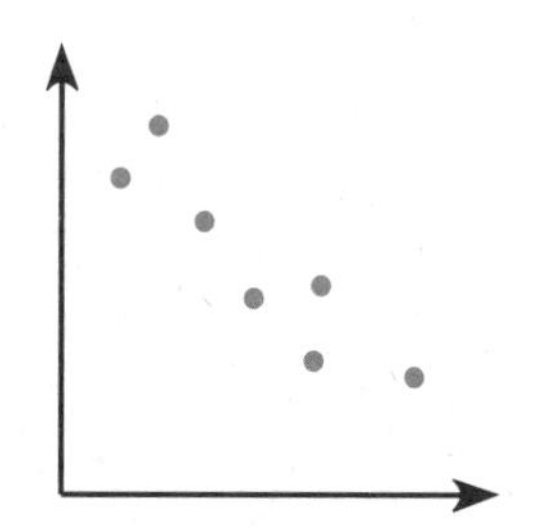

As x-values increase, y-values decrease.

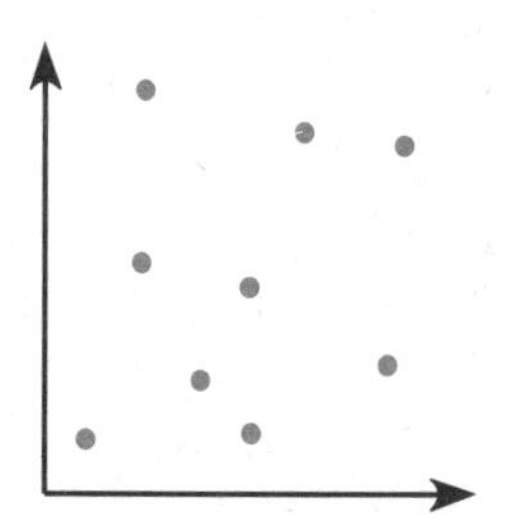

There is no relationship between x-and y-values.

- What happens to the distance the paper airplanes fly as the wingspan increases?

____

Math Talk Mathematical Processes

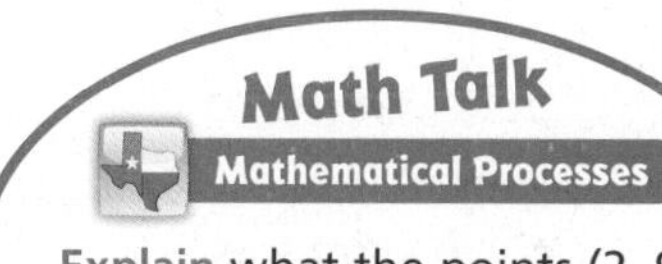

Explain what the points (2, 9) and (2, 12) represent on the scatter plot.

When data shows a trend, you can make a prediction.

Example 2 Solve a multi-step problem.

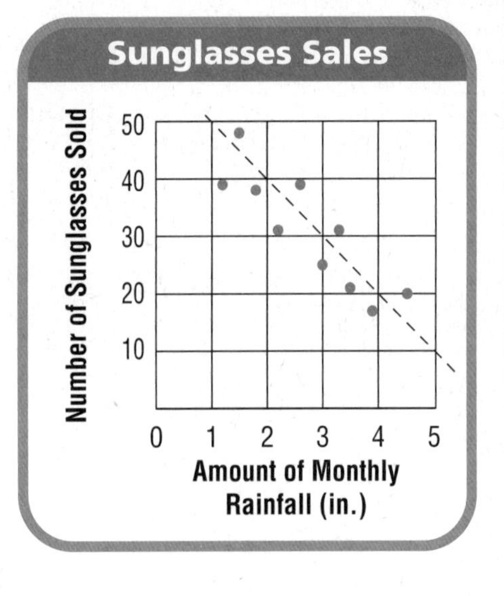

The scatter plot shows the relationship between monthly rainfall and sunglasses sales at a beach shop. About how many sunglasses do you think the shop will sell in a month with 5 inches of rain?

- Draw a line to show the trend. Extend the line past x-coordinate 5.
- Use the line to estimate the coordinates of points that represent the number of sunglasses the shop will sell in a month with 5 inches of rain.

(5, ______)

So, the shop will sell about ______ sunglasses in a month with 5 inches of rain.

Share and Show

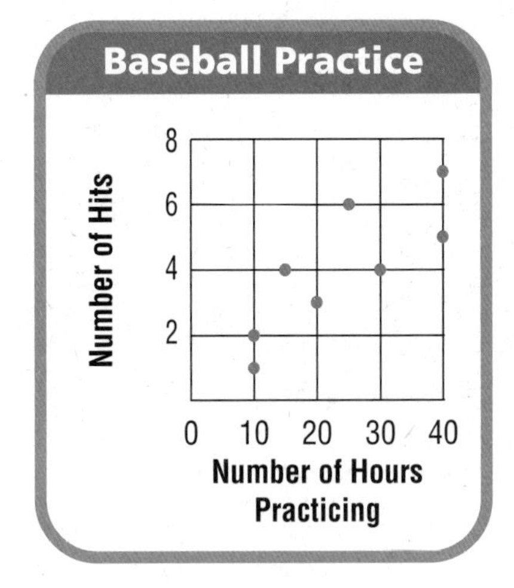

The scatter plot shows the relationship between the number of hours baseball players practiced and the number of hits they got. Use the scatter plot for 1–3.

1. How many hours did the player who got 6 hits practice?

- Write the ordered pair for the player who got 6 hits. (______, 6)

The player who got 6 hits practiced for ______ hours.

2. How many hits did the baseball players who practiced more than 30 hours get altogether?

______

3. As the number of hours of baseball practice increases, does the number of hits increase, decrease, or stay about the same?

______

Problem Solving

4. H.O.T. Generalize Suppose a scatter plot shows the relationship between the number of books in a library and the number of students who play soccer. As the number of books increases, does the number of students who play soccer increase? Does it decrease? Or is there no relationship between the two sets of data?

______

______

Name ______________________

5. H.O.T. **Sense or Nonsense** Terry made a scatter plot to show the relationship between the number of weeks since a seed was planted and the height of the plant. Does this scatter plot make sense for the data? **Explain.**

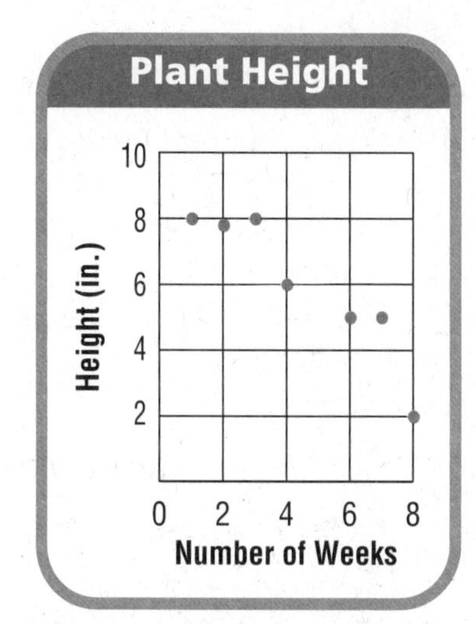

____

____

____

____

6. **Display** Pam is making this scatter plot to show the relationship between the number of minutes students walk in a walkathon and the distance they walk. Graph 8 points on the scatter plot to show the relationship.

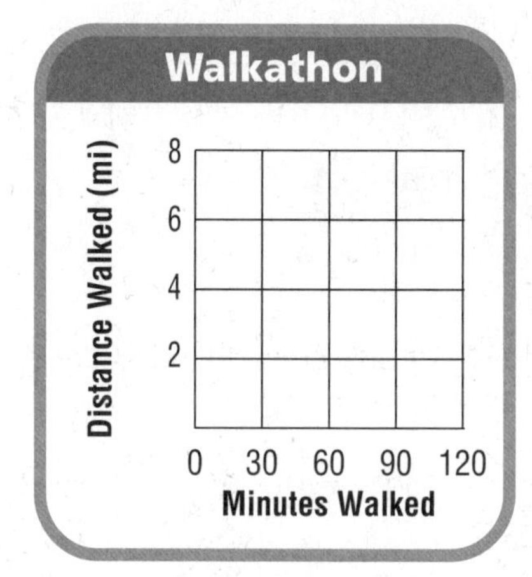

Problem Solving

The scatter plot below shows the relationship between the number of camp counselors and the number of students in each group at camp. Use the scatter plot for 7–8.

7. **Explain** how the number of camp counselors is related to the number of students in each group at camp.

____

____

8. H.O.T. **Multi-Step** About what would you expect the number of students in each group at camp to be if there are 10 camp counselors? **Explain.**

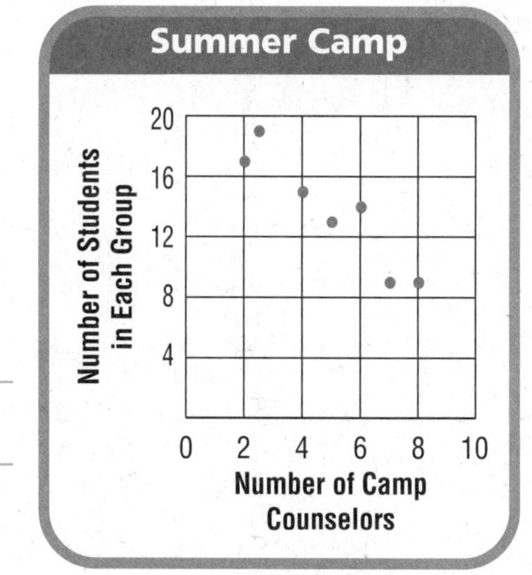

____

____

____

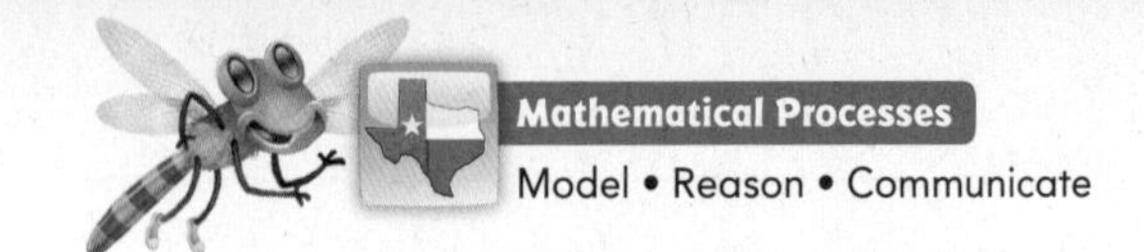

Daily Assessment Task

Fill in the bubble completely to show your answer.

Use the scatter plot for 9-10.

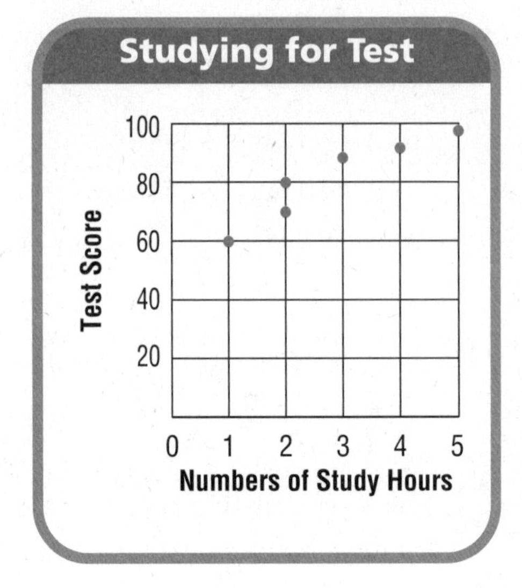

9. Molly collected data about the number of hours students studied and their scores on a test. The results are shown in the scatter plot. Which statement about the data is true?

Ⓐ As study hours increase, test scores decrease.

Ⓑ As study hours increase, test scores increase.

Ⓒ As study hours increase, test scores stay the same.

Ⓓ As study hours decrease, test scores increase.

10. Which is a reasonable prediction of a test score for a student who studied for $\frac{1}{2}$ hour?

Ⓐ 80 Ⓒ 50

Ⓑ 100 Ⓓ 5

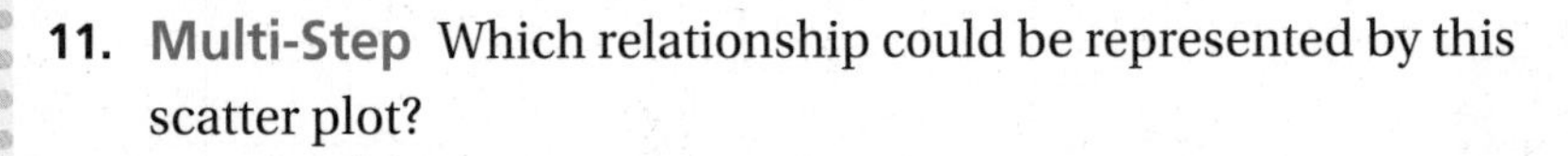

11. **Multi-Step** Which relationship could be represented by this scatter plot?

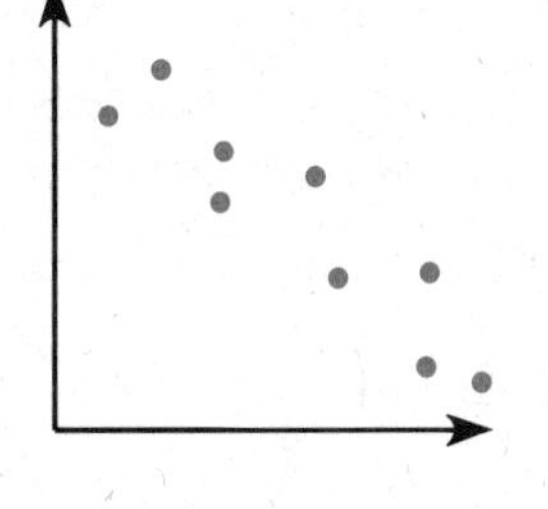

Ⓐ As the number of muffins in a box increases, the price increases.

Ⓑ As the speed of a car increases, the distance the car travels increases.

Ⓒ As the population of a city increases, the number of schools in the city increases.

Ⓓ As the number of daylight hours increases, the number of night hours decreases.

TEXAS Test Prep

12. As the area of a garden increases, what happens to the number of plants in a garden?

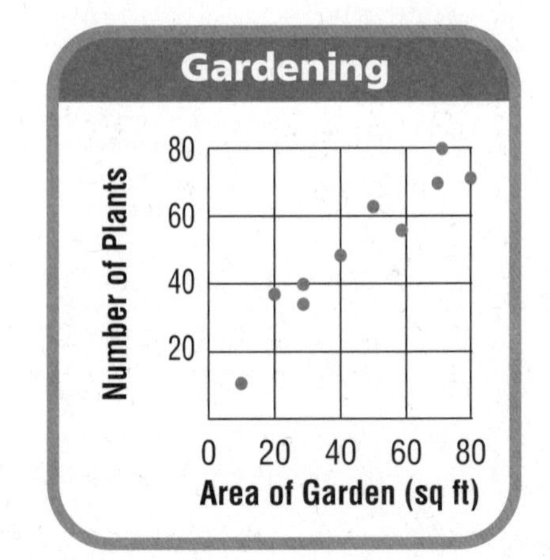

Ⓐ The number of plants decreases.

Ⓑ The number of plants stays the same.

Ⓒ The number of plants increases faster.

Ⓓ The number of plants increases.

TEKS Data Analysis—5.9.C
MATHEMATICAL PROCESSES 5.1.C, 5.1.D, 5.1.F

Name ______________________

16.6 Analyze Scatter Plots

The scatter plot shows the relationship between the ages of the trees in Jane's yard and the heights of the trees. Use the scatter plot for 1–5.

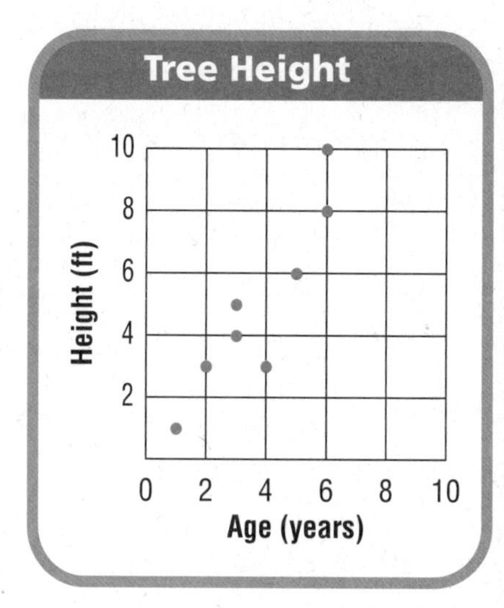

1. What is the age of the tree that is 8 feet tall? ______________
2. How many trees are 3 years old? ______________
3. How many trees are more than 6 feet tall? ______________
4. If a squirrel climbs to the top of each tree that is 6 years old, how far has the squirrel climbed? ______________
5. Which height has the greatest frequency? ______________

Problem Solving

Mr. Sanders has a box of candles. He makes a scatter plot to show the relationship between the number of minutes he burns each candle and the height of the candle when he blows it out. Use the scatter plot for 6–7.

6. Explain how the number of minutes the candle burns is related to the height of the candle.

____

____

7. About what would you expect the height of a candle to be after burning for 2 hours 40 minutes? Explain.

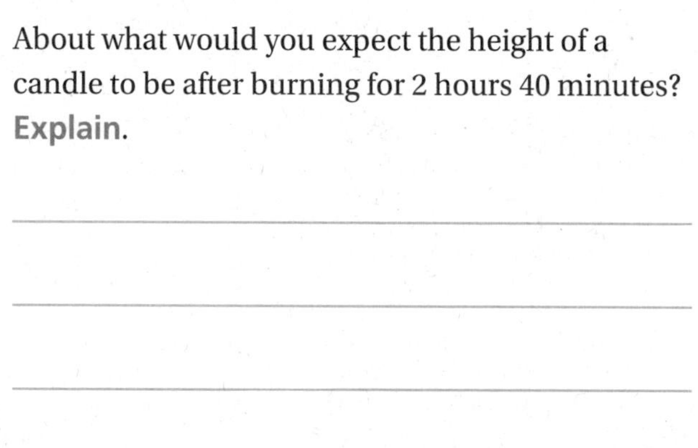

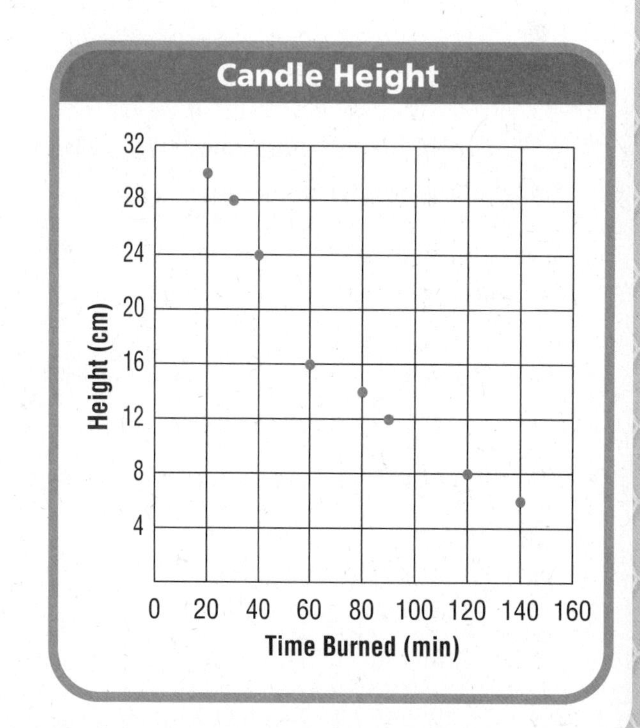

Lesson Check

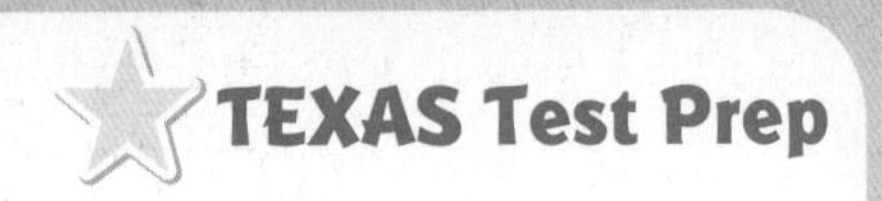

Fill in the bubble completely to show your answer.

8. JoBeth draws a scatter plot that shows as the outside temperature increases, sales at her lemonade stand increase. Which best describes the scatter plot?

Ⓐ The points show that as x-values increase, y-values increase.

Ⓑ The points show that as x-values increase, y-values decrease.

Ⓒ The points show that as x-values decrease, y-values stay the same.

Ⓓ The points show that as x-values decrease, y-values increase.

9. Which of the following best describes a scatter plot that shows no relationship between the x-values and the y-values?

Ⓐ As x-values increase, the points are higher on the graph.

Ⓑ As x-values decrease, the points are higher on the graph.

Ⓒ The points are scattered around the graph.

Ⓓ The points form a horizontal line.

The scatter plot shows the relationship between the hours people shopped online and the number of stores they visited. Use the scatter plot for 10–11.

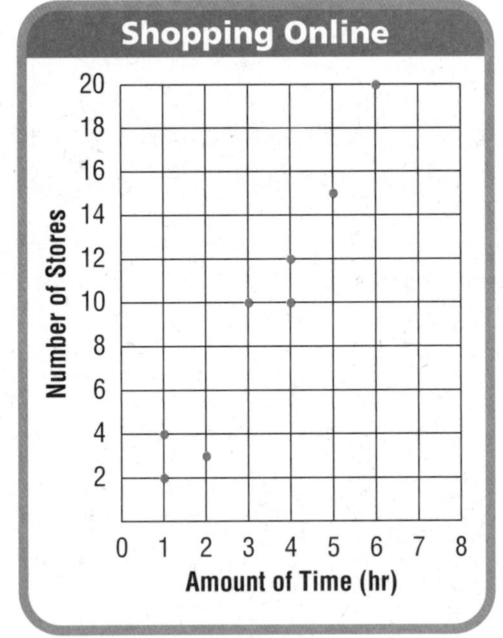

10. **Multi-Step** Which statement best describes the relationship between time shopping online and the number of stores visited?

Ⓐ As the number of hours increases, the number of stores decreases.

Ⓑ As the number of hours increases, the number of stores increases.

Ⓒ The number of hours and the number of stores are about the same.

Ⓓ As the number of hours decreases, the number of stores increases.

11. How much time did the person who visited 3 stores spend shopping online?

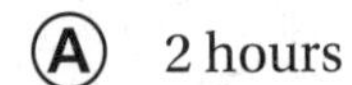

Ⓐ 2 hours

Ⓑ 10 hours

Ⓒ 4 hours

Ⓓ 3 hours

12. **Multi-Step** Mr. Reynosa plans to shop online for 4 hours for two days in a row. What is a reasonable prediction of how many stores he will visit?

Ⓐ 10

Ⓑ 8

Ⓒ 12

Ⓓ 22

Name ___________________________

Module 16 Assessment

Vocabulary

Vocabulary
stem-and-leaf plot
scatter plot
dot plot

Choose the best term from the box.

1. A ________________ is a graph that shows frequency of data along a number line. (p. 571)

2. A ________________ is a graph that shows a relationship between two sets of data. (p. 595)

Concepts and Skills

Use the data and the dot plot for 3–4.

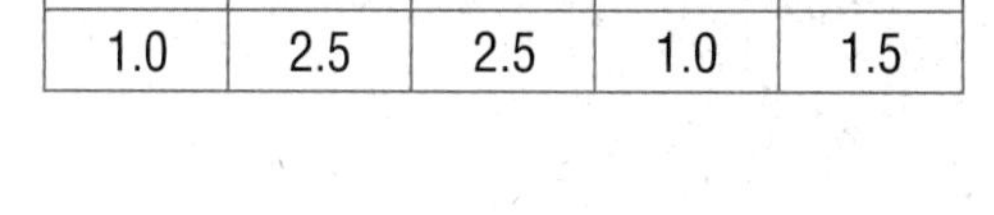

Weight of Pasta Salads (lb)				
2.5	2.5	1.5	3.0	1.0
1.0	2.5	2.5	1.0	1.5

3. Complete a dot plot of the data. TEKS 5.9.A

4. What is the weight of the greatest number of pasta salads? TEKS 5.9.C

____

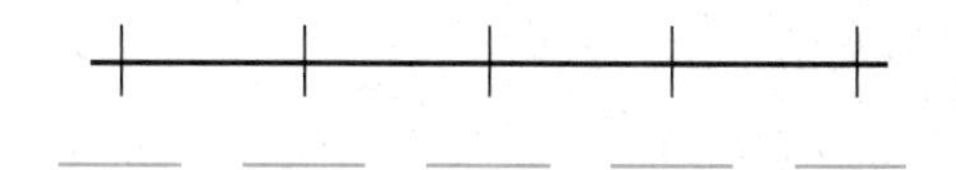

Use the table and the scatter plot for 5–7.

Sally's Vacation Travel							
Time (Days)	2	5	3	4	5	2	3
Distance (mi)	290	700	401	610	799	200	500

5. Complete a scatter plot of the data. TEKS 5.9.B

6. As the number of days traveled increases, does the distance traveled increase, decrease, or stay about the same? TEKS 5.9.C

____

7. About how many miles would you predict Sally would travel in 6 days? TEKS 5.9.C

____

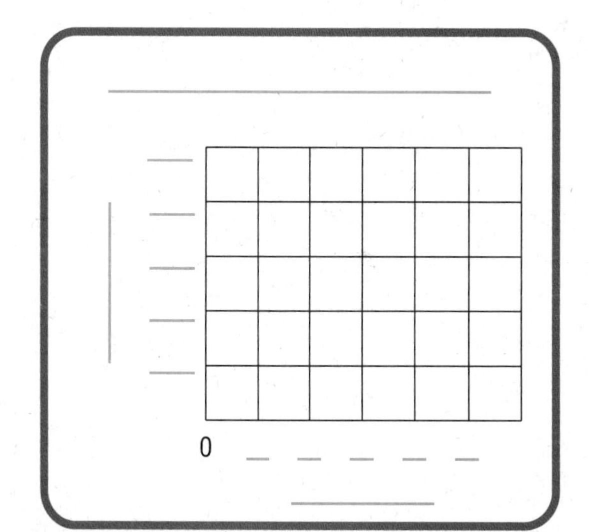

Fill in the bubble completely to show your answer.

The amount of money Tom saved each month in dollars is 23, 18, 24, 32, 27, 31, 25, 20, 14, and 19. Use the data and the stem-and-leaf plot for 8–10.

8. Tom is making a stem-and-leaf plot of the data. What are the leaves for stem 2? TEKS 5.9.A

Ⓐ 3, 4, 5, 7

Ⓑ 0, 3, 4, 5

Ⓒ 0, 3, 3, 5, 7

Ⓓ 0, 3, 4, 5, 7

Tom's Monthly Savings ($)

Stem	Leaves
1	4 8 9
2	
3	1 2

1 | 4 represents 14.

9. For how many months was Tom's savings less than $20? TEKS 5.9.C

Ⓐ 2 months

Ⓑ 5 months

Ⓒ 3 months

Ⓓ 4 months

10. Tom plans to save twice as much next month as he did during the months he saved over $30 a month. How much will Tom save next month? TEKS 5.9.C

Ⓐ $63

Ⓑ $126

Ⓒ $86

Ⓓ $43

Kim bought scraps of ribbon at a discount store. The length of each ribbon in inches is 9, $8\frac{3}{4}$, $8\frac{1}{2}$, $8\frac{3}{4}$, $8\frac{1}{4}$, $8\frac{1}{4}$, $8\frac{3}{4}$, $8\frac{1}{2}$, $8\frac{3}{4}$, $8\frac{1}{4}$, and 8. Use the data and the dot plot for 11–12.

11. Kim is completing the dot plot of the data. How many dots should she put above $8\frac{3}{4}$? TEKS 5.9.A

Ⓐ 1

Ⓑ 4

Ⓒ 3

Ⓓ 2

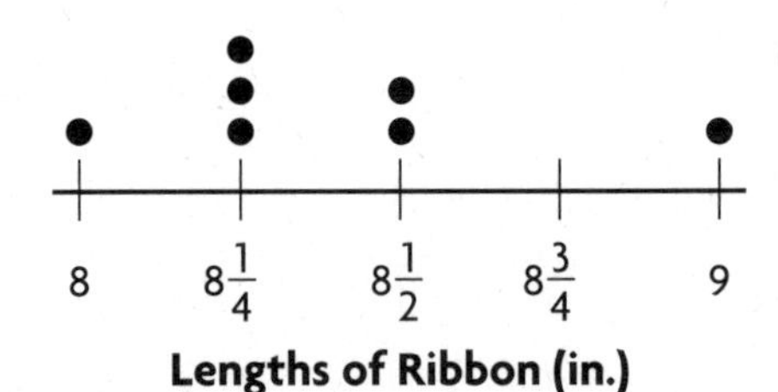

12. What is the range of ribbon lengths in inches? TEKS 5.9.C

Record your answer and fill in the bubbles on the grid. Be sure to use the correct place value.

			.		
⓪	⓪	⓪		⓪	⓪
①	①	①		①	①
②	②	②		②	②
③	③	③		③	③
④	④	④		④	④
⑤	⑤	⑤		⑤	⑤
⑥	⑥	⑥		⑥	⑥
⑦	⑦	⑦		⑦	⑦
⑧	⑧	⑧		⑧	⑧
⑨	⑨	⑨		⑨	⑨

Name ___________________________

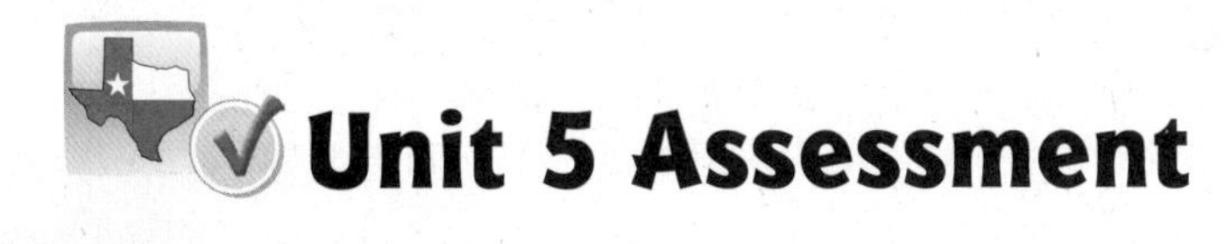

Unit 5 Assessment

Vocabulary

Vocabulary
frequency
prediction
stem-and-leaf plot

Choose the best term from the box.

1. ______________ is the number of times an event occurs. (p. 545)

2. In a ______________________, the data is arranged by place value. (p. 583)

Concepts and Skills

Use the data for 3–6.

Math Test Scores
80, 84, 95, 84, 79, 99, 92, 91, 87, 83, 92, 91, 95, 99, 81, 95

3. Make a dot plot to show the data. TEKS 5.9.A

Math Test Scores

4. Use the dot plot to find how many students scored more than 95 points on the test. TEKS 5.9.C

____

5. Show the data in a stem-and-leaf plot. TEKS 5.9.A

Math Test Scores

Stem	Leaves
___	______________________
___	______________________
___	______________________

___ | ___ represents ___.

6. Use the stem-and-leaf plot to find the range of scores on the math test. TEKS 5.9.C

____

Fill in the bubble completely to show your answer.

TEXAS Test Prep

Use the bar graph for 7–9.

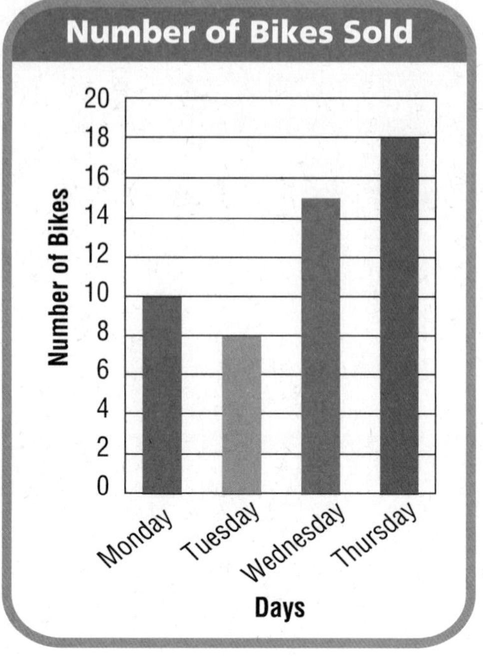

7. How many more bikes were sold on Monday and Tuesday combined than on Wednesday? TEKS 5.9.C

Ⓐ 15

Ⓑ 3

Ⓒ 5

Ⓓ 7

8. Four fewer bikes were sold on Wednesday than on Friday. How many bikes were sold on Friday? TEKS 5.9.C

Ⓐ 15

Ⓑ 11

Ⓒ 19

Ⓓ 20

9. The bike shop owner wants to add another bar to the graph to show the number of bikes sold on Saturday. If the number of bikes sold on Saturday is greater than Wednesday but fewer than Thursday, which of the following could be the height of the bar? TEKS 5.9.A

Ⓐ 14

Ⓑ 20

Ⓒ 17

Ⓓ 33

10. The table shows the time it takes students to complete a math test in hours. How many dots should be placed in a dot plot to show the times greater than $1\frac{1}{2}$ hours? TEKS 5.9.A

Time to Complete Math Test				
$1\frac{3}{4}$	2	$1\frac{1}{2}$	1	$1\frac{3}{4}$
$1\frac{1}{2}$	1	$1\frac{1}{4}$	$1\frac{1}{4}$	2

Ⓐ 5

Ⓑ 6

Ⓒ 4

Ⓓ 1

Use the data and frequency table for 11–12.

Types of Birds				
tern	gull	pelican	gull	gull
tern	egret	pelican	tern	tern
gull	gull	tern	egret	eagle

Number of Birds	
Type of Bird	Frequency
eagle	1
egret	2
gull	5
pelican	2
tern	?

11. Chris uses the data to create a frequency table to show the number of bird sightings on a bird watching trip. Which number belongs in the frequency table for tern sightings? TEKS 5.9.A

Ⓐ 5

Ⓑ 1

Ⓒ 4

Ⓓ 6

12. How many more gulls than egrets does Chris see? TEKS 5.9.C

Ⓐ 2

Ⓑ 5

Ⓒ 3

Ⓓ 7

Use the scatter plot for 13–14.

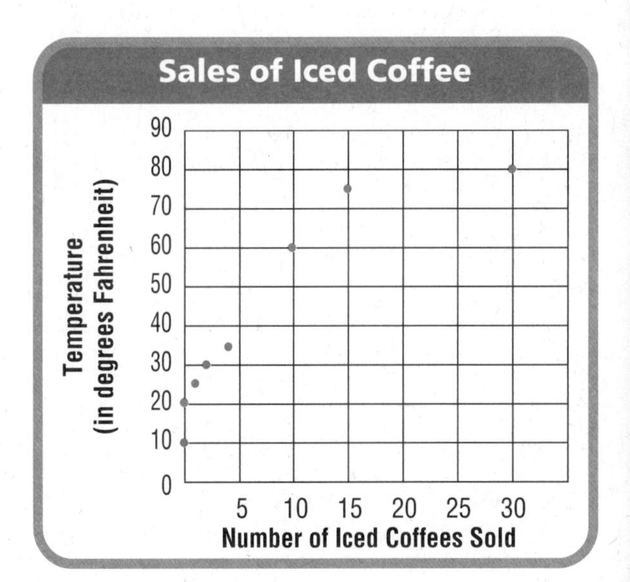

13. How many iced coffees would you predict will be sold when the temperature is 70° Fahrenheit? TEKS 5.9.C

Ⓐ 6

Ⓑ 2

Ⓒ 12

Ⓓ Not here

14. Which of the following ordered pairs could represent the number of coffees sold on a very hot day?

Ⓐ (25, 25)

Ⓑ (1, 90)

Ⓒ (1, 45)

Ⓓ (25, 90)

Use the stem-and-leaf plot for 15–16.

Roller Coaster Speeds (miles per hour)

Stem	Leaves
2	7
3	
4	3 6
5	2 5 5 6
6	2 3 5 6 7 7 7
7	2 2

2|7 represents 27.

15. How many roller coasters are represented in the data? TEKS 5.9.C

Ⓐ 6

Ⓑ 5

Ⓒ 16

Ⓓ 11

16. How many more roller coasters have speeds over 60 miles per hour than roller coasters with speeds less than 60 miles per hour? TEKS 5.9.C

Ⓐ 7

Ⓑ 2

Ⓒ 1

Ⓓ 8

17. Choose your favorite sport. Create a set of data about the sport that could be used to make a dot plot. Make a dot plot of the data. Write a problem that can be solved using the dot plot. TEKS 5.9.A, 5.9.C

Unit 6

Personal Financial Literacy

Show What You Know

Check your understanding of important skills.

Name ______________________________

▶ Subtract Multi-Digit Numbers Subtract.

1. $\begin{array}{r} 18{,}956 \\ -\ 16{,}897 \\ \hline \end{array}$

2. $\begin{array}{r} 35{,}214 \\ -\ 29{,}368 \\ \hline \end{array}$

3. $\begin{array}{r} 72{,}173 \\ -\ 45{,}396 \\ \hline \end{array}$

▶ Multiply 3-Digit and 4-Digit Numbers by 1-Digit Numbers Multiply.

4.

	T	H	T	O
		6	7	9
×				6

5.

	T	H	T	O
	2,	4	7	2
×				3

▶ Add Decimals Estimate. Then find the sum.

6. Estimate:

$\begin{array}{r} \square \\ +\ \square \\ \hline \square \end{array}$ $\begin{array}{r} 1.4 \\ +\ 0.23 \\ \hline \end{array}$

7. Estimate:

$\begin{array}{r} \square \\ +\ \square \\ \hline \square \end{array}$ $\begin{array}{r} 1.78 \\ +\ 0.13 \\ \hline \end{array}$

8. Estimate:

$\begin{array}{r} \square \\ +\ \square \\ \hline \square \end{array}$ $\begin{array}{r} 1.38 \\ +\ 1.21 \\ \hline \end{array}$

GO DIGITAL Assessment Options: Soar to Success Math

Vocabulary Builder

▶ Visualize It

Use the ✓ words to complete the tree map.

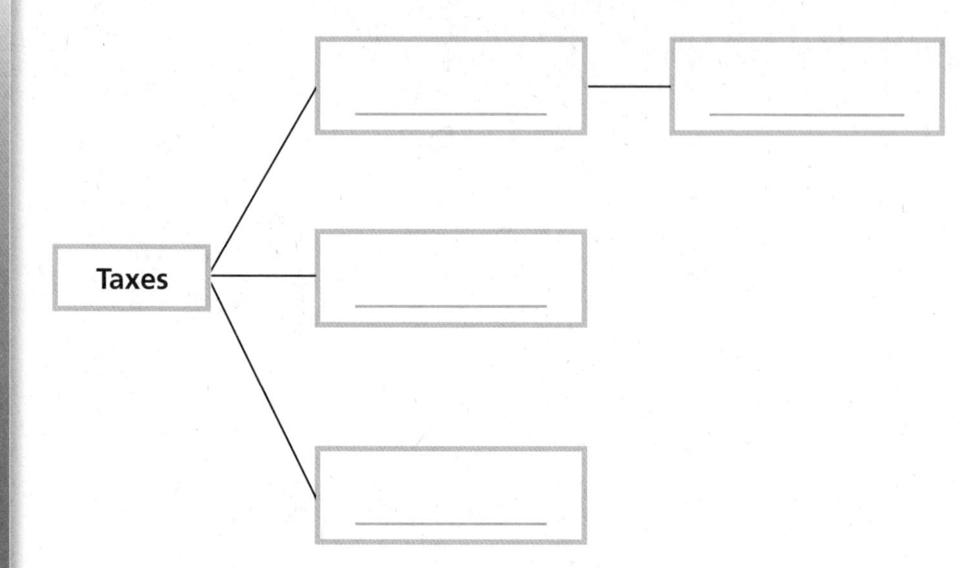

Review Words

- budget
- interest

Preview Words

- check
- credit card
- debit card
- income
- ✓ income tax
- gross income
- net income
- ✓ payroll tax
- ✓ property tax
- ✓ sales tax

▶ Understand Vocabulary

Complete the sentences using the preview words.

1. A ______________ is a fee paid to the government in return for goods and services, such as roads and police protection.

2. ____________________ is the amount of income left after taxes are taken out of the ____________________.

3. ____________________ is the tax withheld from an employee's paycheck.

4. A ____________________ is an identification card issued by a bank that allows a user to immediately use money from an account.

5. A bank may charge interest on the amount of money charged on a ____________________.

6. You can write a ____________________ to pay for a purchase using money in your bank account.

GO DIGITAL
- Interactive Student Edition
- Multimedia eGlossary

Reading & Writing Math

Name ______________________________

Reading When you read a story, you can tell what an unfamiliar word means by the situation being described. When you read about financial matters, you may see a familiar word used in different ways. You may also need to use the situation to understand the word's meaning.

Look at the word **tax** in each of the following situations. Which meaning of the word is used in each sentence? Write the letter of the definition.

- John and Maria live in a big city. They pay **tax** to the city based on how much they earn. ______
- Marcia bought a new coat and hat. She paid $102.96 for the items and $8.49 **tax**. ______
- Kati received her paycheck. Her pay stub showed a total of $67.45 in **tax**es. ______
- The Petersens received a notice that their **tax** would increase because of the new garage they put on their house. ______

A. Payroll tax is money an employer withholds from an employee's earnings.
B. Income tax is the money paid to a city, town, or state government or to the U.S. government (called federal income tax).
C. Sales tax is money added to the cost of items or services.
D. Property tax is a portion of the value of items that is paid to a city or state government. Property tax can be charged on things such as cars, houses, boats, or land.

Writing Choose one of the definitions of *tax* and write your own sentence using the word *tax*. Exchange sentences with a partner and guess the meaning of the word. Then work together to write a math problem based on one of your sentences.

____

____

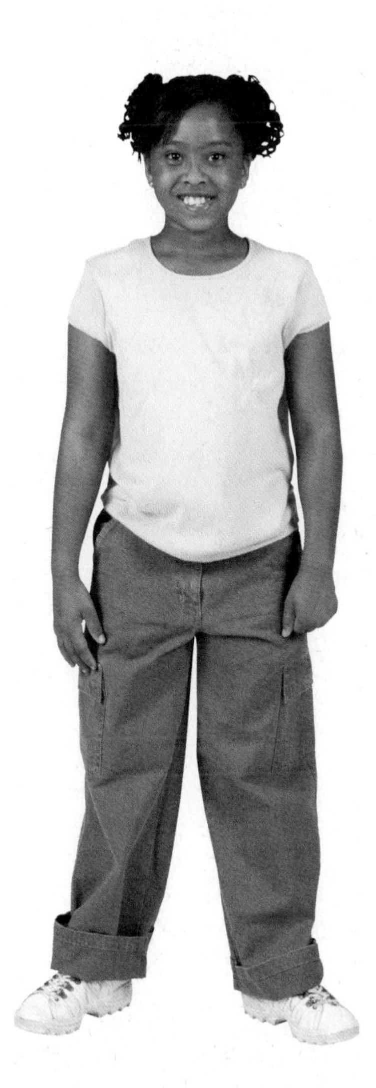

Budget Balance Bingo

Object of the Game Be the first to balance your budget.

Materials

- Number cube labeled 1, 2, 3, 4, 5 and X
- Number cube labeled Red, Blue, Yellow, Green, Orange, and X
- Counters
- *Budget Balance* Game Card

Set Up

Give each player a copy of the game card and some counters. All players begin with $1,675 earnings in their budget.

Number of Players 2 or more

How to Play

1. Each player rolls both number cubes and places a counter on the square named by the color and number. If an X is rolled, the player loses a turn.

2. The first player to cover all the squares in the same row or same column has balanced the budget and wins the game.

3. Variation: Players record each difference as they subtract each expense rolled. They can subtract an expense listed in any square they have covered but cannot subtract the same expense twice. The winner is the person who balances the budget first, even if the squares covered are not all in the same row or column.

	Red	Blue	Yellow	Green	Orange
1	Pay car expenses $225	Savings and donations $150	Pay $750 rent	Pay electric bill $200	Buy food $350
2	Pay $750 rent	Buy food $350	Pay electric bill $200	Savings and donations $150	Pay car expenses $225
3	Buy food $350	Pay car expenses $225	Savings and donations $150	Pay $750 rent	Pay electric bill $200
4	Pay electric bill $200	Pay $750 rent	Pay car expenses $225	Buy food $350	Savings and donations $150
5	Savings and donations $150	Pay electric bill $200	Buy food $350	Pay car expenses $225	Pay $750 rent

Name ____________________

17.1 Income and Payroll Taxes

TEKS Personal Financial Literacy—5.10.A
Also 5.3.K
MATHEMATICAL PROCESSES
5.1.A, 5.1.B

Essential Question

What are income tax and payroll tax?

Unlock the Problem (Real World)

A **tax** is money paid to the government in exchange for services, such as road maintenance and police protection.

Income tax is based on the amount of money you earn, or your **income**. Federal income tax is paid to the United States government. Some states and cities also have an income tax. Workers throughout the United States pay federal income tax, but state or city income taxes vary across the country.

Workers also pay other taxes for government support programs, such as medical care.

Sometimes, these taxes are paid directly to the government. Other times, an employer will withhold these taxes from an employee's earnings and pay the government. The total tax an employer withholds is called **payroll tax**. The amount in an employee's paycheck shows the pay after taxes.

Calculate pay after taxes.

Mia earns $600 per week. When she gets her paycheck, it includes a pay stub that shows total earnings and payroll tax. Find Mia's pay after taxes.

1001

Employee: Mia Goodwin	Total earnings		$600.00
	Federal income tax	$75.45	
	State income tax	$15.17	
Pay period: July 1–July 7	Other taxes	$37.20	
	Total taxes		
	Pay after taxes		

Detach and retain for your records.

Circle the taxes taken out of Mia's paycheck. Add the taxes to calculate the payroll tax.

$______ + $______ + $______ = $______

Subtract the payroll tax from her total earnings.

$600 − $______ = $______

So, Mia's pay after taxes is $______.

Math Talk

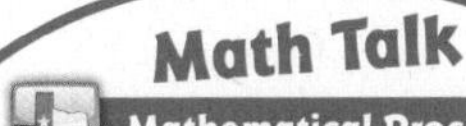

Mathematical Processes

Evaluate Reasonableness How can you check that the amount you found for Mia's pay after taxes is correct?

Example

Rob earns $500 per week. He has payroll tax taken out of his earnings. Unfortunately, Rob spilled kale juice on his pay stub, covering up some of the values. He knows the *Other taxes* are $10. How much state income tax was withheld from Rob's earnings?

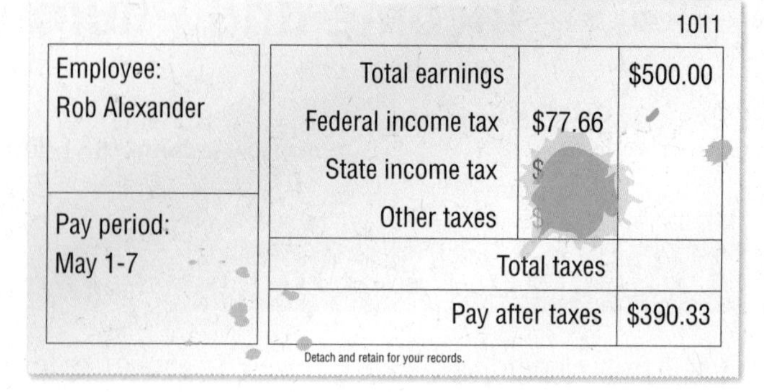

1011

Employee: Rob Alexander	Total earnings		$500.00
	Federal income tax	$77.66	
	State income tax	$	
Pay period: May 1-7	Other taxes	$	
	Total taxes		
	Pay after taxes		$390.33

Detach and retain for your records.

Find the payroll tax withheld from Rob's total earnings.

$________ − $________ = $________.

Add the federal income tax and other taxes.

$________ + $________ = $________.

Subtract the total of federal income tax and other taxes from the payroll tax to find the state income tax.

$________ − $________ or $________.

So, Rob's state income tax is $ ________

Share and Show

Rita works in a state with no state income tax. Use Rita's pay stub for 1–2.

2001

Employee: Rita Logan	Total earnings		$700.00
	Federal income tax	$120.66	
Pay period: September	Other taxes	$15.55	
	Total taxes		
	Pay after taxes		

Detach and retain for your records.

1. Calculate Rita's payroll tax.

   $________ + $________

   = $________

2. Calculate Rita's pay after taxes.

   $________ − $________ = $________

Problem Solving

3. **Write Math** ▶ **Explain** how you can calculate payroll tax if you know total earnings and pay after taxes.

____

____

Name ______________________

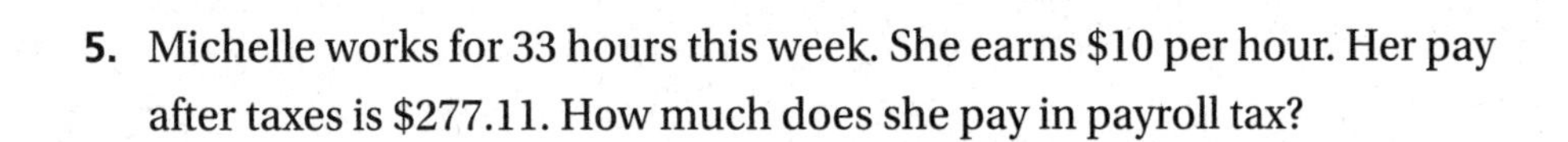

4. Leticia pays federal income tax of $18 for every $100 she earns. How much will she pay as federal income tax if she earns $500? **Explain.**

5. Michelle works for 33 hours this week. She earns $10 per hour. Her pay after taxes is $277.11. How much does she pay in payroll tax?

6. **H.O.T.** **Multi-Step** Oliver lives in a state with no state income tax. He pays $150 in payroll tax each week. If the federal income tax is 0.75 of the payroll tax, how much are the other taxes?

7. **H.O.T.** **Multi-Step** The pay stub shows the payroll tax withheld from Maeve's paycheck. If Maeve gets paid twice a month, how much does she pay in payroll tax in one month? **Explain.**

1351

Employee: Maeve Kelley	Total earnings		$570.00
	Federal income tax	$112.66	
	State income tax	$18.50	
Pay period: January 1–15	Other taxes	$17.35	
	Total taxes		
	Pay after taxes		

Detach and retain for your records.

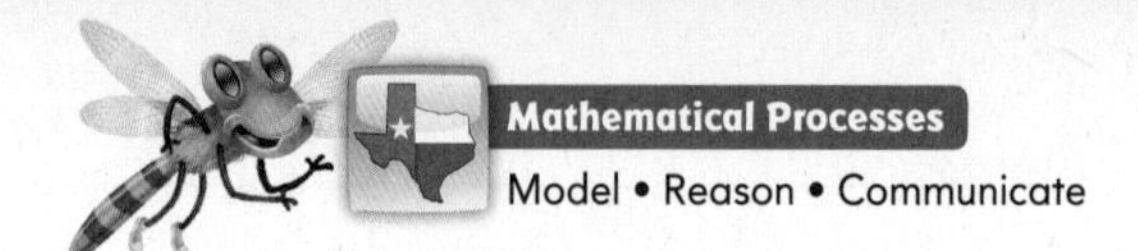

Daily Assessment Task

Fill in the bubble completely to show your answer.

8. Arman works in a state with no state income tax. He earns $625 each week. He pays $38.45 in other taxes. His pay after taxes is $499.61. How much federal income tax does he pay?

Ⓐ $38.45

Ⓑ $76.90

Ⓒ $86.94

Ⓓ $88.72

9. **Communicate** Miranda earns $450.75 at her part-time job. She pays $98.12 in federal income tax and $12.00 in other taxes. How can you determine Miranda's pay after taxes?

Ⓐ Subtract the sum of the taxes from the total earnings.

Ⓑ Subtract the amount earned from the sum of the taxes.

Ⓒ Add all the taxes.

Ⓓ Subtract only the federal income tax from the total earnings.

10. **Multi-Step** Joe has two part-time jobs. At his first job, he earned $200 and paid $42 in payroll tax. At his second job he earned $175 and paid $24 in payroll tax. What is his pay after taxes?

Ⓐ $158

Ⓑ $309

Ⓒ $351

Ⓓ $303

TEXAS Test Prep

11. Mark's pay after taxes is $855.08. If his total earnings are $1,100, how much does Mark pay in payroll tax?

Ⓐ $1,100

Ⓑ $144.02

Ⓒ $244.92

Ⓓ $855.08

TEKS Personal Financial Literacy—5.10.A
Also 5.3.K
MATHEMATICAL PROCESSES 5.1.A, 5.1.B

Name ______________________________

17.1 Income and Payroll Taxes

1. Write an equation to show how to calculate the total amount Sam pays in payroll tax.

____

2. Use your solution in Exercise 1 to write an equation to calculate Sam's pay after taxes if his total earnings are $800.

____

6405

Employee: Sam Brown	Total earnings		$800.00
	Federal income tax	$112.50	
	State income tax	$24.25	
Pay period: January	Other taxes	$12.90	
	Total taxes		
	Pay after taxes		

Detach and retain for your records.

3. Explain how you can calculate total earnings if you know the payroll tax and the pay after taxes.

____

Problem Solving

4. The pay stub at right shows Darla's earnings and taxes this week. Darla says her pay after taxes will be an amount greater than $600. **Explain** how you can use estimation to decide if Darla is correct.

____

____

____

____

____

4675

Employee: Darla Moore	Total earnings		$750.00
	Federal income tax	$119.45	
	State income tax	$30.15	
Pay period: March 14–21	Other taxes	$11.21	
	Total taxes		
	Pay after taxes		

Detach and retain for your records.

5. Adolfo earned $650 last week. He paid $97.50 in federal income tax. He paid one third that amount for state income tax and other taxes combined. What was Adolfo's pay after taxes? **Explain** how you found your answer.

____

____

Lesson Check

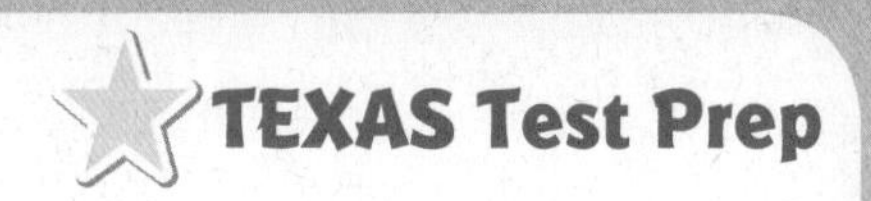

Fill in the bubble completely to show your answer.

6. Martina earns $4,000 per month. Each month, she pays $680 in federal income tax, $160 in state income tax, and $79 in other taxes. What is Martina's pay after taxes each month?

Ⓐ $3,160

Ⓑ $3,081

Ⓒ $3,761

Ⓓ $2,981

7. Lacey earns $680 each week. She pays $91.80 in federal income tax. The other taxes are $17.00. Her pay after taxes is $547.40. How much does Lacey pay in state income tax?

Ⓐ $74.80

Ⓑ $38.60

Ⓒ $115.60

Ⓓ $23.80

8. Which statement about total earnings and pay after taxes is correct, if the payroll tax is withheld?

Ⓐ Pay after taxes is greater than total earnings.

Ⓑ Pay after taxes is less than total earnings.

Ⓒ Total earnings and pay after taxes are the same.

Ⓓ Total earnings are less than the pay after taxes.

9. Each week, Kelly pays $68.45 in federal income tax, $22.81 in state income tax, and $18.75 in other taxes. Which is the best estimate for the payroll tax Kelly pays each month?

Ⓐ $440

Ⓑ $110

Ⓒ $280

Ⓓ $360

10. **Multi-Step** Each week, Desiree earns $925 and pays $148 in payroll tax. How long does it take Desiree to earn at least $3,000 after taxes?

Ⓐ 4 weeks

Ⓑ 3 weeks

Ⓒ 5 weeks

Ⓓ 7 weeks

11. **Multi-Step** Brian works 24 hours this week. His earns $9.25 per hour. He pays $37.30 in payroll tax. He deposits half of his pay after taxes in his savings account. He deposits the other half of his pay after taxes in his checking account. How much money is deposited into each account?

Ⓐ $184.70

Ⓑ $129.65

Ⓒ $92.35

Ⓓ $46.55

Name ________________________________

17.2 Sales and Property Taxes

Essential Question What are sales tax and property tax?

You have learned about taxes that employers withhold from an employee's pay. There are other taxes that are based on the value of certain items. These are usually paid to a city or state government. Just like payroll tax, the government uses these taxes to pay for services.

Math Idea

Sales and property taxes are based on the value of the item. The greater the value, the greater the tax.

Sales tax is the money added to the cost of items and services. It is usually paid when an item is purchased.

Property tax is a portion of the value of items. Property tax can be charged on things such as cars, houses, boats, or land. This kind of tax is paid once or several times a year as long as a person owns the item.

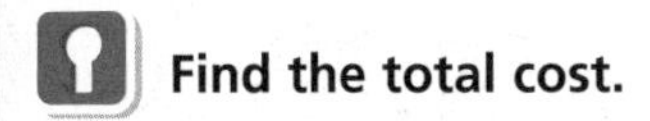

Ethan's favorite book is on sale for $11.98 plus tax. Ethan has $13. Can he buy the book?

Find the total cost.

The store clerk has a sales tax table to determine how much the tax will be.

Read the table. To find the tax, find the price in the table that is close to $11.98, but not less than $11.98. Add the tax to $11.98.

Price of book		Sales tax		Total cost
$________	+	$________	=	$________

The total cost of the book is $12.97.

Ethan has $______, so he ______ buy the book.

Sales Tax Table

Price Through	Add Tax	Price Through	Add Tax	Price Through	Add Tax
$0.06	$0.00	$5.87	$0.48	$11.69	$0.96
$0.18	$0.01	$5.99	$0.49	$11.81	$0.97
$0.30	$0.02	$6.12	$0.50	$11.93	$0.98
$0.42	$0.03	$6.24	$0.51	$12.06	$0.99
$0.54	$0.04	$6.36	$0.52	$12.18	$1.00
$0.66	$0.05	$6.48	$0.53	$12.30	$1.01
$0.78	$0.06	$6.60	$0.54	$12.42	$1.02
$0.90	$0.07	$6.72	$0.55	$12.54	$1.03
$1.03	$0.08	$6.84	$0.56	$12.66	$1.04
$1.15	$0.09	$6.96	$0.57	$12.78	$1.05
$1.27	$0.10	$7.09	$0.58	$12.90	$1.06
$1.39	$0.11	$7.21	$0.59	$13.03	$1.07
$1.51	$0.12	$7.33	$0.60	$13.15	$1.08
$1.63	$0.13	$7.45	$0.61	$13.27	$1.09

Example Find the property tax.

The Green family builds a shed behind their house. The shed will increase the amount the family has to pay in property tax. In their town, the tax is $19.41 per year for every $1,000 of property value. The shed is worth $9,000. If the property tax is paid yearly, how much tax will they pay on the shed in one year?

The shed has a value of $________, which is ________ × $1,000.

So, the tax on the shed is ________ × $________ = $________

Share and Show

1. The price of the dress Bonnie wants to buy is $85. The state has a $0.05 sales tax for every dollar of the price.

   a. What is the sales tax on the dress?

   For $85, the sales tax will be ________ × $0.05 = ________.

   b. What is the total cost of the dress?

   $85 + ________ = ________

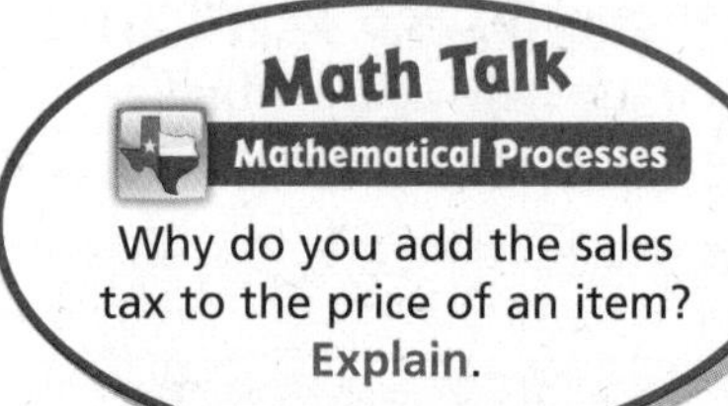

2. Miguel has a small boat that has a value of $3,100. He pays property tax on the boat to his town. The property tax is $4.20 for every $100 of the property value. How much will Miguel pay in tax on his boat?

   $3,100 = ________ × $100

   The tax will be $4.20 × 31 = ________.

Name the type of tax described. Write *income tax, payroll tax, property tax,* or *sales tax.* You may write more than one type.

3. The price of the sweatshirt is $45. The total cost of the sweatshirt is $47.95.

   ____

4. The value of a house is $250,000. The yearly tax on the house is $7,500.

   ____

5. Rolando earns $395. His pay after taxes is $356.

   ____

6. The video game sells for $19.99 plus $0.55 in tax.

   ____

7. Chase pays a yearly tax of $100 on his car.

   ____

8. $21.65 is withheld from Ed's weekly earnings.

   ____

Name ______________________

Problem Solving Real World

9. Write Math ▶ **Explain** the similarities and differences between payroll tax and property tax.

10. H.O.T. **Connect** How can you show that a tax of $0.05 for every $1 is the same as a tax of $5 for every $100? Use an example to help you explain.

11. **Multi-Step** Bill buys a camera for $189 and a tablet computer for $249. The sales tax is $0.08 on every dollar. What is the total cost of his purchases?

12. H.O.T. **Multi-Step** Mr. Kramer buys a new car for $24,000. He will pay a sales tax of $0.06 for every dollar of the price. He will pay a property tax of $14.62 for every $1,000. What are the total taxes on the new car for this year?

13. **Apply** The Norton's home has a value of $150,000. The yearly tax in their city is $28.13 for every $1,000 of value. What will they pay in property tax for the year?

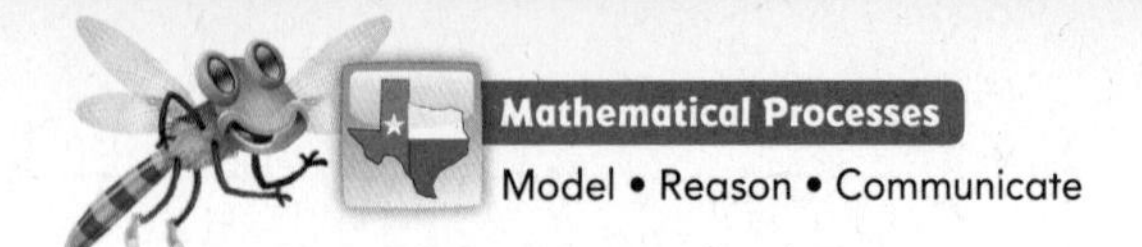

Daily Assessment Task

Fill in the bubble completely to show your answer.

14. At the bookstore, the clearance shelf has a book about explorers. The book has a price tag of $4. The sales tax is $0.05 on every dollar. Which is the total cost of the book?

Ⓐ $4.05

Ⓑ $4.20

Ⓒ $0.20

Ⓓ $3.80

15. Amanda buys a necklace for $280. Which of the following taxes could she have paid on the purchase?

Ⓐ property tax

Ⓑ income tax

Ⓒ payroll tax

Ⓓ sales tax

16. **Multi-Step** The property tax in one town was $6.95 per $1,000 value in the year 2012. The tax increased to $7.71 per $1,000 value in 2013. What effect did that have on the property tax for a house with a value of $100,000?

Ⓐ increase $76

Ⓑ decrease $96

Ⓒ increase $791

Ⓓ decrease $695

TEXAS Test Prep

17. Which statement about sales tax is NOT true?

Ⓐ You can find the amount of sales tax in a sales tax table.

Ⓑ The sales tax is based on the value of an item.

Ⓒ The sales tax is the same as income tax.

Ⓓ You need to know the price of the item to determine the sales tax.

TEKS Personal Financial Literacy—5.10.A
Also 5.3.E, 5.3.K
MATHEMATICAL PROCESSES 5.1.A, 5.1.F

Name ______________________

17.2 Sales and Property Taxes

1. Angelo buys a pair of jeans for $27. He pays $0.07 in sales tax for every dollar of the price. Write an equation to show how to calculate the sales tax on the jeans.

____

Write an equation to show how to calculate the total cost of the jeans.

____

2. The Kleins' home has a value of $120,000. The property tax in their city is $21.30 for every $1,000 of value. Complete the equations to calculate the property tax.

$\$120{,}000 \div \$1{,}000 =$ ____________

The tax will be: $120 \times \$21.30 =$ ____________

3. How do sales taxes and property taxes affect the cost of an item? **Explain.**

____

____

Problem Solving Real World

Use the chart for 4–5.

Outdoor Equipment	
Item	**Price**
Tent	$219
Sleeping bag	$109
Backpack	$78
Lantern	$49

4. Samuel buys an item for his camping trip and pays $0.06 in sales tax on every $1 he spends. His receipt shows a $4.68 charge for sales tax. Which item did Samuel buy?

____

5. On Friday, the tent will be on sale for $15 off the price. What will Amber's total savings be if she buys the tent on Friday? Include $0.06 in sales tax on every $1 when calculating the cost. Show how you found your answer.

____

____

Lesson Check

TEXAS Test Prep

Fill in the bubble completely to show your answer.

6. Some states, including Texas, have a sales tax holiday in which residents do not have to pay a sales tax for a few days each year. If the sales tax is $0.07 on every $1, how much could you save on a purchase of a $19 calculator during the sales tax holiday?

Ⓐ $1.40
Ⓑ $7.00
Ⓒ $0.95
Ⓓ $1.33

7. Which statement about property tax is NOT true?

Ⓐ Property tax is subtracted from the price of the item.
Ⓑ Property tax can be charged on a piece of land.
Ⓒ The greater the value of the item, the greater the property tax.
Ⓓ Property taxes are paid to government.

8. What is the sales tax on an item that costs $33.50, if the sales tax is $0.06 on every $1?

Ⓐ $2.01
Ⓑ $20.01
Ⓒ $0.60
Ⓓ $6.00

9. A pair of laces has a price tag of $7.00. The sales tax is $0.08 on every $1. Which is the total price of the laces?

Ⓐ $7.00
Ⓑ $0.08
Ⓒ $7.56
Ⓓ $7.08

10. **Multi-Step** Mrs. Chan buys a new car for $21,000. She pays a sales tax of $0.06 for every $1. She pays a property tax of $16.80 on every $1,000 of the value. If the property tax is paid once a year, what are the total taxes on the car for the year?

Ⓐ $1,260
Ⓑ $352.80
Ⓒ $1,612.80
Ⓓ $22,612.80

11. **Multi-Step** Rex buys a flashlight for $44 and binoculars for $69. What is the total cost of Rex's purchase if sales tax is $0.07 on every $1?

Ⓐ $113.07
Ⓑ $120.91
Ⓒ $113.00
Ⓓ $116.08

Name ______________________________

17.3 Income

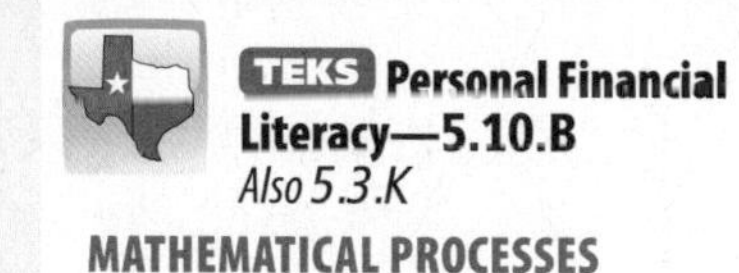

TEKS Personal Financial Literacy—5.10.B
Also 5.3.K

MATHEMATICAL PROCESSES
5.1.A, 5.1.D, 5.1.G

Essential Question What is the difference between gross income and net income?

Income is money you earn, whether from a job, interest from a savings account, or profits from selling items or services. **Gross income** is your total income *before* income or other payroll taxes are taken out of it. **Net income** is the amount that is left *after* taxes.

Taxes based on your earnings, such as income and other payroll taxes, affect your net income. Taxes based on use of items or services, such as sales and property taxes, do not affect your net income.

Unlock the Problem

Jay works at a bank. Use the information in the pay stub to find his gross and net income for the week. The salary from the bank is Jay's only source of income.

3201

Employee: Jay Martin	Total earnings		
	Federal income tax	$115.00	
Pay period: July 1 – July 8	Other taxes	$93.50	
	Total taxes		
	Pay after taxes		$891.50

Detach and retain for your records.

Since Jay has one source of income, his net income is the same as the pay after taxes shown on his pay stub. His gross income is the same as his total earnings.

His weekly net income is ____________.

To find his gross income, add the payroll tax to his net income.

Payroll tax: $__________ + $__________ = $__________.

Gross income: $__________ + $__________ = $__________
(net income) (payroll tax)

So, Jay's gross income for the week is $__________. Write the gross income on his pay stub.

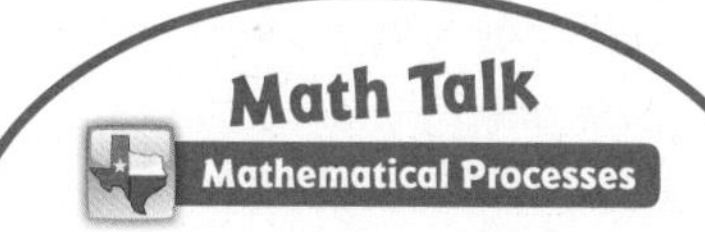

Math Talk Mathematical Processes

Jay pays $3.65 in sales tax for a meal. Does this change his net income? **Explain.**

- If Jay earns $130.56 after taxes during the same week from a part-time job, how does his net weekly income change? **Explain.**

____

Share and Show

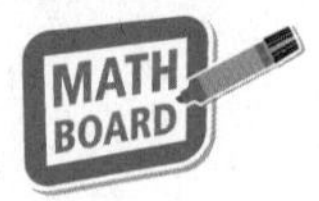

Use the information in the chart for 1–2.

Tina's Finances	
Yearly earnings from part-time job at the bakery	$18,000
Yearly earnings from part-time job at the library	$14,000
Profit from selling pottery	$6,000
Income and other payroll taxes	$5,750.50

1. What is Tina's gross income?

Think: Gross income is Tina's total earnings from all her sources of income.

Gross income:

$__________ + $__________ + $__________ = $__________

2. What is Tina's net income?.

Net income: $__________ − $__________ = $__________

So, her net income is $__________.

Problem Solving

3. Write Math ▸ Daniel works at a grocery store. He earns $8.00 per hour at the deli counter. He works 18 hours each week. If this is Daniel's only source of income, can you find his net income with the information given? **Explain.**

---

4. Use the information in the chart to find Latisha's gross and net income for the year.

Latisha's Finances	
Yearly earnings	$24,000
Profit from selling handmade sweaters	$13,000
Interest from savings account	$214
Income and other payroll taxes	$5,550.16

---

5. **Explain** the relationship between gross income, payroll tax, and net income.

Name ________________________________

Problem Solving Real World

6. **Multi-Step** Eduardo worked for 45 hours last week. His pay is $12 per hour for 40 hours and $18 per hour for any time over 40 hours. His payroll tax was $98.06. If this is Eduardo's only source of income, what was his net income for last week?

____

Write Math ▶ **Show Your Work**

7. **H.O.T.** Emily is a pharmacist. She earns $50 per hour. If she works on a holiday, she gets paid double the hourly rate. Last week she worked for 38 hours, including 8 hours on a holiday. Emily's salary is her only source of income. If her net income last week was $1,947, how much was her payroll tax? **Explain.**

____

____

____

____

____

8. **H.O.T.** **Multi-Step** Charlie's total earnings from his job are $45,000. He also earned $2,000 in profit from selling quilts. He pays $18 tax for every $100 in gross income. What is Charlie's net income?

____

9. **Apply** Geno works at a music store where he earns $16.25 per hour. He works 40 hours per week. Should he take a new job with a gross income of $36,000 per year? Explain your reasoning.

____

____

____

____

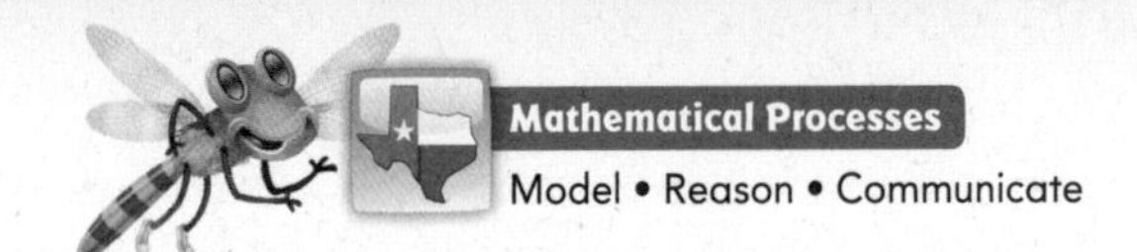

Daily Assessment Task

Fill in the bubble completely to show your answer.

10. The table shows the gross income and payroll tax for the Barker family members for one week. What is their net income for the week?

The Barker Family Income		
	Gross Income	Payroll Tax
Bea Barker	$730	$68.24
Buzz Barker	$654	$50.75

Ⓐ $1,285.01
Ⓑ $1,315.76
Ⓒ $1,264.95
Ⓓ $1,265.01

11. Lana works at the local ice cream store. In the last four weeks, her gross income was $120.75, $118.50, $99.75, and $115.75. Her total payroll tax was $59.70. How can you find her net income for the four weeks?

Ⓐ Find the sum of the gross income. Then add the payroll tax.
Ⓑ Add $59.70 to each of the gross incomes. Then add the sums.
Ⓒ Find the sum of the gross incomes.
Ⓓ Find the sum of the gross incomes. Then subtract the payroll tax.

12. **Multi-Step** Abe earned money mowing lawns. He earned $25 Saturday morning and $75 Saturday afternoon. He earned $100 on Sunday. A payroll tax of $26.25 was withheld each day. If this is Abe's only source of income, what was his net income for the two days?

Ⓐ $73.75
Ⓑ $147.50
Ⓒ $122.25
Ⓓ $173.75

TEXAS Test Prep

13. Sari works in a flower shop for 36 hours each week. She earns $9.75 per hour. The wages from this job are Sari's only source of income. What is her net weekly income if her payroll tax is $73 for the week?

Ⓐ $317
Ⓑ $351
Ⓒ $424
Ⓓ $278

TEKS Personal Financial Literacy—5.10.B
Also 5.3.K
MATHEMATICAL PROCESSES 5.1.A, 5.1.D, 5.1.G

Name ____________________

17.3 Income

Nan Barker lives in a state with no state income tax. Her only source of income is from her job at a technology company. Use Nan's pay stub for 1–4.

7300

Employee: Nan Barker	Total earnings		$1,575.00
	Federal income tax	$236.25	
	Other taxes	$135.40	
Pay period: May 15	Total taxes		
	Pay after taxes		$1,203.35

Detach and retain for your records.

1. What is Nan's gross income for the pay period? ____________

2. What is Nan's net income for the pay period? ____________

3. Nan is paid twice a month. What is Nan's net income each month?

   ____

4. Describe two ways to find the difference between Nan's gross income and her net income for the pay period.

   ____

   ____

Problem Solving Real World

Use Dante's weekly pay stub for 5–6.

904

Employee: Dante Romano	Total earnings		$650.00
	Federal income tax	$78.42	
	State income tax	$35.08	
Pay period: November 1–7	Other taxes	$12.50	
	Total taxes		
	Pay after taxes		

Detach and retain for your records.

5. If the earnings from this job are Dante's only source of income, what is his net income for the week?

   ____

6. What is Dante's annual gross income? **Explain** how you found your answer.

   ____

   ____

   ____

   ____

Lesson Check

★ TEXAS Test Prep

Fill in the bubble completely to show your answer.

7. Keenan worked 45 hours last week. His pay is $20 per hour for 35 hours and $30 per hour for any time over 35 hours. If the earnings from the job are his only source of income, what was Keenan's gross income for last week?

Ⓐ $1,000

Ⓑ $900

Ⓒ $1,350

Ⓓ $700

8. Rita's gross income last month was $2,948.45. She paid $442.45 in payroll tax for the month. How can you find Rita's net income for one week if there were four weeks in the month?

Ⓐ Add the payroll tax to the gross income and multiply by 4.

Ⓑ Subtract the payroll tax from the gross income and multiply by 4.

Ⓒ Add the payroll tax to the gross income and divide by 4.

Ⓓ Subtract the payroll tax from the gross income and divide by 4.

9. Chip works at the amusement park. In the last four weeks, his gross income was $112.25, $98.75, $125.50, and $109.25. His total payroll tax was $62.30. If the earnings from this job are Chip's only source of income, what was his net income for the four weeks?

Ⓐ $445.75

Ⓑ $196.55

Ⓒ $383.45

Ⓓ $508.05

10. Jenna's only source of income is from her job at a car wash, where she works 25 hours each week. She is paid $9.90 per hour. What is her net weekly income if she pays $30.70 in payroll tax each week?

Ⓐ $247.50

Ⓑ $216.80

Ⓒ $278.20

Ⓓ $217.20

11. **Multi-Step** Mr. Jackson's gross monthly income is $4,090 and his payroll tax is $654.40. Mrs. Jackson's gross monthly income is $4,250 and her payroll tax is $680. What is the Jacksons' combined net income for the month?

Ⓐ $8,340.00

Ⓑ $7,005.60

Ⓒ $9,674.40

Ⓓ $6,905.60

12. **Multi-Step** Ari worked for a moving company last weekend. On Saturday, his gross income was $350 and his net income was $307.05. On Sunday, his gross income was $280 and his net income was $246.35. How much did Ari pay in payroll tax last weekend?

Ⓐ $76.60

Ⓑ $103.00

Ⓒ $137.30

Ⓓ $70.00

Name ______________________________

17.4 Paying Bills

Essential Question

What are the advantages and disadvantages of different ways to pay bills?

You go into a store and see something you want to buy. Should you pay with cash, the money in your wallet, or another way?

A **check** is a written order asking a bank to pay a certain amount from your account. Sometimes it takes several days for a bank to pay the amount on a check. In your checkbook, there is a place to record how much you have and how much you spend.

A **credit card** is an identification card issued by a bank that allows a user to buy items and services immediately and pay the cost at a later time. The bank might charge the user interest in exchange for the use of the money.

A **debit card** is an identification card issued by a bank that allows a user to immediately use money from an account. You have a personal identification number (PIN) to keep it safe.

Unlock the Problem

Mrs. Pastella wants to buy an easel for $100 at a store. She has no cash with her. Complete the table below to help her determine the method of payment she should use.

Write the letter of the statements to show the advantages and disadvantages of each method. A statement can go in more than one place.

	Advantages	Disadvantages
Check		
Credit Card		
Debit Card		

A. PIN can make it secure	I. Can buy now and pay later
B. May owe more money than I can pay back	J. Need to remember PIN
C. Could be bulky to carry	K. Need to have enough in my account
D. Less likely to overspend	L. Could lose the card
E. Takes time to write it out	M. Can run out of checks
F. Convenient and easy to carry around	N. May have to pay interest
G. Provides a space to record expenses	O. Could be stolen
H. Easy to forget to record how much I spend	

Example 1

Sometimes it is not possible to use cash or a check. In such cases, you can use a credit card or one of several methods of electronic payment. These methods are especially useful when you shop online.

Some companies offer money transfer services to send money immediately from your account to the seller. There is usually a fee for the service.

Some sellers let you pay the cost in several parts. You set up automatic payments that transfer a set amount of money from your account at specific times. You usually pay a fee for spreading out the payments. Automatic payments are also useful for bills that occur regularly.

Write the letter of the statements to show the advantages and disadvantages of each method of payment. A statement can go in more than one place.

A. Useful for monthly bills
B. Can buy now and pay later
C. May have to pay a fee or interest
D. Convenient and easy to carry around
E. May forget that a payment will be made
F. Fast way to send money
G. May owe more money than I can pay back
H. Need to have enough in my account
I. Could be stolen

	Advantages	Disadvantages
Credit Card		
Money Transfer		
Automatic Payments		

Share and Show

PRICE OF A COMPUTER
C-Mart Computer Store: Cash: $625
ComputerWorld.com
Automatic Payments: 4 easy payments of $150 + $10 fee per payment
Credit Card: $575 + Interest* *Interest: $50

1. The total cost of buying a computer online using automatic payments:

   4 × ________ + 4 × ________ = ________ + ________

   = ________.

2. The total cost of buying a computer online using a credit card:

   ________ + ________ = ________

Math Talk

Mathematical Processes

Which method would you use to buy the computer and why?

Name ______________________

Problem Solving

3. **Apply** Name one method of payment that allows you to use money in your account and one method that alows you to pay the amount at a later time.

4. **H.O.T.** **Analyze** What are the advantages and disadvantages of the methods you chose in Exercise 3?

Problem Solving 

5. **H.O.T.** **Multi-Step** Ty researches how much he would pay if he used various methods of payment to buy a chemistry set. If he pays $0.10 in interest for every dollar on his credit card, which method should he use to buy the chemistry set? **Explain.**

Price of a Chemistry Set

ABC Toys
Cash: $175

Check or Debit Card:
$175 + $5 processing fee

Books.com (free shipping!)
Automatic Payments:
4 payments of $30 + $40 fee

Credit Card: $150 + interest

6. Liam's bank pays the amount on a check five days after it is written. If Liam wants to make a payment immediately, which method of payment could he use? **Explain.**

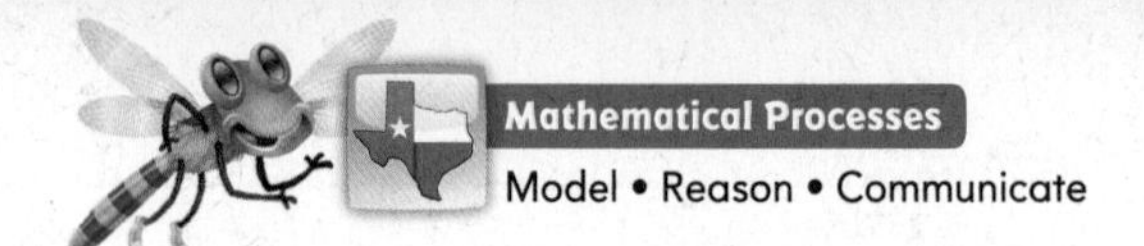

Daily Assessment Task

Fill in the bubble completely to show your answer.

7. Jen wants to buy a camera. Which method will let her buy now and pay later?

Ⓐ check

Ⓑ cash

Ⓒ credit card

Ⓓ money transfer

8. Antoine owes $684. He can make six monthly automatic payments with a $2.50 fee for each payment, or he can pay using a credit card. If he uses his credit card, he will pay $30 in interest. How much money does he save by using automatic payments?

Ⓐ $15 Ⓒ $116.50

Ⓑ $114 Ⓓ $16

9. **Multi-Step** Lester buys a sofa for $560. He pays $200 first and pays the rest over 6 months using automatic payments. How much will he pay each month?

Ⓐ $360

Ⓑ $60

Ⓒ $93.33

Ⓓ $126.67

TEXAS Test Prep

10. Which of the following is an advantage of using a check to pay bills?

Ⓐ You can buy now and pay later.

Ⓑ The money is transferred immediately.

Ⓒ You can pay using money in your account.

Ⓓ You may have to pay interest on the amount.

Name ________________

17.4 Paying Bills

Angelina made a chart to compare the cost of buying a game console using different payment methods. Use the chart for 1–4.

PRICE OF A GAME CONSOLE

Ed's Discount Store: $229

GameStore.com (free shipping)

Automatic Payments:
3 payments of
$75 + $5 per payment

Credit Card:
$219 + $10.95 interest

1. The total cost of buying a game console at Ed's Discount Store is ________.

2. The total cost of buying a game console online using automatic payments: ______ × (______ + ______) = ______

3. The total cost of buying a game console using a credit card: ________ + ________ = ________

4. Why might Angelina choose to purchase the game console using a more expensive payment method?

____

____

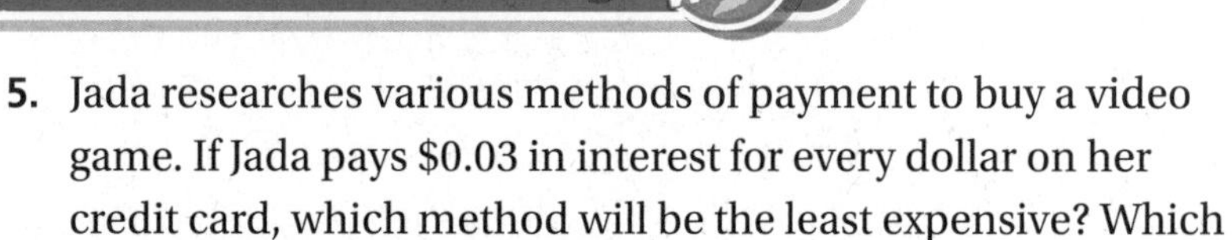

PRICE OF A VIDEO GAME

Paula's Game Store
Cash: $49
Check or Debit Card:
$49 + $5 processing fee

Games.com (free shipping)
Automatic Payments:
2 payments of
$26 + $2 per payment

Credit Card: $48

5. Jada researches various methods of payment to buy a video game. If Jada pays $0.03 in interest for every dollar on her credit card, which method will be the least expensive? Which method is the most expensive?

____

____

____

6. Oliver pays $0.05 interest for every $1 he spends using his credit card. **Explain** how he can use mental math to find the total cost of a $300 tablet computer.

____

Lesson Check

TEXAS Test Prep

Fill in the bubble completely to show your answer.

7. Which of the following is NOT an advantage of using a debit card as your payment method?

Ⓐ You can buy now and pay later.

Ⓑ A personal identification number helps keep your account safe.

Ⓒ It is convenient to carry around.

Ⓓ You are less likely to overspend.

8. Harrison pays $0.02 in interest for every $1 that he spends on his credit card. How much interest will Harrison pay on the purchase of a $78 camera bag?

Ⓐ $1.40

Ⓑ $1.56

Ⓒ $15.60

Ⓓ $79.56

9. **Multi-Step** Charlotte wants to buy some books online that have a total cost of $162. She plans to make six equal monthly payments. Each month, she will be charged a $1.75 processing fee. How much will Charlotte pay each month?

Ⓐ $27.00

Ⓑ $25.25

Ⓒ $28.75

Ⓓ $27.75

10. **Multi-Step** Ethan wants to buy a new watch that costs $112. He pays $0.04 in interest for every $1 that he spends on his credit card. How much will Ethan save by paying with cash?

Ⓐ $2.80

Ⓑ $1.04

Ⓒ $0.45

Ⓓ $4.48

11. **Multi-Step** Enrique buys a jacket for $35 and pants for $29. Sales tax is $0.07 for every dollar of the purchase price. He pays a $2.75 processing fee for paying with a check. How much will Enrique pay for his purchases?

Ⓐ $71.23

Ⓑ $68.48

Ⓒ $71.42

Ⓓ $66.75

12. **Multi-Step** Paige finds a printer for $148 at an online store. The cost of shipping the printer is $20. If Paige plans to make four equal monthly payments for the total cost, how much will she pay each month?

Ⓐ $37

Ⓑ $42

Ⓒ $32

Ⓓ $40

Name ___

17.5 Keeping Records

Essential Question How can you keep track of finances?

A good way to manage finances is to keep track of the money received, paid, and available.

Unlock the Problem (Real World)

Hannah made a chart to keep track of her money. She records her allowance, savings, earnings, and other expenses. Income is added, expenses are subtracted. Use the notes at the right to complete her chart. Include the available funds after each addition or subtraction. How much does Hannah have left at the end of the month?

May 18: baby-sit $15

May 19 movies $6.50

May 25 mow lawns $15

fruit snack $3.97 May 27

May 30 School trip, souvenir $14.75

Hannah's Financial Record: Month of May

Date	Description	Received ($)	Expenses ($)	Available Funds ($)
	Balance: end of April			0
5/4	babysitting	20		20
5/6	allowance	10		30
5/6	save		5	
5/8	3 music downloads		2.97	
5/13	allowance	10		
5/15	snack bar		1.25	
5/20	allowance	10		
5/27	allowance	10		

At the end of the month, Hannah has ___ left.

Math Talk Mathematical Processes

Explain why savings are treated as an expense in Hannah's chart.

Share and Show

Jack keeps a record of his money in July. Use his record for 1–3.

Date	Description	Received ($)	Expenses ($)	Available Funds ($)
	Balance: end of June			0
7/2	yard work	15.50		15.50
7/3	fruit juice		1.75	13.75
7/5	ticket to museum			

1. Jack pays $7.65 for a ticket to a museum on July 5. How much will he have in available funds after he buys the ticket?

   - Circle the available funds Jack has before buying the ticket. Subtract the price of the ticket from the available funds.

     ______ − ______ = ______

   - Record the price of the ticket and the new available funds in the chart.

2. Jack earns $24.00 washing cars on July 8. Complete the next row in the chart to show this information. How much does Jack have in available funds now?

   ______

3. On July 12, Jack gets $15 allowance and spends $4.95 for baseball cards. Complete the chart to show this information. How much does Jack have in available funds now?

   ______

Problem Solving

4. **H.O.T.** **What's the Error?** Ana's financial record shows that she started May with $13.09. On May 4, she earned $18 babysitting and saved $5. Her aunt gave her $10 on May 10. She spent $2.75 for a yogurt bar on May 13. Her record now shows available funds of $43.34. What is Ana's error?

   ______

   ______

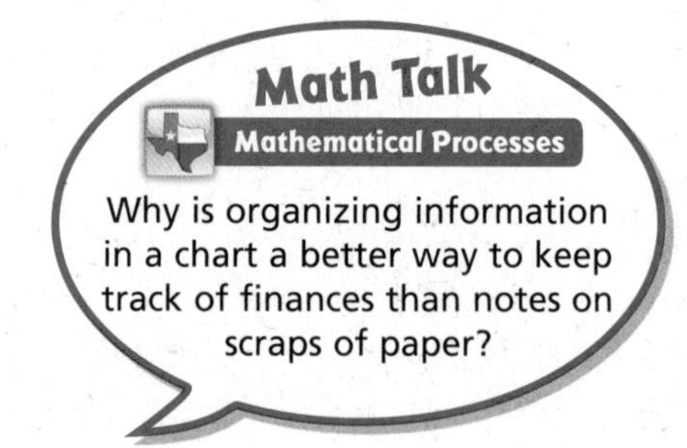

Name ______________________

Problem Solving Real World

Ryan has a dog-walking business. Use the financial information about his business for 5–7.

payment from dog owners - $129 - March 3

buy dog biscuits - $45.98 - March 9

buy leashes - $64.25 - March 12

payment from dog owners - $96 - March 18

pay helper - $140 - March 20

payment from dog owners - $106 - March 26

buy dog food - $84.50 - March 28

5. H.O.T. **Multi-Step** Ryan's goal is to always have $50 or more in available funds. Complete the chart. Did Ryan achieve his goal during the month of March? **Explain.**

____

____

____

Date	Description	Received ($)	Expenses ($)	Available Funds ($)
	Balance: March 1			50

6. **Explain** how you can identify Ryan's expenses by only looking at the available funds column.

____

7. **Multi-Step** Ryan receives another payment from the dog owners on March 31. He also spends $25 on dog treats that day. If Ryan ends the month with $86.27 in available funds, how much money did he get from the owners on March 31? ______________

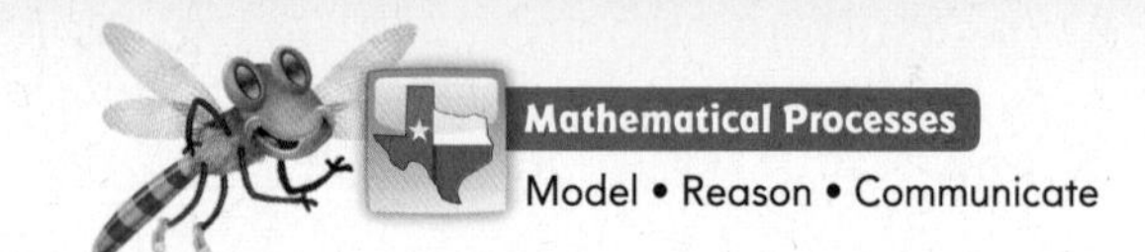

Daily Assessment Task

The chart shows Lisa's finances during the first week in August. Use the chart for 8–10. Fill in the bubble completely to show your answer.

Date	Description	Received ($)	Expenses ($)	Available Funds ($)
	Balance: end of July			0
8/1	allowance	12		12
8/2	orange juice		2.29	9.71
8/3	planting flowers	?		25.96
8/4	comic books		11.65	14.31

8. **Analyze** How much does Lisa earn planting flowers?

   Ⓐ $25.96 Ⓒ $12.00

   Ⓑ $16.25 Ⓓ $35.67

9. Which expression shows how to find the amount of money Lisa has in available funds after she buys orange juice?

   Ⓐ $12 + $2.29 Ⓒ $9.71 − $2.29

   Ⓑ $25.96 − $2.29 Ⓓ $12 − $2.29

10. **Multi-Step** Lisa wins a $25-door prize at a party on August 5. She spends $5.40 for new markers on August 6 and $18 for a soccer ball on August 7. What are her available funds now?

   Ⓐ $21.31 Ⓒ $15.91

   Ⓑ $39.31 Ⓓ $33.91

TEXAS Test Prep

11. Jacob starts June with $20 in available funds. He earns $30 for mowing lawns and gets an allowance from his parents. His expenses for the month were $20.65. If Jacob ends the month with $44.35 in funds, what is his monthly allowance?

   Ⓐ $30.00 Ⓒ $15.00

   Ⓑ $44.35 Ⓓ $45.00

TEKS Personal Financial Literacy—5.10.D
Also 5.3.K
MATHEMATICAL PROCESSES 5.1.A, 5.1.E, 5.1.F

Name ______________________

17.5 Keeping Records

Kimiko makes crafts to sell at a festival in July. Complete the chart using the notes at the right. Use the information for 1–2.

Date	Description	Received ($)	Expenses ($)	Available Funds ($)
	Balance: July 1			45

July 2: purchase craft supplies $27.95

July 5: pay booth fee $15

July 14: earn $125 from craft sales

July 15: earn $52 from craft sales

July 18: pay friend for helping at booth $25

July 22: purchase craft supplies

1. Write an equation to show how to calculate the amount Kimiko has in available funds after purchasing supplies on July 2. ______________

2. **Explain** how Kimiko can calculate her total expenses for July. What were Kimiko's total expenses?

____

____

Problem Solving Real World

Use the information from the chart above for 3–4.

3. Are Kimiko's available funds greater on July 1 or on July 22? **Explain.**

____

4. Kimiko has $15 in additional expenses on July 28. How much more will she need to earn if she wants to have $200 in available funds at the end of July? ______________

Lesson Check

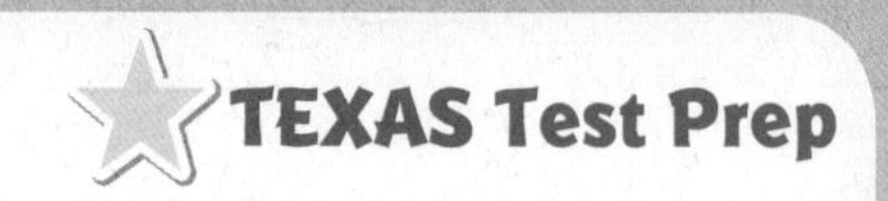

Fill in the bubble completely to show your answer.

5. The chart shows Micah's finances during the first week in May. He earns $25 for babysitting on May 8. He buys another book on May 12 for $9.49.

Date	Description	Received ($)	Expenses ($)	Available Funds ($)
	Balance: May 1			0
5/4	allowance	15		15
5/7	purchase book		12.95	2.05

How much does Micah have in available funds now?

Ⓐ $36.54
Ⓑ $27.05
Ⓒ $15.51
Ⓓ $17.56

Heather sells baked goods. The chart shows Heather's finances for the beginning of June. Use the chart for 6–9.

Date	Description	Received ($)	Expenses ($)	Available Funds ($)
	Balance: June 1			0
6/2	cupcake sales	18.50		18.50
6/3	pie sales	26.74		45.24
6/4	pay for advertising		?	28.99
6/5	pay for supplies		23.97	5.02

6. How much does Heather spend on advertising?

Ⓐ $28.99
Ⓑ $5.02
Ⓒ $16.25
Ⓓ $23.75

7. Which expression shows how to find the amount in available funds after Heather sells some pies on June 3?

Ⓐ $26.74 − $18.50
Ⓑ $18.50 + $26.74
Ⓒ $45.24 − $26.74
Ⓓ $45.24 + $26.74

8. **Multi-Step** What is the difference between Heather's expenses and her earnings?

Ⓐ $5.02
Ⓑ $21.27
Ⓒ $2.77
Ⓓ $7.72

9. **Multi-Step** Heather sells cookies for $14.85 on June 6. She spends $8.99 for packing supplies on June 7 and $5.19 for ribbon on June 8. What are Heather's available funds now?

Ⓐ $5.69
Ⓑ $0.67
Ⓒ $19.87
Ⓓ $5.86

Name ____________________

17.6 Make a Budget

Essential Question How can you make and balance a budget?

Unlock the Problem

A budget is balanced when expenses equal income. Answer the questions, make your choices, and fill in the charts to make and balance a budget.

Make a budget.

Your allowance is $20 per week. Circle one of these ways to earn extra income. Decide how often you will do it in one week.

When you list your expenses, remember to include funds for fun and entertainment, as well as repeating expenses like lunch, bus fare, lessons you pay for, regular donations, savings, and emergency money.

Extra Income!

Mow lawn: $12

Water neighbor's plants: $6.75

Dog walking: $1.50 per dog per day

A **What is your weekly income?**

Description	Amount
Allowance	
Other	
Total	

B **What are your weekly expenses?**

Description	Amount
Total	

Income − expenses = ________

Redo your budget, if needed, to make expenses equal income.

Math Talk Mathematical Processes

Is your budget balanced? Explain what you might do to have more money available at the end of the month.

- You forgot to budget $10 for a birthday gift for your best friend. How can you adjust your budget to fit the new expense?

____

Share and Show

Complete the tables to find Rob's total income and total expenses for the week. Use the tables for 1–3.

Income	
Description	**Amount**
Allowance	$12
Washing windows	$10
Babysitting	$16
Gift	$10
Total	$

Expenses	
Description	**Amount**
School lunches	$8
Field trip	$10
New jeans	$21
Savings	$10
Total	$

1. Is Rob's budget for the week balanced? **Explain.**

2. **Write Math** ▸ How can Rob balance the budget?

3. Rob is saving for a tool kit. He needs $79.99 to buy the kit. If he continues to save the same amount each week, how soon will he be able to buy it?

Problem Solving

4. **Analyze** For every $10 Zain earns, he will budget $2 for savings, $3 for special purchases, $1 for donating to charity, and $4 for his regular expenses. If Zain earns $200, how much will he budget for his regular expenses?

5. **H.O.T.** **Multi-Step** Rhonda budgets for the following expenses each week: $5 for bus tickets, $20 for lunch, $10 for movies, and $5 for savings. Rhonda gets $20 as her weekly allowance and $5 for each garden she weeds. If Rhonda's weekly budget is balanced, how many gardens does she weed each week?

6. **H.O.T.** Hazem's weekly income is $40. He budgets $20 for food and entertainment each week and saves the rest of his income. How much money will he save in 5 months?

Name ___________________________

Problem Solving (Real World)

7. **Multi-Step** The tables show Diana's income and expenses for one week. Find the amount for other expenses that will balance her budget for that week.

Income
Doing laundry for a neighbor: $12 per week
Helping with homework: $5 per hour, 3 hours per week
Selling old board games at a yard sale: $18
Allowance: $7
Gift: $10

Expenses
Donations to the animal shelter: $6 per week
Bus fare: $2 per day, 6 times each week
Savings $10
Snacks/entertainment: $14
Other expenses $

8. **H.O.T.** Mia earns $15 from babysitting and $9 from dog-walking each week. Her weekly allowance is $15. Mia budgets a third of her income each week for savings and the rest for repeated expenses. How much money does she have in her budget for repeated expenses? __________

9. **Record** The tables show Han's monthly budget. Complete the tables to show the total income, total expenses, and the amount of savings if the budget is balanced.

Income	
Description	**Amount**
Allowance	$40
Paper route	$120
Babysitting	$80
Total	$

Expenses	
Description	**Amount**
Lunch and snacks	$125
Entertainment	$25
Savings	$
Total	$

10. Tanja saves $75 each week. Her other expenses are four times the amount she saves. If Tanja's weekly budget is balanced, what is her weekly income? __________

11. **Multi-Step** Yoav earns $8 after taxes for every hour he works at the grocery store. He works 15 hours each week at the store. If Yoav budgets a third of his earnings for art supplies, how much money does he have to spend on art supplies each week? __________

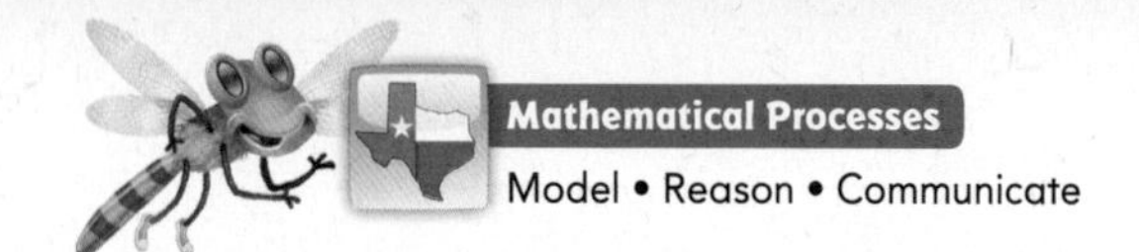

Daily Assessment Task

Fill in the bubble completely to show your answer.
Use the chart for 12–13.

Madi's March Budget	
Income	**Expenses**
Allowance: $40	Book/music downloads: $26
Household chores: $20	Cat supplies: $22
Selling used video games: $10	Savings: $30
Gift: $15	Giving to charity: $15

12. Madi's budget is not balanced. By how much must she reduce expenses to balance her budget?

Ⓐ $85 Ⓒ $93

Ⓑ $18 Ⓓ $8

13. Madi reduces her monthly expense for book/music downloads to $13. How much more money can she put away for savings and still balance the budget?

Ⓐ $13 Ⓒ $30

Ⓑ $5 Ⓓ $35

14. **Multi-Step** Carlos is paid $17 per hour after taxes. He works 25 hours per week. His weekly expenses add up to $476. How many more hours per week would Carlos have to work to balance his budget?

Ⓐ 1 hour Ⓒ 0 hours

Ⓑ 3 hours Ⓓ 28 hours

TEXAS Test Prep

15. Georgette balances her budget by using this plan. For every $100 she earns, she budgets $10 for charity, $20 for savings, $20 for books, and $50 for other expenses. If her income is $500 per week, how much does she give to charity each week?

Ⓐ $500 Ⓒ $5

Ⓑ $50 Ⓓ $250

Name ______________________

17.6 Make a Budget

The chart shows Kristi's January budget. Use the chart for 1–2.

Income	
Description	**Amount**
Allowance	\$50
Shoveling snow	\$40
Tutoring	\$35
Dog sitting	?
Total	

Expenses	
Description	**Amount**
Piano lessons	\$80
Snacks	\$25
Ski rental	\$40
Savings	\$25
Total	

1. What are Kristi's total expenses for January?

____

2. How much will Kristi need to earn dog sitting in January for her budget to be balanced?

____

3. Kristi is saving for a pair of binoculars. The binoculars cost \$125.99. If she saves an additional \$2 each week, can she buy the binoculars in 5 weeks? **Explain.**

____

____

Problem Solving

The chart shows Donald's expenses for one week. Use the chart for 4–5.

Income	
Description	**Amount**
Swimming lessons	\$30
Babysitting	?
Weeding garden	\$10
Total	

Expenses	
Description	**Amount**
School lunches	\$25
Bus Fare	\$15
Movie	\$8
Savings	\$10
Total	

4. What are Donald's expenses for the week?

____

5. How much does Donald earn for babysitting if his weekly budget is balanced?

____

Lesson Check

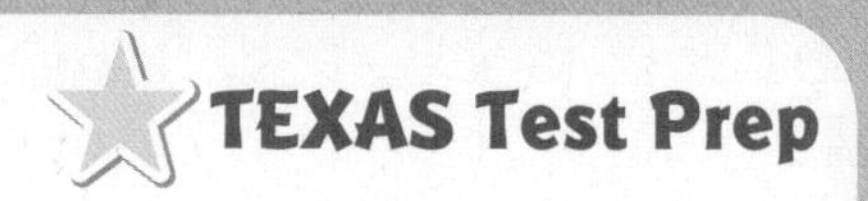

Fill in the bubble completely to show your answer.

6. Pilar has a plan for her budget. For every $10 she earns, she will budget $4 for savings, $4 for her regular expenses, and $2 for special purchases. If her income is $64,000 per year, how much does she budget for special purchases?

Ⓐ $6,400

Ⓑ $25,600

Ⓒ $12,800

Ⓓ $32,000

7. Which statement is true about Mr. Simon's monthly budget?

Ⓐ His budget is balanced when his monthly expenses equal total income for the month.

Ⓑ His budget is balanced when total monthly expenses are greater than his income.

Ⓒ His budget is balanced when total income is greater than his expenses.

Ⓓ His budget is balanced when his weekly expenses are less than his monthly expenses.

The chart shows Ellison's April budget. Use the chart for 8–9.

Ellison's April Budget	
Income	**Expenses**
Allowance: $20	Savings: $20
Yard work: $15	Donation: $10
Garage sale: $18	Baseball tickets: $35
Computer lessons: $16	Club dues: $10

8. Ellison is saving for a skateboard that costs $49.75. If he continues to save the same amount each month, how soon will he be able to buy it?

Ⓐ 3 months Ⓒ 3 weeks

Ⓑ 2 months Ⓓ 2 weeks

9. Ellison decides to ask his parents for an increase in his allowance so he can balance his budget. How much more will Ellison need?

Ⓐ $6 Ⓒ $15

Ⓑ $5 Ⓓ $16

10. Multi-Step Shelley earns $12 per hour after taxes. She works 30 hours each week. Her weekly expenses are $420. How many more hours per week would she have to work to balance her budget?

Ⓐ 6 hours Ⓒ 2 hours

Ⓑ 5 hours Ⓓ 3 hours

11. Multi-Step Tyrone earns $650 per week. This week, Tyrone wants to donate $100 to charity. His weekly expenses are $595. How much will Tyrone need to reduce his expenses in order to make the donation and balance his budget?

Ⓐ $55 Ⓒ $50

Ⓑ $40 Ⓓ $45

Name ______________________________

17.7 Adjust a Budget

Essential Question

How can you balance a budget when expenses exceed income?

Families have many expenses. If they own a home, their budget includes paying for a home loan. They may also budget for food, transportation, utilities (electric, water, or natural gas bills), emergencies, savings, and charitable giving.

Unlock the Problem (Real World)

The Smith family's net monthly income is $3,350. The graph shows the budget for the monthly expenses. The family car needs emergency repairs that cost $725. How might the family change their budget to pay for the car repairs and balance the budget?

Balance the budget.

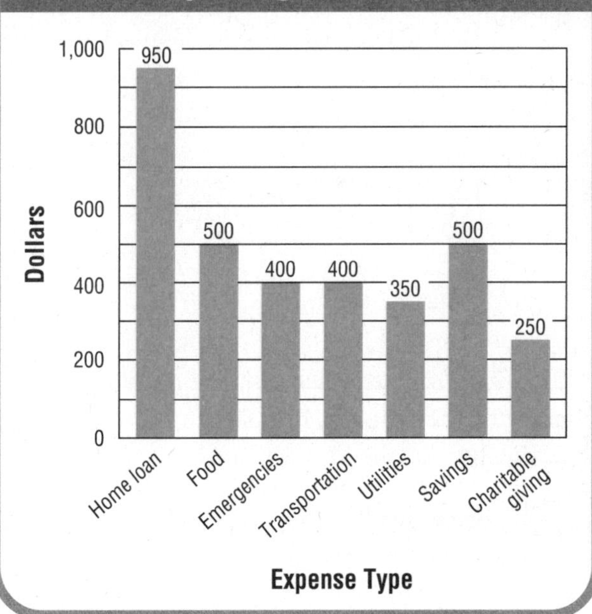

The family income is $3,350.

What is the total of the budgeted expenses?

____

How much money is budgeted for emergencies?

____

So they need __________ − __________ or

__________ more to pay for the car repairs.

The family could try to decrease expenses,

such as ______________________________.

The family could try to increase income

by ______________________________.

The family could withdraw money from their __________ this month and make it up in future months.

Share and Show 

Use the graph at the right for 1–3.

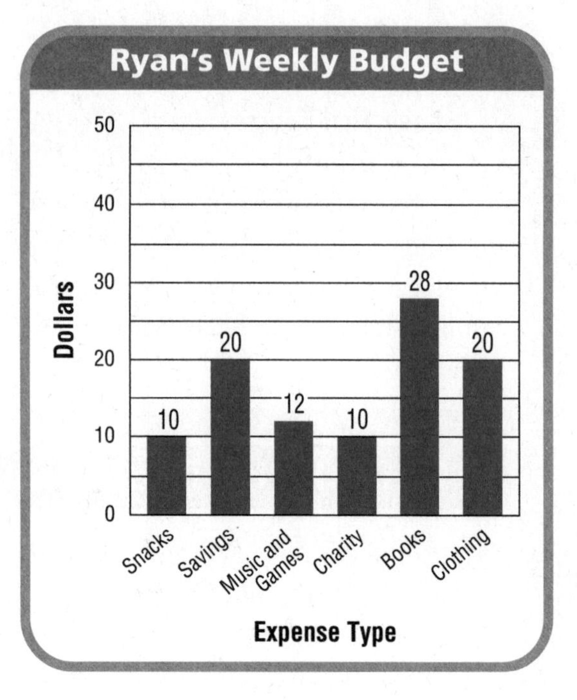

1. Ryan receives an allowance of $15 each week. He works shelving books at the library 4 times a week and receives $20 each time. He also gets $5 each week when he completes his chores at home. Is Ryan's budget balanced? **Explain**.

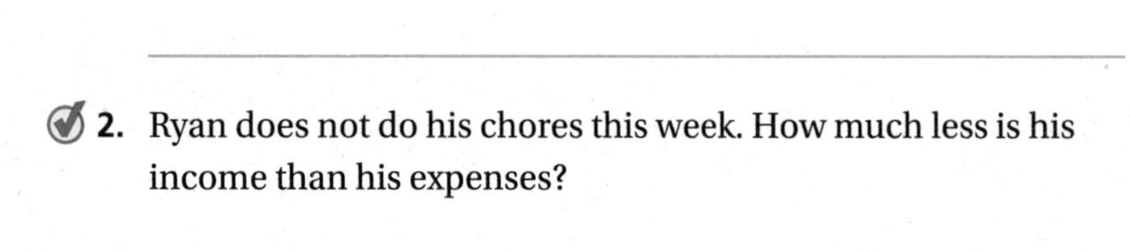

2. Ryan does not do his chores this week. How much less is his income than his expenses?

3. **Explain** two ways Ryan might be able to balance his budget when he does not do his chores.

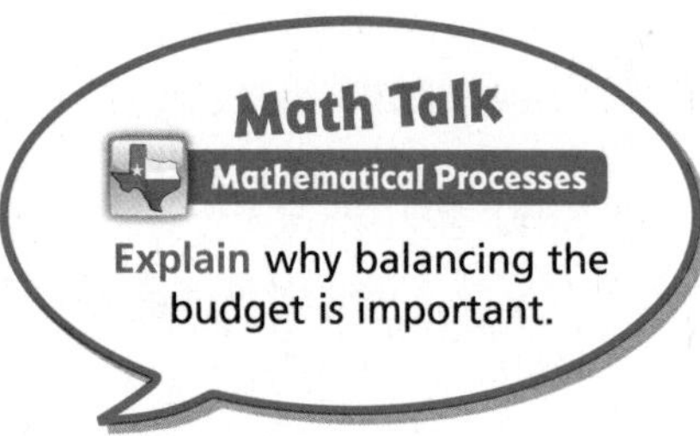

Problem Solving

4. **Write Math** ▸ How can you determine if a budget is balanced?

5. **Write Math** ▸ How can you balance a budget if the expenses are greater than income? Give examples.

6. Think about your weekly expenses. Name an expense that is easy to reduce and one that is not.

Name ___________________________

Problem Solving Real World

Use the table for 7–9.

Michelle's Expenses		
Rent	$675	
Food	$800	
Cable TV and Internet	$45	
Land-line telephone	$29	
Cell phone	$50	
Clothes	$100	
Savings	$200	
Entertainment	$200	
Loan payments	$250	
Education	$150	
Charitable donations	$200	
Pet related	$75	
Transportation	$385	
Gas/oil/electric	$400	

7. **Representations** Michelle is a cook. Her net income is $3,200 per month. Is Michelle's monthly budget balanced? **Explain.**

____

8. H.O.T. **Multi-Step** How can Michelle adjust the expenses in her budget to balance it? Use the column to the right to change amounts so her budget will be balanced.

____

____

9. H.O.T. Michelle decides to give up her land-line telephone and reduce her entertainment budget to $50. She also decides to cater two parties to earn $250 for each party. Use Michelle's numbers to calculate if there is enough money left over to buy an oven for $312. **Explain** your reasoning.

____

____

____

____

____

____

10. **Multi-Step** Alex works in a call center answering phones. He earns $13 per hour after taxes and works 35 hours per week. Each week, Alex is also paid $195 after taxes at his part-time job. If Alex balances his budget, how much are his weekly expenses?

____

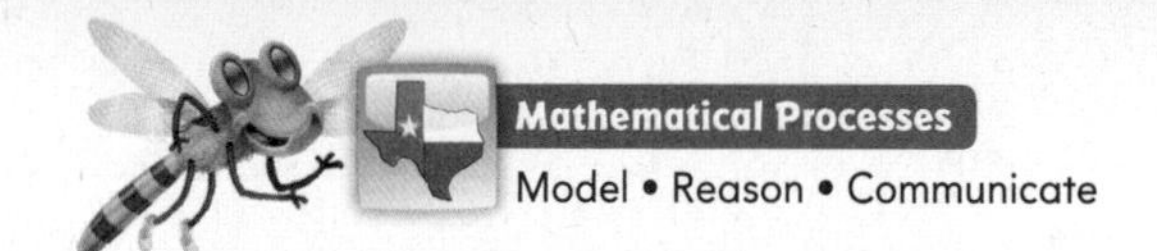

Daily Assessment Task

Fill in the bubble completely to show your answer.
Use the chart for 11–12.

Dean's January Budget	
Income	**Expenses**
Allowance: $25	Monthly cell phone: $18
Paper route: $20	Books: $20
	Movie rentals: $12

11. Which of the following changes can be made to balance Dean's budget?

Ⓐ Decrease the book purchases to $15.

Ⓑ Decrease the paper route income to $15.

Ⓒ Increase the movie rentals to $15.

Ⓓ Increase the paper route income to $22.

12. Multi-Step In February, Dean would like to get a new cell phone plan that costs $30 per month. He can increase his paper route to $25 per month. He would like to continue buying books and renting movies. Which of the following will allow him to keep a balanced budget?

Ⓐ Keep his expenses the same, and increase his income by $10 per month.

Ⓑ Spend no more than $15 on books and increase his income by $5 per month.

Ⓒ Spend no more than $10 on books and $10 on movies.

Ⓓ Spend no more than $15 on books and $7 on movies.

13. Sandy's expenses are greater than her income. Which of the following could Sandy increase in order to balance her budget?

Ⓐ loan payment

Ⓑ music downloads

Ⓒ charitable donations

Ⓓ hourly pay

TEXAS Test Prep

14. Natalia's net income is $28,000 per year. She would like to have a balanced budget. If her other expenses are three-fourths as much as her income, how much can she save each year?

Ⓐ $28,000

Ⓑ $700

Ⓒ $21,000

Ⓓ $7,000

TEKS Personal Financial Literacy—5.10.E
Also 5.9.C
MATHEMATICAL PROCESSES 5.1.A, 5.1.D

Name ______________________

17.7 Adjust a Budget

Use the graph at the right for 1–2.

1. Jordan earns $10 each weekday for chores she completes after school. Her mother pays her $20 on Saturday and $15 on Sunday for helping with her catering business. Is Jordan's budget balanced? Explain.

____

____

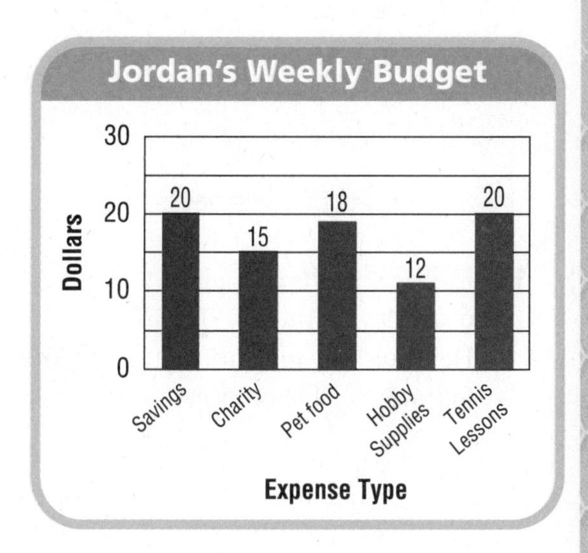

2. Next week, Jordan has a tennis match on Saturday and cannot help her mother. What would be the difference between her income that week and her expenses?

____

Problem Solving

Use the table for 3–4.

3. Jesse earns $2,500 per month after taxes, working at a car repair shop. Is his budget balanced? **Explain.**

____

____

Jesse's Monthly Expenses	
Rent	$795
Food	$750
Cable	$80
Electric bill	$225
Clothes	$125
Savings	$200
Car loan	$200
Gas	$150
Cell phone	$55
Entertainment	$100

4. Sometimes Jesse works on his friends' cars on the weekend and earns an extra $100 per car. How can Jesse balance his monthly budget?

____

____

____

____

Lesson Check

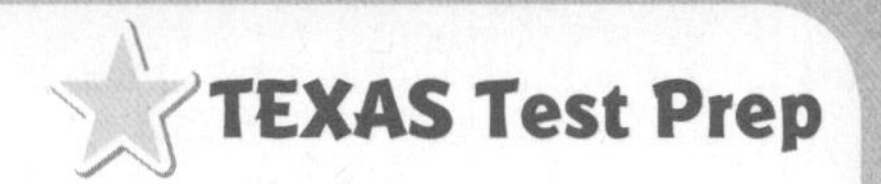

Fill in the bubble completely to show your answer.

5. Mr. Porter wants to spend an extra $150 this weekend on a family outing to the state fair. Which of the following could be a way to adjust his budget to allow for the extra expense?

   Ⓐ Work fewer hours this week.

   Ⓑ Work overtime.

   Ⓒ Give money to charity.

   Ⓓ Increase gasoline usage.

6. Alexis earns $50 a day for five days this week. Her weekly expenses are $280. How can she balance her budget?

   Ⓐ Increase her income $5 each day.

   Ⓑ Increase her income $20 this week.

   Ⓒ Decrease her expenses by $30.

   Ⓓ Decrease her expenses by $20.

Use the chart for 7–8.

Tatiana's March Budget	
Income	**Expenses**
Allowance $40	Sports Equipment $25
House cleaning $25	Meals with friends $35
	Acting lessons $15

7. Which of the following changes can be made to balance Tatiana's budget?

   Ⓐ Decrease spending on sports equipment to $20.

   Ⓑ Increase income from house cleaning to $30.

   Ⓒ Increase spending on acting lessons to $25.

   Ⓓ Decrease spending on meals with friends to $25.

8. **Multi-Step** Tatiana would like to buy soccer shoes that are on sale for $30. She will use her sports equipment budget for part of the cost. Which of the following plans will allow Tatiana to have a balanced budget?

   Ⓐ Increase her income by $15.

   Ⓑ Spend only $15 on meals.

   Ⓒ Spend only $20 on meals and increase her house cleaning income by $15.

   Ⓓ Increase her income by $60.

9. **Multi-Step** Duke works at a grocery store sacking groceries. He earns $12 per hour after taxes and works 24 hours each week. His weekly expenses total $324. How many more hours would Duke need to work to balance his budget?

   Ⓐ 1 hour

   Ⓑ 2 hours

   Ⓒ 4 hours

   Ⓓ 3 hours

Name ____________________

Unit 6 Assessment

Vocabulary

Choose the best term from the box.

Vocabulary
budget
gross income
income tax
net income
property tax
sales tax

1. ____________ is the income that is left after taxes. (p. 629)

2. A ____________ is money added to the cost of items or services. (p. 623)

3. ____________ is a portion of the value of an item, such as land. (p. 623)

4. The total income before any taxes are taken out is ____________. (p. 629)

5. ____________ is money that is paid to a city, state, or the U.S. government based on earnings. (p. 617)

Concepts and Skills

6. The monthly income for a family is $2,000. The family's monthly budget is shown. Describe two ways the family could adjust their budget to put $300 in a savings account each month. TEKS 5.10.E

Monthly Expenses	
Rent	$800
Utilities	$65
Food	$400
Entertainment	$300
Clothing	$300

____

____

____

____

____

7. What are some advantages and disadvantages of using a debit card over a credit card? TEKS 5.10.C

____

____

____

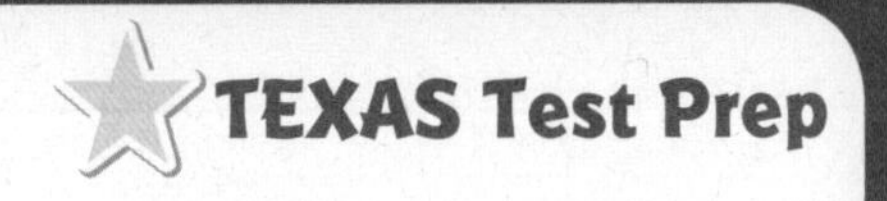

8. A family's monthly income is $2,100. Their monthly budget is shown. How can the family balance their budget if their rent increases by $250? TEKS 5.10.E

Monthly Expenses	
Rent	$900
Utilities	$75
Food	$600
Entertainment	$300
Clothing	$200

9. Martin gets a check for $25 for his birthday on May 8th. The next day, he spends $16 on CDs and $2.50 on stamps. Complete the table to calculate the amount Martin has in available funds now. TEKS 5.10.D

Date	Description	Amount Received ($)	Expenses ($)	Available funds ($)
	Balance: end of April			0
5/4	babysitting	30		30
5/6	allowance	15		45
5/6	save		5	40

10. The total cost of an item is $98. If the item is purchased using automatic payments, the buyer will need to make four payments of $26. How much more does the item cost when using automatic payments? Explain. TEKS 5.10.C

11. Sally got a pay raise. Her gross income increased by $500 and her net income increased by $417. By how much did Sally's taxes increase? TEKS 5.10.B

Fill in the bubble completely to show your answer.

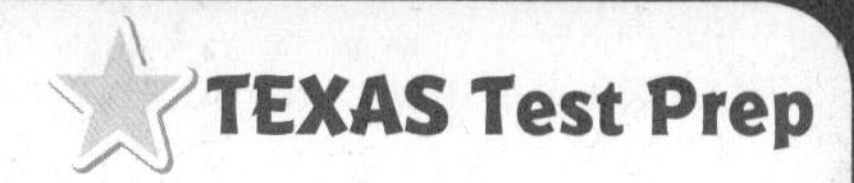

12. Maura pays $0.02 in sales tax for every $1 that she spends. If Maura buys $60 worth of items, what is the total cost? TEKS 5.10.A

Ⓐ $60

Ⓑ $0.02

Ⓒ $1.20

Ⓓ $61.20

13. Raul pays property tax in Dallas. On which of the following might Raul pay property tax? TEKS 5.10.A

Ⓐ clothing

Ⓑ office space

Ⓒ salary

Ⓓ groceries

14. Lorena makes a list of the taxes she pays each month. How much does she pay in payroll tax? TEKS 5.10.A

Lorena's Taxes

Sales Tax: $24.65

Federal Income Tax: $116.24

Property Tax: $216

Other Payroll Taxes: $61.35

Ⓐ $418.24

Ⓑ $21.35

Ⓒ $177.59

Ⓓ $240.65

15. Ralph makes a monthly budget. His monthly allowance is $40. He makes $25 each month from mowing the neighbor's lawn. Ralph's monthly expenses are $75. How much does he need to earn from babysitting to balance his budget? TEKS 5.10.F

Ⓐ $75

Ⓑ $10

Ⓒ $50

Ⓓ $35

16. Which of the following can Chaseedah use to purchase an item if she wants to pay for her purchase at a later time? TEKS 5.10.C

Ⓐ debit card

Ⓑ check

Ⓒ money transfer

Ⓓ credit card

Fill in the bubble completely to show your answer.

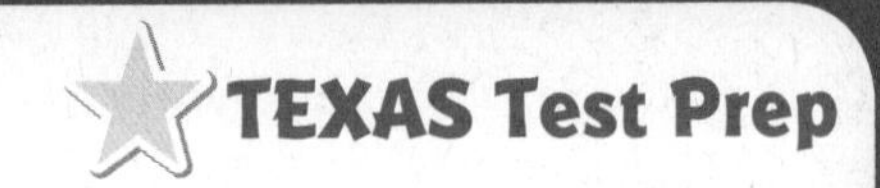

17. The price tags at a clothing store do not include the sales tax in the prices. Chase buys $210 worth of clothing at the store. He hands the cashier $250 and receives three $5 bills and 89 cents in change. How much sales tax does Chase pay on his purchase? TEKS 5.10.A

Ⓐ $24.11
Ⓑ $15.89
Ⓒ $40
Ⓓ $210

18. Reema pays $11.05 in property tax for every $1,000 in value of her land. If Reema's land is worth $100,000, what will she pay in property tax? TEKS 5.10.A

Ⓐ $1,000
Ⓑ $11.05
Ⓒ $100,000
Ⓓ $1,105

19. The Perry family's monthly net income is $2,900. They budgeted $1,200 for rent, $600 for food, $600 for clothing, $500 for entertainment, and $200 for travel expenses. Which of the following actions results in a balanced budget? TEKS 5.10.E

Ⓐ Increase spending on food by $100.
Ⓑ Decrease spending on food by $20.
Ⓒ Decrease spending on entertainment by $200.
Ⓓ Increase spending on entertainment by $200.

20. Gina's gross monthly income is $1,000. The pay stub shows the amount of taxes she pays each month. What is Gina's net monthly income? TEKS 5.10.B

Record your answer and fill in the bubbles on the grid. Be sure to use the correct place value.

2608

Employee: Gina Sanchez	Total earnings		$1,000.00
	Federal income tax	$110.50	
	State income tax	$30.75	
Pay period: November	Other taxes	$18.75	
	Total taxes		
	Pay after taxes		

Detach and retain for your records.

			.		
⓪	⓪	⓪		⓪	⓪
①	①	①		①	①
②	②	②		②	②
③	③	③		③	③
④	④	④		④	④
⑤	⑤	⑤		⑤	⑤
⑥	⑥	⑥		⑥	⑥
⑦	⑦	⑦		⑦	⑦
⑧	⑧	⑧		⑧	⑧
⑨	⑨	⑨		⑨	⑨

Glossary

Pronunciation Key

a	add, map	f	fit, half	n	nice, tin	p	pit, stop	yo͞o	fuse, few
ā	ace, rate	g	go, log	ng	ring, song	r	run, poor	v	vain, eve
â(r)	care, air	h	hope, hate	o	odd, hot	s	see, pass	w	win, away
ä	palm, father	i	it, give	ō	open, so	sh	sure, rush	y	yet, yearn
b	bat, rub	ī	ice, write	ô	order, jaw	t	talk, sit	z	zest, muse
ch	check, catch	j	joy, ledge	oi	oil, boy	th	thin, both	zh	vision, pleasure
d	dog, rod	k	cool, take	ou	pout, now	th	this, bathe		
e	end, pet	l	look, rule	o͝o	took, full	u	up, done		
ē	equal, tree	m	move, seem	o͞o	pool, food	û(r)	burn, term		

ə the schwa, an unstressed vowel representing the sound spelled a in above, e in sicken, i in possible, o in melon, u in circus

Other symbols:
- • separates words into syllables
- ′ indicates stress on a syllable

acute angle [ə•kyo͞ot′ ang′gəl] **ángulo agudo** An angle that has a measure less than a right angle (less than 90° and greater than 0°)
Example:

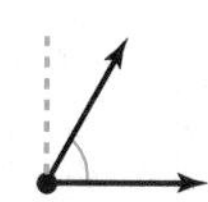

Word History

The Latin word for needle is *acus*. This means "pointed" or "sharp." You will recognize the root in the words *acid* (sharp taste), *acumen* (mental sharpness), and ***acute***, which describes a sharp or pointed angle.

acute triangle [ə•kyo͞ot′ trī′ang•gəl] **triángulo acutángulo** A triangle that has three acute angles

addend [ad′end] **sumando** A number that is added to another in an addition problem

addition [ə•dish′ən] **suma** The process of finding the total number of items when two or more groups of items are joined; the opposite of subtraction

angle [ang′gəl] **ángulo** A shape formed by two line segments or rays that share the same endpoint
Example:

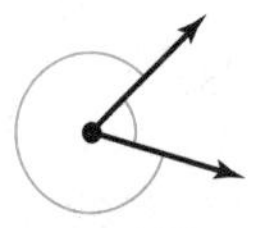

area [âr′ē•ə] **área** The measure of the number of unit squares needed to cover a surface

array [ə•rā′] **matriz** An arrangement of objects in rows and columns
Example:

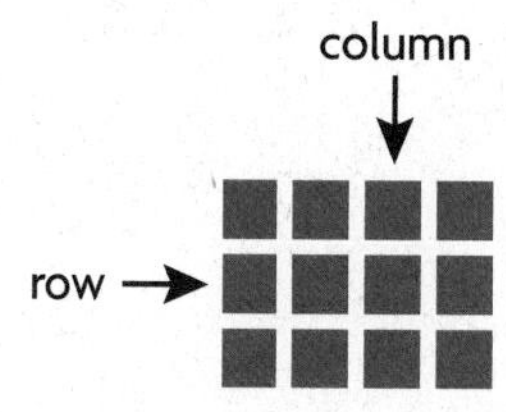

Associative Property of Addition [ə•sō′shē•āt•iv präp′ ər•tē əv ə•dish′ən] **propiedad asociativa de la suma** The property that states that when the grouping of addends is changed, the sum is the same
Example: $(5 + 8) + 4 = 5 + (8 + 4)$

Associative Property of Multiplication [ə•sō′shē•āt•iv präp′ər•tē əv mul•tə•pli•kā′shən] **propiedad asociativa de la multiplicación** The property that states that factors can be grouped in different ways and still get the same product
Example: $(2 \times 3) \times 4 = 2 \times (3 \times 4)$

balance [bal′əns] **equilibrar** To equalize in weight or number

bar graph [bär graf] **gráfica de barras** A graph that uses horizontal or vertical bars to display countable data (p. 557)
Example:

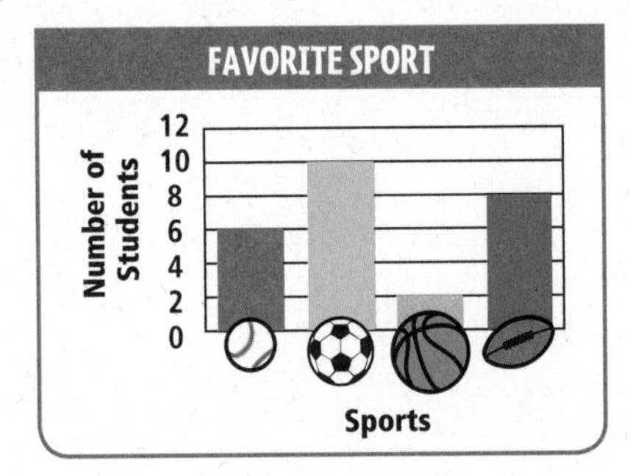

base (geometry) [bās] **base (geometría)** In two dimensions, one side of a triangle or parallelogram that is used to help find the area. In three dimensions, a plane figure, usually a polygon or circle, by which a three-dimensional figure is measured or named
Examples:

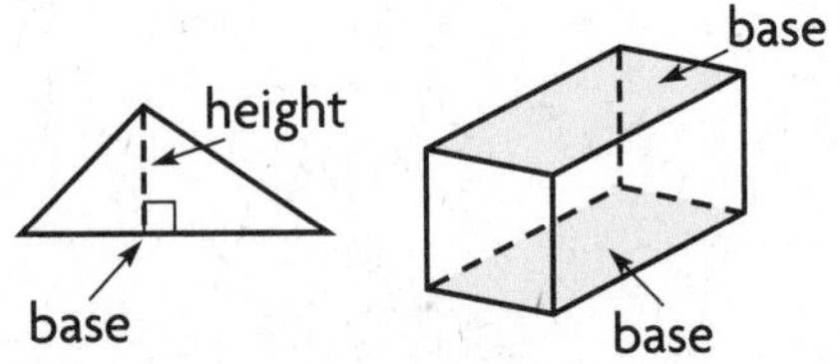

benchmark [bench′märk] **punto de referencia** A familiar number used as a point of reference

budget [bŭj′it] **presupuesto** An organized plan for spending and saving money

capacity [kə•pas′i•tē] **capacidad** The amount a container can hold when filled

Celsius (°C) [sel′sē•əs] **Celsius (°C)** A metric scale for measuring temperature

centimeter (cm) [sen′tə•mēt•ər] **centímetro (cm)** A metric unit used to measure length or distance
0.01 meter = 1 centimeter

closed figure [klōzd fig′yər] **figura cerrada** A figure that begins and ends at the same point

check [chĕk] **cheque** An order in writing to a bank asking that a certain sum of money be paid out of one's account (p. 635)

common denominator [käm′ən dē•näm′ə•nāt•ər] **denominador común** A common multiple of two or more denominators (p. 213)
Example: Some common denominators for $\frac{1}{4}$ and $\frac{5}{6}$ are 12, 24, and 36.

common factor [käm′ən fak′tər] **factor común** A number that is a factor of two or more numbers

common multiple [käm′ən mul′tə•pəl] **múltiplo común** A number that is a multiple of two or more numbers

Commutative Property of Addition [kə•myōōt′ə•tiv präp′ər•tē əv ə•dish′ən] **propiedad conmutativa de la suma** The property that states that when the order of two addends is changed, the sum is the same
Example: $4 + 5 = 5 + 4$

Commutative Property of Multiplication [kə•myōōt′ə•tiv präp′ər•tē əv mul•tə•pli•kā′shən] **propiedad conmutativa de la multiplicación** The property that states that when the order of two factors is changed, the product is the same
Example: $4 \times 5 = 5 \times 4$

compatible numbers [kəm•pat′ə•bəl num′bərz] **números compatibles** Numbers that are easy to compute with mentally

composite number [kəm•päz′it num′bər] **número compuesto** A number having more than two factors (p. 291)
Example: 6 is a composite number, since its factors are 1, 2, 3, and 6.

congruent [kən•grōō′ənt] **congruente** Having the same size and shape (p. 410)

coordinate grid [kō•ôrd′n•it grid] **cuadrícula de coordenadas** A grid formed by a horizontal line called the *x*-axis and a vertical line called the *y*-axis (p. 511)
Example:

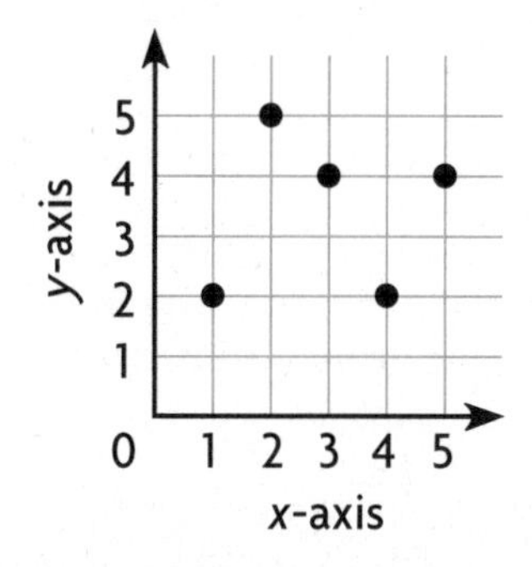

counting number [kount′ing num′bər] **número positivo** A whole number that can be used to count a set of objects (1, 2, 3, 4, . . .)

credit card [krĕd′ĭt kärd] **tarjeta de crédito** An identification card issued by a bank that allows a user to buy items and services immediately and pay the cost at a later time. The bank might charge the user interest in exchange for the use of the money (p. 635)

cube [kyo͞ob] **cubo** A three-dimensional figure with six congruent square faces
Example:

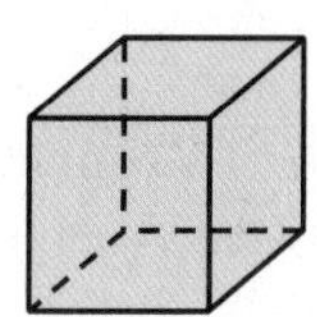

cubic unit [kyo͞o′bik yo͞o′nit] **unidad cúbica** A unit used to measure volume such as cubic foot, cubic meter, and so on (p. 355)

cup (c) [kup] **taza (tz)** A customary unit used to measure capacity
8 ounces = 1 cup

data [dāt′ə] **datos** Information collected about people or things, often to draw conclusions about them

debit card [dĕb′ĭt kärd] **tarjeta de débito** An identification card issued by a bank that allows a user to immediately remove money from an account (p. 635)

decagon [dek′ə•gän] **decágono** A polygon with ten sides and ten angles
Examples:

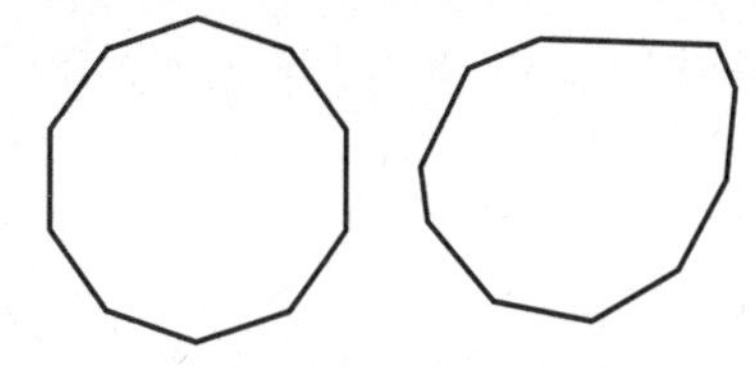

decimal [des′ə•məl] **número decimal** A number with one or more digits to the right of the decimal point

decimal point [des′ə•məl point] **punto decimal** A symbol used to separate dollars from cents in money, and to separate the ones place from the tenths place in a decimal

decimal system [des′ə•məl sis′təm] **sistema decimal** A system of computation based on the number 10

decimeter (dm) [des′i•mēt•ər] **decímetro (dm)** A metric unit used to measure length or distance
10 decimeters = 1 meter

degree (°) [di•grē′] **grado (°)** A unit used for measuring angles and temperature

degree Celsius (°C) [di•grē′ sel′sē•əs] **grado Celcius (°C)** A metric unit for measuring temperature

degree Fahrenheit (°F) [di•grē′ fâr′ən•hīt] **grado Fahrenheit (°F)** A customary unit for measuring temperature

dekameter (dam) [dek′ə•mēt•ər] **decámetro (dam)** A metric unit used to measure length or distance
10 meters = 1 dekameter

denominator [dē•näm′ə•nāt•ər] **denominador** The number below the bar in a fraction that tells how many equal parts are in the whole or in the group
Example: $\frac{3}{4}$ ← denominator

difference [dif′ər•əns] **diferencia** The answer to a subtraction problem

digit [dij′it] **dígito** Any one of the ten symbols 0, 1, 2, 3, 4, 5, 6, 7, 8, 9 used to write numbers

dimension [də•men′shən] **dimensión** A measure in one direction

Distributive Property [di•strib′yoo̅•tiv präp′ər•tē] **propiedad distributiva** The property that states that multiplying a sum by a number is the same as multiplying each addend in the sum by the number and then adding the products (p. 6)
Example: $3 \times (4 + 2) = (3 \times 4) + (3 \times 2)$
$3 \times 6 = 12 + 6$
$18 = 18$

divide [də•vīd′] **dividir** To separate into equal groups; the opposite operation of multiplication

dividend [div′ə•dend] **dividendo** The number that is to be divided in a division problem
Example: $36 \div 6$; $6\overline{)36}$ The dividend is 36.

divisible [də•viz′ə•bəl] **divisible** A number is divisible by another number if the quotient is a counting number and the remainder is zero (p. 292)
Example: 18 is divisible by 3.

division [də•vizh′ən] **división** The process of sharing a number of items to find how many equal groups can be made or how many items will be in each equal group; the opposite operation of multiplication

divisor [də•vī′zər] **divisor** The number that divides the dividend
Example: $15 \div 3$; $3\overline{)15}$ The divisor is 3.

dot plot [dät plät] **diagrama de puntos** A graph that records each piece of data along a number line (p. 571)
Example:

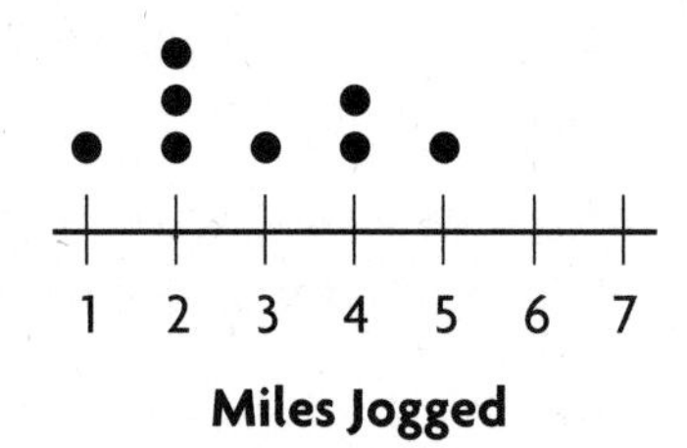

edge [ej] **arista** The line segment made where two faces of a solid figure meet
Example:

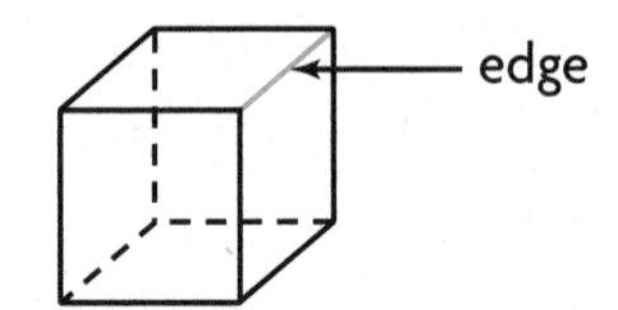

elapsed time [ē•lapst′ tīm] **tiempo transcurrido** The time that passes between the start of an activity and the end of that activity

endpoint [end′ point] **extremo** The point at either end of a line segment or the starting point of a ray

equal to (=) [ē′kwəl too̅] **igual a (=)** Having the same value

equation [ē•kwā′zhən] **ecuación** An algebraic or numerical sentence that shows that two quantities are equal

equilateral triangle [ē•kwi•lat′ər•əl trī′ang•gəl] **triángulo equilátero** A triangle with three congruent sides (p. 415)
Example:

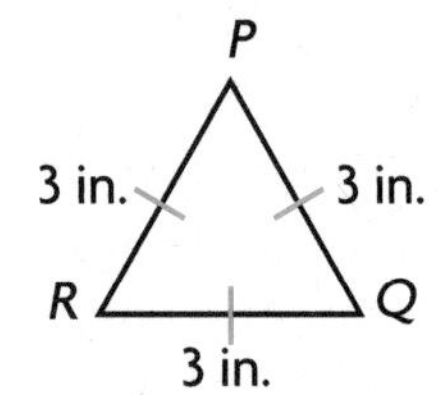

equivalent [ē•kwiv′ə•lənt] **equivalente** Having the same value

equivalent decimals [ē•kwiv′ə•lənt des′ə•məlz] **decimales equivalentes** Decimals that name the same amount
Example: $0.4 = 0.40 = 0.400$

equivalent fractions [ē•kwiv′ə•lənt frak′shənz] **fracciones equivalentes** Fractions that name the same amount or part
Example: $\frac{3}{4} = \frac{6}{8}$

estimate [es′tə•mit] *noun* **estimación (s)** A number close to an exact amount

estimate [es′tə•māt] *verb* **estimar (v)** To find a number that is close to an exact amount

even [ē′vən] **par** A whole number that has a 0, 2, 4, 6, or 8 in the ones place

expanded form [ek•span′did fôrm] **forma desarrollada** A way to write numbers by showing the value of each digit
Examples: $832 = 800 + 30 + 2$
$3.25 = 3 + 0.2 + 0.05$

expression [ek•spresh′ən] **expresión** A mathematical phrase or the part of a number sentence that combines numbers, operation signs, and sometimes variables, but does not have an equal sign

face [fās] **cara** A polygon that is a flat surface of a solid figure
Example:

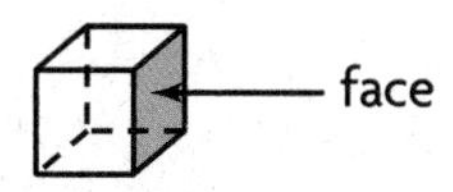

fact family [fakt fam′ə•lē] **familia de operaciones** A set of related multiplication and division, or addition and subtraction, equations
Examples: $7 \times 8 = 56$; $8 \times 7 = 56$;
$56 \div 7 = 8$; $56 \div 8 = 7$

factor [fak′tər] **factor** A number multiplied by another number to find a product

Fahrenheit (°F) [fâr′ən•hīt] **Fahrenheit (°F)** A customary scale for measuring temperature

fluid ounce (fl oz) [flo͞o′id ouns] **onza fluida (oz fl)** A customary unit used to measure liquid capacity
1 cup = 8 fluid ounces

foot (ft) [fo͝ot] **pie (ft)** A customary unit used to measure length or distance
1 foot = 12 inches

formula [fôr′myo͞o•lə] **fórmula** A set of symbols that expresses a mathematical rule
Example: $A = b \times h$

fraction [frak′shən] **fracción** A number that names a part of a whole or a part of a group

fraction greater than 1 [frak′shən grāt′ər than wun] **fracción mayor que 1** A number which has a numerator that is greater than its denominator
Example:

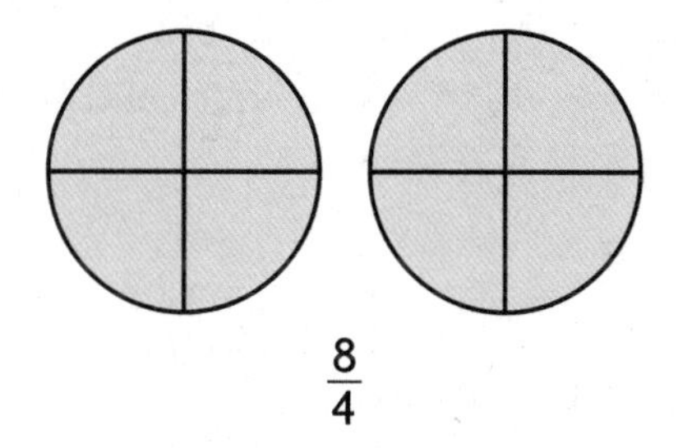

$\frac{8}{4}$

frequency [frē′kwən•sē] **frecuencia** the number of times an event occurs (p. 545)

frequency table [fre′kwən•sē tābəl] **tabla de frecuencia** A table that uses numbers to record data about how often something happens (p. 545)
Example:

Favorite Color	
Color	**Number**
Blue	10
Red	7
Green	5
Other	3

gallon (gal) [gal′ən] **galón (gal)** A customary unit used to measure capacity
4 quarts = 1 gallon

general quadrilateral [jen′ər•əl kwä•dri•lat′ər•əl] **cuadrilátero general** See *quadrilateral*.

gram (g) [gram] **gramo (g)** A metric unit used to measure mass
1,000 grams = 1 kilogram

greater than (>) [grāt′ər than] **mayor que (>)** A symbol used to compare two numbers or two quantities when the greater number or greater quantity is given first
Example: $6 > 4$

greater than or equal to (≥) [grāt′ər than ôr ē′kwəl to͞o] **mayor o igual que (≥)** A symbol used to compare two numbers or quantities when the first is greater than or equal to the second

greatest common factor [grāt′əst käm′ən fak′tər] **máximo común divisor** The greatest factor that two or more numbers have in common
Example: 6 is the greatest common factor of 18 and 30.

grid [grid] **cuadrícula** Evenly divided and equally spaced squares on a figure or flat surface

gross income [grōs ĭn′kŭm′] **ingreso bruto** Income before any taxes are taken out of it (p. 629)

height [hīt] **altura** The length of a perpendicular from the base to the top of a two-dimensional or three-dimensional figure
Example:

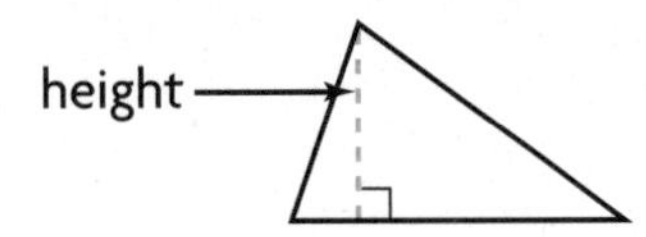

heptagon [hep′tə•gän] **heptágono** A polygon with seven sides and seven angles (p. 409)

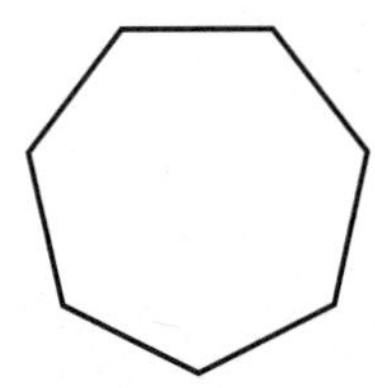

hexagon [hek′sə•gän] **hexágono** A polygon with six sides and six angles
Examples:

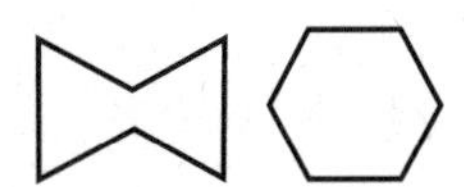

horizontal [hôr•i•zänt′l] **horizontal** Extending left and right

hundredth [hun′drədth] **centésimo** One of 100 equal parts
Examples: 0.56, $\frac{56}{100}$, fifty-six hundredths

Identity Property of Addition [ī•den′tə•tē präp′ər•tē əv ə•dish′ən] **propiedad de identidad de la suma** The property that states that when you add zero to a number, the result is that number

Identity Property of Multiplication [ī•den′tə•tē präp′ər•tē əv mul•tə•pli•kā′shən] **propiedad de identidad de la multiplicación** The property that states that the product of any number and 1 is that number

inch (in.) [inch] **pulgada (pulg)** A customary unit used to measure length or distance
12 inches = 1 foot

income [ĭn′kŭm′] **ingreso** Money earned (p. 617)

income tax [ĭn′kŭm′ tăks] **impuesto sobre el ingreso** Money paid to a city, town, or state government or to the U.S. government based on income (p. 617)

inequality [in•ē•kwôl′ə•tē] **desigualdad** A mathematical sentence that contains the symbol $<$, $>$, $\leq$, $\geq$, or $\neq$

interest [ĭn′trĭst] **interés** The additional money paid by a borrower to a lender in exchange for the use of the lender's money. For example, you earn interest from a bank if you have a savings account and you pay interest to a lender if you have a loan

intersecting lines [in•tər•sekt′ing līnz] **líneas intersecantes** Lines that cross each other at exactly one point
Example:

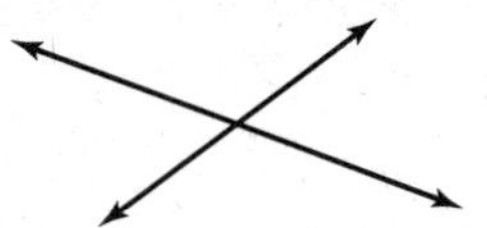

interval [in′tər•vəl] **intervalo** The difference between one number and the next on the scale of a graph

inverse operations [in′vûrs äp•ə•rā′shənz] **operaciones inversas** Opposite operations, or operations that undo each other, such as addition and subtraction or multiplication and division (p. 41)

isosceles triangle [ī•säs′ə•lēz trī′ang•gəl] **triángulo isósceles** A triangle with two congruent sides (p. 415)
Example:

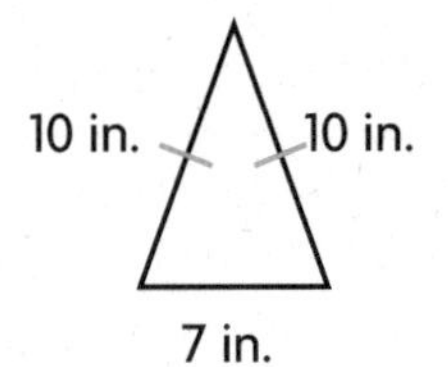

key [kē] **clave** The part of a map or graph that explains the symbols

kilogram (kg) [kil′ō•gram] **kilogramo (kg)** A metric unit used to measure mass
1,000 grams = 1 kilogram

kilometer (km) [kə•läm′ət•ər] **kilómetro (km)** A metric unit used to measure length or distance
1,000 meters = 1 kilometer

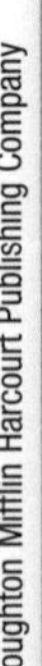

least common denominator [lēst käm′ən dē•näm′ə•nāt•ər] **mínimo común denominador** The least common multiple of two or more denominators
Example: The least common denominator for $\frac{1}{4}$ and $\frac{5}{6}$ is 12.

least common multiple [lēst käm′ən mul′tə•pəl] **mínimo común múltiplo** The least number that is a common multiple of two or more numbers

less than ($<$) [les than] **menor que ($<$)** A symbol used to compare two numbers or two quantities, with the lesser number given first
Example: $4 < 6$

less than or equal to ($\leq$) [les than ôr ē′kwəl to͞o] **menor o igual que ($\leq$)** A symbol used to compare two numbers or two quantities, when the first is less than or equal to the second

line [līn] **línea** A straight path in a plane, extending in both directions with no endpoints
Example:

line segment [līn seg′mənt] **segmento** A part of a line that includes two points called endpoints and all the points between them
Example:

linear unit [lin′ē•ər yo͞o′nit] **unidad lineal** A measure of length, width, height, or distance

liquid volume [lik′wid väl′yo͞om] **volumen de un líquido** The amount of liquid in a container

liter (L) [lēt′ər] **litro (L)** A metric unit used to measure capacity
1 liter = 1,000 milliliters

mass [mas] **masa** The amount of matter in an object

meter (m) [mēt′ər] **metro (m)** A metric unit used to measure length or distance
1 meter = 100 centimeters

mile (mi) [mīl] **milla (mi)** A customary unit used to measure length or distance
5,280 feet = 1 mile

milligram (mg) [mil′i•gram] **miligramo (mg)** A metric unit used to measure mass
1,000 milligrams = 1 gram

milliliter (mL) [mil′i•lēt•ər] **mililitro (mL)** A metric unit used to measure capacity
1,000 milliliters = 1 liter

millimeter (mm) [mil′i•mēt•ər] **milímetro (mm)** A metric unit used to measure length or distance
1,000 millimeters = 1 meter

million [mil′yən] **millón** 1,000 thousands; written as 1,000,000

mixed number [mikst num′bər] **número mixto** A number that is made up of a whole number and a fraction
Example: $1\frac{5}{8}$

multiple [mul′tə•pəl] **múltiplo** The product of two counting numbers is a multiple of each of those numbers

multiplication [mul•tə•pli•kā′shən] **multiplicación** A process to find the total number of items made up of equal-sized groups, or to find the total number of items in a given number of groups. It is the inverse operation of division

multiply [mul′tə•plī] **multiplicar** When you combine equal groups, you can multiply to find how many in all; the opposite operation of division

net income [nět ĭn′kŭm′] **ingreso neto** Income that is left after taxes are taken out of the gross income (p. 629)

nonagon [nän′ə•gän] **eneágono** A polygon with nine sides and nine angles (p. 409)

not equal to ($\neq$) [not ē′kwəl to͞o] **no igual a ($\neq$)** A symbol that indicates one quantity is not equal to another

number line [num′bər līn] **recta numérica** A line on which numbers can be located
Example:

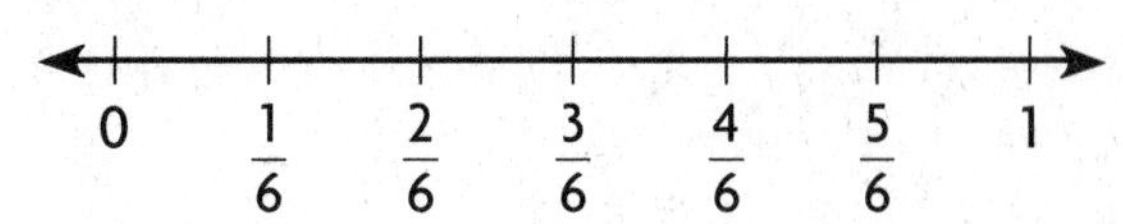

numerator [no͞o′mər•āt•ər] **numerador** The number above the bar in a fraction that tells how many equal parts of the whole or group are being considered
Example: $\frac{3}{4}$ ← numerator

numerical expression [no͞o•mer′i•kəl ek•spresh′ən] **expresión numérica** A mathematical phrase that uses only numbers and operation signs (p. 303)

obtuse angle [äb•to͞os′ ang′gəl] **ángulo obtuso** An angle whose measure is greater than 90° and less than 180°
Example:

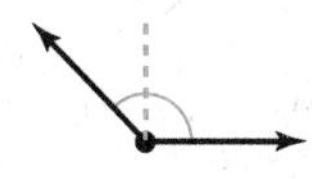

obtuse triangle [äb•to͞os′ trī′ang•gəl] **triángulo obtusángulo** A triangle that has one obtuse angle

octagon [äk′tə•gän] **octágono** A polygon with eight sides and eight angles
Examples:

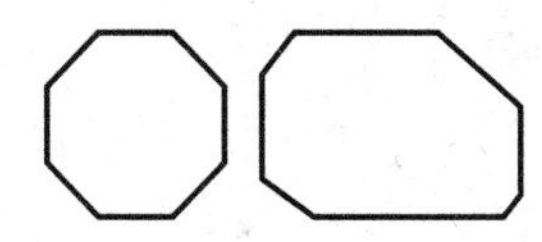

odd [od] **impar** A whole number that has a 1, 3, 5, 7, or 9 in the ones place

open figure [ō′pən fig′yər] **figura abierta** A figure that does not begin and end at the same point

order of operations [ôr′dər əv äp•ə•rā′shənz] **orden de las operaciones** A special set of rules which gives the order in which calculations are done in an expression (p. 309)

ordered pair [ôr′dərd pâr] **par ordenado** A pair of numbers used to locate a point on a grid. The first number tells the left-right position and the second number tells the up-down position (p. 511)

origin [ôr′ə•jin] **origen** The point where the two axes of a coordinate plane intersect (0, 0) (p. 511)

ounce (oz) [ouns] **onza (oz)** A customary unit used to measure weight
16 ounces = 1 pound

overestimate [ō′vər•es•tə•mit] **sobrestimar** An estimate that is greater than the exact answer

pan balance [pan bal′əns] **balanza de platillos** An instrument used to weigh objects and to compare the weights of objects

parallel lines [pâr′ə•lel līnz] **líneas paralelas** Lines in the same plane that never intersect and are always the same distance apart
Example:

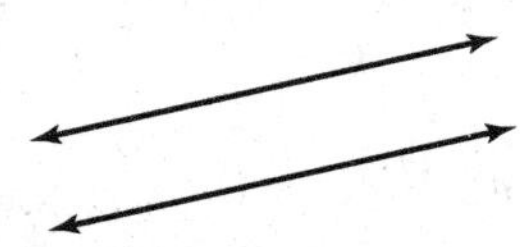

parallelogram [pâr•ə•lel′ə•gram] **paralelogramo** A quadrilateral whose opposite sides are parallel and have the same length, or are congruent
Example:

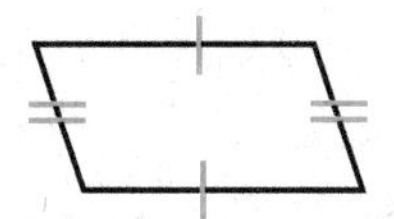

parentheses [pə•ren′thə•sēz] **paréntesis** The symbols used to show which operation or operations in an expression should be done first

partial product [pär′shəl präd′əkt] **producto parcial** A method of multiplying in which the ones, tens, hundreds, and so on are multiplied separately and then the products are added together

partial quotient [pär′shəl kwō′shənt] **cociente parcial** A method of dividing in which multiples of the divisor are subtracted from the dividend and then the quotients are added together

pattern [pat'ərn] **patrón** An ordered set of numbers or objects; the order helps you predict what will come next
Examples: 2, 4, 6, 8, 10

payroll tax [pā'rōl' tăks] **retención sobre el salario** Money an employer withholds from an employee's earnings (p. 617)

pentagon [pen'tə•gän] **pentágono** A polygon with five sides and five angles
Examples:

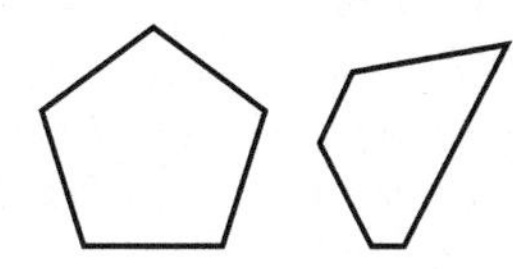

perimeter [pə•rim'ə•tər] **perímetro** The distance around a closed plane figure

period [pir'ē•əd] **periodo** Each group of three digits separated by commas in a multi-digit number
Example: 85,643,900 has three periods.

perpendicular lines [pər•pən•dik'yōō•lər līnz] **líneas perpendiculares** Two lines that intersect to form four right angles
Example:

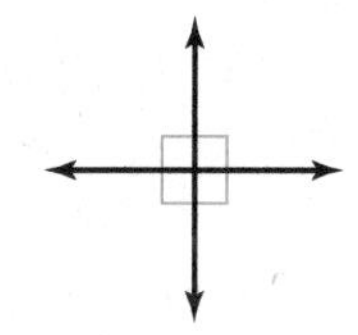

pictograph [pĭk'tə·grăf'] **pictografía** A graph that uses pictures to show and compare information
Example:

HOW WE GET TO SCHOOL

Walk	❀ ❀ ❀
Ride a Bike	❀ ❀ ❀ ❀
Ride a Bus	❀ ❀ ❀ ❀ ❀ ◖
Ride in a Car	❀ ❀

Key: Each ❀ = 10 students.

pint (pt) [pīnt] **pinta (pt)** A customary unit used to measure capacity
2 cups = 1 pint

place value [plās val'yōō] **valor posicional** The value of each digit in a number based on the location of the digit

plane [plān] **plano** A flat surface that extends without end in all directions
Example:

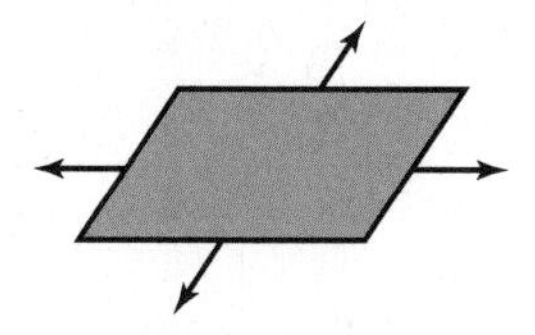

plane figure [plān fig'yər] **figura plana** See *two-dimensional figure*

point [point] **punto** An exact location in space

polygon [päl'i•gän] **polígono** A closed plane figure formed by three or more line segments (p. 409)
Examples:

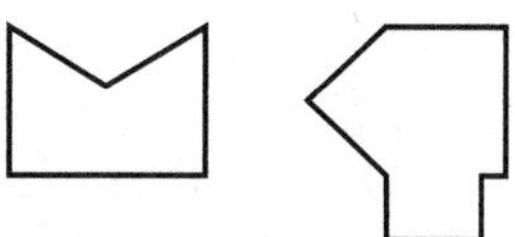
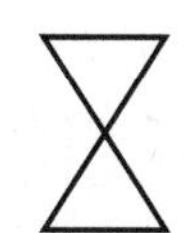

Polygons Not Polygons

pound (lb) [pound] **libra (lb)** A customary unit used to measure weight
1 pound = 16 ounces

prime number [prīm num'bər] **número primo** A number that has exactly two factors: 1 and itself (p. 297)
Examples: 2, 3, 5, 7, 11, 13, 17, and 19 are prime numbers. 1 is not a prime number.

prism [priz'əm] **prisma** A solid figure that has two congruent, polygon-shaped bases, and other faces that are all rectangles
Examples:

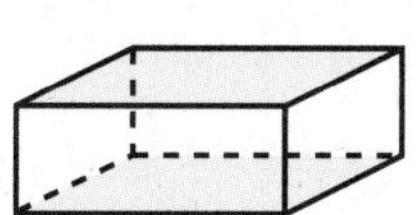
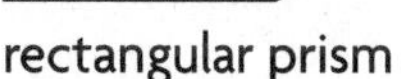
rectangular prism

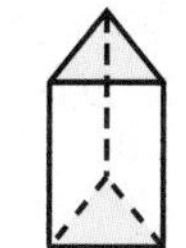
triangular prism

product [präd'əkt] **producto** The answer to a multiplication problem

profit [prŏf'ĭt] **ganancia** The amount left after all the expenses are subtracted from the amount of money received from selling an item or service

property tax [prŏp′ər·tē tăks] **impuesto sobre la propiedad** A portion of the value of items that is paid to a city or state government. Property tax can be charged on things such as cars, houses, boats, or land (p. 623)

protractor [prō′trak•tər] **transportador** A tool used for measuring or drawing angles

quadrilateral [kwä•dri•lat′ər•əl] **cuadrilátero** A polygon with four sides and four angles
Example:

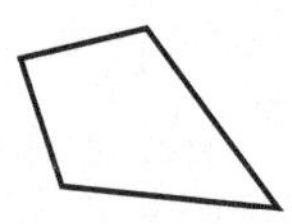

quart (qt) [kwôrt] **cuarto (ct)** A customary unit used to measure capacity
2 pints = 1 quart

quotient [kwō′shənt] **cociente** The number, not including the remainder, that results from dividing
Example: $8 \div 4 = 2$. The quotient is 2.

range [rānj] **rango** The difference between the greatest and least numbers in a group (p. 577)

ray [rā] **semirrecta** A part of a line; it has one endpoint and continues without end in one direction
Example:

rectangle [rek′tang•gəl] **rectángulo** A parallelogram with four right angles
Example:

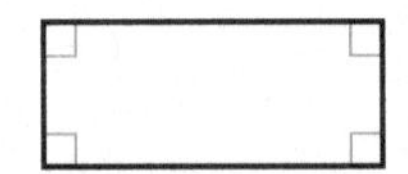

rectangular prism [rek•tang′gyə•lər priz′əm] **prisma rectangular** A three-dimensional figure in which all six faces are rectangles
Example:

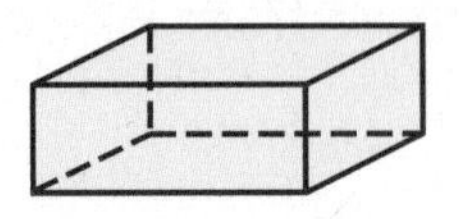

regroup [rē•gro͞op′] **reagrupar** To exchange amounts of equal value to rename a number
Example: $5 + 8 = 13$ ones or 1 ten 3 ones

regular polygon [reg′yə•lər päl′i•gän] **polígono regular** A polygon in which all sides are congruent and all angles are congruent (p. 410)

related facts [ri•lāt′id fakts] **operaciones relacionadas** A set of related addition and subtraction, or multiplication and division, number sentences
Examples: $4 \times 7 = 28$ $\quad 28 \div 4 = 7$
$7 \times 4 = 28$ $\quad 28 \div 7 = 4$

remainder [ri•mān′dər] **residuo** The amount left over when a number cannot be divided equally

rhombus [räm′bəs] **rombo** A parallelogram with four equal, or congruent, sides
Example:

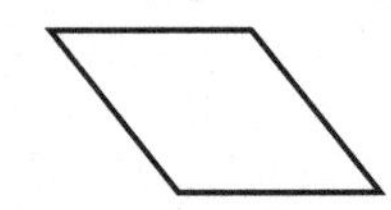

Word History

Rhombus is almost identical to its Greek origin, *rhombos*. The original meaning was "spinning top" or "magic wheel," which is easy to imagine when you look at a rhombus, an equilateral parallelogram.

right angle [rīt ang′gəl] **ángulo recto** An angle that forms a square corner and has a measure of 90°
Example:

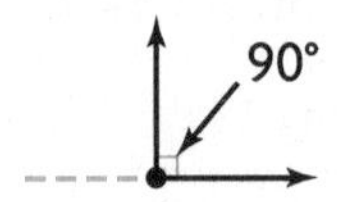

right triangle [rīt trī′ang•gəl] **triángulo rectángulo** A triangle that has a right angle
Example:

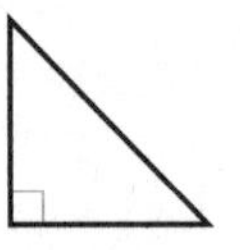

round [round] **redondear** To replace a number with one that is simpler and is approximately the same size as the original number
Example: 114.6 rounded to the nearest ten is 110 and to the nearest one is 115.

sales tax [sāls tăks] **impuesto sobre las ventas** Money added to the cost of items or services. Sales tax amounts vary from state to state and from city to city (p. 623)

scale [skāl] **escala** A series of numbers placed at fixed distances on a graph to help label the graph

scalene triangle [skā′lēn trī′ang•gəl] **triángulo escaleno** A triangle with no congruent sides (p. 415)
Example:

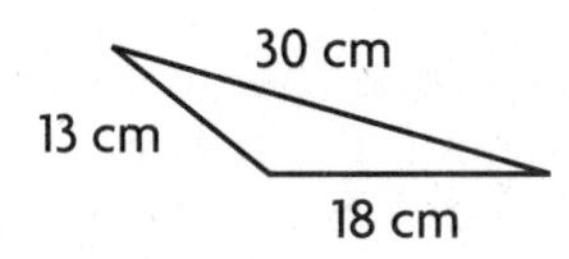

scatter plot [skăt′ər plŏt′] **diagrama de dispersión** A graph that shows a relationship between two sets of data (p. 595)

second (sec) [sek′ənd] **segundo (s)** A small unit of time
60 seconds = 1 minute

simplest form [sim′pləst fôrm] **mínima expresión** A fraction is in simplest form when the numerator and denominator have only 1 as a common factor

simplify [sĭm′plə·fī′] **simplificar** To find the value of a numerical expression (p. 309)

skip count [skip kount] **contar salteado** A pattern of counting forward or backward
Example: 5, 10, 15, 20, 25, 30, . . .

solid figure [sä′lid fig′yər] **cuerpo geométrico** See *three-dimensional figure*

solution [sə•lo͞o′shən] **solución** A value that makes an equation true

square [skwâr] **cuadrado** A polygon with four equal, or congruent, sides and four right angles

square unit [skwâr yo͞o′nit] **unidad cuadrada** A unit used to measure area such as square foot, square meter, and so on

standard form [stan′dərd fôrm] **forma normal** A way to write numbers by using the digits 0–9, with each digit having a place value
Example: 456 ← standard form

stem-and-leaf plot [stĕm ənd lēf plŏt] **diagrama de tallo y hojas** A graph that shows groups of data arranged by place value (p. 583)

straight angle [strāt ang′gəl] **ángulo llano** An angle whose measure is 180°
Example:

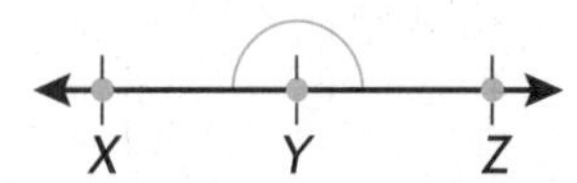

subtraction [səb•trak′shən] **resta** The process of finding how many are left when a number of items are taken away from a group of items; the process of finding the difference when two groups are compared; the opposite of addition

sum [sum] **suma o total** The answer to an addition problem

tablespoon (tbsp) [tā′bəl•spo͞on] **cucharada (cda)** A customary unit used to measure capacity
3 teaspoons = 1 tablespoon

tax [tăks] **impuesto** Money paid to the government in exchange for services, such as road maintenance and police protection (p. 617)

teaspoon (tsp) [tē′spo͞on] **cucharadita (cdta)** A customary unit used to measure capacity
1 tablespoon = 3 teaspoons

tenth [tenth] **décimo** One of ten equal parts
Example: 0.7 = seven tenths

thousandth [thou′zəndth] **milésimo** One of one thousand equal parts (p. 11)
Example: 0.006 = six thousandths

three-dimensional [thrē də•men′shə•nəl] **tres dimensiones** Measured in three directions, such as length, width, and height

three-dimensional figure [thrē də•men′shə•nəl fig′yər] **figura de tres dimensiones** A figure having length, width, and height
Example:

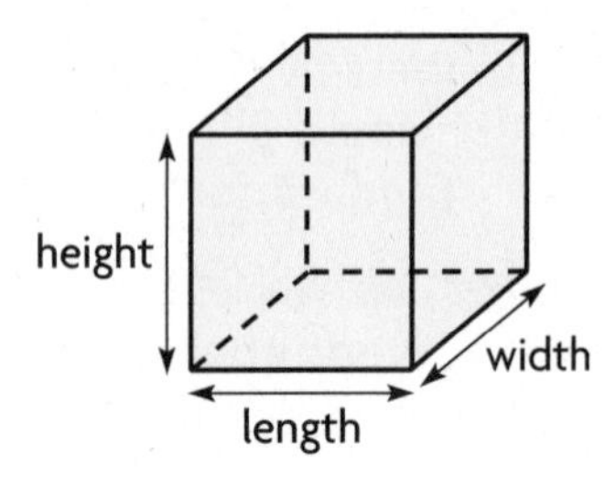

ton (T) [tun] **tonelada (t)** A customary unit used to measure weight
2,000 pounds = 1 ton

trapezoid [trap′i•zoid] **trapecio** A quadrilateral with exactly one pair of parallel sides
Examples:

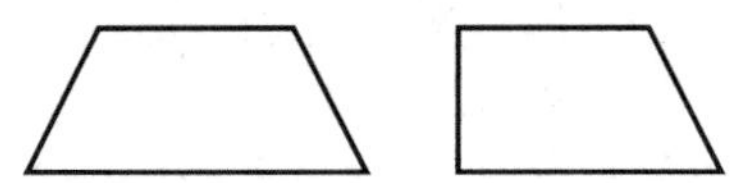

triangle [trī′ang•gəl] **triángulo** A polygon with three sides and three angles
Examples:

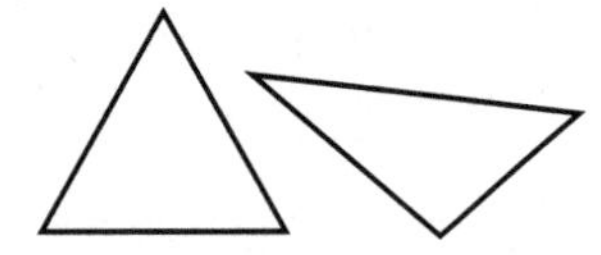

two-dimensional [to͞o də•men′shə•nəl] **dos dimensiones** Measured in two directions, such as length and width

two-dimensional figure [to͞o də•men′shə•nəl fig′yər] **figura de dos dimensiones** A figure that lies in a plane; a figure having length and width

underestimate [un•dər•es′tə•mit] **subestimar** An estimate that is less than the exact answer

unit cube [yo͞o′nit kyo͞ob] **cubo de una unidad** A cube that has a length, width, and height of 1 unit (p. 435)

unit fraction [yo͞o′nit frak′shən] **fracción unitaria** A fraction that has 1 as a numerator

variable [vâr′ē•ə•bəl] **variable** A letter or symbol that stands for an unknown number or numbers

Venn diagram [ven dī′ə•gram] **diagrama de Venn** A diagram that shows relationships among sets of things
Example:

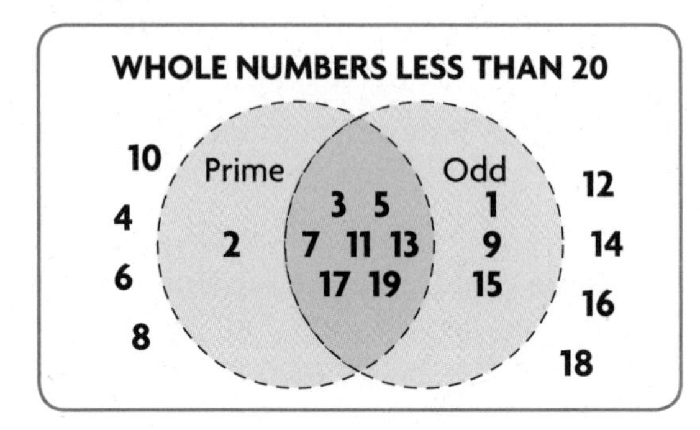

vertex [vûr′teks] **vértice** The point where two or more rays meet; the point of intersection of two sides of a polygon; the point of intersection of three (or more) edges of a solid figure; the top point of a cone; the plural of vertex is vertices
Examples:

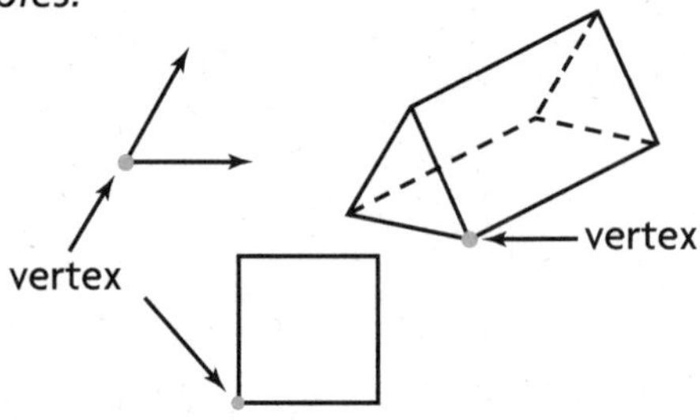

Word History

The Latin word *vertere* means "to turn" and also relates to "highest." You can turn a figure around a point, or ***vertex***.

vertical [vûr′ti•kəl] **vertical** Extending up and down

volume [väl′yo͞om] **volumen** The measure of the space a solid figure occupies (p. 355)

weight [wāt] **peso** How heavy an object is

whole [hōl] **entero** All of the parts of a shape or group

whole number [hōl num′bər] **número entero** One of the numbers 0, 1, 2, 3, 4, . . . ; the set of whole numbers goes on without end

word form [wûrd fôrm] **en palabras** A way to write numbers in standard English
Example: 4,829 = four thousand, eight hundred twenty-nine

x*-axis** [eks ak′sis] **eje de la *x The horizontal number line on a coordinate plane (p. 511)

x*-coordinate** [eks kō•ôrd′n•it] **coordenada *x The first number in an ordered pair; tells the distance to move right or left from (0, 0) (p. 511)

yard (yd) [yärd] **yarda (yd)** A customary unit used to measure length or distance
3 feet = 1 yard

y*-axis** [wī ak′sis] **eje de la *y The vertical number line on a coordinate plane (p. 511)

y*-coordinate** [wī kō•ôrd′n•it] **coordenada *y The second number in an ordered pair; tells the distance to move up or down from (0, 0) (p. 511)

Zero Property of Multiplication [zē′rō präp′ər•tē əv mul•tə•pli•kā′shən] **propiedad del cero de la multiplicación** The property that states that when you multiply by zero, the product is zero

Table of Measures

METRIC	CUSTOMARY
Length	
1 centimeter (cm) = 10 millimeters (mm)	1 foot (ft) = 12 inches (in.)
1 meter (m) = 1,000 millimeters	1 yard (yd) = 3 feet, or 36 inches
1 meter = 100 centimeters	1 mile (mi) = 1,760 yards, or 5,280 feet
1 meter = 10 decimeters (dm)	
1 kilometer (km) = 1,000 meters	
Capacity	
1 liter (L) = 1,000 milliliters (mL)	1 cup (c) = 8 fluid ounces (fl oz)
1 metric cup = 250 milliliters	1 pint (pt) = 2 cups
1 liter = 4 metric cups	1 quart (qt) = 2 pints, or 4 cups
1 kiloliter (kL) = 1,000 liters	1 gallon (gal) = 4 quarts
Mass/Weight	
1 gram (g) = 1,000 milligrams (mg)	1 pound (lb) = 16 ounces (oz)
1 gram = 100 centigrams (cg)	1 ton (T) = 2,000 pounds
1 kilogram (kg) = 1,000 grams	

TIME
1 minute (min) = 60 seconds (sec)
1 half hour = 30 minutes
1 hour (hr) = 60 minutes
1 day = 24 hours
1 week (wk) = 7 days
1 year (yr) = 12 months (mo), or about 52 weeks
1 year = 365 days
1 leap year = 366 days
1 decade = 10 years
1 century = 100 years
1 millennium = 1,000 years

Table of Measures

SYMBOLS			
$=$	is equal to	$\overleftrightarrow{AB}$	line AB
$\neq$	is not equal to	$\overrightarrow{AB}$	ray AB
$>$	is greater than	$\overline{AB}$	line segment AB
$<$	is less than	$\angle ABC$	angle ABC, or angle B
(2, 3)	ordered pair (x, y)	$\triangle ABC$	triangle ABC
$\perp$	is perpendicular to	$^\circ$	degree
$\parallel$	is parallel to	°C	degrees Celsius
		°F	degrees Fahrenheit

FORMULAS			
Perimeter		**Area**	
Polygon	P = sum of the lengths of sides	Rectangle	$A = b \times h$, or $A = bh$
Rectangle	$P = (2 \times l) + (2 \times w)$, or $P = 2l + 2w$		
Square	$P = 4 \times s$, or $P = 4s$		
Volume			
Rectangular prism	$V = B \times h$, or $V = l \times w \times h$		
B = area of base shape, h = height of prism